Praise for *The Scoundrel Harry Larkyns*

'A fascinating piece of historical detective work ... that brings the extraordinary Larkyns to life'

HWA Non-Fiction Crown Judges

'Gripping, cinematic, tragic and tender ... A hugely enthralling story of a life richly lived ... a contender for one of the best books of the year'

Declan Burke, *Irish Times*

'There's much to enjoy in this painstakingly researched account of a forgotten and troubled ne'er-do-well; it's a story that is as eventful as it is tragic'

PD Smith, *Guardian*

'Harry Larkyns's life at times reads like fiction ... Full marks to Rebecca Gowers for bringing this contradictory and little-known figure properly under the lens'

Max Décharné, *Spectator*

'The fantastical twists and turns in Larkyns's life are brilliantly, and coolly, recovered by the author ... Strange, brilliant, quirky and illuminating, books such as this remind us, if we need reminding, that books matter'

Jason Goodwin, *Country Life*

'This is a cold case investigation into a true crime of passion with a family history twist that r...
finally puts the unlucky Larkyns' si...

D1331699

'Gowers has taken the cold embers ...
them to create a portrait of a fascinating, contradictory figure'

The Oldie

The Scoundrel Harry Larkyns

Rebecca Gowers is the author of *The Swamp of Death*, a narrative analysis of a striking 1890 murder case, shortlisted for the CWA non-fiction Golden Dagger award; and of two novels, *When to Walk* and *The Twisted Heart*, both longlisted for the Orange Prize. In 2014, she became the fourth editor of Plain Words, a classic guide to the use of English by her great-grandfather, Sir Ernest Gowers; and she followed this with her own, anti-establishment guide to the misuse of English, *Horrible Words*. *Scoundrel* takes her back to her fascination with nineteenth-century literature, history and crime, and is both a non-standard biography, and a radically new exploration of a seminal murder.

Also by Rebecca Gowers

Fiction

When to Walk
The Twisted Heart

Non-fiction

The Swamp of Death
Plain Words (revised edition)
Horrible Words

The Scoundrel Harry Larkyns

and his Pitiless Killing by the
Photographer Eadweard Muybridge

REBECCA GOWERS

WEIDENFELD & NICOLSON

First published in Great Britain in 2019 by Weidenfeld & Nicolson
This paperback edition published in 2020 by Weidenfeld & Nicolson
an imprint of The Orion Publishing Group Ltd
Carmelite House, 50 Victoria Embankment
London EC4Y 0DZ

An Hachette UK Company

1 3 5 7 9 10 8 6 4 2

A CIP catalogue record for this book is
available from the British Library.

ISBN (Mass Market Paperback) 978 1 4746 0643 1
ISBN (eBook) 978 1 4746 0644 8

Typeset at The Spartan Press Ltd,
Lymington, Hants

Printed and bound in Great Britain by Clays Ltd,
Elcograf S.p.A.

www.orionbooks.co.uk
www.weidenfeldandnicolson.co.uk

Contents

List of Illustrations

The author and publisher are grateful for permissions given to reproduce the following illustrations: **p. 3** Getty Images/George Eastman Museum; **p. 26** Getty Images; **p. 39** London Borough of Merton; **p. 47** Alamy Stock Photo/The Picture Art collection; **p. 118** Bibliothèque nationale universitaire de Strasbourg; **p. 140** Getty Images/Bettmann; **pp. 152, 153, 176, 211, 232, 250, 303 and 307** The Bancroft Library, University of California, Berkeley; **p. 159** Hathi Trust Digital Library; **p. 181** California State Library; **p. 183** Oakland Museum of California/Albumen Photographs: History, Science and Preservation; **pp. 194, 203, 205, 208, 209, 218 and 228** Iris & B. Gerald Cantor Center for Visual Arts at Stanford University; Museum Purchase Fund; **p. 309** Getty Images/ University History Archive/UIG. All other illustrations are taken from the collection of the author: those on **pp. 7, 12, 13, 67, 93 and 274**, copyright © the author.

Introduction

For well over a century, a shady figure known as Harry Larkyns has been loping his way through books and newspaper articles too numerous to count. Occasionally he shows up in the wall notes of exhibitions. He is also embedded in *Stillanovel*, an art poem by Carl Andre. He stars in *The Photographer*, a chamber piece by Philip Glass, and plays his part in a film or two besides. Yet this Larkyns trails next to no history behind him, so that scholars have doubted 'Larkyns' was even his true name. All they really have on him is that the man was a fraudster who appeared out of nowhere in Nevada in 1872, telling tales of an improbably daring life; and that, reaching San Francisco shortly afterwards, he traded in spurious Old World glamour until it destroyed him. What more likely, they suggest, than that the image he projected of himself was a calculated deception, hiding a background of no great interest at all?

Even when Harry Larkyns was alive, the stories that circulated about him were received by many with raised eyebrows. He made himself out to be an orphan from a wealthy English family, short of funds after a theatrical investment gone awry, but with entangled riches waiting for him in a bank in China, or perhaps Japan. And he gave himself the title of Major, though whether arising from purported service with the British Army in India, or from equally suspect antics fighting under the notorious General Bourbaki in France, well, who could confidently say? As for the Légion d'honneur that he awarded himself for valour shown during the Franco–Prussian War: how likely was that bauble to be real?

Original doubts about Harry Larkyns have become overwhelming since. The cultural commentator Rebecca Solnit, in her acclaimed book *River of Shadows*, is typical in being profoundly unimpressed, describing him as 'a rogue whose tales of his life before San Francisco are heroic beyond the reach of credibility'. She notes with derision that he even pretended to have fought with Garibaldi, and concludes:

'As a pure fiction, he was ready for the West.' Edward Ball, a Yale professor, in his popular work *The Inventor and the Tycoon*, is also wary about a life history he labels implausibly 'grandiose', while the performance artist Brian Catling, dropping a 'Major Larkyns' into his twisty novel *The Vorrh*, makes no more of him than is conveyed by the single bourgeois judgement 'despicable'. And so it goes on.

Any serious account of Larkyns concedes that, in his day, he won himself many devoted friends. But in death his charisma was obliterated, leaving all the glamorous stories to fail. As for commonly agreed facts about him, these are now strikingly few, even among writers who approach him with scholarly intent. Such as they are, however, the facts do terminate for certain with his death in darkness on 17 October 1874. And what continues to give interest to this slender reckoning decades later is how his story ended that day. Because, whoever he really was, Harry Larkyns got himself shot, with a bullet, by the brilliant and celebrated photographer Eadweard Muybridge.

Muybridge is still popularly half remembered, and by those who study photography, revered, as the person who first proved what the eye unaided could not see: that a horse moving fast enough lifts all four feet simultaneously off the ground. By improving shutter mechanics, and using cameras triggered by trip-threads, he then went on to snatch images in sequence of horses at speed, revealing the true nature of the animal's gait, previously misrepresented in innumerable works of art. After this, in 1879, Muybridge invented what he came to call the zoöpraxiscope, a device by which the series images of his locomotion studies, transferred in paint to the rims of spinnable disks of glass, could be beamed life-size in super-rapid succession on a wall. He was, that is, the first person to create a machine that projected the illusion of a moving photograph, 'putting his pictures again in motion', as he himself explained it, so that he is now also credited as a forefather of 'moving pictures', or the cinema. In addition, he is venerated simply as an artist, not least for his images of the sublime Yosemite wilderness in California, where he pushed both himself and his equipment to the limit.

Photographs by Muybridge continue to be widely exhibited

and reproduced, and exhaustively analysed too. Yet his character, marked by a set of unresolvable questions, remains elusive. Did head injuries in 1860, after a terrible stagecoach accident, really leave him cheerlessly volatile, liable to lose self-command, and perhaps not altogether sane? And, considering the numerous sequences he went on to photograph of barely clad or entirely naked women and men, himself included, is it fair or ridiculous to question the impulses behind his later studies in human locomotion? Again, what are

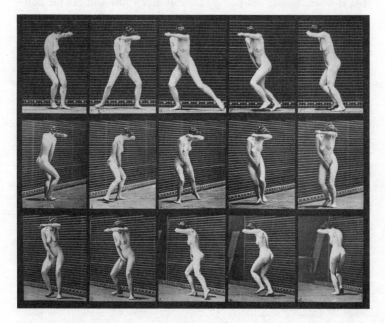

'Turning around in surprise and running away. (Movements. Female).'

we to make of the fact that on 17 October 1874 he travelled, with indisputable premeditation, through a long afternoon and deep into the night, to commit a brazen and pitiless act of murder?

What are we to make of that killing? Well, not too much, is the clear consensus. In the 1870s, experimental photographers were finding thrilling new ways to capture what was real. Muybridge was among those in the vanguard. Why lament the shadowy character, apparently concocted out of fictions, who stood for a moment in his path?

*

It may seem fair enough to want to view the matter in this light – except that Muybridge scholars are inclined to skew the available evidence, treating partisan newspaper accounts of the murder as neutral, and suspect testimony from Muybridge's trial as dependable, while omitting to explain how far their subject himself deliberately subverted the truth. In this way, standard accounts of Muybridge, executioner, reflect what their authors perhaps fail to grasp in full: that the killing was marked by critical deception on both sides.

This tendency to misrepresent the surviving evidence is particularly unhappy given the value placed on that same evidence by students of Muybridge. Those keen to ponder his interior life soon discover that, in the main, it must be deduced from a reading of his photographs. There is no great stash of diaries; no substantial hoard of personal letters; whole years of his existence go unrecorded. The one knockout exception to this deficit is the reporting of the murder he committed and of his subsequent trial, giving the best account we now have of Muybridge's mind and soul as they were ever captured in words. In this way, the killing becomes a boon to Muybridge scholars. Had their man not shot someone down, their understanding of him would be significantly less. Solnit describes the knowledge gained this way as 'priceless'.

That is easy to say. Yet the knowledge bought by Muybridge's act of murder is only really 'priceless' if the life he stole was worth nothing. And what if we are no longer quite so ready to accept that this is true?

Muybridge's zoöpraxiscope works because the eye, confronted at sufficient speed by successive static images, misses the gaps and instead perceives fluid motion. This is the reason we understand even the flickery films of long ago as representing something real. And the same flickering model can be applied to the story of Harry Larkyns. As he followed his resolutely wayward course he made a powerful impression on bystanders, and many of their written snapshots remain, so that he can be traced from one reported sighting to the next.

Harry lived an extraordinary life, filled with radical changes of circumstance, including three or four stints behind bars, wild romances and knife-edge adventures. In the process, he passed through what today can seem like completely distinct worlds; worlds we may well know best from the works of authors as diverse as Charlotte Brontë, Emile Zola and Mark Twain. Given the gaps that remain in Harry's record, and those phases where he left no more than a faint shadow behind him, what follows is necessarily not a balanced account. Yet by laying out, in order, the surviving fragments of his existence, it is possible to create a narrative zoöpraxiscope in waiting. Spin the whole, and we can imagine him careering crookedly between each damning or dazzled glimpse. The resulting story is quite as far-fetched as anything that cinema has thought to dream of since. But the tale is true, and it explains how 'Harry Larkyns' came to take a bullet through the heart.

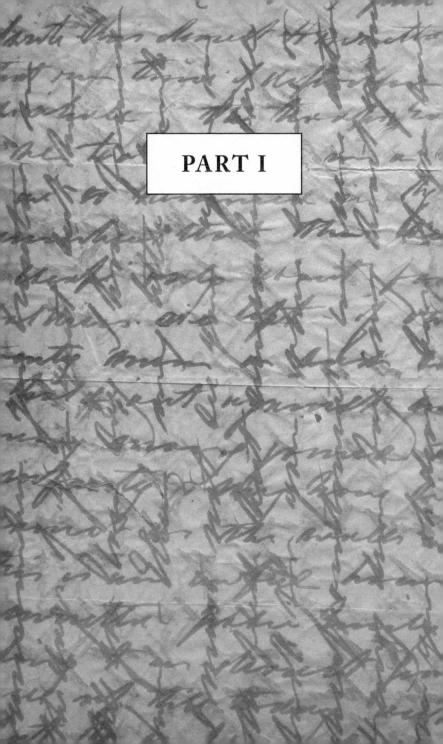

PART I

1: Childhood

Harry Larkins had a childhood no one could envy. It began to go wrong when he was not quite three. He and his sister Conny were left with relatives in London, and that was that: the two of them never saw their parents again. There are a few early glimpses of him in his mother's subsequent correspondence, but she makes him a pitifully marginal figure, so that it really does seem to be true, as was later said of him, that he was left 'to fight the battle of his life alone'.

Harry was born on 18 October 1843 in Meerut, in the East India Company's Bengal Presidency. He was christened Henry Thomas Larkins. Conny, also born in India, was older by a year.

The wider Larkins family had for generations been deeply implicated in Company business, with combined Larkinses down the years owning many great ships, the famed 'Indiamen'. Individual family members, too, became notable sea captains, or served as prominent Company soldiers, lawyers and civil servants, ranging far across the world. In their fortunes, that is, the Larkinses were essentially piratical, though among them, George Larkins, Harry's father, an officer in a regiment of the Bengal Horse Artillery, was comparatively an undistinguished specimen.

Harry's parents had married in 1838, also in Meerut. His mother was Scottish, born Ewart Carnochan, but known as Emma. Her father had been controller of HM Customs, Greenock, while in the Ewart line she was related to William Ewart, Liverpool merchant and slaver, and the man after whom John Gladstone, prolific fellow slaver, in 1809 named his son, the future Prime Minister, William Ewart Gladstone.

When George and Emma wed, George was thirty and a widower, having recently buried a young wife and two baby sons, presumably lost to sickness. Emma was almost thirty herself, and as this was considered old for a bride, she may well have gone out to India in the hope of snagging a husband, as part of the so-called fishing fleet. But even if there was pragmatism at the start of their union, the marriage proved affectionate and strong.

In the autumn of 1842, George survived being sent into Afghanistan as part of a force intended to terminate the extraordinarily bloody and senseless First Afghan War. Otherwise, scuppered by persistent ill health, his military record was destined to amount to very little. In fact it was on 'medical certificate' that, in February 1844, George took Emma, Conny and an infant Harry home, 'per *Queen*, for London'. For most of the next two years they lived cheaply in a rented house in Ardpatrick, Argyllshire, presumably to be near Emma's relations. And it was there, in the spring of 1846, that Emma gave birth to another child, Alice Schaffalitzky Larkins, her name a gesture to an influential godparent. But when the time came to return to India that October, George and Emma took only the baby with them. The other two children they left to the mercy of various Larkinses in England.

In the summer of 1849, when Harry was still only five, Emma sent a joint letter to him and Conny reminding them of their duty 'to strive at all times to please & approve yourselves to your kind uncles & aunts that we may be made happy from time to time with good accounts of your efforts & behaviour'. They had countless uncles and aunts, but were currently under the wing of the formidable pair known as Uncle and Aunt Larkins, who effectively headed the family in London.

'Uncle Larkins', John Pascal Larkins, was actually George's much older first cousin. He had joined the Bengal Civil Service in 1796, aged about sixteen, and thirty years later was President of the Marine Board, a director of the Board of Customs, Salt and Opium, and masonic Grand Master of Bengal. In 1825, in the teeth of disdainful opposition from Company directors at home, he laid the foundation stone of what was destined to become a great intellectual institution, Sanskrit College, Calcutta. But after winning this battle to value 'Asiatic knowledge', in 1826 he went on furlough to England, and, still in his forties and apparently unwell, there he remained, retiring on an annuity. Aunt Larkins, born Mary Ann Robertson, happened to be a first cousin of William Ewart Gladstone, and she loomed as large in the Larkins family as her husband.

One of the last of Emma's letters to place Conny in this household was delivered by a distant Ewart relative in 1849: 'My dearest Conny, I have just seen Colonel Ewart who is going home to England and he has promised to see you & write & tell Mama all about you.' Emma explained in passing that she had promised Harry twenty shillings, 'if he would send me a nicely written note which he did'. In another letter soon after, Emma told Conny that, as well as Ellen Mona Larkins, born the year before, God had now given Mama and Papa 'another little lamb to bring up for Him': Jessie Douglas Larkins. Alice, meanwhile, had just learnt 'C for Conny, H for Harry, B for Baby, A for Aunty and P for Papa'.

After this, Harry, now aged about six, slips right out of Conny's correspondence. Presumably he had been parcelled off to one of the many small, cheap schools known for taking the sons of 'Indian families', and it would be years before the two of them next met.

Conny herself soon left London to live with George's sister Henrietta, who was in her early fifties with no children of her own. As a young woman, Henrietta had been left £2,000 a year, worth about £150,000 today, by a cousin called Mrs Samuel Knip, on the whimsical condition that she must always keep a carriage and pair. And despite this fortune, or perhaps because of it, Henrietta had remained single until she was forty, when she married the banker John Dimsdale. Conny joined the two of them in their splendid dwelling, Greenham Lodge, Newbury, and remained there until the autumn of 1850 when, aged eight, she was dispatched to join a Devonshire cousin, Julia Luke, in a little school in Plymouth.

Every month or so, Emma Larkins sent a packet of letters to England, including correspondence for her children. Her letters to Harry have not survived, but, isolated as he was, he must have received his own bulletins of her captivating talk about leopards, bears, tigers, and 'immense crocodiles' on the banks of the Ganges, the 'ugliest creatures I ever saw'; her descriptions of huge journeys,

Emma Larkins, 1840

sometimes travelling by elephant, and of camping out, during the 'Relief' marches of the cold season when regiments shifted military station; paragraphs with scattered references to mangoes, custard apples, Mysore candy, acidulated raspberry drops, rhododendrons, fireworks and regimental weddings, not to mention happy children's games on the shaded verandah. 'I don't think I have seen anything more impressively lovely', she wrote one time, 'than the dew of an early morning in India, every leaf, twig & blossom, <u>laden</u> with beautiful globules that sparkle in the light.'

She also began to relay messages to Conny and Harry from their siblings in India, verbatim transcripts, so that the little voices come leaping off the page. Where necessary, as their first language was 'Hindoostanee', Emma also gave bracketed translations. Two of these notes for Harry, unforwarded, survive: 'My dear Henry, I did saw a great many birds' nests in the garden called the Tailor birds nests they are "coup sooret bunna" (beautifully made) as if sowed by a tailor with fine thread and hanging "muza" (gracefully) from a tree. I cannot say any more. Your Affectionate Sister Alice.' And: 'Henry Baba Kelona daga or churia. Jessie Douglas. (Henry my child I will give you toys and birds.)'

Amid the tantalising details, a sorry strand in the letters concerned Papa's rheumatic ill health. The family spent months in the hill station of Naina Tal in hopes of his recovery, even though on one visit the cold so profoundly shocked his system that for days he could not be undressed, apart from his boots, 'not his gloves even! the pain he endured was very great & he was all that time unable to move hands or feet'. For weeks at a time, he was obliged to use crutches. Perhaps not surprisingly, Papa's Naina Tal doctor and his wife became close friends, leading to an intriguing anecdote: 'We have had very heavy rain lately for three days so heavy & constant that Dr. Payne's house became filled with water to the height of five feet & Dr. Payne got into a boat & rowed about from one room to another & in & about his garden.'

For all the beguiling talk of elephants, crocodiles and custard apples, Emma also burdened her correspondence with darkly religious strictures. She had her absent children closely monitored by the adults who looked after them, creating a points system for their failings and naughtinesses. As these accounts and scores, and her responses to them, were sent wearyingly back and forth in posts that

George and Alice Larkins, Christmas 1851

took more than a month in each direction, her admonitions would resurrect crimes that were weeks in the past. She sent dire messages when the news was bad, explaining, 'I cannot help shedding tears when thinking that my dear absent children may be disobedient.' She believed that 'insubordination is the root from which every sin springs', and made free with half-remembered biblical snippets: 'a foolish man despises his mother', and 'still more awfully', she said, 'The eye that mocketh at his Father and despiseth to obey his mother, the ravens of the valley shall pick it out and eagles eat the same.'

After her first term at school, Conny returned to Greenham for Christmas. But John Dimsdale was ill, and he died in the new year of 1851. Emma later wrote approvingly that she gathered Conny had 'behaved discreetly and properly at that time'. However, Conny was soon sent back to school in Plymouth. The national census, taken at the end of March, captures Harry, aged seven, swept up with several Devonshire Larkins relatives on dutiful visit to his bereaved aunt in Greenham. But no one had seen fit to engineer a reunion between him and his sister.

The next year, Alice, now aged six and still barely able to read or write, was sent from India to be educated in England. Henrietta decided to recall Conny, and to employ a governess, Miss Elsie, to teach the two girls together in Greenham. Pathetically, on first encountering Alice, what Conny most wanted to know was whether, if she were to meet her own mother, she could expect to be embraced. Conny copied Alice's reply into a letter to Emma, receiving the brisk yet hedged response: 'Alice was quite right I would certainly embrace you & each of my good children if they came to us in India but this will be first in England I think.' Conny's prospects of physical affection if she failed to be a 'good child' were left less than wholly clear; but talk of a family visit to England was something to cling to.

Emma's letters to Alice would prove distinctly warmer than those she wrote to Conny, in part because Emma sought to maintain links between Alice and the servants who had largely brought her up. A typical string read: 'The Dhi, Munna, Rosan, Ramdeen & Surag the Buskery Wallah send many salaams to their little mistress.' Of these,

Alice's second mother had been Munna, who sometimes added special messages of her own: she conveyed through Emma 'many salaams to her little Alice Bee bee', or 'many salaams and hopes to go home with Mama to see you', or begged 'her pious salaam to Alice & hopes to send the silver junka (earrings) soon'. It had been Munna, and no one else, who had taken Alice hundreds of miles to Calcutta to put her on the boat for England, and Munna, therefore, who was the last to say goodbye.

Emma described Henrietta to Conny one day as someone 'to whom God has bound you and me by ties of gratitude more than human efforts almost can ever satisfy'. And that debt increased in 1854, when Ellen Larkins, now aged six herself, was also sent to England. Between them, the three girls would go on to preserve a correspondence of over a hundred letters from India, mostly written by their mother. Increasingly, Emma urged study on her children, writing to Conny, for example: 'I have just been reading your list of schoolbooks some of them are rather formidable, Philosophy for instance however I hope you give due attention to all I used to be very quick at parsing as a little girl & generally at the top of the class.' She also let it be known that: 'I am very desirous that you should be diligent and spend all your leisure time at the piano. All of you—for dearest Papa expects you all to play well.' God, however, came first: 'His glory must always be the beginning, continuing & ending of all studies, separate them & they become at once low & grovelling, so much time & reasoning faculties prevented & utterly wasted.' Even in passing Emma was repressive, writing to Conny: surely 'you would never pain me by the selfish gratification of an evil inclination'; or to Alice: 'believe in my own alterable love as long as you are good'. As for Ellen: 'I hope dear Ellen you have quite learnt never to tell a falsehood: it is an odious vulgar thing to do'; after all, 'God hates a lie and can never love a liar, a word that we even dislike to pronounce it is ugly, deformed, repulsive', and on, and on.

The Larkins sisters continued to visit Aunty and Uncle Larkins on holiday trips to London, but Harry was never there too. In 1851, Conny was taken to see the Great Exhibition at the Crystal

Palace in Hyde Park. And in the summer of 1854, she, Alice and Ellen all went to visit the 'Brazilian in Bloomsbury', as Dickens's *Household Words* dubbed the first ever living giant anteater to be displayed in the city. In the autumn of that year, Henrietta married Major-General Guy Carleton Coffin, who came to live with her and the girls at Greenham Lodge. His previous wife of over forty years had been one of Henrietta's many first cousins, and he was a generous man, buying the girls a pony which they called Pug. Then at last, on 18 December, after five years, Emma included this in a letter to Conny: 'I hope you enjoyed having dear little Henry and that you were kind to him remembering that his lot in life hitherto has not been so pleasant as your own. I hope to have a nice account of him in your next letter.' Conny must have obliged only very sketchily. On 1 April 1855, Emma's response was: 'What a surprise when you were told the little stranger was your brother; what did you think of him I wonder.'

Harry was by now eleven; Conny, twelve. What exactly his less pleasant lot had been all this time is not entirely clear. But there is a clue in one of Emma's letters to Alice, in which she insisted that Alice was luckier than 'many dear little girls' sent from India, who, rather than being placed with relatives, were dispatched to schools where they were forced 'to seek happiness & consideration amongst <u>strangers</u>'.

Harry made a second visit to Greenham in the summer of 1855, Emma this time responding to the information breezily: 'we are glad indeed to hear that dear Henry is to spend some time at Greenham & sincerely trust he will leave regretted'. Writing afterwards to Ellen, and remembering her son aged two, Emma was cooler still: 'Your Brother Henry has paid you a visit ere this I think: what impression did he make I wonder: I hope he is more gentle and discrete than I recollect him when he used to take Conny round the waist and drag her round the room.'

The year 1856 proved bleak for the family, when both Uncle Larkins and General Coffin died. Some months later, writing to a brother-in-law, Emma mentioned Henrietta's loss, and said: 'we all regret him & justly—his good feelings to our children boy & all—was valuable—of course not for our sakes—but that of his wife—but the benefit reached our hearts all the same'. The expression 'boy & all' here is characteristically opaque. Was Harry a particular challenge to 'good feelings', or was it just that he was hardly ever there to receive them? Or did she mean that it had been at the General's urging that Harry was invited to Greenham at all?

On Alice's arrival in England in 1852, Emma had written to Conny: 'I am made happy by your joy at having a dear sister to love.' But it is unclear whether there was anyone for Harry to love when he was a child, let alone someone who might have loved him back. Certainly his family in India must have struck him as more or less intimate strangers. He was presumably sensitive to the fact that, in with the dismal paragraphs of advice and criticism from his mother, with their endless talk of the immanence of death and of an inescapable, punishing God, the standards she expected of her English children, by whom she was so ready to be disappointed, scarcely matched the warm and unbuttoned picture she painted of his little siblings still in her care. For Harry, this difference must have been especially compelling when it came to his only brother, ten years younger than him, known in the family as Georgie.

After Jessie Douglas, and in 1850, a fifth daughter, Augusta Emily, George Lestock Larkins was born in 1853. He had nut-brown hair, a face 'just like an angel's', and was, as Emma indulgently put it, 'full of mischief'. As a two-year-old in oppressive heat, he 'frequently during the day all of a sudden slips through his dress and then he appears quite naked', she wrote. A year later, 'Sailing down the Soonderbunds', fellow passengers called him 'a very attractive child' and petted him 'very much': he spoke 'broken English so strangely', she said, 'that everyone asks him questions just for the pleasure of hearing him talk'. Georgie was a compulsive prankster. After the family received a new dog, Rajah, from Cousin William, a son of Uncle and Aunt Larkins, and another Bengal Army officer, Little Georgie 'tied his bed sheet round Rajah's neck and got up on the bed holding the end of the sheet and told the dog to go'. Rajah 'dragged his coachman after him and Georgie's poor nose was nearly broken'. Another time, he threatened to leap off a table in order to make the servants dash to save him: for a small boy to enjoy 'the discomfiture of his attendants' was 'not usual', said Emma, with an implicit smile. Georgie had his own servants, she explained, including 'the good Dhi', who 'keeps by her little master', never thwarting him, so that 'he orders her about and has quite the upper hand'. He even had a delinquent dog of his own called Pixie.

Glimpses of Georgie's happy relationship with his father must have been no less painfully alluring to the neglected son in England. 'Papa sometimes when playing with him calls him jolly dog in fun', wrote Emma; while Jessie Douglas, in one of her dictated messages, noted: 'Georgie bumptious boy Papa does call he does ride upon Papa's horses sometimes he teases us very much.' He did once in a while fall foul of his mother. Aged four, he stole ten small rice biscuits, and as Emma wrote: 'the enjoyment was soon over and then came the punishment I whipped him severely and I was sorry to see the dear little face full of suffering and indeed Mama shed tears with her little boy'. But to Harry, even this may have sounded like a reasonable price to pay for the luxury and freedom of his brother's existence.

In his twenties, after witnessing a mother bully her small child on a tram, Harry wrote feelingly that some people 'never seem to realise that children are individuals with whims and fancies of their own—very innocent, too, many of them—but they appear determined to crowd them into a certain groove, and make them over after a pattern'.

Harry himself, as he grew up, so thoroughly rebelled against being crowded into a certain groove that it seems fair to imagine considerable resistance, and even sparks of wilful disorder, scattered across the early, missing phases of his story. But whatever else, it is certainly true that, in the satellite existence to which his family condemned him, the seeds were sown for what he later became, a 'brilliant waif'.

2: Rebellion

For almost all of his early childhood, Harry was kept isolated from his immediate family, including his sisters in England. Even so, the events of his thirteenth summer would teach him how much more deprived it was possible for him to be. A desperate convulsion was about to take place in India, and whatever dreams he might have cherished about his birthplace, they were set to be overwhelmed by bloodshed and horror. After this, his idea of himself, too, could never be the same.

In January 1856, while travelling, Emma Larkins sent a letter to England in which she said: 'we are near Cornpore and hope to learn something of a future home there. I have asked God to fix it for us and to enable us to be happy in his decision.' Cawnpore, a military station on the Grand Trunk Road and on the banks of the Ganges, though strategically important to the British, had been rather neglected by the authorities, leaving it with a reputation as simply a pleasant garrison town. God fixed things so far as to provide a home there at the start of 1857, and Emma was soon writing giddily to her brother-in-law, about George, that she had 'a good account to give of my dearest one. He commands the Cawnpore Artillery division.' With this new posting, she thought, 'If health be granted us, we ought ere long to be rich', although 'it is wonderful to notice how an officer's expenses increase with rank'.

In England, Henrietta Coffin and the three Larkins girls also moved home, from Greenham closer in to London, 'in a very gay neighbourhood, Aldenham Park, Elstree'. It was there that Emma sent an apologetic letter to Conny at the end of February: 'It is a very long time since I have written to you or the other two dear girls and this has been remembered occasionally with dissatisfaction to myself.' Papa, she added, 'seldom requires a stick now which is a great change'. Emma was delighted that she and George had been singled out by the elderly but battle-hardened commander of the Cawnpore garrison and his wife: 'We dined with General Sir Hugh & Lady Wheeler last night and spent a very pleasant evening we were the only guests: their son Captain Wheeler is Sir Hugh's A. D. C. and a remarkably attractive man we thought.' More was promised, too. 'Tomorrow we have a musical party consisting of Miss Wheeler and her younger sister who plays <u>well</u>; Miss W—sings well.' An invitation also arrived from Mr Hillersdon, the District Magistrate and Collector, and his wife Lydia. 'We were highly delighted with her performance on the piano & concertina', wrote Emma, betraying perhaps a wisp of envy when she went on to explain that General the Hon. George Anson, head of all the British forces in India, had 'begged' to hear Mrs Hillersdon when he passed through Cawnpore en route for Simla. 'He asked Colonel Ponsonby to invite her to his house that he might hear her and both he and Mrs. Anson were charmed.'

On 14 April, *The Times* of London printed a piece by its Calcutta correspondent, sent a month before but just now received, reporting on 'this cartridge question' currently 'travelling northward'. A rumour had spread among the sepoys, the lowest-ranking Indian soldiers, that the cartridges of the army's new-issue Enfield rifles came greased with tallow and lard, fat from cattle and pigs. A cartridge was usually bitten to release its powder. Thus, if the rumour was true, the new ordnance threatened to defile both Hindus and Muslims. As the *Times* piece put it, the matter seemed likely to 'excite every Sepoy regiment in India, until in some station a determined Brigadier gives the men the option of obedience or death'. To the author of this sentence, death seemed just the thing to end the quibbling. After all, he wrote, 'Every man feels to the bottom of his heart that the safety of the empire hinges on the instant suppression of mutiny in whatever shape it may appear.'

In practice, the role of 'determined Brigadier' fell to Colonel George Carmichael-Smyth, commander of the elite 3rd Light Cavalry in Meerut. On 24 April he abrasively insisted that ninety of his men should perform a firing parade using the suspect cartridges. Any rumours about animal fat he declared to be false, but he allowed that, for this particular exercise, the blanks could be hand-torn.

The concession was not enough. All but five of his men refused, and over the next ten days the eighty-five whom he had driven to resist him were locked up, court-martialled and found guilty of disobedience. Most were sentenced to ten years' imprisonment with hard labour, a small handful receiving five-year terms, and on 9 May, in front of the other soldiers of the station, they were assembled on one of the parade grounds, publicly shackled and led away to jail.

The next day, their fellow sepoys broke them out again and put the station to the torch.

On 14 May Emma wrote to Conny. Cawnpore was now 'burning hot', she said: 'your sisters & Georgie dislike the confinement they undergo for not until the sun is down and the twilight gone are they allowed to go out'. Two days later Emma composed a note for Ellen, a deluge of chit-chat about plants, kid goats, and the new baby of Dr and Mrs Payne, now in Calcutta, before adding teasingly, 'I very often talk to dearest Papa about going home, would you not welcome us?' In her pell-mell manner she also added: 'Dearest Aunty will tell you all of our unhappy position at present in consequence of a misunderstanding among the Native soldiers <u>regarding</u> the motives of their Officers regarding their religion, many lives have been sacrificed within the last week and many houses have been burnt down, at Meerut.'

On 19 May, Emma wrote to Cousin William Larkins, currently in England on furlough, disgorging more particulars of these events. Every regiment of Native Infantry had 'plundered & burnt every bungalow in the N.I. & Cavalry lines, killed every European they could find, amongst whom Captain & Mrs. MacDonald of the 20th N.I. Colonel Fenn Mrs. Courtney of the hotel—also a niece of hers', as well as an army wife, 'the lady killed by a <u>butcher</u> who was caught by sweepers and burnt on the spot'. And she gave a similar litany for Delhi, where the Meerut rebels had taken their uprising next, ending: 'and many others whose names I know not, the poor bodies were stripped, thrown out on the streets of the city and exposed till night when their respective servants crept out and hid them from view, the insurgents are now in the Fort with 30 lacs of rupees and possession of the Powder Magazine: the other Mr. Willoughby blew up and it is feared blew himself up also'. Nevertheless, in Cawnpore, she wrote, 'we hope better things, the Artillery surely remain faithful'.

This uneasy hope was an extension of her faith in her husband. As early as 22 April, George had sought permission of General Wheeler to place a Native guard over his loaded guns 'to shew confidence', and the station had been on edge ever since. Stingingly, higher command had derided these precautionary measures, General Anson writing to Wheeler that he considered him 'an "Alarmist"', at which Wheeler was 'most <u>wroth</u>', Emma said. She went on: 'who has shown wisdom and who not. General Anson is now forced from the Hills and marching with the three Regiments of Europeans to <u>retake</u> Delhi.' She little knew that Anson would be dead in a week from cholera. George believed the continuing orders from on high were 'imbecile', and Emma attributed the 'whole calamity' to 'clumsy blundering'. But this was to identify a fault in the exercise of power, not in the fact of wielding it at all; and when she added, 'how distressing to know these dear lives sacrificed nothing can redeem them', she did not mean that punishment would be redundant. Mentioning 'numbers of the infatuated' supposedly 'begging for pardon on the plea that they did not kill their own officers', she wrote: 'Justice is Charity and I hope they will suffer they have forfeited life and must not live poor wretched criminals.' Despite the fearful uncertainty of the times, she closed by remarking to Cousin William, 'if you come back soon I hope for tidings of our dear little girls'.

About her dear little boy, by contrast, Emma said nothing, and it seems Harry was far enough removed from the rest that she saw no prospect of his being folded into a family gathering. As for any letters that Harry himself might have received from his distracted mother that year, they were presumably few. With or without this, however, news from India would soon be inescapable.

Writing shortly afterwards to Henrietta, Emma asked: 'What will you say to our being obliged to fly from our houses and take refuge in a barrack guarded by George's artillery and every European soldier at the place.' On the night of the retreat there, 21 May, George had been out for hours waiting to receive a phantom detachment of European reinforcements from Lucknow. Then the order came: 'Prepare for defence.' He was to abandon the watch and mastermind the transport of guns. With the alarm raised, Emma soon found her house disordered with panicking strangers, before they all hastily extracted themselves and fled.

Lydia Hillersdon, also writing home, explained that at first she had hoped that she and her children might take refuge with a friendly local dignitary, the Nana Sahib, in whom her husband placed full trust. But instead she stopped briefly at the house of Colonel Ewart and his wife, the same Colonel Ewart who in 1849 had carried a letter to England for Conny and Harry. And along with everyone else, she was then ordered to hasten to the barracks. 'There was an immense number of ladies and gentlemen assembled there, and oh! what an anxious night it was; the children added much to our distress and anxiety; it was some hours before I could get them to sleep. I did not lie down the whole night.'

With the artillery shifted, an unidentified officer described how the men were 'kept standing by them all night through the rain, expecting an instant attack'. The cantonments now stood empty, with hundreds of residents removed, foreshadowing a greater vacancy to come: 'At night, everything is so quiet it seems like a large cemetery', he said. To show confidence in the sepoys by putting yourself at their mercy was to risk death, he explained; but demonstrating lack of confidence by attempting to disarm them was to risk provoking the very attack you sought to avoid. He described how Wheeler now had 'a trench and earthen parapet' thrown up round the barracks, the second formed by digging out the first, and added: 'No officer can look forward with any degree of pleasure to a struggle with men whom he lately commanded, and took pride in, and implicitly trusted.' Everyone knew that the Cawnpore station was 'built on a dead level', with no fort or 'place of refuge', making it 'in every respect ill-adapted for defence'.

On 31 May, Colonel Ewart wrote home to the current guardian of his son that 'if the troops do mutiny, my life must almost certainly be sacrificed'; in that event, he said, 'think kindly of me. I know you will be everything a mother can be to my boy. I cannot write to him this time, dear little fellow; kiss him for me.' That same day, Wheeler sent word to Calcutta stating that he had victuals for three weeks, and counted 400–500 women and non-combatants, with, to defend them, 'not more than 150 fighting men', a total number of refugees in the entrenchments since calculated to have been considerably higher.

The next day, writing to Henrietta, Emma noted that, 'the sepoys here are not to be depended on more than at other places'. She believed that, 'were they to rise they would only destroy property and plunder the Treasury. The only fear is of pressure from without.' But this secondary fear was great, especially as 'every bungalow at Lucknow was burnt last night', and the Lucknow mutineers had since departed that nearby station. All in all, she wrote, 'should overpowering numbers assail this place we know not what would be the result'. She added, 'you would be sorry dearest Henrietta to look at us crowded up together and not a bathroom even, but we are here to save our lives and we all feel how solemn is our situation.'

The first of June, the date of this letter, was the last day before the Cawnpore postal system collapsed. This final correspondence would be stowed on the Bombay steamer on the 11th, reaching England in mid July.

The revolt properly began in Cawnpore on 5 June. The British had long denied the Nana Sahib hereditary privileges on the grounds that he had won his title through being adopted. To appease him, though, they had allowed him to hold several large guns. When Cawnpore's rebel sepoys, lacking artillery, left town to march on Delhi, he met their column and offered them the weapons they needed. Also potentially available to them was a vast quantity of ammunition, stored on boats in the Cawnpore canals, which the British had failed to blow up. With the added promise of the wealth of the treasury, equally vulnerable to capture, the sepoys turned back to fight.

Jonah Shepherd, a Christian, and, in the language of the times, a Eurasian, who had retreated within entrenchments, was later able to describe how the barracks there were now slowly 'scattered to atoms by the 24-pounder balls that were incessantly fired by the enemy'. Many people, he said, simply 'died under the walls. Day and night the guns were kept playing upon us without ceasing for a moment', and 'The existence of those that remained alive was spent in perpetual dread and fear.'

Charles and Lydia Hillersdon were among those killed early. Charles Hillersdon was 'standing in the verandah of the puckah-roofed barrack in conversation with his wife' when a round shot 'completely disembowelled him'. Lydia, who had recently had a baby, died a couple of days later, 'killed by a number of falling bricks dislodged by a shot and causing concussion of the brain'. General Wheeler's son and ADC, Godfrey, whom Emma had considered 'remarkably attractive', died inside the barracks. He lay 'fainting from a wound he had received in the trenches; his sister was fanning him, when a round shot entered the doorway, and left him a headless trunk'.

Georgie had just turned four, and Jessie Douglas was shortly due to turn eight, while 9 June was Augusta Emily's seventh birthday. Three days after that, the roof of the hospital barrack caught fire. Numbers of the sick and injured languishing there burned to death, and the hoarded medical supplies, including vital implements for amputations, were almost completely destroyed. Many women and children were now forced to migrate to the outer trench for safety, using whatever rags they could muster to protect them from the scorching sun. By this point, according to Lieutenant Mowbray Thomson, an officer who survived, 'our fifty-nine artillerymen had all been killed or wounded at their posts'. George, however, because of the 'shattered state' of his health, had already been forced to withdraw from active duty, no doubt extending his chances. By now, Thomson wrote, there was a terrible stench of the 'putrefying remains of the dead', as well as an 'unusually great influx of flies', though scavenging birds helped to mitigate the 'frightful aggravations' of epidemic diseases. 'Wives', he added, 'saw their husbands' bodies mutilated in the most awful manner', and husbands 'saw their wives suffering the most excruciating agonies from wounds they were unable to heal. Then there was the screaming of children after their dead parents. Poor little things, how it unnerved one to see them!'

The siege went grinding on in this desperate fashion for almost three weeks. Only when the water supply was completely exhausted did Wheeler accept terms. The survivors inside the entrenchments were offered safe passage out of Cawnpore, by boat along the

Ganges, so long as they disarmed first. And what choice did they have, when 'to remain there was to die'? A ceasefire came into force on 25 June. According to Thomson, after the 'incessant bombardment', the 'stillness was actually painful'.

Destroyed barracks and verandah, Cawnpore

Two days later, on the morning of the promised embarkation, 'day-break disclosed to view hosts of adjutant birds and vultures gloating'. Those assembling to leave for the boats were filthy and emaciated, some of them now half mad, and most half naked too, having torn up their clothes for bandages and given their stockings as impromptu containers for grapeshot. Colonel Ewart, wounded early on, so as to be 'entirely disabled from any participation in the defence', was with his wife at the tail end of the ragged procession. Ramshackle attempts to convey the wounded to the ghat by the river 'must have caused them greatly aggravated torture', wrote Thomson. And Ewart, in a parlous physical state, accepted an offer of help made by sepoys from his own regiment. They carried him to one side, and 'after mocking and repeating to him the angry expressions he sometimes used towards them on parade, they cut him to pieces with swords, and afterwards slew Mrs. Ewart also'.

For lack of rain, the river was extremely low. But it was only after many had clambered into the forty or so waiting vessels that the truth struck home, that almost all the boats were immovably lodged in the mud. 'The infernal treachery of our assassins', wrote Mowbray Thomson, now led to a scene that 'beggars all description'. The thatched roofs of these vessels, notionally designed to shield passengers from the sun, were set alight, and 'Alas! the wounded were burnt to death.' Of those fit enough to jump back out, some waded for safety into deeper water, and even attempted to swim away; but they were picked off by gunfire from the banks, or hacked down by enemy fighters on horseback, many dying of their wounds or drowning. Men who staggered through the mud back ashore were immediately killed also.

Reports on Wheeler's fate proved contradictory. All plausible sources concurred in saying that, with his wife and daughters, he made it to the boats. But individual bias or scruple must explain the disparity in the accounts of how shamingly he was butchered thereafter, or how honourably he took his killing, in one version beheaded by the single stroke of a sword.

One of Wheeler's two daughters, both of whom had struck Emma so pleasantly, was among a very few young women who now escaped, only to be abducted by enemy troopers. According to Jonah Shepherd, they were selected for their 'dark complexion': as Lady Wheeler was Eurasian, so her daughters were too. Whichever of the girls was taken, 'Miss Wheeler' became a near-mythic figure as the story got abroad that, to avoid 'dishonour', she had secured her abductor's sword, 'and with it, after killing him, his wife, and three children, threw herself into a well and was killed'. A later police investigation concluded that this story was 'mere fabrication' and that in truth she had surrendered to her fate, and lived.

A hundred and sixty-three other women and small children who survived the slaughter at the boats were removed by the Nana Sahib to a small building back in town, known as the Bibighar. And there, for the time being, he kept them, barely alive.

*

Because of the lengthy delay in getting information to Britain, only compounded by the destruction of large parts of the Indian telegraph system, it was not until 24 June, the day before the Cawnpore capitulation, that *The Times* in London first reported: 'burning of the barracks and of the houses of the European officers at Meerut'. Across the country, newspaper readers must have prayed that this had been a local uprising in response to a misconstrued slight. But the causes of 'disaffection' in India ran far deeper than the incendiary matter of the cartridges, and as the summer wound on, the British press went from relaying out-of-date details of ever more 'mutinies' by diverse scattered regiments, to speaking of a unitary 'Indian Mutiny' or 'Sepoy Rebellion', until, four months in, the *Evening Standard* saw fit to describe the ever-escalating nightmare as 'the vortex of the Indian War'. For those miserably awaiting each further news bulletin, not least the extended Larkins family, the lag in communications must have been unbearable.

Henrietta's move to Elstree had given her readier access to the society of numerous relatives, including her youngest sister, Jane Emma, married to the Rev. William Streatfeild, the vicar of East Ham; and the Streatfeild daughters, too, were a good match for Conny, Alice and Ellen. On 3 August, there was a family gathering when, in a church in Marylebone, Streatfeild assisted at the marriage of Cousin William Larkins to a Louisa Southey. But the event cannot have been wholly cheerful. That morning's *Times* carried an unreservedly inflammatory account of depredations outside Delhi: 'Give full stretch to your imagination—think of everything that is cruel, inhuman, infernal, and you cannot then conceive anything so diabolical as what these demons in human form have perpetrated', it said. Women fleeing the city had been stripped, 'violated', murdered, butchered, then left unburied to be eaten by wild animals. And children had been butchered too. 'We found a pair of boots, evidently those of a girl 6 or 7 years of age, with the feet in them. They had been cut off just above the ankle.'

The Streatfeild family had their own fears, as Robert, the oldest son, was in India with his regiment. And their concern would shortly be justified. Helping to disarm the 14th Native Infantry in Ghelum, he was terribly injured. A few days afterwards, he somehow penned a note home, saying: 'Do not grieve, dear ones—God's will be done! I am quite happy, and looking forward to home always.' A brother officer was more explicit: 'Poor young Streathfield, the bravest of the brave, got a bullet through both knees, smashing the right one to atoms and going through the other. The right leg was amputated at the thigh.'

But Robert was not the only one. On 18 August, William Streatfeild sent a sorrowful letter to one of his young daughters: 'Dear Mamma and her sisters are, as you may suppose, extremely anxious about their brother George, his wife and children, who are supposed to be at Cawnpore, besieged by a large number of these sanguinary mutineers', resignedly adding, 'All communication is cut off, so that we cannot hear from Major G. Larkins.' Perhaps not, but there was evidently no attempt to conceal from the children the awful stories appearing almost daily in the press, so that Conny, Alice, Ellen, and surely Harry too, must have been left horribly anxious by chaotic increments of undependable information.

Day after day for most of the rest of August, inconsistent stories from India appeared in *The Times*, often out of chronological order, until on 27 August the paper announced definitively: 'Sir Hugh Wheeler has been killed at Cawnpore. The garrison, pressed by famine, surrendered the place to Nena Sahib, by whom, in violation of his solemn promise, all were massacred.' The paper called this news 'most lamentable', and added the hope that Wheeler had died in advance of the capitulation, 'and that he finished his long and brilliant career a soldier, and not as the helpless victim of a hideous butchery'.

The Streatfeild daughters would later describe how, when finally it came, 'the appalling news of the massacre at Cawnpore was a fresh and fearful blow to our parents, as it was by this time almost a matter of certainty that so many dear ones had perished'. Yet to this blow a new dread was immediately added, that Emma, and even Jessie Douglas and Augusta Emily, might have suffered the 'yet direr fate' for which some women were said to have been reserved in the Bibighar, a possibility that left 'sudden and violent dissolution' comparatively to be desired.

On 2 September, *The Times* was able to explain that relieving forces under General Havelock, who might have saved the Cawnpore garrison, had been delayed by the need to put down mutinies in Benares and Allahabad. The paper finally supplied a hopelessly patchy list of the dead, with the appended comment, unsupported by anything other than general incredulity: 'We still believe, however, that many returned as murdered will be found to have escaped.' The name 'Larkins' was nowhere to be seen.

The Streatfeild parents now went to stay with Henrietta in Aldenham Park, from where, on 16 September, William Streatfeild wrote despairingly: 'We think the last gleam of hope has vanished in respect to the doomed victims at Cawnpore! There is another horrifying letter in the paper about the massacre there. It is most affecting. My spirits are not very exalted.' That day's *Times* carried an especially gruesome article describing the 'soul-harrowing spectacle' of the Bibighar, as discovered by the British soldiers who retook Cawnpore: a picture of 'barbarously slaughtered' women, 'stripped naked, beheaded, and thrown into a well'. Some children, now dead, appeared to have been 'hurled down alive upon their butchered mothers, whose blood yet reeked on their mangled bodies'. The *Times* predicted, accurately, that no matter what other new 'prodigies and horrors' might emerge from the Rebellion, Cawnpore, which had seen 'put to death in cold blood one thousand Europeans and Christians', was destined to stand in British consciousness as 'the crowning atrocity' of them all.

The response of many of the soldiers who arrived too late to prevent these acts was to commit random atrocities of their own. And 'if they should in future be accused of cruelty in their vengeance, it need only be replied—Remember Cawnpore!' wrote *The Times*. Two days later it put its own palliative to the test, reporting on the actions of Colonel James Neill, who was left to hold Cawnpore while Havelock pushed on. Neill ordered that any 'high-caste Brahmins' among those whom he deemed guilty for the carnage at the Bibighar should be compelled by the lash to 'wash up the blood from the floor', meaning that they should be made to pollute themselves by licking up that human blood, before being hanged. Neill's indiscriminate, baroque and repulsive punishment, said *The Times* glibly, had 'gained him great credit'.

On 19 September, the paper printed a remarkable first account from Cawnpore by Jonah Shepherd, who had endured almost the whole of the siege within the entrenchments, before escaping. After making it out, he was immediately caught, imprisoned, and thereafter temporarily starved. One of his children had been shot in the head on 12 June. Once liberated by the British, he learnt of the deaths of the rest of his family inside the entrenchments, apart from a daughter, 'inhumanly butchered' at the Bibighar: 'Oh! when I think of it how my heart breaks,' he wrote, 'I get beside myself, and wish I had not been spared.'

Two days later, *The Times* provided a translated list of names compiled by an Indian doctor who at some point had assessed the women and children in the Bibighar. While some died in there of cholera or dysentery, including, incredibly, the mother of a two-day-old baby, by far the majority were killed in the final massacre on 16 July. Gruellingly, their many names were supplied by *The Times* in small, dense print, in no discernible order. Added to this, there was the high likelihood of misspellings. But as a mercy for members of the Larkins family, once more there was no name included that looked anything like their own.

A further, small news item on the same page of the paper may have eluded many of those reeling from its disclosures. Word was just starting to spread that two young lieutenants, Mowbray Thomson and Henry Delafosse, had somehow managed to escape from the massacre at the boats. And the story was true: they had been on the one boat to launch successfully down the Ganges, thereafter hunted along the banks for several days by men with guns. Most of their fellow passengers had either been picked off with bullets, or had simply died from existing injuries and exposure. But through shattering physical effort, blind luck, and the kindness of strangers once they crept ashore, Delafosse and Thomson became the sole British officers to survive.

At the end of September, senior members of the Larkins family issued a death notice, subsequently reproduced in countless newspapers. As printed, it read: 'Major George Larkins and his wife Emma Ewent [*sic*], with their children Jessie Douglas, Augusta

Emily and George Douglas Lestock, at Cawnpore, in June last, (supposed to have perished in the general massacre).' The caveat 'supposed to have perished' might ordinarily be taken to imply the hope that one or more had possibly survived. But this was not the point of what became a standard equivocation. The hope was that they really had all perished in the 'general' massacre at the boats, with none reserved to face the further atrocities in July. And yet, even supposing all five had lasted until 27 June, how much mercy would there have been in that?

It is possible that when they issued this announcement, the family in England had received advance notice of lists being published in the journal the *Homeward Mail*. When George Smith launched this fortnightly title at the start of 1857, with its digest of Indian news, he can scarcely have imagined the information he would soon be called on to broadcast. On 16 September he printed a first list, compiled 'with considerable care and pains', of those believed dead 'up to the present time during the disastrous revolt in India'. A second list, on 1 October, at last named George, Emma and the three children.

For the four Larkins children in England, the shock of Cawnpore must have been absolutely immense. At the same time, what it meant to them individually cannot have been anything like the same. Alice and Ellen had both lived in India until the age of six, brought up in a household with their mother, father and younger siblings, not to mention a whole family of servants too. Conny and Harry, by contrast, can have had few living memories of their parents, few if any memories of India, and their three youngest siblings they had never met at all.

At least, in the unremitting bleakness of their losses, however they experienced them, Conny, Alice and Ellen had each other. But if Harry spent any time with them at Aldenham Park, as hope dwindled across that terrible summer, he was not long to remain there. In fact, exactly coincident with the first specific announcements in the press of the deaths in his far-off family, he was himself sent away to a little boarding school in Belgium.

3: School

When Charles Dickens was writing *Our Mutual Friend* and needed to put the young John Harmon out of the way, he decided to have him 'cheaply educated at Brussels'. And it is possible that Harry's fate, too, at the hands of his underfunded parents, had for some years been a *pensionnat*, or Continental boarding school. Many of them advertised the inestimable benefit of 'No Vacations', or 'No Vacations unless desired', perhaps explaining Harry's conspicuous absence in England. But whatever the truth of this, from now on he was 'brought up by his aunt, Mrs. Coffin', so that it was Henrietta's decision, in the autumn of 1857, to send him to a new school abroad, on his own. Here, not for the first time, and certainly not for the last, he would be forced to reinvent himself among strangers, a faculty he was developing as an art in itself.

Getting to Brussels from England was an overnight journey. According to Charlotte Brontë, who with her sister Emily sought cheap instruction there in the 1840s, the view from Ostend onwards was characterised by 'reedy swamps' and patches 'like magnified kitchen gardens', with pollarded willows, canals, 'painted Flemish farmhouses; some very dirty hovels; a grey, dead sky'. The sisters intended to improve their language skills, so that rather than the drudgery of governessing, they might open their own school at home. And they had the name of Mrs Jenkins, wife of the British Consul in Brussels, to help them to secure 'a cheap and decent residence and respectable protection'. Mrs Jenkins afterwards reported that she would invite the sisters to come for Sundays and holidays, 'until she found that they felt more pain than pleasure from such visits'. And Charles Edward Jenkins, one of her sons, was still dining out on Charlotte's peculiarities a decade later: 'his province as a lad, was to escort her back to school, after evenings spent at their house. A purgatorial process, he declares it was, from her invincible taciturnity. He remembers her, too, in the family circle, screwing her chair round by degrees, till her face was to the wall.'

Brontë's first novel manuscript, *The Professor*, completed in 1846, and concerning a pair of impoverished expatriate teachers in Brussels, was, she felt, summed up in the line: 'He that is low need fear no fall.' The conditions she portrayed were harsh, with instruction 'extremely cheap there on account of the number of teachers', but by the end her hero has plans for his own *pensionnat*, and the promise of being able to eke out his income through additional private tutoring. Every publisher to receive the manuscript turned it down. However, the same George Smith who would later launch the *Homeward Mail* had 'Currer Bell' encouraged in kindly terms to 'submit another effort', a proffered crumb of hope that won him the inestimable plum of publishing *Jane Eyre*.

A child's view of the typical *pensionnat* can be found in the memoirs of one of Dickens's sons, Henry. Between 1853 and 1860, Dickens sent four of his seven boys, not to Brussels, but to Boulogne. The institution he chose was run along standard lines by two English clergymen, promising low costs, superior instruction in French and a reassuringly Protestant ethos. And there the boys remained, a year at a time, returning only in the summers. When Henry Dickens later wrote about his experiences, he recalled the language-teaching as dismal and the meals as absolutely awful too: 'very pale veal with very, very watery gravy', followed by 'stick-jaw pudding', all served on plates of tin.

Some months after squiring Charlotte Brontë through the streets of Brussels, C. E. Jenkins left the city to go to school at Shrewsbury. He subsequently went to Cambridge, becoming a 'Second Classman' in Classics, after which, in 1851, he was ordained a priest by the Bishop of Ely. But he had been 'Born and established on the Continent for life', as he put it, and so he returned to Brussels, where he was appointed English Chaplain in 1856, a position previously held by his father. There was no Anglican church in the city, so for services, at odd hours, he rented out the Chapel Royal. He also set up his own *pensionnat*, before casting around, like Brontë's unhappy hero, for further pickings. And though his school survived him, when Jenkins died in 1873 aged forty-six his total worth was reckoned at £20.

Stick-jaw pudding or not, it was to Jenkins's *pensionnat*, in its earliest incarnation at 14 rue des Champs Élysées, Brussels, that Harry was sent by Henrietta. His later records confirm that he was a highly adept scholar with a particular flair for languages, making it extremely unlikely, unless they bored him, that he found his lessons a struggle. But while Brontë certainly suggested that a bad Brussels school could be stultifying, marked by 'deadness' and a 'sameness of life's daily ongoings', so that her hero falls prey to the 'morose nurselings' of depression, she omitted to mention cricket. And Jenkins was at least a great advocate of a game that Harry himself later wrote about as inspiring 'pure love'. The school was developing its own Champs Élysées Club, and the boys, sometimes aided by visiting Anglican clerics, pitted themselves against teams representing 'Brussels' or 'the English'. After all, as one match account put it, 'Though not indigenous to the green fields of Belgium, the noble game may flourish in them as an exotic.'

Brussels was by no means insulated from news of India. Just a week after Harry arrived, Queen Victoria engineered a national paroxysm in the form of a Day of Humiliation and Prayer, with railways and businesses suspended, hand-wringing and tub-thumping from the pulpit, and long reports in the press. Copies of those same newspapers, sent to expatriates clustered abroad, continued to serve up graphically frightful stories of the Rebellion, even as the slogan 'Remember Cawnpore!' became totemic among the British. On 17 October, copies of *The Times* reached Brussels containing a deposition by Henry Delafosse, one of the two lieutenants to have escaped Cawnpore and lived. He named everyone he could remember among the besieged, with, where he knew it, a terse cause of death: apoplexy, smallpox, sunstroke, fever, or often simply 'killed'. Instantly striking as the third of over a hundred entries was 'Major Larkins, Mrs. Larkins and children', though how they had died, Delafosse did not say. If Harry was by any chance still clinging to the minuscule possibility of a miraculous escape by someone in his family, this ended all rational hope.

The day after his orphanhood was in this way effectively sealed, he turned fourteen.

One further direct shock of this kind awaited Harry, and it came from a dreadfully unexpected source. That Christmas, after a wandering journey of half a year, an extraordinary last letter written by Emma finally reached England. It confirmed that the family must be dead, 'if any confirmation had been needed'. But for Harry, it also carried a terrible added sting.

The letter itself consisted of a single frail sheet of paper covered in almost impenetrably crossed lines. And it was dated 9 June, meaning that Emma had composed it inside the entrenchments, after several days under enemy bombardment. She started breathlessly: 'I write this dearest Henrietta in the belief that our time of departure is come the whole of the troops rose here & we took refuge in a Barrack We are so hemmed in by overpowering numbers that there seems no hope of escape only about forty European soldiers are left—of one hundred & twenty men a sad sad number to hold out against such an awful enemy.' With no idea how much more endurance lay ahead, she explained:

> The walls are going—This is an awful hour my darling Henrietta—Jessie Emily & Georgie cling to us dearest George has been well up till to-day out day & night But he is I grieve to say obliged to abandon his post This is to me a grief many brave men have fallen to day the siege has lasted four days!—and let this be a warning to your government never again to place British officers & men in such a pitiable position—only 120 European soldiers at Cawnpore! It is sad & painful to reflect on that our lives are to be sacrificed in such a condition.

She then scribbled valedictions to various friends, before contemplating to her four distant children:

> give my love to my sweet girls—tell them there is but one thing needful—tell them to seek sorrowing that faith sure & steadfast an anchor of the soul—Conny darling your Mama has longed to see

& know you—seek your God & heaven in <u>spirit</u>—Alice my sweet child remember your Creator in the days of your youth seek Him till you can say I have found Him—Ellen my little lamb I must not see you again in the flesh but remember I will look for you where sorrow & disappointment can never enter Henry dear boy my heart yearns over you oh dear boy if you saw the position your little brother & sisters are in at this moment you would weep over ever having pleased your own desires seek your God & serve Him & please Him & always hate whatever is sinful

With a helpless expression of gratitude, she then added: 'dearest Henrietta we leave them all in the hands of God & your tender watching.'

The letter itself was not quite all. Inside the triangular flap of its tiny envelope, Emma scrawled a further fragmentary message: 'I have given this to Munna—who hopes to escape also I hope to give her my pearls & little jewels to hand to you', across which, on a diagonal, was a direction to her friend, now in Calcutta, Mrs Payne.

The envelope scribble looks yet more chaotic than the letter itself, as though dashed off under extreme duress, with Emma dipping her pen into ink dregs or wet dirt every two or three words. Jonah Shepherd's account confirms that, with the siege under way, 'there was no ink or pens to be had for love or money', making it likely that Emma composed the letter some days before Munna's decision to flee provided the means by which to attempt to smuggle it out.

It might be thought natural that Munna would endeavour to escape. Though the barracks provided only feeble protection, with their walls 'so sadly riddled that every safe corner available was considered a great object', social distinctions were ruthlessly enforced, so that 'native servants had to remain in the open air at night'. Shepherd saw seven servants out on a verandah struck by a shell that 'hopped in the midst of them and burst with tremendous effect, causing instant death to five'. At the same time, any attempted flight required immense courage. Apart from the immediate danger of being shot, anyone captured alive by opposing forces risked being incarcerated, interrogated, tortured, and possibly then killed anyway. And even surviving all these dangers, servants risked reprisals, after

Cawnpore was retaken, from British soldiers who took the view that they had cruelly abandoned their duty to their 'defenders'. In this light, Emma's last scribbled note about Munna stood to save her life. James Neill, who oversaw blood-licking and mass reprisal killings, wrote with complete confidence in a letter: 'I find the officers' servants behaved shamefully, and were in the plot.' They 'deserted their masters and plundered them'. He described peremptorily hanging anyone he believed to be a rebel, who could not immediately prove a defence.

The Streatfeild girls wrote later that Emma's last letter was 'entrusted to a native servant to take down to the coast, and post for England'. Conny, perhaps more reliably, recorded that 'the ayah gave the letter to one of General Havelock's officers', who then took four months to get it to Calcutta. Alice, however, all her life cleaved to a story in which Munna walked the 600 miles to Calcutta, only to be refused a hearing when she arrived; after which, 'Bursting into tears she called on Heaven to witness her Faithfulness, gave the packet to a servant and weeping turned away Never to be heard of again.' Various misconceptions make this tale factually unlikely. However, to Alice Munna was not simply a 'native servant', or 'the ayah', but her second mother, imparting metaphorical truth to this tale of unrewarded fidelity and love; and by insisting on her version, Alice could sorrow for a loss in India that she was given no other means to acknowledge.

Harry's bereavement, by contrast, though extreme, must have felt bizarrely abstract; and in this light, Emma's last letter was surely horribly alienating. To her 'sweet girls' she had offered love and the promise of heavenly reunions. To Harry she had sent a public rebuke, and a call for ceaseless self-denial. Moreover, she tried to associate his future pleasures in life with the slaughter of his little brother and two smallest sisters, a message from beyond the grave that she clearly hoped would haunt him for ever.

It is at least possible to lay out how the East India Company weighed Harry's losses for him. In April 1858, its 'Home Accounts' for the latest financial year included a list of 'Special Pecuniary Grants' payable to the dependants of officers recently killed in action. Under the heading 'Bengal Establishment', one of many grim entries read: 'The four orphan children of Major George Larkins, of the Artillery, who with his wife was killed by the mutineers at Cawnpore on the 27th June 1857, 20*l* per annum each': a little under £2,000 today. The sums were determined by an officer's rank, and when it came to the Larkins children, it formed no part of the calculation that they had lost their mother too.

On 1 July 1858, after nine months in Brussels, Harry returned to England. Henrietta had decided to invest more in his education, in the process angling him towards a career. The Wimbledon School, where she sent him next, was housed in a mansion built by Robert Bell, a founder member of the East India Company and an exact contemporary of Shakespeare. The building had been converted into a school in 1790, with Georgian dormitories and offices added on. And in 1803, Arthur Schopenhauer had been sent there aged fifteen, principally to improve his English, though it had the more important effect of provoking him to revolt at its insistent religiosity. After passing through several hands, in 1850 the school was acquired by the Rev. John Brackenbury, one of the original assistant masters

The Wimbledon School

at Marlborough College, founded seven years earlier. 'Brackenbury's' soon earned a reputation as an outstanding army crammer, and when Harry arrived for the new term in September 1858, it was at full capacity, with about sixty-five pupils.

The curriculum was designed to prepare most boys for the competitive examinations that faced candidates who wished to become officer cadets. And though cricket, football and athletic sports were encouraged, it was the academic classes that held sway. Brackenbury professed to dislike cramming, if this implied knowledge 'more superficial than sound'. But he admitted ruefully to an Education Commission in 1866 that, compared with the more famous public schools, 'you may call us, perhaps, somewhat of a hotbed of instruction'. He believed that, above all, the 'study of language, itself the expression of all the complex powers and emotions of the mind, and the severe process of mathematical reasoning, strengthen and develop the intellect'. As in Schopenhauer's day, the timetable was heavily overlaid with Christian teaching, including daily doses of scripture, Greek Testament classes, and two church services on a Sunday with hours of religious study in between. But in any spare time, boys could roam the countryside, checked by two-hourly roll-calls.

At Marlborough College, where Brackenbury learnt his trade, 'The "natural enmity" theory between boys and masters' prevailed: 'public and promiscuous caning' with 'a weapon of hideous length and terrible circumference' was used as a 'tremendous engine of discipline', and became 'a thrilling and leading feature of the daily task'. Brackenbury, though, preferred 'the government to a great degree of boys by boys', and instituted a system in his own school where the ten top pupils, known as 'censors', formed their own court. They had 'the power of the cane' over any boy up to the age of fifteen, and only after this did a teacher inflict the punishment. Harry, therefore, to begin with, would have faced the court.

Dickens also attempted to round off four of his sons at Brackenbury's, 'educating expensively', as he put it. He wrote: 'I don't think I ever saw boys more closely stoned than at that eminent Grinder's by the bye', 'stoned' here meaning 'sharpened on a whetstone'. Despite the jocular tone, this was the language he had used in *Dombey and Son*, with its school of the 'Charitable Grinders', whose pupils were 'huffed and cuffed, and flogged and badged, and taught, as parrots are, by a brute jobbed into his place of schoolmaster'.

Harry overlapped there with the second of Dickens's sons to attend, Alfred D'Orsay Tennyson Dickens; and presumably any of the Dickens boys emitted a touch of proximate dazzle. When Henry Dickens wrote about being punished for talking in the dormitory in Boulogne, he conjured up a fellow pupil prompting him riskily in the darkness: 'Now young Dickens, spin us a yarn.' Alfred attended Brackenbury's for three years, but was eventually found wanting, and at seventeen went to work in the London office of a China merchant. Two years later he was sent to Australia and never saw his father again. Henry Dickens, who was younger, went to Brackenbury's from 1861, rising to become Head Censor. Against strong opposition from his father, he won permission to apply to Cambridge to read maths, and became the sole brother to go to university. In fact, it was only the first of the Dickens boys to go to the school, Walter Savage Landor Dickens, who profited from its military cramming. Weighing up Walter's prospects there, Dickens predicted correctly that he would pass the cadet exams after two years, 'as soon as he is old enough – which will be at the expiration of that time'.

An 1857 volume, *The Choice of a Profession*, declared in its chapter on the army that 'Fortune, safety, comfort, the enjoyment of domestic affections, must be almost entirely erased from the pictured future of the military cadet.' In exchange, a young man of the officer class could expect 'alternations of hope and fear', and, perhaps, 'the brilliant, though fleeting reputation, or, as it is termed, "honour" to be won by military achievements'. The author explained that the usual route into the East India Company's forces was through its military training academy at Addiscombe, and added that Company officers were unfairly 'looked down upon by the Queen's officer'.

Addiscombe had been the path taken by Harry's father, George Larkins. George, second-youngest of at least ten siblings, had been eleven when his father died in 1818, aged sixty-two. John

Pascal Larkins, after whom 'Uncle Larkins' was named, had been owner-manager of several Indiamen; but in his will he spoke of having been made 'subject to great losses' through the duplicity of a partner. He therefore recommended George to the 'particular attention' of his older brother Tommy Larkins, who had already received the command of a family ship, *Marquess Camden*; unless, that was, George's 'dear mother shall be of a different opinion'. And it seems she was, as he attended Dr Burney's in Greenwich instead, a school founded by the brother of the novelist Fanny Burney, proceeding from there to Addiscombe. George then graduated as a cadet in 1825 under the superintendence of Major William Henry Carmichael-Smyth, Thackeray's stepfather, and a brother of the Carmichael-Smyth whose inflexible stance over Enfield cartridge blanks would later help to spark the Rebellion in India.

Apart from Addiscombe, there was only one other way to become an officer in the East India Company's forces: what was called a 'direct cadetship'. In a system of unabashed patronage, a few of these were handed out annually by the Company's directors, though from 1851 direct cadets, like their Addiscombe peers, also faced stiff entry exams with a high attrition rate. A young man who could pull the right strings, and who passed, was sent straight to India to learn his soldiering on the job, a shadow system that bypassed the huge expense of the academy. This benefit, tinged as it was with charity, tended to be conferred on the sons of Company families in need. But Walter Dickens, for example, in 1856, received the nomination of director John Loch through the good offices of the philanthropist Angela Burdett Coutts, a friend of Dickens, and a major Company shareholder.

In 1858, in response to the Rebellion, the British government dismantled the East India Company and transferred its armies to the service of the Crown. But the direct cadetships briefly survived, in the gift of a new Council of India. The president could award two annual nominations, and the fifteen other members, one each. It was to this body of men, therefore, in November 1859, that Harry's sponsors turned. They had left it extraordinarily late. Walter Dickens had his nomination in the bag for over a year before he sat his cadet exams, and Dickens attempted to secure a second nomination for

Alfred when the boy was only eleven. Harry, by contrast, won his with just two weeks to spare. This left him awfully little time to prepare for the certainty of sitting the exams, let alone for what would speedily follow if he passed. Still, on 21 November 1859, 'on the recommendation of his Aunt, Mrs. Coffin', Harry received the sole nomination of Sir Frederick Currie as a direct cadet in the Bengal Infantry.

In the consequent paperwork, Henrietta declared, against a baroque set of subclauses, that, together with Mrs J. P. Larkins, she had gained this nomination through 'gratuitous solicitation', which is to say without bribes. The ties between the four people concerned were highly convoluted. Mrs J. P. Larkins, 'Aunt Larkins', was the second wife of Henrietta's first cousin, the second John Pascal Larkins. He had had two daughters with his first wife before she then died; and one of these, Susannah, had been the first wife of Sir Frederick Currie, before she too died. Thus Susannah Larkins, Currie's deceased first wife, had been one of Harry's endless second cousins, giving Currie himself ample reason to confirm that he was well acquainted with Harry's 'Character, Family, and Connexions'. As an endorsement, this was hard to beat. From being a director of the East India Company, Currie had risen to play the part of its last ever chairman. And now, having advised on the complex transfer of Company powers to the Crown, he had just been made Vice-President of the Council of India. In this way, Harry's nomination represented the full imprimatur of the old guard in its final gasps of power.

He had little time to absorb any of this. C. E. Jenkins sent word vouching for his satisfactory conduct in Brussels; and the Wimbledon School agreed that the conduct of 'Mr. H. T. Larkins' had been 'entirely satisfactory'. Harry passed a medical test in Harley Street. Then on 5 December, now scrambling, he swore before a police magistrate at Bow Street that he was above the lower age restriction for a cadet: though he lacked paperwork documenting his birth, from information, 'which Information I verily believe to be true', he declared that he had indeed recently turned sixteen.

The very next day, Harry faced an intimidating array of Addiscombe professors waiting to examine him. Military admissions encompassed exams in 'gentlemanly' subjects, such as French, English, classics and history, but also demanded an unusually high standard in mathematics. Most boys faced down this challenge after two or three years of cramming. Harry had had one. His five subjects were mathematics, classics, French, Hindustani and fortification, the last two presumably learnt from scratch. No matter: his intellectual flair sufficed, and he carried the day.

Regular Addiscombe seminarians were treated to uplifting farewell speeches. That year, Sir Charles Wood, Secretary of State for India, told them that 'a more fearful calamity than the Indian mutiny had never overwhelmed any other country in the world'. And now, he said, because of the disproportion between the number of rulers and the ruled, 'more depended on the conduct of an individual in India than in any other part of the globe'. Each new cadet must 'endeavour to maintain his character as an English gentleman', that he might thereby 'sway the natives' and become one of the 'saviours' of empire. Next, the Archbishop of Canterbury said that although they must not interfere with 'revolting superstition' in India, he hoped that by 'letting in the light of Christianity' the 'gross darkness which covered that country might be dispersed'.

A cadet acquired his rank from the date of sailing, and this had to be within three months of qualifying and being sworn. Dickens, when he imagined Walter so swiftly off to India, wrote: he 'will fall into that strange life "up the country", before he well knows he is alive, which indeed seems to be rather an advanced stage of knowledge'. Walter eked out his three months by learning to shoot, swim, ride and more; and Dickens was perhaps comforting himself above anyone else when he wrote that a quick departure would be better for Walter than lingering 'with unsettled purpose on him and a cloud of departure hanging over him'. He accompanied Walter to Southampton, and wrote that his son was 'as little cast down as, at 16, one could reasonably hope to be with the world of India before one'. As the ship sailed, Dickens was left to wonder mournfully 'whether the best definition of man may not be, after all, that he is (for his sins) a parting and farewell-taking animal'.

Thomas Nicholls Walker, one of Harry's many cousins, who had set out to join the Bengal Army in 1854, wrote of a rather different style of leave-taking when he paid a last visit to his great-uncle, one of the family's elderly sea captains, 'Fighting Tom' Larkins. Having told the young cadet that India was 'the finest country in the world', the old man added in valediction: 'live generously, my boy, live generously. Always drink a bottle of beer a day, and when you can afford it drink two.'

Harry, later celebrated for his witty stories, recorded virtually nothing about his childhood. The earliest memory he ever put in print dated from the Easter before he too set sail as a cadet. Aged fifteen, during his year at school in Wimbledon, he was taken to a Good Friday concert at the Crystal Palace, now re-erected in south London. Before an audience of thousands, and against a backdrop of gushing fountains in the naves, the chorus of the Italian Opera and the orchestral band of the Coldstream Guards had performed Handel, Mendelssohn and Rossini. The lead soprano was Madame Anna Bishop, whose decades-long affair with Nicholas-Charles Bochsa, a much older musician and criminal on the run, was later taken to have inspired the fiction of Trilby and Svengali. Harry was so enraptured by the music that he never forgot it, nor Anna Bishop's voice, which, with 'electrical effect', he said, had 'floated easily through the vast space, pure and serene'.

4: Bengal

Harry received confirmation of his cadetship on 21 December, and sailed a fortnight later, on 4 January 1860. As his vessel left Southampton, he gained the rank of ensign, and with this his military career began. The wise old heads of the Larkins family could congratulate themselves on having set him up for life, or so they presumably believed. What Harry himself might have been thinking is harder to imagine. An 1856 volume, *Advice to Officers in India*, warned that for an embarking cadet, 'The past is all a dream, the present a chaos of doubts, and hopes, and perplexities —and the future beyond the scope of his comprehension.' Harry, though, would have known too well that he faced having to reinvent himself yet again, this time in an army many of whose men had recently revolted, leading to the massacre of half his family. The very paperwork of his cadetship enshrined the strangeness of his position by requiring him to contribute to the Bengal Presidency Military Orphan Fund. In effect, he was being compelled to repay in increments the same pension that, as an East India Company orphan himself, he was simultaneously set to receive for another two years. Despite these uncomfortable facts, the Bengal Army would ideally function something like a new family for its latest adolescent recruit. However, in its care Harry was to receive an education not only in fighting skills, but also in fecklessness, so that it is a wonder he lasted in India for much time at all.

Harry's Larkins heritage would have marked him out to old Company hands no matter what. His great-grandfather, William Larkins, had been an East India Company sea captain, and the eventual owner of the Indiaman, the *Lioness*. William's oldest son, Captain Thomas Larkins, had then put the family money into many more vessels. Thomas's brother, another William Larkins, went into the Bengal Civil Service, becoming Accountant General at Fort

William in Calcutta for nineteen years, notably under Warren Hastings. And when Thomas Larkins died in 1794, the shipping business fell to the third and youngest brother, also a sea captain, Harry's grandfather, the first John Pascal Larkins. After he too died, the family ships were managed by Harry's grandmother, sometimes referred to as the Rosebud of Kent. The man Harry had known as 'Uncle Larkins' was a son of Captain Thomas Larkins. So too was 'Fighting Tom' Larkins, a nickname he gained in 1806 after a voyage back from China during which 'Fighting Tom' battled valiantly to resist the capture of his ship by a French frigate *La Piémontaise*. Harry's grandfather subsequently named one of the family fleet the *Larkins* in honour of his nephew's boldness, a vessel, in 1860, still out ploughing the waves.

The Indiaman Larkins, *1843*

Even without this constellation of Larkins brigands serving the East India Company down the decades, the Civil Service and regimental lists in India were still peppered with the names of Harry's cousins. But if his connections had helped to get him this far, he did now need to carve out his own career.

*

Harry travelled the overland route between Alexandria and Suez, and reached India on 12 February by a ship called *Nemesis*. His understanding of his family heritage must have acquired an exhilarating new charge out on the high seas, and sailing up the Hooghly River into 'the metropolis of British India', Calcutta. By all accounts, it was overwhelming to come in on the flood tide for the very first time, past fleets of merchant ships, wharves and warehouses, exquisite palaces and parks, with people half naked under palm trees, alligators lounging on the banks, and decaying corpses in the surrounding waters, perched on by vultures, who treated as rafts what they simultaneously ate; past, that is, a heady mix of horror and pomp, stink and beauty, lushness, heat and grandeur.

Landing, a cadet stepped into a crush of coolies and palanquin-bearers, with jackals, pariah dogs and five-foot adjutant birds lurking, like those that had 'gloated' over the pickings at Cawnpore. Yet no matter how otherworldly all this might have seemed, Harry could still wander down Larkins Lane, named for his great-uncle William, or drift past Sanskrit College, whose foundation stone had been laid by Uncle Larkins. Still, there would be little opportunity for idling. Once the superintendent of cadets at Fort William had claimed his charges, they were soon on their way.

The army Harry now joined was in a state of unrest. The *Bombay Gazette*, on the current 'condition of India question', noted in a madly blinkered analysis that 'The mutual feelings of suspicion and dislike which the mutiny first developed between black and white still subsist in their full force.' At the same time, the imposition in 1858 of direct rule by the British government had delivered an unwelcome new challenge to authority. Erstwhile East India Company or 'Local' soldiers were surprised to find themselves nominally transferred into the Queen's army, without a by-your-leave, but with diminished prospects and insulting conditions. Under the slogan 'discharge or bounty', many demanded either the free right to go home, or a bonus payment to acknowledge a new enlistment. This was 'blunderingly resisted' before an offer finally came of discharge with a free passage home, and in the spring of 1860, a remarkable and unforeseen 6,000 of the 10,000 existing British Bengal soldiers chose to quit. They were sent to England in ill-equipped troop ships, familiarly known as 'sea-hearses'. Dickens met one of these vessels in Liverpool, and found that its passengers, having subsisted on 'the excrement of maggots', had succumbed to dysentery, gangrene and simple starvation, sixty of them dead in transit. He watched the rest, 'awful to look on', with 'hands of ivory' and 'lips of lead', taken to a workhouse in open carts in the freezing rain, the wretched workhouse inmates struggling to drag them in. And yet, he added furiously, these same men were being vilified in the press as improvident drunkards who had effectively killed themselves. 'No punishment that our inefficient laws provide, is worthy of the name', he declared, 'when set against the guilt of this transaction.'

It was against exactly this background that Harry was appointed to the infantry of the Bengal Establishment. He was in the highly anomalous position of being one of the last young officers to join the old Bengal Army before its amalgamation into the Queen's army was fully achieved. At the same time, rather than being attached to a particular regiment, as of old, reforms already instituted meant that he was placed on a 'general list' of officers who could be sent to 'do duty', in stints, with any regiment in the Bengal Presidency, whether a Local regiment or one of Her Majesty's regular regiments of the line. George Larkins had stalled for years on a modest income in part because his advancement in his regiment had depended on the promotion, retirement or death of a limited list of officers ranked above him. But though the new system broadened a young officer's experience, and allowed for promotion to be organised more fairly, a young man in Harry's position was now denied the anchoring effect of belonging to a single regiment.

After some muddle, a directive confirmed: 'Ens H. T. Larkins, gen. list, to do du. with H.M.'s 73rd.' The redoubtable 73rd Foot, soon to be renamed the Black Watch, was one of the British regiments that had been hastily drafted to India in 1857. It was currently stationed at Dinapore on the Ganges, midway between Cawnpore and Calcutta, the headquarters of one of Bengal's eight military divisions. Here, Harry would need more than ever to put his wits and charm to the fore. Being a probationer, or 'griffin', and, worse, a direct cadet with no Addiscombe training, he would be at the mercy of those in power over him, not to mention, if he lacked flair, of those he was learning to command as well. He faced a life dominated by rising at dawn, on the signal of gunfire, followed smartly by drill practice, target practice and parades, as well as local-language and other studies, not to mention endless paperwork, 'The amount of official correspondence on all matters of duty' being 'very great'. But this life had awful longueurs in it as well, when he would have to choose between the mess, with its coffee, newspapers, billiards, whist, Allsop's Pale Ale and pegs of brandy, or sporting and other civilian distractions: picnics, cricket, sunset promenading, perhaps a regimental band performance, the bazaar. His life, that is, looked set to alternate between being challengingly arduous and challengingly dull. Except that he was about to find himself witness to a storm that came to be called the White Mutiny.

The military exodus described by Dickens left a surplus of officers in Bengal, leading in turn to a hasty and poorly managed recruitment drive for privates from Britain. And by the time Harry arrived in India, several newly formed Bengal regiments were in a state of unrest. The larger stations, with their sprawling cantonments, could be several miles across, providing a home to six or more regiments. And like HM's 73rd Foot, the 5th Bengal Europeans, one of the most recalcitrant of the new regiments, soon came to be stationed at Dinapore.

On 25 October 1860, a week after Harry turned seventeen, William Johnson, a private of the 5th, found himself on duty on the barrack pickets 'for the express purpose of taking into custody disorderly characters'. However, faced with fellow soldiers running amok and demanding discharge, he 'absolutely refused to do his duty', after which, temporarily, 'all discipline was at an end'. Four days later, Johnson's fellow malcontents were sentenced to various terms of penal servitude, but because he had defied direct orders while on duty, Johnson himself was sentenced to be shot.

By chance, Sir Hugh Rose, the new Commander-in-Chief of the whole army in India, reached Dinapore on 7 November, sweeping through the Upper Provinces as part of a grand tour of inspection. He was 'highly delighted with H.M.'s 73rd Regiment', and 'publicly praised them on parade', but he gave the 5th Bengal Europeans 'a regular jobation'. The military court there had recommended mercy for William Johnson on the grounds of his youth and good character, but Rose 'declined to accede'. He ordered the commander of the station, Brigadier Welchman of HM's 73rd, to carry Johnson's sentence into execution.

At dawn on 13 November, the band of the 73rd Foot, drums muffled, played the 'Dead March' from Handel's *Saul* while Johnson 'marched round the square in rear of his coffin'. He 'acknowledged the justice of his sentence', and was executed on his knees, 'shot dead at the first volley'. Immediately, the men of the 73rd oversaw the risky task of disarming the 5th, after which Welchman pronounced the regiment's doom. Many old soldiers, 'draughted from the old Bengal and from Royal regiments', now 'sobbed like children at this terrible disgrace', and 'Even upon the spectators the effect was very great.'

This drastic event was not the only one to raise questions about continuing botched authority in Bengal. Soon, too, there was the calamity of widespread famine. Those in charge blamed drought and 'inferior grain', with little acknowledgement of the contributory ill effects of forcing agriculture away from food crops and towards crops that served British commerce, including indigo and opium. The people of Britain donated substantial funds for famine relief, but many hundreds of thousands of souls nevertheless perished. In English newspapers, the blow to the British exchequer consequent upon the crop failures was represented as an equal disaster to these deaths, or even a worse one.

Late in 1860, while the 5th Bengal Europeans were still careering towards disbandment, one of the 'little wars' of the period, as the British dismissively called them, appeared to be brewing on the northern border with the small Kingdom of Sikkim. This period saw frequent incursions and 'insolent threatenings' across India's Himalayan frontier, and a British reporter observed loftily that 'The lion has whisked away the fly so tenderly that it considered itself invited to return.'

Now, skirmishers from the 'wretchedly poor' Sikkim had afforded 'insults and injuries' to British subjects, killing some and imperilling hundreds more. The nearest concentration of military personnel was in the civil station of Darjeeling, site of one of the British Army's main convalescent depots. The superintendent there, Dr Campbell, was authorised on 1 November to cross the border in reply. With about 100 Native soldiers, and demonstrating 'the bravery of rashness', he notionally annexed a vast swathe of Sikkimese territory that he found it immediately impossible to defend. Within a month, he had been forced to retreat by fighters largely armed with poisoned arrows; some forty of his men were dead; and he had allowed the shameful abandonment of his guns. 'We are rather in a mess here just now', wrote a fraught correspondent in Darjeeling. 'Urge the Government not to drop the affair', wrote another. There were daily appeals for reinforcements from the nearby station at Julpigoree, or else perhaps 'A second Cawnpore drama may be expected.' British command concluded irritably that Campbell had rendered it imperative not only to make Darjeeling safe, but also to 'efface' his 'seriously embarrassing' failed invasion.

On 12 December, Harry was reassigned to do duty with 73rd Native Infantry at Julpigoree. After roughly a year of griffinage, it was standard for a cadet to be transferred into a Native regiment, allowing him to hone his colloquial language skills, as well as his abilities in command. Even so, this posting might ordinarily have felt like something of a banishment. Julpigoree was supposed to 'overawe Bhotan', but was still thought of as little more than a rudimentary outstation on the banks of the Teesta River flowing down from Sikkim. The place was infested with snakes and mosquitoes, and its buildings, even its jail, were bamboo huts 'with walls of matting, and roofs thatched with grass', raised up off the ground to allow for torrential flooding during the rains.

For Harry, though, this posting looks like a reward, with his new regiment supplying some 450 troops for an active campaign. A rough total of 1,500 British soldiers, including 800 Sikhs and 400 Europeans, was gathering on the Sikkim border. And these forces were to be led by Lieutenant Colonel Gawler, who had commanded Harry's previous regiment.

Their invasion began in early February 1861. Under enemy fire, much of it from stolen British guns, Sikh soldiers, covered by the 73rd N.I., constructed a raft bridge across the churning border river, the Runjeet. Gawler had already taken a small force over the water higher up, and he hoped to mount a pincer attack on the embedded Sikkimese snipers, having concentrated them by means of the provocation of the bridge. But the terrain was so dense and exhausting that he arrived too late: the 73rd N.I. had already blasted the Sikkimese out of their positions. The retreat of bands of enemy fighters thereafter was feared as a positive guerrilla tactic. The British followed them ever further into what Gawler described as a land of 'snowy peaks, deep dark valleys, foaming torrents and interminable forests'. Not only did the Sikkimese leave booby traps in their wake, but there was the perceived danger that they planned to strand the British forces far inside 'waste country', before doubling back to make an attack on Darjeeling.

Conditions were arduous, though word circulated quickly among the men that Lieutenant Delafosse was somewhere among them, totemic survivor against all odds at Cawnpore. 'Hill coolies' proved recalcitrant. Mules were unequal to the extreme terrain. Roads had to be exhaustingly cut, and bridges dangerously constructed, to enable the passage of large guns. 'Wretched cold', food shortages and a dearth of greatcoats and tents for the soldiers meant dire 'exposure and privation'. Then, after several gruelling weeks, and nothing like a battle, the 'passively hostile' Rajah of Sikkim signed a treaty in tactical surrender. One outside commentator wrote that it was 'greatly to be deplored' that funds had been squandered on this dreadful misadventure when thousands were starving in Bengal: 'By such successes as these we lose more than we gain.' Gawler was left to argue in reply that a lack of much bloodshed in the enterprise was a mark of skill and success, not a humiliation. With Sikkim reduced to a 'vassal state', the British hoped at least for 'commercial intercourse with Thibet', and trade in borax, musk, turquoise, gold and more. Gawler was therefore ordered to extend road construction to the far border of Sikkim. Sepoys from Harry's regiment refused to do this work, leading some to be court-martialled. And perhaps they baulked because cholera was rife. As the British progressed, they left Native corpses 'rotting on the roadside'.

Harry soon became seriously sick himself. The 73rd N.I. left Sikkim at the end of April, and on 20 May he was issued a four-month leave of absence to go to Darjeeling on medical certificate. Though there was cholera in Darjeeling too, the climate there was understood to be healthful. One doctor wrote rhapsodically: 'The scenery of these hills is, I believe, the most stupendous, the most sublime in the world;—valley scooped out of valley, hill raised upon hill, crag hung upon crag, and mountain piled upon mountain, far above the limit of man's existence', with the only 'visitants' the 'avalanche, the thunderbolt, and the sunbeam'.

Harry reappeared in official notices on 1 January 1862, when he was promoted to lieutenant. This put him on a basic rate of pay of Rs 225 per month, with the promise, if he served another twenty years, of an annual pension in England of £191 and 12 shillings. A new directive shortly after ordered him to Benares, attached to the 9th Native Infantry.

Benares was another of Bengal's main division stations, though the British cantonment, along the Ganges at Secrole, was a couple of miles from the city itself, with its crowded ghats, narrow streets, mosques and profusely carved temples. In this relatively metro-politan posting, Harry faced once more an inevitable 'dull, listless, routine'. Ordinary privates, from the agonies of tedium, were reputed to 'chop off their fingers; put out their eyes; and malinger incorrigibly, in the hopes of getting invalided'. And alcoholism and drug-taking were 'prevalent in all classes'. But the 'passions of manhood and the penalties entailed upon their gratification', principally syphilis, were said to cause 'more broken constitutions than all other indiscretions put together'. Nevertheless, the army accepted that there must be brothels in the bazaar.

All this time, Harry had been banking up 'privileged leave' of one month in six, privileged in that it did not count against a soldier's record of service. But so far he had taken none of it; and he took none in 1862 either, staying put in Benares through the summer, even as the plains grew insufferably stormy and hot. The only stir in the cantonment was caused by its amateur theatricals: 'had it not been for the punkahs, you might, without any great stretch of imagination, have fancied yourself "in the Strand'". Even this, though, was in feeble contrast to reports from the theatres of the hill stations, especially Simla, on its 'bungalow bestudded steep'. There, 1862 saw a visit by no less than the San Francisco Minstrels. Though this troupe served up its usual 'burnt cork' blackface and ludicrous transvestism, it switched material from American to local subjects, triumphantly satirising the risible attempts of Eurasian men and women to imitate the no less risible affectations of the British sahib and his wife.

If the layers of offence here were tangled almost to absurdity, another event of Simla's 1862 season, a charitable concert 'in aid of the unfortunate Lancashire operatives', betrayed its own contortions and blindnesses. The American Civil War was now a year in, and with the North blockading Southern ports, imports into Britain of cheap, high-quality, raw American cotton had almost completely ceased. British trade in cotton fabrics was therefore foundering, leading to extreme hardship among mill workers, though notably in Manchester, starving cotton operatives supported the embargo, standing with the Union cause against the 'foul blot' of slavery. In India, the new Viceroy, Lord Elgin, battled to be allowed to send home a £20,000 surplus from the very same Famine Fund recently collected in vain by the British people to relieve Bengal. And though the home authorities strongly resisted this gesture, wishing the money to stay in India against the inevitability of new famines, Lord Elgin won the day. As there was suddenly a market in Britain for relatively low-quality Indian cotton, India's growing districts were now expanded, at the expense of food production, and many livelihoods previously dependent on Indian cloth works were destroyed for lack of raw materials. Those, meanwhile, who feared future Indian famines were proved right as soon as 1866, when maladministration coupled with fresh crop failures led to uncountable hundreds of thousands of people in Orissa being left to starve to death.

On 21 October 1862, after less than a year in Benares, and having just turned nineteen, Harry received orders that he would hence-forth be attached to the 7th Native Infantry, one of the few Native regiments not to have mutinied in 1857. As it was headquartered at Banda, in the Cawnpore division, this put him relatively near to Cawnpore itself. Though the corpses of his family had almost certainly been scavenged by birds and dogs, or washed down the Ganges with the crocodiles and fishes, he could visit the cross erected over the dry well in Wheeler's entrenchment, where many bodies had been dumped during the siege, which bore an inscription from Psalm 141 starting, 'Our bones are scattered'. And he could also visit the 'Massacre Ghat' on the river itself. There was, too, a second monument being raised over the Bibighar well, surrounded by an ornamental garden, though the platform still lacked the statue of a sorrowing angel that was to become its most famous feature. Alice, all her life, would keep a leaf from a peepul tree, labelled 'Picked at Cawnpore in the garden'.

In February 1863, Harry was among nineteen candidates, including several captains and a major, to pass the half-yearly superior exam in Hindustani. Then in April, having earned himself the maximum allowable break of six months, he finally took privileged leave and travelled to Simla. Civil power, represented by Lord Elgin, and

The 'Massacre Ghat', Cawnpore

military, represented by Sir Hugh Rose, arrived there on 4 April. Lord Elgin's journey had been marked by levées and durbars, though a new railway line threatened to render it 'the last of those obtrusive pageants called the Viceroy's progress'. He inaugurated the season proper in Simla on the 20th, with a grand ball to celebrate the marriage of the Prince of Wales, Queen Victoria's oldest son, known as Bertie. By then the hill station was 'full of dusty fugitives from the plains', with rents at 'a figure never previously heard of'. Those who had not gone there to recuperate from sickness set about picnics, parties, promenading, card games, dancing, riding and simple 'rinking' or prowling about, and hoped for society to be enlivened by the odd snub, duel, 'police matter' or elopement, and perhaps one or two fellows going smash.

Harry would later dine out on the apocryphal-sounding story of a 'very splendid' fancy-dress ball given there by his 'chief' in India. An officer whose wife had suffered the loss of her costume in the posts from Europe, sent a note to ask whether she might defy stringent rules and attend the ball without one, eliciting the quip in reply, according to Harry, that she could expect to find herself stopped at the door if she really planned to come as Venus. July brought heavy rains to the hills, whereupon amateur theatricals were 'the order of the day, or rather of the night', a dearly loved pastime in Simla, where small theatres were built to host these performances.

One visitor, struck by all the subalterns there on privileged leave, or on bogus medical certificates, wrote: 'The very lax notions of discipline and decency of these young men' and 'the excesses of their conduct' would not be endured 'in any place where a sound public opinion existed, or indeed any public opinion at all'. But there was something beyond this licensed dissipation to attract a young lieutenant. John Lang, whose essays Dickens published in *Household Words*, wrote of overlooked officers struggling against all odds 'in the hope of prepossessing one or other of the Great Authorities'. In more jaundiced language, Simla was where 'the place-hunter' desperately tried to ingratiate himself with 'great personages', who therefore found themselves followed about by 'a host of minor swells'.

*

Harry abandoned his leave half way through, and from 25 July took up a short posting, as paid doing duty officer, with the 44th Native Infantry. If this was a reward for his charm in Simla, it almost certainly reflected a dearth of funds as much as any zeal for soldiering. At any rate, he now journeyed to a rainy Assam on the south-eastern frontier, where the 44th N.I. had just helped to terminate the so-called Cossyah Rebellion. Resistance to British rule had broken out months earlier in the hills beyond Cherra Poonji. 'The desperadoes are thirsting for blood', a local correspondent wrote, and across a ravine 'their cooking fires bespangle the jungle in all directions'. But, 'joking apart', he added, several boxwallahs and Bengalis had been murdered and British buildings destroyed, and without immediate countermeasures 'the British *raj* will be at an end for some time'. To bring this 'long neglected rebellion' to an end, the British had recently wielded 'overpowering strength' against the 'contemptible resources of the rebels', and after four months hundreds of fighters had surrendered in a terrible state of 'suffering, privation and depression'. Then in March, the British and an opposing rajah had signed a treaty of peace.

Several regiments were retained in Assam to enforce that peace, or continuing suppression, including an artillery regiment 'equipped for hill and jungle warfare'. When Harry joined the 44th, its men were divided between Cherra Poonji, Cachar and Munnipore. Days before his arrival, reports in the press indicated fresh trouble: 'Those invincible rebels the Cossyas are again in the field.' But the British hung fire, fearful of the fevers of the jungles in the rainy season, and tried to counter locally the 'depredations' of those they called robbers and marauders.

Harry spent three months in Assam in these unsettling and risky conditions, being the unused balance of his leave. Then on 21 October 1863, just after his 20th birthday, he was reassigned to do duty with the 7th Dragoon Guards, currently on the move to Benares. Geographically, this was a backwards step. But on the positive side, time in one of HM's 'dragoon' or cavalry regiments would allow him to acquire 'a knowledge of cav. duties', as the listings put it, as well as honing glamorous skills in 'equitation' or horsemanship, and in cavalry drill.

*

Walter Dickens had taken the same path into military service as Harry: Brackenbury's, and a direct cadetship at sixteen. But, being three years older, he had set sail for India in July 1857. Though the first reports of uprisings in Bengal had already reached London, no one there yet guessed the full implications. When, a few weeks later, news did come through of events in Cawnpore, Charles Dickens's celebrated compassion for the downtrodden radically failed him. In a private letter, he wrote with awful passion: 'I should do my utmost to exterminate the Race upon whom the stain of the late cruelties rested.' I should, he said, 'blot it out of mankind and raze it off the face of the Earth'.

A year later, rather than battle wounds, a combination of 'sun-stroke, a passing attack of small pox, and smart Fever' saw Walter dispatched to a sanatorium in the hills. He survived this sickness to be rewarded with a lieutenancy at seventeen, and thereafter remained permanently attached to the 42nd Highlanders. Four years later, when Dickens sent a friend an account of the family, his view of his son's career was unforgiving. Walter, he said, 'spends more than he gets and has cost me money and disappointed me'. At the end of 1863, as Harry was travelling back to Benares, Walter once more became so ill that he was sent to Calcutta, in order to return home on extended medical leave. A typical invalid passed through the city 'with the hectic flush upon his cheek, his sinews unstrung, and his raiment a world too wide for his shrunk shanks, preparing to embark for a more congenial climate'. Walter pitched up at the Officers' Hospital, and there, just before sailing, on the last day of the year, aged twenty-two, he suffered a sudden haemorrhage and died.

A few weeks later, several Indian newspapers noted that on 4 February 1864, at Trinity Church, Paddington, Alice Schaffalitzky Larkins wed Raymond Percy Pelly. No doubt she married from Henrietta Coffin's new home at 25 Cleveland Square, one of an array of spectacular mansions recently built around a central garden, in the London style, with an adjacent mews for carriage and horses. This move into town seems to have been prompted by Joseph Cockfield Dimsdale, a nephew of Henrietta's first husband and a thriving banker himself, who advised her on her money affairs, and who also lived in Cleveland Square.

Alice's match had come about as a result of family connections in Upton, East Ham, home of her Streatfeild cousins. The Pelly family had acquired the Upton estate in the eighteenth century, raking in immense fortunes through both the Hudson's Bay and the East India Companies. And Sir John Henry Pelly, grandfather of Alice's new husband, Ray, had not only been Governor of the Hudson's Bay Company for thirty years, but also, briefly, Governor of the Bank of England. Over the decades, Upton and East Ham were settled by members of several other righteous banking families, including Quaker families, leading to a mare's nest of intermarriage. Thus, Ray Pelly was also a grandson, on his mother's side, of another resident there for many years, the Quaker reformer Elizabeth Fry.

The marriage was to prove a happy one, though Alice found herself in a fierce new family embrace against which she sometimes struggled. A thread in the congratulatory letters to Ray's parents, who had no daughter of their own, concerned her orphan status, and the indulgence of her therefore becoming 'so wholly yours'. Despite his Quaker connections, Ray was destined for the Anglican priesthood, and in this way Alice became a vicar's wife.

On 7 February 1864, Charles Dickens turned fifty-two. A letter arrived for him that day, five weeks in the post, from Walter's commanding officer. 'It is my most painful duty to inform you', he wrote, 'of the sudden death of your son, Lieut. Walter Landor Dickens', adding, 'Life became extinct in a few seconds by the rush of blood which poured from his mouth.' Walter had been buried in the hospital graveyard in Calcutta. In a second letter, the same officer forwarded Walter's unpaid mess bills, along with a record of his outstanding debts at the regimental stores, debts for billiards, orderlies, and so on: 'I feel I could not do my duty if I withheld these from you', he remarked politely, before explaining that Walter had been 'a favourite with us all; and not all his difficulties in pecuniary matters, which appear to have begun immediately after he came to India, affected or in any way diminished our regard for him'.

It was notoriously difficult for young officers to survive on their pay in India, and they received many warnings to 'balance the debit and credit side of their accounts to the utmost farthing'. Dickens was appalled to discover what was owed, and distressed altogether by 'poor Walter's wretched affairs – utterly incomprehensible, as they always have been'. The outstanding regimental debt was for £65, or about £7,500 today.

For the British military, 1861 had been intended as 'the great amalgamation year', when the Queen's Indian Army would be consolidated with the East India Company's old Presidency forces. But this was 'a measure never really accomplished', and in Bengal the Local soldiers were condemned as embodying a 'moral delinquency' that rendered them unfit for 'the honour of bearing arms'. Many long-standing Company officers, publicly impugned as 'old women and fossils', felt driven to resign, with happy savings for the military purse when they forfeited large pensions. But on 1 March 1864, as a sop to persistent ill feeling, the surviving men of the old Presidency armies were finally accorded equal rank with their counterparts in the British Army as a whole.

For Harry, this felicity was followed by an exciting new appointment. On 17 March he was confirmed as doing duty officer with the most glamorous of all the old Indian regiments, now the 1st Bengal Cavalry, but originally Skinner's Horse. The Yellow Boys, as they were also known, on account of their canary uniform, were hardbitten warriors top to bottom, famed for their élan and endurance. Far from mutinying in 1857, they had undertaken the dangerous work of disarming rebel infantry regiments, staunchness of a kind to inspire crass doggerel from the not-yet-ennobled Alfred Tennyson: 'Praise to our Indian Brothers, and let the dark face have its due! / Thanks to the kindly dark faces who fought with us, faithful and few,' etc. Harry was ordered to join them at their new headquarters, the Nowgong station, south of Cawnpore.

What happened next is opaque, but Harry cannot have spent much more than a month with the Yellow Boys before taking a short spell of leave. Then on 9 June came a fresh announcement. In an abrupt dimming of reflected glory, it read: 'The appointment of Lieut. H. T. Larkins, gen. list, inf., as doing duty officer with the 1st Bengal cav., announced in G.O. of March 17 last, is canc.'

All was decidedly not well, and after a muddle about where he should go next, on 9 July he was ordered to rejoin the 7th Native Infantry, the regiment to which he had been attached two years earlier. Logistically, this was an easy shift to the nearby Banda station. And Harry was now under the stern hand of one Colonel D. Pott, not, it seems, a man to be taken lightly, having been removed from another regiment for organising a summary execution after a Native soldier killed a Native lieutenant: or rather, 'for having had a sepoy, who shot a jemadar through the heart, tried by a drum-head court-martial, and hanged on the spot, half an hour after the cowardly deed was perpetrated'.

It is only now that Harry's record reveals quite how far his time in India had been an education in utter irresponsibility. At the end of September, Ray Pelly wrote to his parents giving a glimpse of the enormous trouble engulfing the brother-in-law he had not yet met. Given postal time lags, the information Ray relayed had presumably been sent to Henrietta Coffin by Colonel Pott in August. And Ray's picture of Harry all round can only have been supplied to him by members of the Larkins family. Alice scribbled 'Private!' beside the relevant paragraph: 'Master Henry Larkins is in debt over £2,000 & lots of people are clamouring for at Aunty for bills they have backed, the Coll of H's regiment says if Aunty does not at once pay H will go to prison, which as he has been in the habit of stealing all his life appears to be the best place for him poor fellow.' £2,000 happened to constitute an entire year's income for Henrietta from the inheritance bequeathed to her by Mrs Samuel Knip.

Every shift between regiments would have required Harry to win over a new set of brother officers, and this had plainly tempted him into some extremely expensive habits. When Dickens came to weigh up Walter's miserable fate, he laid some of the blame for his son's troubles on lack of oversight: 'I suppose the Regiment to have been ill looked after by the Colonel.' And by contrast with Walter, Harry had had nothing like a constant eye kept on him. Even so, £2,000 in 1864 was a simply astronomical sum, exceeding Walter's debts many times over, equivalent today to a figure not far short of £200,000.

Advice to Officers in India gave as a 'sacred maxim' that a young officer, 'if possible', should live within his pay. But it also conceded that, below the rank of captain, this required 'great moderation and economy', while 'no pleasure is so fascinating as entertaining one's comrades at frequent champagne parties, or taking a lead in the expensive gaieties of the fashionable world; and nothing is more easy than to raise money for such purposes'. Temptation was all around, and: 'It is a lamentable fact that a large proportion of Indian officers are deeply involved in debt, and that the monthly stoppages made from their pay in the pay-office to meet bank loans, leaves them but a scanty sum on which to exist.'

This raises questions of how Harry managed to run up debts on quite so ruinous a scale, and of what brought the matter to a crisis. The answers may have been linked. Though cartels of impoverished officers often stood security for one another in a ring, a trick by which all risked failing at once, it seems that Harry had beguiled many people into backing his bills, and that their joint patience was finally exhausted after he returned to the plains in 1864, and lived successively with two sets of high-caste cavalry officers. As he was fast approaching his twenty-first birthday, he may have traded on the promise of a patrimony; though if so, this was a seductive lie. Just a month before entering the Cawnpore entrenchments, Emma Larkins wrote to her brother-in-law that 'but for a remnant of debt—which will soon disappear—we should now be putting some away "to the good"'; while a post-Rebellion 'Inventory of Estates' reckoned George's final worth at about £220.

Almost more striking than Harry's debt, in the letter that reveals it, is the phrase: 'as he has been in the habit of stealing all his life'. This casually absolute detail is the only surviving clue as to why, in her dreadful final communication, Emma should have appealed to Harry to 'weep over ever having pleased your own desires'. This was a call he had clearly rejected outright. And in doing the exact opposite, his desires had surpassed to a stunning extent his ability to pay for them.

Harry turned twenty-one at just about the time that Henrietta's reply should have reached Colonel Pott. Unlike Ray Pelly, she did not blithely regard prison as 'the best place' for her nephew, and she must have raised the funds to keep him clear. Presumably she informed

Harry that nothing like this must ever happen again. Presumably he replied that nothing like it ever would. New Presidency division orders came in soon afterwards, confirming that he must move yet again. Henceforth he would be attached to the 38th Native Infantry, headquartered at Barrackpore, just north of Calcutta, not far from where he had washed up in India five years before.

In his period of duty so far, Harry had served in seven regiments, travelling thousands of miles between division stations, outstations and hill stations, in conditions of threatening unrest and, for him, perhaps equally risky peace. Along the way he had seduced others into standing security for him as he racked up unthinkably vast debts. Now, having reached his majority, and having been given a new start, his best bet and only hope was going to be to keep his head down, severely restricting his expenses.

The 38th was a recently established regiment, but was nevertheless respected for its soldiery, made up of 'Brahmans, Rajputs, Jats, and the like'. Eight months after Harry joined, command was bestowed on Lieutenant-Colonel Alexander Bagot, for whom this was something of a return from the wilderness. In 1857, he had commanded the Nusseeree Battalion, 'principally Goorkhas', and was assigned to the defence of Simla. But his men broke out into 'semi-mutiny', and according to one account 'scared half Simla into the jungles'. This was doubly disturbing to the British as Bagot's forces had no conceivable religious objection to the Enfield cartridges. In 1858, Sir Hugh Rose engineered Bagot's semi-permanent leave in England, and permission to return to duty came only when Rose's tenure as Commander-in-Chief ended. Bagot sailed for India at once, receiving command of the 38th N.I. on 20 June 1865.

Bagot was a man for his pleasures. The *Oriental Sporting Magazine*, dedicated to cricket, boa constrictors, pig-sticking and other such topics, related how he once followed a wounded tiger on foot, showing 'more enthusiasm than discretion', only for it to turn and charge him down, puncturing his leg with its teeth. He was saved only by the immediate and accurate shot of a sepoy, whereupon 'the beautiful beast made one bound into the air and fell dead on the spot'.

For about a year, Harry appears to have flourished under Bagot's command. In September 1865 he was appointed to officiate as the 38th's quartermaster, and then again in March 1866; and the following August he officiated as 1st doing duty officer also. But despite his presumably efficient shouldering of these responsibilities, Harry was once more getting adrift.

A decade later, an officer called R. B. Cumberland happened to mention in a book of his travels how he had entertained people at a party one night by 'narrating the story of the late lamented Colonel Bagot and "Harry Larkins"'. With notable poetic justice, Bagot had just died on a tiger-hunting expedition after his cook accidentally made breakfast chupatties using the arsenic meant for curing the animal skins. What the amusing story about Harry and Bagot actually was, Cumberland passed over in print; but he did say that Harry had been 'wild', that 'volumes might be published of his extraordinary escapades and daring games in India', and that these escapades would have 'brought many a man a dozen times to the gallows'.

Whatever the truth of this excitable flourish, Harry's Indian games were now, finally, terminal. It seems he himself later put it about that, 'Not being able to agree with his colonel, he threw up his commission.' Alice's more plausible version was that Harry 'had to resign on account of some serious breach of discipline which took place at the Officers' Mess of the Regiment', though she did also remember a fanciful tale that, afterwards, 'he joined the Indian police, and when pursued for debts incurred when in the Army, actually travelled about with a warrant for his own arrest in his pocket, hunting the culprit'.

In the bald terms of the army listings, on 17 September 1866, orders from Simla included the following note: 'Larkins, Lieut. H.T. of the gen. list Inf 2nd doing duty officer 38th (the Agra) N.I. is perm. to resign the serv., subject to H.M.'s approval.' In the old days of the East India Company, officers were 'permitted to resign the service' to avoid disgrace, and would 'slip out of sight unnoticed', surviving on subsistence pay until they could get themselves home. As this dodge had continued despite all formal efforts to end it, a similar slinking departure may have been Harry's fate too. Certainly he was penniless, and he would now also lose all the future benefits accrued from his six years of military service. But he was still young. And so he soon set sail for England, arriving back with the rest his life before him.

5: London

Harry returned to London in 1867, aged twenty-three. For the last decade, since being orphaned, he had led an extraordinarily itinerant life, transplanted between one school and the next in different countries, and then between eight military regiments in six years, all across Bengal. This unmoored life had given him opportunity, and very good reason, to refine his bonhomie and charm. But although his ability to win people over at short notice was to prove one of his greatest assets, it was unquestionably also his most dangerous.

Some Bengal soldiers worried that 'We Indians', returning home after a 'sojourn of some years in that benighted country', and confronted by such wonders as London's new Underground Railway, would appear idiotic, 'to the amusement of the London dandy'. But if Harry initially seemed rough around the edges, a London dandy is exactly what he now became. For the next two years, off and on, he lived at 25 Cleveland Square with Henrietta and Conny. And more than ever, he did what his mother had urged him not to, and 'pleased his own desires'.

In the glimpses of him that survive from this period, he flashes forth as simply a footloose spendthrift. If Henrietta gave him an allowance, he far exceeded it. If he somehow earned more besides, he exceeded that too. The press in Europe, and then America, when summing up this indulgent spell, agreed that he had 'an aunt, colossally rich, at whose expense he lived a joyous life in London', and that he pursued the usual dissipations at the usual fashionable haunts of 'the Cremorne Garden, Argyle Rooms, and all of the Clubs of London'. A Larkins cousin, after talking to Alice, later reported: 'Extravagance was evidently his weak point. Endowed by nature with an excellent physique, good looks and a ready wit, he was nevertheless generally in debt.' Apparently, 'Many times his debts were paid either by his aunt or by his sisters who, in spite of his weaknesses, loved him dearly.'

Harry racked up those London debts early, and in 1867, Tom Hadwen, 'bookseller', sued him 'for 120*l.*, being the balance of 196*l.*, which he owed on an account from February to May, for opera tickets, &c.' Further tickets would have ranged from high-minded

Henrietta, Conny and Ellen

concerts to variety shows featuring burlesques, farces, melodramas, ballets, satire, and ladies with their legs on show. A successful bookseller rented theatre boxes and seats by the season, paying considerably under the nominal price in the hope of selling on the tickets, and profiting from the difference. From this, the impresario putting on a show was guaranteed desperately needed funds ahead of its opening, as well as help in filling the theatre when the season began. Even so, spreading risk in this way remained a highly chancy business for all concerned, especially when a bookseller's customers, in turn, took tickets without immediately paying for them. Harry's huge line of credit with Hadwen, £196, is evidence of just how plausible he could be. Only the year before, Gladstone, by this point Chancellor of the Exchequer, in the great debate of the time on widening the franchise, had disputed that respectable, vote-worthy male artisans should be defined by an annual income of £96 or above. 'Many an able, industrious, and skilful workman,' he said, 'using his best exertions all his lifetime, would and must fail to attain to such an income', and so he advocated the alternative figure of just above £67 a year as a sum still high enough to exclude all ordinary labouring men. Sixty-seven pounds was a third of what Harry had shelled out, on account, for opera tickets and related indulgences, in four months flat.

The question arises of whether Harry, with Hadwen's complicity, had actually speculated on renting a theatre box himself; the cheapest second-tier box at Covent Garden, for example, cost 100 guineas for the season. Claire Clairmont, the testy stepsister of Mary Shelley, and once the adolescent mother of a baby by Lord Byron, spent £4,000 in middle age on buying a box outright at Her Majesty's Theatre, hoping to secure herself a decent income for life. But what it actually secured her was a miserably obsessive interest in the fortunes of the theatre, a poisonous hatred for her agent and, she believed, irreparable damage to her health. After nearly two decades of this, she wrote to a friend in 1862 that her terrible gamble was still forcing her to get by on a 'mere pittance of bread, cheese, and fire in the winter and sun in the summer'.

It would seem that the outstanding debt of £120 in Hadwen's legal suit was expunged by one of Harry's womenfolk; and this particular suit was almost certainly symptomatic of other similar but unrecorded entanglements.

The wild way that Harry was so impetuously embracing was captured with great frankness by George Moore, the louche Irish aristocrat and writer, who declared that 'the life of the theatre—that life of raw gaslight, white-washed walls, of doggerel verse, slangy polkas and waltzes—interested me beyond legitimate measure, so curious and unreal did it seem'. He wrote of nights of brandy and soda, dawns of champagne and cigarette smoke, hansom cabs, pet names and low-necked dresses. This was, he said, an era of 'fabulous Bohemianism; a Bohemianism of eternal hardupishness and eternal squandering of money—money that rose at no discoverable well-head and flowed into a sea of boudoirs and restaurants, a sort of whirlpool of sovereigns in which we were caught, and sent eddying through music-halls, bright shoulders, tresses of hair, and slang'. Less poetically, he noted: 'I lived at home, but dined daily at a fashionable restaurant: at half past eight I was at the theatre. Nodding familiarly to the door-keeper, I passed up the long passage to the stage. Afterwards supper. Cremorne and the Argyle Rooms were my favourite haunts.'

William Acton's grand tome investigating prostitution in this period confirms that at the Cremorne, a famous pleasure garden, the setting of the sun would cause respectable folk to clear out before the arrival of 'westward Hansoms freighted with demure immorality in silk and fine linen'. And now, by the light of a thousand gas

Cremorne Gardens, Chinese Platform

lamps, 'men of the upper and middle class' danced on 'monster platforms' with harlots 'more or less *prononcées*'. Back in town, Acton described the Haymarket, with its ulcerous looseness, and the Argyll Rooms, lure of the upper current of 'the fast life of London', as being 'at once the Alpha and the Omega of prostitution'. Persons of a certain mind, he remarked dryly, found that both places, being adjacent to the Opera House, came 'betwixt the wind and their fine sensibilities'. And it was in the environs of the Argyll Rooms that Gladstone, in his own words, put himself 'peculiarly in the way of contact with exciting causes'. Notoriously, he 'courted evil' there, hunting for prostitutes whom he might endeavour to redeem.

*

On 30 July, a blow fell on the Larkins family with the death of Aunt Larkins, first foster-mother to Conny and Harry. She left the four Larkins orphans no remembrances; no bracelets of carbuncles or lumps of plate. Nevertheless, the severing of this link must have cast a shadow when, four days later, Ellen married a lawyer called Edward Cutler. Cutler, at thirty-six, was almost twice Ellen's age of nineteen. But socially he was a reasonable match, being a well-established barrister of the Stone Buildings, Lincoln's Inn, and an accomplished musician. Despite this, their union seems to have inspired a certain *froideur* in the family. Ray Pelly's correspondence contains remarkable instances of bald reluctance at the thought having Ellen and Edward to stay, with repeated and hopeful 'puttings off' by him and Alice. And when Henrietta drew up her will, she turned for help not to Ellen's husband, after all a lawyer, but to her Dimsdale and Streatfeild connections instead. Indeed, until the day that the will was read out loud, Alice was fearful that Henrietta might have cut Ellen out of it altogether. And all she did eventually leave her was a few small trinkets.

A French newspaper later stated that Harry spent part of 1867 picking up his Parisian French, usually thought 'inimitable', but which he spoke with unusual 'absence d'accent étranger'. It is true that the English *beau monde* was drawn to Paris that year in particular because of the staging, from 1 April, of the *Exposition Universelle*. Gossip flowed steadily back to the British press, especially when Bertie, the Prince of Wales, attended. There he took in a performance by the diva Hortense Schneider in the title role of Offenbach's new extravaganza *La Grande-duchesse de Gérolstein*, so that even the *Cheltenham Mercury* reported to its no doubt avid readers that, amid many 'drolleries', the Prince had 'seemed much amused' by her. What the paper omitted to spell out, but everyone soon knew, was that, unconstrained by his recent marriage, the future Edward VII was no less amused by la Schneider's performances in private. His attentions, compounding those of many a nobleman and potentate, contributed to her acquiring as a lewd nickname the title of a glassed shopping arcade in central Paris, the 'Passage des Princes'.

*

Towards the end of the year, Harry found himself in new difficulties. This time, Ray Pelly tentatively stepped in. On 1 November he wrote a letter to Alice, his 'own darling', who was staying in Cleveland Square. As though troubled in his mind, he cut across an account of the litany he had read in church that morning, to say:

> Alice tell Aunty that I deeply feel poor Harry's claim is far more than Edwards. Besides, Edward can afford a house of his own & I think ought certainly to do so rather than hint at turning one whose true home it is, out of doors. Edward acknowledges his being with Aunty is a temporary arranget & this is all it is. Harry is Auntys adopted son. I am clear darling that rather than H. should go into lodgings we will offer him our Prophets Chamber—but be cautious about offering it too freely, let us rather see 1st if he must be driven out like poor Hagar into the Wilderness. It may be God's will he should come to us let us wait & see.

There is no obvious candidate for the Edward of this letter, unless it was Edward Cutler, now three months married to Ellen.

Ray himself currently had a meagre living in Wanstead. The 'prophet's chamber', a biblical reference, was in common parlance a spare bedroom: 'Let us make a little chamber, I pray thee, on the wall; and let us set for him there a bed, and a table, and a stool, and a candlestick: and it shall be, when he cometh to us, that he shall turn in thither.' The allusion to Hagar, meanwhile, Abraham's concubine, though appearing self-explanatory, was perhaps more complex. Hagar, at first made welcome in Abraham's household, is thrown out when pregnant, and for centuries she has been swathed in unresolvable questions about whether or not she was responsible for bringing this exile on herself.

Whatever the ructions at Cleveland Square, six weeks later, on 11 December, Ray wrote exultantly to his parents: 'Harry came to us for Sunday, & O there is such a blessed change in him, I never saw a man so earnestly seeking, now there is no pretence about it. I expect daily to hear he has found peace. We had most interesting conversation together. He thinks of nothing else.'

The 'blessed change' in Harry was not destined to last. But Ray may still have been right to detect a lack of peace in his brother-in-law, a weariness of soul and a desire for redemption. Equally, Harry may have drawn momentary comfort from the beliefs of his sister's husband. They were only two years apart in age, and Ray had a questing intelligence of his own. The remark of his that seems least persuasive is the last: 'He thinks of nothing else.'

Harry did end up temporarily in the prophet's chamber; but the routine in Wanstead must rapidly have palled. Ray and Alice already had a three-year-old, a two-year-old and a baby, their 'precious lambs', Doug, Mabel and Kattie, who wobbled between being in 'good pluck' and being afflicted with colds, boils, sore gums and scarletina. Alice, herself oppressed by bouts of ague, was caught up in 'mothers meetgs', church working parties, efforts to adapt her piano skills to the church organ, and the pressing matter of whether to buy a dining-room carpet at the Baker Street Bazaar. Ray fretted over his sermons, dilatory congregants, and the deaths of his parishioners, and involved himself in cottage lectures, prayer meetings, children's monthly services, and a nearby school for gypsies. He also worried about keeping the church warm enough for Alice's organ practice, how to find lamps for the pony chaise, and, endlessly, about how he was ever to secure himself a more comfortable living.

Ray was heavily dependent on the charity of his father, who was terminally stingy in response to appeals from his son. It was only a year, too, since a disastrous run on the discounting house of Overend Gurney had staggered British financial confidence when it collapsed under immense unsecured debts. Ray's wider family had had reason to be particularly shaken by this upset. Samuel Gurney, who managed the business successfully for decades, until he died in 1856, was a brother of Elizabeth Fry, making him Ray's great-uncle; and several Quaker cousins lost a great deal of money when the business went down. Ray regularly pleaded with his father for £10 handouts, and in 1871 wrote with impressive humour of being 'deeply grieved to hear that dear daddy should let pecuniaries worry him so much'. In fact, when the old man died in 1886, his property, plus wealth in Imperial Continental Gas, and in West Ham Gas shares, turned out to have the colossal value of £87,555, six shillings and eight pence. For the time being, though, Ray and Alice struggled.

George Moore waxed caustic about the type of life they led, and what he called the 'villa' mentality. 'Respectability has wound itself about society, a sort of octopus, and nowhere are you quite free from one of its suckers', he said. Even his cherished theatres were increasingly dependent on attracting a middle-class audience, so that now, appallingly in his view, 'overfed inhabitants of the villa in the stalls' sought 'gross excitements to assist them through their hesitating digestions'. He considered suburban hypocrisies shameful, and wrote defiantly that 'subtle selfishness with a dash of unscrupulousness pulls more plums out of life's pie than the seven deadly virtues. If you are a good man you want a bad one to convert; if you are a bad man you want a bad one to go out on a spree with.'

In Wanstead, Harry had put himself in the hands of a thorough-going good man, but the siren call of badness was not long coming. In a letter of 9 March 1868, Alice remarked to her mother-in-law: 'My brother is in the Isle of Wight with some of his numerous friends. He says "no power on earth will bring him back to Ray and me" he is too ashamed of himself.' It seems telling that 'he is too ashamed of himself' should fall outside Alice's quotation marks, making this her exasperated judgement, and not a confession by her reckless brother.

There is no record of where Harry went after this spree with his 'numerous friends', though by the summer, Hortense Schneider, playing the Grand Duchess of Gérolstein, was stunning packed houses at the St James's Theatre in Piccadilly. This was again news across the land. In the *Wiltshire Times and Trowbridge Advertiser* for 4 July 1868, a London gossip writer, in villa mode, and deploying all-too-typical anti-Semitism, described how the Prince of Wales 'not only wears as many rings as a Jew merchant, but also wears bracelets'. Possibly worse: 'I was sorry to notice that his Royal Highness patronized Mdlle. Schneider at the French plays on Saturday night, especially as this fast Parisian actress has now given way to the clamour of a portion of the audiences, and dances the *cancan* nightly.'

If Harry got caught up in this whirl, later press accounts neverthe-less agree that in 1868 he largely stayed out of England, explaining in vague terms that he 'traveled extensively in Europe', and became 'familiarly acquainted with the attractions and points of interest in the principal cities of the continent'. The *New York Times* expanded on this to say: 'He had a handsome face and figure, winning ways, captivating manner, and a vast variety of accomplishments. Floating around in Europe, he added to his knowledge of the classics com-plete mastery of many modern languages, a familiarity with human nature, and thorough acquaintance with the rare art of pleasing.'

Alice had a tale about Harry in which, 'when in Italy, he posed as a great personage at Florence and received such [*sic*] hospitality from the English society there. In return for this he gave a magnifi-cent ball which was attended by all the notabilities of the City. On the following morning when the account had to be settled, Henry Larkins was not to be found.' This story is so lacking in detail that all it really confirms is the appeal of Harry's battered reputation. Yet he himself did later describe having seen Contessa Rattazzi at a 'brilliant fancy ball' in Florence, 'one of the most original women in Europe', attired 'in a leopard skin, quiver, bow and arrows and nothing more, not even so much as a touch of violet powder'.

Under the hand of Henry James, a Florentine narrative about the bamboozling of expatriate notabilities would no doubt have been splintered into an agonising trail of impenetrable nuances and regrets, with a dastardly protagonist attempting to win himself the fortune of an ingénue heiress. But in all the records Harry left behind him, there is not one whisper to suggest that he ever tried to solve his difficulties by marrying money, and his interest in ingénues would appear to have been nil. Instead, he continued to rely on his charisma to save him, no matter what, a strategy that was about to get him into the most spectacular trouble.

6: Paris

In January 1869, Harry stopped at the opulent Grand Hôtel in Paris, known as one of the city's new 'monster establishments'. He was meant to be merely passing through, but remained until his purse ran dry, whereupon he resorted to what the British press would call 'unpleasant dodges'. The villa mentality was unimpressed; but it has to be said that in the shadowy adventure that followed, he showed extraordinary nerve, earning himself a riot of sympathisers and friends.

The Grand Hôtel had over 700 rooms, five lavish dining rooms, 'magnificently furnished saloons', baths if you really cared for them, billiards rooms, smoking rooms with foreign newspapers, an integral telegraph office. It occupied an entire block, and sat next to the grandiose new opera building, now near the end of its construction, at the very heart of Napoleon III's staggering redesign of the city.

The Opéra under construction

The Prince of Wales liked to stay there. And with its front entrance facing the exclusive and anglophile Jockey Club de Paris, it had also become a notorious hub for a set of raffish, aristocratic gamblers from England.

In an occasional column about the 'distinguished fashionables' making Paris their playground that spring, *Baily's Magazine of Sports and Pastimes* noted that, already, various young swells were inclining towards their 'usual parliamentary sittings' in the hotel's courtyard. One luminary of this set was Lord Charles Hamilton, younger brother of the 12th Duke of Hamilton. When the 11th Duke, their father, died in 1863, aged fifty-two, after falling drunkenly down the back stairs at Paris's famous Maison d'Or restaurant, Queen Victoria wrote to her daughter, 'How shocking'. Charles Hamilton, sixteen then, was now twenty-one. A couple of decades later he would die as a chloral addict on the Riviera.

According to Harry's later testimony, he was meant to be on his way to take up a position in Japan, but unexpectedly ran into old friends, 'de la plus haute aristocratie d'Angleterre', according to one report, including 'MM. Hamilton et d'autres gentilshommes'. And so he moved down into a better room at the hotel, and 'abandoned himself with all the élan of his passions' to the pleasures of the city. In January, as the racing season had not yet begun, English society took over Paris's boulevards for velocipede races 'at a maddening rate of speed', their bicycles referred to as 'flying horses'.

Harry himself described Paris as a 'fairy city' where 'perfect contentment' could be found in idling outside a café on the Champs-Élysées over dominoes and cigarettes, or absinthe and ices, watching the pretty women go by. But then, a fellow could do more than simply watch the women of the *demi-monde*, 'the highest class of questionable company'. *Baily's* mockingly distinguished the top quarter of this half-world as the 'semi-hemisphere', presumably the women who wore velvet and diamonds, when dressed; who lived under zinc chandeliers and among silk flowers scented with ambergris; who smoked cigarettes themselves, ate burnt almonds and drank champagne. Then again, above even this upper division, a fabled few formed their own select firmament known as '*la garde*'.

Manet's *Olympia*, first revealed to a disgusted public in 1865, was an eye-wateringly modern interpretation of the classical Venus. His subject, the courtesan Victorine Meurent, stared back with riveting lack of concern at those entranced by her nudity. And the hand she rested with such cool possession across her naked lap was matched by lush flowers set within oval folds of paper, brazenly representing what her hand appeared to conceal. In these vibrantly disturbing forms of equilibrium, Manet enshrined the ambiguous distribution of power whereby a successful courtesan chose as much as she was chosen. The more desirable she became, the more she could be wilful, offensive and outrageous.

Harry's aristocratic friends were blamed for introducing him to Adeline Markowich, but he could just as well have met her at the Bal Mabille, the pleasure garden in Paris that most resembled the Cremorne in London. He later recounted a quip about the Mabille, capturing the original wordplay in his translation. A *habituée* was asked why the women there sometimes fought each other with 'hands full of hair being scattered to the breezes'. Her reply, he wrote, was that 'the worst result is, the employes [*sic*] take us out, but if we fight outside, the police take us in'.

A first ghostly image of Harry in Paris, and in trouble, places him early one morning in la Markowich's rented apartment at 31 rue Vernet near the place de l'Étoile, an elegant four-storey building with long windows and little wrought-iron flower balconies. She was of a 'beauté ravissante', in the view of reporters, her hooded gaze helping to explain why, for her pleasure, several small fortunes were stolen and an extraordinary number of duels fought. *Le Pavé*, a paper aimed at boulevardiers, had announced her at the start of the year as a new queen among the courtesans of the city. La Barrucci was a waning figure, she who had famously once stripped naked, unasked, in front of the Prince of Wales at the Maison d'Or; and the sceptre was slipping from the hands of Cora Pearl, among the most famous of them all, drawn into this life as a girl by the proprietor of the Argyll Rooms in London. Their power, said *Le Pavé*, was being assumed by the younger, crazier, Polish 'Marcowitch'.

La Markowich's origins were predictably obscure, with talk of an abduction, followed by a trip to Naples with an Italian protector. She earned the passing soubriquet *la femme au nègre* when she took to flaunting a black servant round the artificial lake in Napoleon III's newly created park, the Bois de Boulogne. But this affectation was unoriginal. The maid who displays the suggestive bouquet in *Olympia*, for example, has been rendered so dark by Manet that she appears almost as her mistress's photographic negative. After this, therefore, the nickname that came to define la Markowich, to the dangerous amusement of the press, was *la fée aux giffles*, or the 'slap fairy', a title she made no perceptible effort to live down. It may have been Markowich whom Harry had in mind when he described a 'well known and very fair Parisian blonde' who caused a 'sensation' by including a live green snake in her coiffure. At any rate, for now she was notorious, though her fame would not last.

Wearied tradesmen formed queues early up the stairs of such women, hoping to extract money from their slippery customers before they left for the day. Harry happened to be with *la fée aux giffles* the morning Collier, a horse dealer, talked his way into her salon, demanding to be paid. She owed him the balance on a pure-bred worth 2,500 francs, equivalent to £10,000 today. From her bedroom she yelled out to Harry: 'Pay, or don't pay', sounding indifferent on her own account, but perhaps a little threatening on his. Gallantly, Harry produced the required sum, no doubt aware that among shady types, milking an admirer in this way was known as the 'bill trick'. And yet, with this unforeseen loss, Harry had just bought himself Collier's trust. Using drafts on a bank in England, he went on to purchase two horses of his own from the dealer, valued at another 2,500 francs each, then hired a carriage and pair, which he reserved for use at night.

An English 'clubman' commenting on the courtesans of the Second Empire remarked dryly that they 'diffused an atmosphere of sumptuous immorality which intoxicated many who were unable to withstand its fragrance'. Harry, falling in with this life, now also became an acknowledged *adorateur* of Hortense Schneider. Though she was the great star of Offenbach's operettas, her voice was widely criticised by purists; but she carried the day, in Paris, London and Cairo, with her salacious, frivolous interpretations. 'Beaux in her

Hortense Schneider as the Grand Duchess of Gérolstein

string she naturally will have', wrote *Baily's* that spring. She herself confessed to thinking the English droll for going 'into fits' about her now that she was old, 'but how old!', and plain, 'but how plain!' Harry wrote that, off stage, she was 'a little, insignificant-looking woman', and *boulotte*, dumpy, 'but very conversational and witty'. One of her anecdotes, which he repeated, concerned her *femme de chambre*, Niquette, who, during a performance, became pregnant by the theatre fireman in a dark corridor. When later she begged that he should be made to marry her, 'Poor Niquette fell on the floor aneantie', or annihilated, wrote Harry, on learning that a different fireman worked at the theatre every night. As for the thrill imparted by la Schneider in performance, to attempt to describe this, he said, 'would be useless'. She may have been thirty-five, and therefore past her prime, but to her the attentions of a delightful young suitor were evidently welcome, even as Harry was able to enjoy the company of a creature for whose favours princes had squandered millions.

*

It was mid March when Harry was first taken by his gang of affluent friends to the shop of the jeweller Kramer, at 31 rue Neuve-Saint-Augustin, among the glamorous streets nested around the Grand Hôtel. In 1853, Kramer had been among those commissioned by Napoleon III to disassemble an antique collection of jewellery and reset the gems as modish wedding adornments to be worn by his bride, Empress Eugénie. Though Kramer ever afterwards advertised himself as 'joaillier de l'Impératrice', in June 1866 he had fallen into near-ruin when, somewhere in Marseilles, couriers mislaid an underinsured box of his diamonds, bound for Egypt. Even now, he was struggling to recover from these losses.

Harry now bought a few exorbitant trinkets from Kramer for a total of 5,000 francs in cash, then took his winking purchases and pawned the lot for 4,000 francs. At the cost of the 1,000 francs thrown away in this transaction, he hoped to establish himself in rue Neuve-Saint-Augustin as someone with money, and to spare. He was soon back again. He presented Kramer with a drawing of a *parure*, a splendid jewellery ensemble. How quickly could it be copied? Kramer said he could have the *parure* ready in under a week. Could it be made up in diamonds? It could. And the cost? In diamonds, Kramer ventured, the cost would be 36,000 francs.

The true value of this commission would be conveyed by Maupassant in his famous story 'La Parure', first published in 1884. In it, Mathilde Loisel, dissatisfied with her lot as the wife of a lowly civil servant, borrows the diamonds of a happier friend to wear to a party, and is then aghast to find that she has lost them. In agony, Mathilde and her husband resolve to buy new diamonds, and secretly return these instead. Obliterating an inheritance, begging friends for help, and borrowing further sums at dreadful rates of interest, they effect the switch, then fall into hopeless poverty. Only after ten years do the Loisels finally clear the debt; and it is now that Mathilde, a haggard wreck, accidentally discovers that the jewellery she was originally lent had been made of glass. As for the sum that has destroyed her and her husband: Maupassant valued the replacement diamond *parure* at 36,000 francs.

*

In the third week of March, Harry went to collect his commission. Kramer refused to relinquish the *parure* for anything less than an immediate cash payment of 20,000 francs, with the balance due on 5 July. Harry consented, proffering drafts for the cash sum, to be drawn on a banking house in London. But Kramer had his doubts, and insisted on being given time to make enquiries first, to see whether the bank drafts would stand up. Harry had little choice but to agree. He left the shop minus both his drafts and the diamonds, putting him in a highly precarious position.

Easter Sunday was set to fall that year on 22 March, and this was also to be the date of the premier of *La Diva*, an operetta written by Offenbach in fulfilment of a long-standing promise to Hortense Schneider. The new work presented a florid version of her own life, and she was to star in it at her old stamping ground, the lavishly sleazy Théâtre des Bouffes-Parisiens. Fashions were changing, however, so that the production represented an anxious roll of the dice.

After a day or so, Harry returned to tell Kramer that he needed the *parure* at once. It was to be a gift for la Schneider, and he wished to hide it in an Easter egg from the famous confectionery house Siraudin, at 17 rue de la Paix. Harry had already been round the corner, he explained, to this luxurious and 'célèbre boutique', with its sweeping stairway and potted palms, and the confectioners needed the diamonds to do their work. He showed Kramer a letter from his brother-in-law in England that warned him not to draw further on his English bank, for fear of too greatly disheartening his family in London. Obligingly the letter concluded: if you need funds, let me send you £2,000.

Kramer suggested that Harry should send for the money at once. Harry replied airily that a telegram would do. Give me some paper, and I shall write out a message, he said; and if you like, you can set the ball rolling by dispatching the request yourself.

With the clock supposedly ticking, Kramer at last gave way and, in return for a few scribbles, handed Harry his diamonds.

In France at this time, pawnbroking was organised on the *Mont-de-Piété* system: not for the profit of the lender, that is, but on controlled and charitable lines, with the interest rates kept low. As a further safeguard, in Paris there was a cap on lending of 10,000 francs. But a 'devoted friend' who 'knew all about this sort of thing' tipped Harry the wink that the *Mont-de-Piété* in Versailles gave more. Thither Harry went. And there Kramer's *parure* blessedly realised 15,000 francs.

It is not hard to imagine the sinking feeling of M. Collier, the horse dealer, when he discovered that Harry's bank account in London was empty, making his drafts invalid. Added to this, Collier heard on the grapevine that Harry had given the horses hired for his night carriage to the great singer, Hortense Schneider. Collier laid charges. But by the time he caught up with the young Englishman, Harry's fortunes seemed to have changed. All the little difficulties between them were quickly smoothed away.

Being flush now, Harry pressed home his advantage. Even as Kramer awaited the happy result of the telegram, Harry returned to 31 rue Neuve-Saint-Augustin to make a couple of new purchases. He needed a watch chain, and selected one at 250 francs. Then he pushed his luck and asked about a pair of lady's diamond cufflinks, priced at 3,500 francs. Kramer agreed to accept a deposit on them, on the understanding that if they were not agreeable to the lady, Harry could bring them back. And if she liked them, he would return to make good the difference.

These cufflinks Harry really did give to Hortense Schneider. To a woman more used to diamonds like decanter stoppers, they were perhaps no great matter. And yet the first night of *La Diva* was torn to pieces in the press, and was received by the public with unprecedented coolness. As a mark of devotion from a young admirer, therefore, the little trinkets can only have touched the troubled star. After this, Harry somehow never did find time to stroll back round to see Kramer and make good the transaction.

Early in April, Kramer went one evening to the Grand Hôtel planning to corner Harry and demand payment. But he had just missed his quarry, who had packed his trunks and disappeared, leaving no forwarding address that anyone could find. To compound the bad news, hotel staff recalled that the young Englishman had sent a servant and some luggage ahead to Brussels.

Kramer hurried back out into the night, past the Café de la

Paix, and out across the great open *place* before the new opera building. A mountain of cladding had recently been removed from the front, and in the glow of Paris's globular gas lamps its over-whelming façade was almost ready, though four great sculpture groups on plinths were yet to be revealed. Kramer's fastest route took him down the majestic avenue de Napoléon, then left on a zigzag into rue Monsigny, home to the front entrance of the Théâtre des Bouffes-Parisiens. *La Diva* was still playing, Hortense Schneider struggling on woefully as herself. Though *Baily's* wrote that 'nobody but Schneider could have saved Offenbach', and that she had 'decided it was to be a success', in truth the only question was when the show would fold. Her need for applause had never been greater. But if Harry spent time there that evening, dallying among the cocottes, he was dallying there no longer.

Kramer set off again at a run, perhaps out of the back of the theatre and through the passage Choiseul, the seedy arcade that lay behind. If so, it yielded nothing, and he was soon hurrying on north towards the boulevard des Italiens. And it was on this grand street, outside the Café Anglais, that Kramer's luck turned. Of all the great restaurants in Paris, in 1869 the Café Anglais reigned supreme, its head chef, Adolphe Dugléré, described by Rossini as 'le Mozart de la cuisine française'. Like the Maison d'Or, along the same street, it had not only a superb public dining room, but also a maze of *cabinets particuliers*, or private rooms, with pianos and divans, reached via an occluded entrance, hidden staircases and a warren of corridors. Here, the rich could idle discreetly with their lovers, and aristocratic adultery of every feather was put in play.

Drawn up outside, Kramer spotted the *coupé* Harry had hired from Collier, the 'cut-small' pleasure carriage, with its open perch for the driver and, behind, an enclosed space for two. True, a jeweller could not simply rush in and play the outraged creditor. But Kramer was prepared to wait.

If Harry was really planning an escape to Brussels, then he was being extremely careless about it. Not until 2 a.m. did he and his companions rise from their supper, leaving the cloistered naughtiness and glimmering splendour of their *cabinet particulier* to slip back outside into the cool night air. As he no longer had a room at the Grand Hôtel, perhaps one of his 'partners in pleasure', as they were coyly called, proposed her bed for the next several hours. But those few steps out into the chill started him inexorably on a different path, towards the vast and awful panopticon prison that was Mazas.

Harry was plucked from amid his friends, arrested, and conveyed through the streets of Paris to the sound of horse hooves clopping in the night, swiftly passing over a bridge to the Île de la Cité, where he was ushered into the 'seething anthill' that was the Dépot de la Préfecture de Police.

It was said that every kind of human misery washed through this building at one time or another, those detained at night crammed into underground cells. A few months later, the poet Rimbaud, aged seventeen, would also be processed at the Préfecture, recording that in a courtyard full of the accused, he was forced to fight off the sexual advances of other men.

Morning saw a great circus of prostitutes, destitutes, crooks and drunkards waiting to be interrogated by the examining magistrate. Harry must have prayed through the dark hours that when his turn came, he would somehow escape this unfolding disaster. But if so, his prayers availed him nothing.

Mazas, in the east of Paris, was a 'model' institution only completed in 1850; a remand prison designed to hold 1,200 men in solitary confinement. Isolation was its overpowering rationale, and its rule was silence. Even a few days in there left a crushing impression on those subjected to what Victor Hugo called its 'philanthropie doctrinaire'. The theory was that preventing all association between inmates preserved the better among them from the pernicious influence of the worse, while halting the spread of disease and removing the risk of violence. However, prisoner after prisoner experienced the regime at Mazas as a form of violence in itself. And there was no defence against harsh treatment by the guards.

Thomas Cook's guide called the exterior 'gloomy and repulsive-looking', and in 1900 Mazas would be razed to the ground as a gigantic, ill-conceived eyesore. But when Harry was sent there, the prison was in its prime. Its iron gate was set in a hulking great block of wall that loured grimly over those who passed beneath. New inmates were first dumped into holding cells in an administration building, after which they gave their details and had their loose possessions removed. Then they were stripped, washed, shaved, and issued with a rough prison suit and cap. Their own clothes, often tattered and reeking, often crawling, were given a 'fumigation sulfureuse', then stored in little packets side by side on a high wall of shelves, in a bleak parody of the prison itself. After this: a short walk to the actual prison, and in.

Mazas was by all accounts joltingly cold and dismal, but also imposing, huge, even grand, illuminated with dotted gas flares, high windows and distant skylights. By day it resembled a giant tank; by night, a vault. Its sepulchral silence was so oppressive that even the guards spoke in a murmur, as though among the sick. From the towering circular hall at its heart radiated six immense corridors, or 'divisions', on the pattern of an open fan, blading away to distant vanishing points. These corridors were three storeys high, with the

A three-tier corridor at Mazas

upper two tiers served by vertiginous iron balconies that seemed to hang suspended in the air. At any one time, each division held roughly 200 muted men.

Marooned at the centre of this deadened facility sat the 'bureau central de surveillance', a glazed rotunda incongruously decorated like a kiosk in a public park. Inside the bureau, a fresh inmate was registered for the second time, and once he had given his name here, it was gone. His sole identity became the zinc plaque bearing his cell number, which he carried as he was led, newly anonymous, into one of the six vast divisions to be locked away.

No amount of Grinderesque discipline at Brackenbury's, no military discipline in India, could have prepared Harry for the relentless deprivation that faced him now. By day, the sleeping hammock was stowed by order on a shelf. Victor Hugo explained how, in a cell at Mazas, with its dim light, jaundiced whitewash and 'odeur infecte', the choice was therefore either to pace incessantly like a caged wolf, or simply to sit, like a lunatic in an asylum. Blessed are they who remain desperate, wrote the anarchist Jules Vallès, remembering time spent in a Mazas cell in 1853. A prisoner needed that despair to fuel resistance, he said, but not so much of it that his mind abandoned him altogether. He recalled obsessively counting over and over again the bricks of his cell floor, and described his brain collapsing, stupefied, as though drowning in mud, the experience akin to swallowing, and vomiting back up, ceaselessly, a thick, awful nothingness.

The relentless lack of real human contact was made worse by lack of privacy. Repeatedly during the day and four times each night, softly shod guards padded the metal galleries, and would silently open and stare through the *judas* or peephole set in steel in each cell door. Anyone caught breaking a rule was punished, at worst put in a 'dungeon' cell in the sixth division, with the meagre furniture removed, and no light.

There was, each day, just one hour of respite, in the outdoor *promenoirs*, circular walking yards built in the gaps between the six hulking divisions. Like the prison itself, the *promenoirs* were panopticons, with a watchtower in the middle of each, from which radiated twenty high walls, like the spokes of a wheel. This allowed for 100 men, across the five yards, to exercise in simultaneous isolation. Any attempt by prisoners to communicate was punished; but on a good day, Harry could loaf for an hour in a strip of early-summer sun, drawing on a pipe if he had the money to pay for it, and perhaps watching the odd bird fly over, or listening for the sounds of the city beyond the prison's encircling walls.

Otherwise, on Sunday mornings, each prisoner had his cell door bolted open two and a half inches, so that, if he chose to, he could peer towards the central rotunda. On its roof, incongruously, and protected by no more than an ornamental balustrade, was an open chapel, with an altar, a golden sculpture of the Madonna and Christ, and torches. And from there a weekly religious service was held, the priest's voice travelling into the anguished, tomb-like silence of the divisions, and dying before it reached the end.

There were also set visiting hours in the week, and for these the divisions were hidden behind six gigantic curtains. Across the shrouded hall, and up a flight of stairs, was a row of 'parlours', through the bars of which a general visitor could talk to any inmate to whom visits had not been denied. Separately, there were also two cells per division reserved for meetings between prisoners and counsel, where cases could be discussed and trial strategies devised. Bearing the zinc plaque with his number, without which he was not allowed to move, it would have been inside one of these cells that Harry came face to face at last with the renowned lawyer on whom he must now depend, to spring him from this nightmare and help him walk free.

Harry was in Mazas for over a month before he was shaved, restored to his own garb and sent for trial. What the press called 'le high-life' that he had previously been living, among the gorgeous restaurants and raddled theatres of the city, now found its dark reflection in a courtroom at the Palais de Justice. The great star of the Bouffes-Parisiens herself had decided to engineer a deft dramatical turn. While Harry waited, word arrived out of the blue that a *grande-duchesse* had 'proved the nobility of her blood', as a reporter sneeringly wrote, and had just rushed to return a pair of diamond cufflinks to the jeweller Kramer. 'Unbelievably', it seemed that other forms of restitution had also recently been made on Harry's behalf: his crazy friends loved him enough to see him straight. Thus, with no time to spare, Kramer at last stood fully compensated.

If Harry momentarily hoped that he was now in the clear, those hopes were dashed at once. He stood accused of obtaining goods under false pretences, a fraud charge. Restitution made no difference. Still, his trial was put back by a week, and he was summarily returned to jail.

In 1869, after a grand reworking, the Palais de Justice was near to complete. Tourist guides recommended sweeping up the grand staircase into the main concourse, with its pillars and statues, the 'Salle des Pas-perdus', to catch the amusing sight of black-robed lawyers trying to cut deals for their clients with prosecuting victims. From this huge hall, a visitor could then pass into one of the many courtrooms or *chambres* for further entertainment.

When Harry, under municipal guard, was returned there for his trial proper, he was taken up an impressive double staircase to the seventh *chambre correctionelle*. The room was packed, with the press out in force, and many reporters now fell under the spell of 'Henri-Thomas Larkins'. He was, they said, 'un fort joli garçon', a fine-looking young man, highly educated, beautifully dressed, 'élégant', and altogether, 'le spécimen le plus complet du gentleman'. *Le Figaro* said he was so good-looking, and so clearly from the best circles, that seeing him with common vagabonds and swindlers on the 'banc des accusés' could only inspire pity. And when Harry spoke, the impression was yet more striking. His French was excellent, with only the slightest of accents, and he talked with 'real distinction and great discretion', a discretion that inspired particular respect because it stood to harm his defence. Come what may, he refused to name either of the women who had been dragged into the affair, or to reveal any details about them that he considered private. As their identities were nevertheless an open secret, this formality was taken to be exquisite.

In sum, Harry stood accused of fraud and abuse of trust. Moreover, at point of arrest, he had appeared to be mere hours from fleeing to Brussels. M. Lancelin, president of the court, began with

questions to establish the basic facts of the case. Harry said that he
had served for six years in India as a British Army officer, but that,
after disagreeing with his colonel, he had resigned and returned to
London. He was an orphan with a wealthy aunt: he expected to
be her sole heir. He had stopped in Paris on his way to take up an
advantageous position, secured for him by a relative, in Japan. M.
Lancelin raised the incident where Harry had succumbed to the
foot-stamping of a certain lady: once he had paid the horse dealer
Collier the balance on her pure-bred steed, had he not manoeuvred
over horses for himself? And had he not then offered two of these
horses to an actress? Harry explained that, as the horses belonging
to the second lady had been unwell, he had lent her a pair for a
ride in the Bois; that was all. Lancelin conceded that Collier had
withdrawn his complaints against Harry: there was no crime to
answer there, but the prosecution had put in Collier's testimony to
demonstrate Harry's exorbitant style. After this, Lancelin finally
laid out the purported facts of Harry's dealings with Kramer: that
he had pawned one set of diamonds, the *parure*, for which he had
paid nothing, and had then given away a pair of diamond cufflinks
for which he had paid merely a deposit.

It was now the turn of the imperial prosecutor, M. Cazeaux,
to throw an uncomfortable light on the details. Harry had so far
abused his aunt's generosity in London that she had felt compelled
to 'expatriate' him to Japan, he said. She had 'filled his pockets
with banknotes' to enable him to reach this faraway land, expressly
forbidding him to stop in Paris. But instead, Harry had surrendered
to 'outrance', or excess, in the city, followed by crooked 'manoeuvres'.
Harry had represented himself to Kramer as a captain, when he
was merely a lieutenant, said Cazeaux. And he had claimed to
be an attaché at the British Embassy in Japan: also untrue. His
companions had been of the kind to 'throw their money out of
windows', so that Harry had seemed wealthy by association, and
he had then applied fraudulent pressure to make Kramer hand over
his valuables. Deposits had been violated, trust despicably betrayed,
and a criminal exit planned.

This assault was punctuated by Harry's explanations. His aunt
indeed had a fortune. The British Ambassador to Japan really was

his relative. His behaviour had been imperfect, he admitted, but he had always planned to honour his arrangements with Kramer by 5 July, as agreed between them. As for the cufflinks, the jeweller had granted that if they found favour with a certain artist, she was to keep them. *Le Gaulois* called Harry's calm demeanour under questioning 'perfect'. But a nagging difficulty remained. How did he explain secretly quitting the Grand Hôtel, and sending his luggage out of France?

It must have struck Harry that he could use the fact that he had been so easily caught outside the Café Anglais as grounds for asserting that he had never planned to escape in the first place. He attempted to clear the decks by saying that he had, of course, left a forwarding address at the Grand Hôtel especially for M. Kramer: 37 rue Le Peletier, Paris. What he said next, though, was a truly risky move by which he aimed to trade the appearance of one form of duplicity, material to the case against him, for the admission of another, perversely calculated to strengthen his defence. Sending a man to Brussels, he explained, with a little of his luggage, had been a charade, intended to convince his family in England that he was finally quitting France. By this means, he had hoped to persuade them to forward him funds that would set him straight again. The Brussels *manoeuvre* was not evidence of an attempt to escape his debts, but the opposite: it represented his attempt to clear them.

If true, this was a shabby confession. If untrue, it was an extremely neatly conceived lie. Either way, it wrong-footed Cazeaux. Weakly he pointed out that, even now, Harry's family had not come to his aid. Instead, it had been Harry's wild friends who, after he was carted away to prison in the night, had had a whip-round, redeeming the *parure* in Versailles the very next day, Cazeaux conceded, and afterwards paying off the balance of its cost. As for the 'fashionable actress' to whom the cufflinks had been given, 'and who accepted them as a tribute to her talent, I'm sure', added Cazeaux, provoking a ripple of amusement in the court, it was also true that she had now returned them. But the charge of fraud still stood unanswered, he said doggedly. He ended: 'we marvel to see, here in this court, a well brought up young man from one of the foremost families of England. We regret that he was carried away by the ardour of his age into forgetting not merely all delicacy, but even the simple probity that every honest man both grasps and observes.' It was a stinging rebuke, yet it hinted at understanding.

Harry was represented in court by Charles Lachaud, thirty years into an outstanding career, and famous for his part in several sensational trials. He had come to prominence in 1840 with the case of Marie Lafarge, tortuously related to the then royal family of France, and accused of poisoning her brutal husband by means of a cream cake laced with arsenic. Though her defence failed, Lachaud, only twenty-two at the time, had stood out among her legal team. He became notorious in the years that followed for arguing without notes and using dramatic gestures, every speech 'éloquente et passionnée' as he switched between the powerful and the caressing. After Lafarge, his more prominent cases had included a theft to the tune of six million francs, an attempted servant murder, aristocratic defamation, fatal duelling, and the spattering of sulphuric acid over a mistress by a jealous wife; not to mention baby theft, bigamy, further poisonings galore, and so on.

In the present case, Lachaud's strategy was to replace one humiliating cliché with another. Rather than a cunning gentleman crook, he suggested, Harry was a foolish young blade. He was descended from Scottish royalty, had entered the army in the service of his queen, and in a brilliant career in Bengal had reached the rank of lieutenant, before returning, young, ardent and penniless, to be close to his family. When he then embraced the gaieties of life in London, his aunt generously paid his expenses. M. Charles Laffitte, said Lachaud, a founder member of the Jockey Club de Paris, and from a fabulously wealthy banking family himself, was ready to attest that she was rich and childless, and wished to be thought of as Harry's adoptive mother. Venturing a little wordplay, Lachaud added that if there were *fils de famille*, well, there were also *neveux* or nephews *de famille*, the term 'son-of-family' all too often invoking a well-born rascal who rashly depended on a future inheritance to clear his debts. Still, one fine morning, Harry and his aunt had agreed that it was time for him to leave for a career in Japan. He had imprudently passed through Paris, and had run into friends, who had introduced him to others; and with every temptation thrown in his path, his stay had extended itself, until his situation had become 'difficile'. Of fraud, however, said Lachaud, there had been not a shadow, and Harry had never intended any harm. By what misadventure, therefore, did he now find himself among the recidivists on the correctional bench?

Harry had tied his lawyer's hands somewhat by his marvellous discretion. Lachaud did no more than gesture to the idea that two ladies had set out to enrich themselves by leading the passionate young officer astray. But he was under no such constraint with Kramer, and launched into a diatribe against merchants who acted as parasites on a seamy trade. The market in luxury goods, he said, was built on insane credit, offered to the sons of great families, yes, but also to ladies of no family at all. And when young men like Harry found themselves ensnared, the parasitical merchants turned mercilessly to the courts, where they pitted the honour of their clients against their own exaggerated prices.

In the single most important sentence of his speech, Lachaud smoothly declared that it had been the patronage and wealth of Harry's titled friends, and not some letter from his brother-in-law, that had decided the canny jeweller on making a customer of the young man. And had Kramer's seedy gamble not paid off? Had those same friends not expunged Harry's debts? A young man who inspired such fidelity in these difficult circumstances, said the lawyer, turning the tide of his speech, could not possibly be dishonest. He was guilty of imprudence, to be sure, but not of any crime. And may his gratitude act as a safeguard in times to come, concluded Lachaud, getting slightly ahead of himself. He will leave this perilous city tomorrow, he said, carrying the memory of the verdict with him, and in distant latitudes a high opinion of French justice will prevail.

Though the packed *chambre* met this final flourish with a round of applause, Harry, left waiting for the judgement of the court, had reason to be deeply fearful. But at least that judgement was not long in coming. M. Lancelin returned from deliberations in short order, and pronounced an acquittal, and Harry's immediate release.

Again, applause: the satirical yet celebratory ethos of the Bouffes-Parisiens once more infected proceedings. *Le Gaulois* dubbed the decision of the court 'légitime et indulgente', raising the nice question of how far it could really be both. Certainly, the degree to which indulgence won out may be judged by the response of Harry himself. The handsome young Englishman, admired throughout the trial for his coolness, and reserve 'tout britannique', was, in the moment of his release, all undone. He wept. And this was the first time, the press remarked, that he seemed prey to powerful emotion. As his tears fell, and his frailer self stood revealed, there was a murmur of sympathy through the court.

Still, once again, authority had let Harry Larkins slip away.

The general view afterwards was that Harry had acted the crazy rake, but if he had been led to the 'extreme limits of delicacy', by implication he had not quite gone over the edge. And anyway, whatever his guilt, his time in Mazas was surely punishment enough. *Le Figaro*, in a crime column written by the novelist René de Pont-Jest, now took the lid off this 'comedy of manners'. Pont-Jest named la Markowich and Hortense Schneider, and commented that both must feel a little embarrassed at having mistaken the resources of their admirer, a skill in which they were usually so adept. Then

Adeline Markowich

again, as a positive, the exposure arising from Harry's trial had turned photographs of la Markowich into top sellers. Not many men could afford the original, and those who did have the money might not have the nerve, was the smirking comment. She was, after all, known for being an 'amiable vampire'. When her doctor prescribed exercise to repair her lost appetite, how did she respond? She ordered her maid, before morning chocolate, to 'Bring in the nobility of Europe, waiting in my antechamber. I shall whip them.'

The day after Harry's release, la Markowich threw a spectacular party for him at her home in rue Vernet, bringing together 'tous les lions du *high life*' to celebrate 'the return of an English captain wrongfully accused of fraud'. The startling guest list included the famous ballerina Angelina Fioretti and the opera star Marie Sax, who had premiered roles in works by Wagner and Verdi. No less striking was the presence of Blanche d'Antigny, Caroline Letessier and Cora Pearl, *ruineuses* of the first water, notorious *grandes horizontales* of the Second Empire, undisputed members of '*la garde*'. In Zola's novel *Nana*, published in 1880, concerning a consummately destructive courtesan, he synthesised the scandalous histories of several of these women, threw in elements of Hortense Schneider too, and added colour trawled from Pont-Jest's crime columns. In particular, Zola gave d'Antigny's death, aged only thirty-four, to Nana. D'Antigny would spend her final ghastly weeks dying of perhaps smallpox, or typhoid, at the home of Caroline Letessier, Letessier herself reputed to have slung plates at Lord Charles Hamilton in a *cabinet particulier* at the Café Anglais. But Zola restaged the death in a top-floor room of the Grand Hôtel, depicting Nana there as a suppurating carcass. When Manet painted the character of Nana in her prime, he too used d'Antigny as his model.

The compliment to Harry of such a gathering in his name could hardly have been greater. And la Markowich received her own compliment that night, a clash between two of her admirers so severe that it provoked a duel. There would be several more of these over the summer, her most violent suitors including M. de la Poëze, Baron Malortie, a member of the Russell family, a Pemberton-Grund, and one of the Hamilton brothers too. The fights were never fatal, but there were slash wounds and loose bullets, and M.

de la Poëze, fighting Russell in Chantilly, suffered a punctured lung, until *la fée aux giffles* acquired a new name: *la Déesse de la guerre*, or the Goddess of War.

On 26 July, with great fanfare, the last of the cladding came off the façade of the sumptuous new opera building. The massed spectators who had gathered to see the four huge sculpture groups unveiled were enormously shocked by one: Carpeaux's *La Danse*. Far from the cool classicism they expected, the work seemed to show a mad, sozzled whirl of yielding flesh. A furious debate ensued

Carpeaux's La Danse *revealed to the public and assaulted with ink*

about its merits. Carpeaux's admirers valued either his positive, radical breach with the artistic norms of the past, or, somewhat contradictorily, his subtly Republican condemnation of the lascivious excesses of the hated Second Empire. His detractors were more straightforwardly appalled by a vulgar, filthy vision that called to mind the most abandoned cocottes entertaining their immoral protectors: 'Tourne-Crême, Fifine du Casino, la Markowich et les autres'.

With the figure he cut among the crooks in the Palais de Justice, Harry managed to win over the court, most of the press, the 'semi-hemisphere' and several infamous *grandes horizontales*, all in one go. But was his engaging candour quite what it seemed? Perhaps he really was the presumptive heir of Henrietta Coffin, but if so, this meant little. Her wealth came in the form of annuities that would not survive her, and she was disinclined to save much of her income on the way. Meanwhile, though the family might well have conspired to send Harry to the East, he could not possibly have been offered the role of a consular attaché in Japan. Such a post required years of study, and was won through competitive Foreign Office examinations. If there was really a job waiting for him in Yokohama, it was more likely to have been along the lines of a clerkship in a dockside silk house. Still, these caveats would probably have seemed to Harry like quibbling. His aunt was rich and childless and she gave him money. For generations his relatives had had influence in the East. And even if he did take dubious steps to keep a creditor happy, was the money not paid in good time, according to his word?

There can be no doubt that Harry's tears were genuine when he was spared the horror of an immediate and lengthy return to prison. But he was far from chastened by this adventure. And to find that he could walk from the court, not merely forgiven, but publicly celebrated as both a gentleman and a handsome ne'er-do-well to boot: in the cementing of his character, this appears to have been a perilous outcome all of its own.

7: Alas! Mr. Larkin

Local newspapers across Britain, from the *Bath Chronicle* to the *Oban Times*, syndicated a reasonably balanced account of Harry's trial and acquittal in Paris. In London, though, the *Morning Advertiser* made merry at his expense, quipping: 'Alas! Mr. Larkin, why were you so given to your own synonym?' At least the piece did end by congratulating him on his 'fortunate escape'. And this winking attitude to his shady exploits was evidently enough for Harry. He took the risky decision to return to a city where he had been 'given to larking' in the past, a decision that would soon prove to be a disturbing mistake.

Emily Soldene, in her day a famous singer, first came to prominence in London in the 1860s in roles originally written by Offenbach for Hortense Schneider. Then in April 1870, she starred at the Lyceum as Marguerite in *Little Faust*, an Anglicised burlesque on Gounod's opera *Faust*, written by Offenbach's great rival, the singer-composer Hervé. When Soldene later dished up a blizzard of only fitfully censored gossip in her sensational *Recollections*, she described a typical Lyceum show as starting off 'perfectly proper', before, 'Bing-bang-boom!', a 'bunch of graded Venuses' with 'natty' newspaper-stuffed bosoms would shoot out their naked legs in all directions. She also recalled the Lyceum Greenroom, where one of 'the girls' charged sixpence for a peep at what she swore was her 'Royal baby'. It was par for the course to find, lurking backstage, a select handful of aristocrats and other ardent followers, and Soldene scandalously named many of them. But it was the 'charming author-actor' Dion Boucicault whom she described in detail. He had run a silent hand down the back of her Marguerite costume, fitted to her 'like the paper on the wall', producing a euphemistic shiver that she never afterwards forgot.

Little Faust debuted on Easter Monday, 18 April. Advertisements promised a 'gorgeous kaleidoscope of pretty faces, pretty dresses, magnificent scenery, and witty dialogue'. It was set in a 'startlingly fashionable ladies' school in Peckham', and featured a lady whistler and a man who imitated orchestral instruments. Girls played boys, ladies, young men, and Mephisto was a delightful Mlle Debreaux. However, with Faust disguising himself as a Peckham schoolgirl, and with the man-hunting schoolmistress being performed by a Mr Odell, critics agreed that the public was starting to look askance at male actors in 'petticoat parts'. In Soldene's own account, various performers sang wonderfully, acted winningly, moved sultrily, or looked ravishing, but rarely all four together, and not necessarily even two. That said, one of the uncontested 'landmarks of the representation' was little Jennie Lee, as a Street Arab, giving a first taste of the 'unapproachable glory' of her career to come. Besides the performers, wrote Soldene, Leonide Leblanc was in town, one of the *grandes horizontales* of Paris, who 'would often come and stand in the prompt entrance'. And 'Amy Sheridan, too, used to come.' As Sheridan was performing a nightly turn at the Globe mere minutes away, she must have migrated to the Lyceum when she

Amy Sheridan

was through. Suggestively, Soldene capped this account by saying, 'Captain Harry Larkin was largely interested in the show, and also a little in her, I think.'

Well might Harry have been interested in Amy Sheridan. In *Punch*, 'Our Representative Man' lauded her as 'gorgeous, merry, sparkling', though as her star waned she would start to attract less obliging titles, such as 'that Goddess of Material Love'. Finally, the *Sporting Times* declared that: 'This lady's legs are as freely displayed and as symmetrically moulded as of yore, whilst her voice is as harsh and her artistic merit as slight as ever', and that, on stage, she should 'cast significant glances with less frequency towards some of the private boxes'.

Pirated copy of a photograph showing Amy Sheridan as Lady Godiva

For Soldene to have remembered Harry as a Lyceum 'masher' after thirty years, when she committed her recollections to print, he must have been greatly enamoured of *Little Faust* and of Amy Sheridan too. Once more, he was squandering his frail resources on salacious operetta, and on the company of a celebrated actress, no doubt in the face of disquieted Larkins relatives. Soldene's note confirms what was turning into a pattern, by which Harry would seek a place for himself among a different sort of family, made up of witty, passionate and sexually unbuttoned theatre folk, and their knot of often influential followers.

A few days after *Little Faust* opened, an attendant in the saloon at the Lyceum, Eleanor Coulton, served a gentleman and his two companions, whom she understood to be 'gay ladies' or prostitutes. The pair had taken a private box facing that of the Prince of Wales, and Coulton later recalled that 'one was dressed in green satin, and the other in mauve satin'. They asked for a brandy and split. 'Then', she said, 'they asked had we a ladies' room? I said, "Yes, madame—follow me."' The next night, the same two gay ladies went to the Strand Theatre, one now wearing a 'low necked evening dress of white and crimson silk and flaxen wig', the other still in green. In their box, with their backs to the stage, they were observed 'nodding and smiling to gentlemen in the stalls'. This time, when they left the theatre, they were arrested and hauled up before a magistrate in a police court, where they did not deny that they were both young men. They now found themselves charged with 'intent to commit felony' in a place of public resort. In the small hours they were removed to a secluded room, where they were made to strip and were examined by a waiting police surgeon. He required them to bend over, and in silence sought to determine by examination whether or not they were sodomites. Their new address, for some weeks to come, would be the brick catacombs of the House of Detention in Clerkenwell. The desperate case of 'The Men in Women's Clothes' had begun.

A couple of weeks into the run of *Little Faust*, Harry, too, was arrested. Typically for the period, this was a private prosecution, meaning that the plaintiff had gone before a magistrate to argue for the granting of an arrest warrant. There were no misappropriated diamonds in the case, or even horses; but a year after Mazas, Harry found himself back behind bars, pending preliminary hearings. Among the lower courts, with their feckless, dissolute clients, Marlborough Street stood out. Though it sat among the very thoroughfares deemed most likely to draw in the 'idle, the vicious, and the intemperate', closely followed by the 'predatory classes', those held there were not just an endless parade of tuppenny uprights, child-beaters, area sneaks and the like. Many an 'easy-going, slangish' swell also passed through, giving the court a 'more dandified aspect'. In Dion Boucicault's latest melodrama, *Formosa; or the Railroad to Ruin*, a wicked cad was shown to baulk amusingly at being removed to Bow Street: 'It sounds so low! Marlborough Street is the fashion!'

Bow Street was where, in December 1859, Harry had sworn in advance of his cadet exams that he was really sixteen. And it was where the already infamous pair, 'The Men in Women's Clothes', were now being subjected to their own set of preliminary hearings. In the case of 'Regina v. Park and others', the court wished to establish whether Frederick Park, twenty-three, law student, son of a judge, wearer of green satin, and known to some as Fanny, and his companion Ernest Boulton, no occupation, but otherwise Miss Stella, had had some purpose in dressing up 'beyond that of mere larking'. Public fascination grew frantic when it emerged that Miss Stella seemed to live as though the wife of Lord Arthur Pelham-Clinton, bankrupt brother of the 6th Duke of Newcastle, and Gladstone's godson. Counsel for Boulton, together with Frederick Park's brilliant young lawyer Douglas Straight, argued impatiently that while 'filthy imputations had been insinuated', they were 'not supported by one tittle of evidence'.

As Mr Poland, for the Crown, pressed on with his case, Douglas Straight went on the attack, extracting from the police doctor that he had made his internal physical examinations on no authority but his own. Straight angrily called this conduct, and that of the compliant policemen present, a 'gross outrage'. Poland countered weakly that it had been necessary to establish that Boulton and Park really were men. At this, the magistrate piped up farcically that when the two, still in their dresses, had stated that they were not women, he had not fully believed them, and had clung to the hope this was a lie.

Preliminary hearings in the case drew to a close on the intensely hot morning of Saturday, 21 May. Throughout, a second renowned young lawyer, Montagu Williams, had held a precautionary 'watching brief' on behalf of a Mr Haxell, a hotelier on the Strand, who was fearful that stray testimony in the case, not least his own, might lead to his arrest. Poland pressed Haxell to describe a 'little fancy dress affair' that he had helped to organise in the hotel, paid for by Albert Westropp Gibbings. Some of the fifty guests had come 'in drag', including Boulton and Park; but there had been, said Haxell with anxious emphasis, 'not an atom of coarseness'. At the close, defence counsel demanded to be told of what crime, exactly, their clients stood accused. Poland replied that it was 'a general one—of having entered into a conspiracy to commit an abominable offence with divers persons'. And, vague as this was, it was allowed to stand. A corrupt and tortuous legal process would now have to play itself out.

Douglas Straight, still only twenty-five, and Montagu Williams, not much older, were familiarly known as 'The Twins'. They frequently fought the same cases, opposed or otherwise. Both, for example, had defended clients in trials resulting from the collapse of the discounting house Overend Gurney. They might quarrel 'like cat and dog', but in truth they were 'the most intimate and the staunchest of friends'. Williams had a story of battling Straight in court one morning, then walking out with him afterwards, laughing arm in arm, off to have lunch together at the Garrick. To his abiding amusement, he overheard outraged bystanders muttering, 'ain't we been sold!', and 'it's all a put-up job', which it was.

That same hot Saturday, 21 May 1870, Straight and Williams made their way across town to Marlborough Street, where they were lined up to fight a tawdry little afternoon fraud case, arguing before the renowned senior magistrate Alexander Andrew Knox. Straight held the prosecution brief, and the defence had been entrusted to Williams.

The Marlborough Street courtroom was on the small side, with 'rail compartments mapping out the centre of the room into pens for witnesses, prosecutors, attorneys and prisoners'. Harry must already have been processed by a clerk of the court, but it was only now that press reporters took note of his case, and their truncated accounts are the sole record to explain what happened next. One began with the summary: '*Mr. Harry Larkins*, formerly holding a commission in the Indian army, was charged on remand with obtaining 10*l.*, by fraudulent means, from Mr. Hadwen, librarian, 1., St. James's-street.'

Again: Tom Hadwen. He had gone up in the world since his underwriting of Harry's opera tickets and other entertainments three years earlier. He was now in partnership with George Lock, a well-established bookseller somewhat his senior. Remarkably, as Lock & Hadwen, the two had succeeded in taking over the 'most commandingly situate' St James's Street business of William Raymond Sams, who for over two decades had had the disposal of some of 'the best boxes and stalls for the Italian Opera by the night or season', also subletting private boxes and stalls for Drury Lane, the Haymarket, the Lyceum 'and all the theatres in London'. Sams had recently retired to concentrate on charitable works, and when Lock & Hadwen took over the premises, and the goodwill of his extensive enterprise, they prudently adopted the tag 'formerly W. R. Sams'. In fact, 1 St James's Street would continue to be known as 'late Sams' for years to come.

Douglas Straight might have fought hard for Miss Fanny that morning, in the face of police malpractice, press revulsion and a prurient public, but he was not about to flag in prosecuting Harry. He explained to the court that 'the charge against the prisoner was for obtaining 10*l.* from Mr. Hadwen by means of a cheque drawn on the bank of Messrs. Twining some time after the account was closed, he having had notice that it was closed'. Hadwen took the stand and stated 'that the prisoner was a customer of his. The cheque in question was given to him in 1867, and he gave the prisoner 10*l.* in exchange for it.' Hadwen had presented the cheque to Twining's, he said, but 'it was endorsed "account closed," and returned to him'. Asked why he had let three years elapse since this failed transaction, Hadwen explained that the 'prisoner had, in the meantime, been on the continent', but 'as soon as he ascertained the prisoner was in town he obtained a warrant against him'.

Montagu Williams now cross-examined Hadwen, drawing out from him the details of the original debt in 1867. And just as Charles Lachaud had defended Harry in Paris by turning on Harry's accuser, so too Williams endeavoured to position Hadwen squarely among 'the predatory classes'. Hadwen agreed that he had sued Harry for £120, 'and obtained judgement, but the 10*l.* cheque had not been included in the account'. That outstanding £10 was comparatively a negligible sum, but gaining it by fraud, rather than as a debt, constituted a serious crime, and if found guilty of deliberately 'uttering' a bad cheque, Harry faced a prison sentence of one to two years. Williams's questioning was therefore designed to suggest that Hadwen could easily have recovered all his money in 1867, but had kept Harry's cheque in reserve for three years, waiting for an opportune moment to exploit it. Moreover, exploiting it in a certain way would constitute a crime of its own. To extort money from a defendant in return for dropping charges was 'compounding a felony'.

Still, none of this exculpated Harry from the charge of fraud. Williams therefore pressed harder, forcing Hadwen to explain that 'The prisoner called on a Thursday, and obtained 6*l.*, and afterwards sent the cheque for 10*l.*', dispatching it 'after banking hours'. It arrived 'with a request for the balance of 4*l.* which was sent to him'. Here Williams rightly pointed out that if Hadwen lent the initial six pounds before any cheque was produced, then legally that was a debt, and the fraud charge 'resolved itself into one of obtaining only 4*l.*' Fraud might be fraud at any price, but Hadwen had laid charges against Harry at two and a half times the correct sum.

Douglas Straight now produced a prosecution witness, Donald King, clerk of Messrs Twining's bank. Twining's had a reputation as one of the best private banks in London. It sat next to the family's tea and coffee warehouse in the Strand, the two linked by a communicating door, and a client who cashed a cheque on the bank side was offered the option of realising its value in notes and coins, or measures of coffee and tea. Straight wanted Donald King to challenge the idea that Harry could ever have believed the cheque he had sent Hadwen to be valid. But in the less definitive words of one court reporter, King simply 'proved that notice had been sent to the prisoner, prior to this transaction, that his account was closed'.

Montagu Williams had no defence witnesses to call. But he pointed out that in law fraud required an intent to deceive, meaning that 'the whole question was whether the prisoner had reasonable grounds for believing that at the time he gave the 10*l.* cheque there were funds at the bank sufficient to meet it'. Who could say that Harry, a fine young gentleman, had not been innocently deceived himself as to the validity of his cheque? Putting aside any imputations against Hadwen, Williams told the court that he had been 'instructed that the prisoner's relations were highly respectable, and that the presumption was the prisoner believed he had funds at the bank'.

Douglas Straight, making free with his own interpretation of inconclusive facts, here countered that he 'thought it was evident that the prisoner had left the country to avoid legal proceedings', some irony given that Harry's foreign wanderings had landed him in the hellhole of Mazas. Nor does it ring true to suggest that he had spent three years on the run, when minimally he passed time in Wanstead and Cleveland Square in 1868 and 1869. But if he did, nevertheless, lingeringly fear a prosecution all this time, he must finally have deluded himself that the danger was past. After all, making himself a devoted follower of *Little Faust* at the Lyceum was no way to hide from a bookseller whose business depended on knowing the theatre audiences of London. Despite these flaws in his argument, Straight sought to paint Harry as an absconder, to which Williams responded forthrightly by saying that if Knox decided to send the prisoner for trial, 'he hoped he would admit him for bail'.

Williams's strongest strategy was his appeal to gentlemanly understanding. As he himself later put it, his early legal career served him numerous 'impecunious upper and middle class men' whom he 'duly whitewashed', and he had reason to hope that the whitewash might stick here too. Only a couple of months earlier he had held the prosecution brief in a starry case also presided over by Knox, in which Dion Boucicault had brought libel charges against George Smith, publisher of the *Homeward Mail* and of *Jane Eyre*. Smith was also now the proprietor of the *Pall Mall Gazette*, which had printed an anonymous denunciation of Boucicault's play *Formosa*. 'Azamat-Batuk' described this work, about a meritorious courtesan, as 'completely tedious'; while unlike 'a lady of camelias', it conveyed 'no moral sense at all'. Its 'palpable notions about various dirty nests in London' revealed Boucicault to be, not a 'dramatist', but 'a photographer of ugliness only', and given that a writer who belonged to the 'so-called natural school' depended 'on the medium in which he lives', it followed that Boucicault must have had 'no opportunity of seeing better subjects'.

Knox agreed that these comments appeared libellous. But, the parties being gentlemen, he felt sure, he said, that those connected to the journal would be 'first to repair that wrong'. Under pressure, Montagu Williams agreed on his client's behalf to accept an avowal that no libel had been intended, and Knox suggested counsel should retire to devise 'an amicable settlement of the matter', with a suitable statement to appear in the *Pall Mall Gazette*. Knox, that is, engineered that the matter should be resolved out of court, leaving George Smith privately 'much exhilarated' by the sense that the 'practical victory' had been his.

When it came to latitude in the present case, and Harry's gentlemanly *bona fides*, there were reasons for the magistrate to be sympathetic again. Knox was a generation older than those lined up before him, and as a parentless scholarship student at Cambridge in the early 1840s, 'proud & sensitive to a fault', he had formed a friendship with Shelley's robust and cheery son, Percy Florence. Mary Shelley, then a widow in her forties, had virtually adopted Knox, repeatedly allowing him to fall, as she put it, 'rather heavily on my purse'. And when, in 1845, she was threatened with blackmail over indiscreet letters she had sent to a persuasive young Italian called Gatteschi – fearing that if they came to light they 'wd destroy me forever', she said – Knox agreed to follow Gatteschi to Paris and make the problem go away. Astonishingly, not to mention illegally, he manipulated the French secret police into making a pretended political raid on Gatteschi's rooms. The letters were recovered, Knox evidently afterwards burned them, and the whole affair, Mary later admitted, 'looked very shocking'. She continued to fund Knox while despairing at his behaviour: 'half', she wrote, 'is all thrown into the waste gulph of prodigal useless expenditure'. Knox fancied himself as a poet, and writhed at the need to 'catch the proper tone of common place' when he was reduced to writing for the *Morning Chronicle*, the paper on which Dickens had begun his career under the pen name 'Boz'. Then in 1849, on a month's acquaintance, Knox married Clara Clairmont, niece of Mary Shelley's stepsister Claire Clairmont, owner of a box at Her Majesty's Theatre. The marriage caused a breach between the two older women that never really healed, in part because Claire believed that Mary had had an affair with Knox too. Clara died of pulmonary consumption in 1855. Knox started writing leaders for *The Times*, and became a magistrate five years later. By 1870, whatever rackety thrills he had experienced in his youth, it seems he vibrated to those thrills no longer. His decision in Harry's case was harsh: 'Mr. Knox intimated that he should send the case for trial. He consented to take bail, two sureties in 200*l*., and the prisoner in 400*l*.'

This was a sum equivalent today to roughly £80,000, perhaps not quite enough to be absolutely sure of keeping Harry behind bars until his full criminal trial, but a figure evidently designed to squash any idea in the mind of a chronic absconder of forfeiting bail by slipping away. Montagu Williams wrote of Knox that 'at times, with the heavy strain of a very busy Court upon him, he was inclined to be irritable'. And this particular ruling stung Williams into protest. 'The bail required was excessive,' he said, 'the amount obtained being in reality only 4*l*.' Knox, though, 'declined to alter his decision, and committed the prisoner for trial'.

Despite Knox's ruling that day, Harry never did face a criminal trial over his Twining's cheque. There is the very slender possibility that, with the bail paid, he did, in fact, abscond. But no good evidence survives to suggest this. Edward Henry Park, older brother of Frederick Park, or Miss Fanny, had absconded from bail back in 1862, aged nineteen, after failing to appear at trial on a charge of exposing himself to and indecently assaulting a policeman. When he was finally caught eight years later, living in Scotland under a false name, he responded indignantly, 'They had the "tin," had they not?' But that 'tin', or forfeited bail, did not void the criminal charge against him, and two months after Harry's Marlborough Street hearing, Edward Park was sentenced to a year in prison with hard labour. By contrast, when the case of his younger brother and Ernest Bolton, Miss Stella, came to trial a year after that, the jury found the pair on all counts not guilty. Lord Arthur Clinton, Miss Stella's ostensible husband, had not dared to hope for this outcome, and was reported to have died of scarlet fever just beforehand, though many commentators believed his death to have been a suicide. Then again, another strong rumour got about that his funeral itself had been a sham.

Assuming Harry did not abscond, then this gives traction to what Montague Williams implied about Hadwen's motives. In a parallel case the following year, one that also muddled debt and fraud, and was also argued by Straight and Williams before Knox, Williams, for the defence, again pointed out that the plaintiff had begun proceedings in a civil court, before abruptly transferring the matter to Marlborough Street, 'parties thinking their remedy more convenient in a police court'. Less guardedly, Williams's second remarked 'that the police-courts were too often made the means of extorting a settlement of claims'. And Knox agreed, in principle, replying from weary experience that he 'had no doubt' that 'frequently' plaintiffs shifted court in pursuit of 'compensation of claims and more than compensation'. This was a practice, he said, that he 'set his face against, and would do his best to put an end to'. But it was not an easy dodge to outsmart, and authority was not above quietly concluding, 'let the thieves pick each other's pockets'.

Hadwen may well have had compelling reason by 1870 to wish to swindle 'more than compensation' out of the Larkins family, so that moral justice and his lost £10 would not do. Within two years of laying charges against Harry, he and his partner, Lock, were declared bankrupt, owing in excess of £3,000. Against securities provided by the wider Lock family, the final offer to creditors would be a paltry four shillings in the pound. And Hadwen, at least, never recovered from this disaster. Instead he maundered through the rest of his days in successive dingy little households, often 'out of employ', though ending up as an elderly waiter in a hotel outside Reading.

Knox himself valued public disgrace as an element in justice, as he made clear one day when forced to free a defendant whom he believed to be guilty. He remarked to reporters that he 'hoped the facts would go forth to the public', alerting the world to how the man in question, technically innocent, was nevertheless 'surrounded by falsehoods'. And if nothing else, reports of Harry's hearing left him disgraced too, in the crime columns of the London press, all the way up to the *Pall Mall Gazette*. Even so, it is a moot point how far he was likely to have accepted that, by his own acts, he was 'surrounded by falsehoods'. Courtesy of Montagu Williams, he had once again been defended as a fine young fellow ensnared in shabby dealings; largely sinned against, if also modestly sinning. Moreover, this time the true sum at issue had been a miserable £4, however he happened to come by it. No doubt it was a strain to find himself again behind bars, and in the dock, with the threat of the Old Bailey; but it seems unlikely that he would have felt an overpowering need to repent.

Trials in London and Paris over the summer of 1870 led to traffic both ways across the Channel. On 26 June, *Reynolds's Newspaper* reported from France that la Markowich had 'at last' been ordered out of Paris by the police. London should beware her arrival, it said, before adding that 'if perfidious Albion has deprived us of our Leonide Leblanc and Markowitz, she has enriched us in turn with Mr. Gibbings, of Park and Boulton notoriety'. The same Albert Westropp Gibbings who had paid for a drag party at Haxell's hotel on the Strand had recently been seen, 'remarkably lady-like', with a grey-haired escort at the Mabille.

After the run of duels the summer before, la Markowich had temporarily left Paris in the autumn to lurk about the gaming tables of Homburg and Baden, where she had benefited from the generosity of a young American called Ely. He was then put on trial in Paris for having stolen from his employer the 126,500 francs that had funded his stupendous spree; and though retaining Charles

Lachaud to defend him, he was found guilty and sentenced to five years in jail. As for la Markowich, court reporters noted that her protectors had grown less liberal, so that she had been struggling to raise money equal to her dissipations. She let it be known that she had kept an embarrassing register of all her clients, prospectively worth its weight in gold, but the ploy did not serve her, nor prevent her expulsion from the city.

Reynolds's referred to her as 'Madame Adeline Hankey (a notorious courtezan), or Madame Markowitz, or Madame Alias'. No doubt 'Hankey' was meant to raise the spectre of Frederick Hankey, infamous pornographer, unkindly described as 'a second de Sade *without the intellect*'. It aligned her, that is, with Sadism, or what was known at the time as 'the English vice', giving a literal turn to the idea of her working up an appetite by whipping aristocrats, and raising a further question about her nickname, 'the slap fairy'. A sanctimonious strand in the Indian letters of Emma Larkins about whipping the children she kept with her, for filching biscuits, or telling little lies, goes some way towards explaining the contorted yen for flagellation recorded by many a prominent Victorian. Gladstone, to take a single example, compulsively scourged himself after becoming aroused by his own prowling after prostitutes, marking his diary with a whip symbol, like a zeta with a handle, after each session of calmative violence.

No matter the truth of these scurrilous hints about la Markowich's services, it is clear that by 1870 her reputation had grown internationally sordid. There is no saying where she went after Paris, but if she did travel to London that hot summer, perhaps hoping for a reunion with some of her old admirers, she would have found that the 'fort joli garçon', at least, was about to disappear.

8: War

On 19 July 1870, two months after Harry's turn in the dock at Marlborough Street, France declared war on Prussia. Four days later, Ray Pelly sent a letter to his parents from the Queen's Hotel in Scarborough, where he had taken a heavily pregnant Alice for sea air. In it, he included one of his oblique asides about his scapegrace brother-in-law: 'As I suspected Master Harry's latest is likely to prove as much an imposture as the rest.' However, the dates here make it virtually certain that Ray was reading the situation wrong. Whether for the adventure of it, to redeem himself, or both, Harry had determined to go to war. But the pursuit of death or glory would require fresh funds. And as he was in a state of 'beggary', a request for help may well have made the whole romantic cause look like a convenient deceit. In truth, though, not even lack of money could have prevented Harry taking up arms for his beloved France.

Napoleon III declared war on Prussia in order to check Bismarck's expansionist ambitions. On paper the opposing forces were fairly well matched, though as Prussian military organisation was far superior, the case has been made ever since that Bismarck cannily provoked a conflict he had every reason to expect to win. Immediate troop mobilisation in France was chaotic, with army command unprepared for the logistical challenges of keeping its men properly armed, clothed and fed. As a result, France made no forays across its eastern frontier until early August. Despite triumphing in a very few first clashes, within a week, French troops were in retreat before a full invasion by the enemy massing on its border. On 6 August, Marshal MacMahon, leaving one regiment to stiffen Strasbourg's antiquated defences, led his men back through the mountains of the Vosges, and west. On 14 August, some 40,000 Prussian troops under General Werder reached Strasbourg and put it to siege.

A French newspaper later described how, governed by the 'esprit aventureux' that never left him, Harry hastened to Paris, with whatever funds he had mustered, and there solicited the right to be killed for his country of 'prédilection'. Though the French Foreign Legion was hastily expanding its numbers, and would have offered a form of asylum with no 'curiosités indiscrètes', Harry sought admission as an officer in the regular French forces. But this gave rise to 'difficultés', so that he was advised to leave his details with the War Office, and to enlist, for the time being, as an ordinary soldier, a move that would reduce him, in the slang of the day, to a shady 'gentleman ranker'. Instead, Harry cast about for a prospect with more style.

On 15 August, *Le Figaro* ran an advertisement explaining that, by the authority of the Interior Minister and the Minister of War, the Vicomte d'Abzac and M. Macaire de Verdier sought volunteers to form an independent 'free corps' of forty men, so-called *francs-tireurs* or freelance sharpshooters operating outside the bounds of the regular army. They must be ready to depart shortly, to fight in the Vosges mountains, and would need to be self-financing, paying 1,000 francs each into a common fund. Their task would be to harass the enemy, especially at night, hunting down and disrupting convoys, either as snipers, or if need be attacking with knives: in short, classic guerrilla tactics, or fighting 'à l'américaine'. As well as Frenchmen, foreign officers were welcome to apply. There had already been a launch meeting in the Café Helder, at 19 boulevard des Italiens. Anyone else was invited to leave his name there with M. Félix.

A few days later, in a crushing blow to national morale, well over 150,000 French soldiers were defeated in battle in northern Lorraine, outside Metz. On 19 August the survivors retreated within the city's ring of forts, where, along with the civilians of Metz, they were now encircled and blockaded by an enemy force of comparable size.

The next day, 20 August, the Interior Minister fully authorised *Les Quarante*, or *Les 40*, though enlistment was still not complete. A further announcement declared that it was proving impossible to source the breech-loading rifle of the French army, the *chassepot*. *Les 40* must use American rifles instead. The aim of the band was once again advertised as being simply to harass the Prussians in the Vosges, 'with not a bullet wasted', a pragmatic motto given that they were now condemned to using non-standard ammunition.

Those who came forward, *bigarrés*, or a motley lot, were mostly young, were necessarily well to do, and in many cases were indeed foreign. They included mining engineers, a journalist, a doctor, a merchant from Alexandria, six or seven Englishmen, a possibly fraudulent Austrian aristocrat, Count Philippe Draskowitsch, James Fowler, a decidedly eccentric American dentist and nautical sportsman, and a number of ardent French 'gens de famille'. Harry slightly jigged his surname, perhaps to leave behind complications in his paperwork, and signed on as a new entity, 'Harry Larkyns'. But he was still a charming one-time lieutenant of the Bengal Infantry, up on guerrilla tactics in Sikkim and Assam, making him much better qualified for what lay ahead than many of his new brothers-in-arms. A final press announcement in Paris on 30 August gave sole command of the unit to M. de Verdier. As for *Les 40* themselves: bearing rifles, rockets, wicks, wires and dynamite, they had already embarked on what was in truth a fantastically dangerous *mission secrète*.

After his swift retreat back through the Vosges, Marshal MacMahon took his army north-west. Dithering between the imperatives of defending Paris and of attempting to relieve Metz, he fell back on Sedan, a small town near the Belgian border. There he joined forces with Napoleon III; and there, 1 September witnessed total Imperial defeat. The French were demoralised, disorganised, outnumbered, trapped and crushed. Napoleon III capitulated, and the next day, with his army, surrendered. He was removed from France a prisoner, leaving some 150,000 Prussian troops free to march on Paris.

Many roving bands of *francs-tireurs*, all sporting their own uniforms, had chosen to fight outside the regular French lines of command; some 60,000 men, and numbers of women too. Maupassant's famous story 'Boule de Suif' portrays provincial *francs-tireurs* as a mix of the merchant class and ill-contained lowlifes, all adopting the air of bandits and grouped under such vainglorious names as 'Partakers of Death', or 'Citizens of the Tomb'. But *Les 40* were different. Dressed discreetly in wide-pleated grey shirts, grey trousers with a black stripe, grey kepi and solid hunting shoes, they were closer to the sorts of *francs-tireurs* encountered by the war correspondent of the *Evening Standard*, G. A. Henty. The sharpshooters he came across struck him as 'capital material for guerrillas', men who had clearly 'smelt powder in their time', and who exuded 'a certain dash and self-reliance'.

Les 40 took a train to Dijon, and in short order the raw recruits among them were put through basic training in skirmishing, in how to bivouac, and so on. Lieutenant Girard, formerly a Zouave in Africa, became their practical leader, down to proffering remedies for blistered feet and shoulders bruised by their deadweight haversacks. 'G. L.', an engineer, and one of the amateur members of *Les 40*, printed a memoir two years later that included letters he had composed at the time. His boss at *Gaz de Paris*, in an 'effluve de patriotisme', had promised to keep his job open and to pay him double in his absence. G. L. was obsessed by food and drink, and filled his correspondence sorrowfully with the lard, potatoes, salt meat and biscuits they were compelled to buy from peasants along the way. Nor was it a laughing matter to have to learn everything from Girard so fast, he said, simultaneously aware that France was being overwhelmed by 'ces désastres'.

The fourth of September saw the proclamation in Paris of the Third Republic. With the bulk of the regular French army now either trapped at Metz or having surrendered at Sedan, the Prussians granted three weeks for an election to be held, in order that there should be a valid National Assembly with which to negotiate a peace settlement. But as Prussian terms included an unwavering demand that France should cede Alsace and part of Lorraine, the new Republic chose instead to continue to fight, using local defence forces and volunteers, existing *francs-tireurs* units, and any remnants of the regular army still in the field. There now followed, too, the conscription of, in the end, over half a million more men.

On 5 September, though knowing that the Second Empire had fallen, under whose aegis they had been assembled, Harry and his new companions set out from Dijon for the Vosges. It took two infuriating days to travel 150 miles in a military train, left endlessly idling at various stations. But at last they made it to the ancient town of Colmar. Given that they were well equipped and armed, and full of beguiling enthusiasm for their plot, two forestry agents from the local defence force, Mabaret and Michaud, bearing their own *chassepots* and revolvers, agreed to join them as guides.

Their *mission secrète* was crystallised in a café in Colmar. The Imperial Minister of War had provided plans, and had ordered them to blow up the railway tunnel of Saverne, which ran on a curve some 400 metres through a mountain under Lutzelbourg Castle. Intact, the railway offered the enemy a vital supply line all the way from Strasbourg to Paris. And back in July, the Eastern Railway Company had agreed to mine the tunnel. But no clear authority for its destruction had yet arrived when Marshal MacMahon made his abject exodus through the Vosges; nor did he mitigate his retreat with this one critical act of sabotage. Random bands of *francs-tireurs* could cut sections of rail as often as they liked, but such damage was easily repaired. By contrast, if *Les 40* could collapse a mountain tunnel on the line, the obstacle of the Vosges would present the Prussians with 'les difficultés sans nombre'.

Mabaret undertook to lead them secretly through the mountains all the way to their goal, and *Les 40* left Colmar knowing conditions were about to get inestimably tougher. They had with them a little dun horse and a mule, along with a two-wheeled cart, to help transport their baggage and ordnance, and two shepherd dogs as additional sentinels. Word circulating in Colmar made it clear that Prussian columns would be pouring into France before and behind them. Worse, with other bands of *francs-tireurs* already active in the Vosges, General Werder had released detachments of his Strasbourg siege corps to defend lines of communication into France, while mounted soldiers, known as Uhlans, were criss-crossing the mountains, hunting down and killing any guerrilla fighters they could find. Even so, wrote G. L., out on the road at last, *Les 40* walked towards danger 'like a bride who runs to a first kiss'.

They went by Riquewyhr before entering the hill ranges extending north from Ribeauvillé, through the forest of Kintzheim and on, Mabaret consulting local rangers as they went, who guided them along hidden trails. G. L. remained jovial even as hardship began to bite, calling them 'touristes militaires'. He also suggested that 'Harry L***' and Count Draskowitsch became a sort of double act as the band's presiding field cooks. With what deliberation, that is, Harry placed himself at the heart of this new family. But the life was exhausting for all, and they never knew when or where it would next be safe to sleep. A bed of anything other than straw or fir branches was now a dream.

Francs-tireurs prepare a meal

As September unfolded, G. A. Henty was outraged to report in the *Evening Standard* on 'a new element of horror to this already sufficiently bloody struggle'. The Prussians had announced that French fighters must wear regular military uniform to be entitled to 'the treatment of soldiers'. This rule meant that if any of *Les 40* were caught, they would be classed as murderers, 'without the privilege of surrender', and would be lucky to be shot rather than hanged. But their outfits of grey were essential camouflage. When, for safety, they moved through the forests at night, each wore a white neckerchief as a glimmering guide to the man behind.

They became used to waiting, hidden, guns poised, with the enemy nearby, in a 'fever of calm'. And when they were presented with an early opportunity to ambush a unit of Prussians, their strategy of 'silent devotion' barely outweighed the attractions of demented valour. Regretfully, G. L. wrote that the courage of a lion was for others. For them, it was the wiles of a fox. In one frightening incident, as they crossed an exposed road in fog, Prussian voices loomed out at them, and they dreaded that their little dun horse might answer a nearby neigh.

On 12 September they found themselves in a tiny mountain village where they were greeted with 'Vive l'Empereur!' by villagers who had no idea that France was now a republic. The news made them so angry that they supplied *Les 40* with nothing better than black bread, nuts and white cheese. G. L. himself was hardly more favourable to the new government of honest citizens, he wrote, whose leading lights symbolised everything from tears, vanity and ridicule to 'massacre, pillage et pétrole'. Yet as they set off again, surrounded by the cool green beauty of the Vosges, he found it hard to believe in the horrors of war; in disembowelled bodies and looted villages, and the women of Lorraine heaped dead upon the corpses of their children. A madcap spirit overcame *Les 40* on one high plateau where a signpost gave directions to three different *départements*. As they hopped round the post, they switched between speaking French and German, the gourmands declaring themselves for Strasbourg and *foie gras*, the artists for the Vosges, and each 'Aramis' for the Meurthe, and the lace of Nancy. Years later, one of the forest agents, Michaud, described how, from the crest of another mountain, they also saw Strasbourg in its agony under Prussian bombardment, and watched the city burn.

At last, they entered the forested mountain *massif* that took them the final stretch of their journey. On the way, in the village of Dabo, they discovered that Prussian soldiers, up ahead in Garrebourg, had demanded the delivery of two oxen, threatening otherwise to come the next day and requisition four. M. de Verdier ordered the mayor of Dabo to deliver nothing, then issued 'avis à nos cuisiniers, Larkyns et Draskovitsh': they were to pull together a celebratory menu that night, after which *Les 40* would make a show of marching out of the village, before stealthily settling down nearby to catch themselves some Prussians.

They must have hoped to local gain enemy intelligence; and in the worst case, hostages would give them latitude to threaten reprisal killings. But after many hours of sequestered discomfort, they deduced that no Prussians were coming to Dabo. Doubling back, they discovered that the mayor had secretly delivered two oxen to Garrebourg despite them, and though M. de Verdier was livid at this 'serviteur servile', in truth the mayor had good reason to collaborate with the stronger side. As *Les 40* abandoned Dabo for the second time, the villagers armed themselves as best they could against the possibility of a revenge attack by the *francs-tireurs* themselves.

On 27 September, word caught up with them of a 'barbaric line' of Prussians that now encircled Paris. The siege there had actually begun on the 19th, and this desperate news added a certain edge to the happiness of *Les 40*, and no doubt to Harry's feelings too, when, shortly after, they at last reached their destination. They bivouacked in a mountain perch above Lutzelbourg, huddled there, wrote G. L., like a clutch of eaglets under a protective escarpment. What

The Saverne Tunnel

the Eastern Railway Company had begun, they intended to bring to a dramatic conclusion.

They had endured a month of draining stealth and hardship, combined with stretches of extreme danger. But, abruptly, their expedition now ended in 'le cruel désenchantement d'un demi-succès', or rather, no success at all. A small party slipped down the mountain in disguise, aiming to take stock of the tunnel entrance, only to find that the Prussian guard post had been reinforced in such overwhelming numbers that no attack by their own forces could possibly hope to succeed. The Prussian 'cynique système' of torching local houses in response to *francs-tireurs* attacks confirmed that they must resist any urge to indulge in suicidal half-measures. Small comfort, against the gall of simply having to creep away again, that their discretion would in the end be praised as merciful.

In the full weight of their bitterness, *Les 40* now confronted the disclosure that the dramatic increase in the tunnel guard had resulted from a betrayal of their mission by the 'infâme commerce' of Vinkel, the traitorous schoolmaster of Garrebourg. Although this information came in the form of a voluntary betrayal by one informant of another, M. de Verdier, thwarted and incensed, decided on revenge. And he was prepared to risk lives to achieve it. Garrebourg was not far, and was only lightly occupied by the enemy. He called for two men, in the garb of peasants, to enter the town that evening as spies. Chancing instant execution if unmasked, they were to find out where Vinkel lived.

Harry and Count Draskowitsch, who was Austrian, both, it seems, spoke German 'comme Schiller'. It was therefore they who were chosen to go in and perform this exceptionally dangerous stunt. Lieutenant Girard, heading a squad of six men, hid nearby and awaited their findings. In the guise of convivial Alsatian woodcutters, Harry and Draskowitsch had settled themselves in at a Garrebourg tavern when five Prussian soldiers entered and demanded to know who they were. Their horse could not pull its load, they replied, and they had come into town to seek help. They bought the corporal a drink, then proceeded to try to persuade all five men out into the forest to help them. Half seduced, the enemy soldiers deliberated over whether or not to abandon their posts, bringing a second horse with them. But when eventually they drew straws, the result was that they should remain.

This spontaneous attempt by Harry and Draskowitsch to lure the enemy into an ambush showed extraordinary bravado. But so too did the plan already in hand. And within two hours, deploying 'beaucoup d'audace et d'habileté', much audacity and skill, they and Girard's unit had successfully abducted Vinkel under the noses of enemy patrols, dragging him from his bed and smuggling him out of town. Once reunited with the rest of *Les 40* in the depth of the forest, there was talk of shooting Vinkel dead. But, lacking absolute proof of his guilt, they held him prisoner instead.

In early October, Léon Gambetta, Minister of the Interior in the new Republican government, escaped the Paris siege by hot-air balloon, then travelled to Tours, where he became *de facto* Minister of War. From there, he dedicated 10,000 francs to a new scheme to blow up the Saverne tunnel; but as neither this nor any subsequent plan succeeded, the daring shown by *Les 40* left theirs as the 'plus connue' or best-known attempt. A wider idea of their mission was partly down to G. A. Henty, of the *Evening Standard*, who had recently begun a second career as an author, and who was destined to become famous over the years for a huge output of rampantly imperialist children's literature. In 1872, he published *The Young Franc-Tireurs*, in which he made the undercover exploits of Harry and Draskowitsch a central event, though Henty substituted his own imaginary, adolescent heroes, the pure but fervent Barclay brothers, Ralph and Percy. As in life, Henty depicted the vastly increased guard on the 'rock tunnel' as a disaster for the guerrilla unit. Without this, his fictional captain remarks, 'We should have saved France, and immortalised ourselves.' But if history could not be revised here, Henty did at least allow himself the luxury of improving the Vinkel episode. Because Ralph and Percy speak excellent German and look too young to be military spies, it is they who are disguised as peasants and sent in to track down the 'sallow, cunning' schoolmaster, conveniently found with blood money and an incriminating letter in his pocket. Back in the forest, Henty's *francs-tireurs* take a vote on Vinkel's guilt. Vinkel wastes his final few minutes on cries and imprecations, and then, after a 'brief struggle', a 'deep silence' reigns. They leave his body swinging from the branch of a tree, with a note pinned to the breast: 'So perish all traitors.'

Vinkel hanged

The ludicrously decent Barclay brothers may have been suited to their juvenile audience. But with his history of charm, nerve and deception, Harry would seem a far more plausible candidate for the task that he really did perform of spying in Garrebourg. As for the possibly fake 'Philippe comte de Drascowitz': in murky circumstances, in Marseilles, he would later be denounced as an enemy informer himself.

The retreat of *Les 40* after Garrebourg was as perilous as their outbound journey. They were, reflected G. L. glumly, but little atoms in an immense war. And as Strasbourg had just fallen on 28 September, thousands more enemy troops had now been released to pour in through the Vosges. As fast as possible, therefore, they retraced their route, with provisions as ever a pressing challenge, especially after they picked up a dozen escaped French fighters, including two Turks, whom they found starving in the mountains. G. L. composed a wilfully cheerful letter one evening to a 'Chère Amie', to say that Count Draskowitsch had mercifully just stolen a sheep. G. L. himself was being called on to help with the butchering. But, he noted hastily, he would be counting on 'le talent de notre camarade Harry L***, un officier de l'armée anglaise dans les Indes', well practised in the art of skinning 'les rhinocéros et les éléphants!' For Harry, a sheep should be a mere 'bagatelle', thought G. L., adding that one of the great challenges of war was to eat a good meal made with bad things, and that a malnourished soldier was effectively beaten. He could hear rifle fire down the mountainside, he said, interrupting himself to finish with 'Voilà Harry L…', come to torment him into lending a hand.

Rather than return to Colmar, *Les 40* were ultimately now heading to Saint-Dié, where they planned to hand over Vinkel to the French authorities. On arriving, they learnt that the new Republican government had prohibited *francs-tireurs* companies from acting independently. Instead, they must now put themselves at the disposal of the nearest regular military leader. Despite this, M. de Verdier gave his men their freedom to depart and fight under any flag they pleased. Some ten of them dispersed, including G. L. and Draskowitsch. But the rest, Harry among them, agreed to rendezvous at the small fort town of Épinal, the current rallying point of a new Army of the Vosges.

Its leader was General Cambriels. At Sedan, Cambriels had received a head wound so severe that the Prussians let him go. But he had recovered sufficiently since to be awarded notional command of the disparate forces, perhaps 20,000 in number, now fighting in the east. Their avowed task was to cut Prussian lines of supply and communication while defending the region's fortified towns, which were currently doubling as supply depots and as bases from which to protect vital rail routes still held by the French.

The nominal Army of the Vosges lacked food, footwear, ammunition, and basic military training. And October brought terrible weather too, with frequent rainstorms and snow, abysmal conditions for bivouacking, apart from anything else. It was against this back-drop, out in the field, that the remaining members of *Les 40* caught up with their new commander. Despite their weeks of trekking, they were immediately marked out as 'volontaires admirablement équipés', and acquired a new nickname, *Les Gris*, or the Greys. Like other French commanders, Cambriels found his efforts in battle hampered by extremely poor communications. Given the demonstrated verve of the new recruits, the fact that they were well educated and that many were good horsemen, he decided that, rather than squander them in the front lines, he would make them his 'cavaliers d'ordonnance' or dispatch riders, vital work, and often highly dangerous too.

In the first week of October, Cambriels pitted his forces against General Werder's men in the heights and forests of the western Vosges. But his poorly supplied and undisciplined army was no match for the enemy, and soon large convoys of the wounded were being carted away. The French now retreated hastily to Épinal, reducing the town to a state of unspeakable confusion. But Cambriels knew that staging a battle there would render the town liable to complete destruction. And so, with his Sedan head wound conspicuously afflicting him, he ordered a second rapid retreat to a stronghold further south. There, Cambriels elevated members of *Les Gris* to positions on his staff, conspicuously M. de Verdier and Lieutenant Girard. But not Harry, who was still in Épinal four days after the evacuation, when the Prussian forces arrived.

Épinal had no garrison. Cambriels had left the retired soldiers among its citizenry to lead a local Guard force. On the morning of 12 October, a dreaded bugle call and alarm bells led to panic and futile exhortations by the city fathers, as the assembled fighters, lacking leadership, and ammunition, milled in disarray. Only the *francs-tireurs* among them seemed to act decisively. The rest of the defence force took up random positions, either within Épinal's forti-fications or outside in ditches and behind farm walls. The Prussians, under General Werder, were soon upon them, with disordered skirmishing in the forests round about. But despite individual acts of bravery, the French were no match for their formidable enemy.

Within hours, under dazing batteries of incessant fire, the French were routed, and Épinal fell.

A decade later, incidental comment in *Le Figaro* would give a glimpse of Harry's place in this catastrophe. Édouard Philippe, a well-regarded Paris playwright originally from Alsace, had gone east to fight in the war, and was acting as a guard inside Épinal when Werder's forces entered in triumph. Confronted by this sparkling swarm of pointed helmets, Philippe recognised an acute danger, and risked his life to rescue 'MM. Pistor et Larkyns', two unimpeachably brave officers, he wrote, who were sheltering wounded in an inn, unprotected by any ambulance flag. M. Pistor, a youth from Metz, had acted with memorably crazy valour under MacMahon at the very start of the war, rescuing a machine gun from Prussian hands on the battlefield at Froeschwiller. He had then been injured on 6 October, leaving him unfit to fight again for two months. The linking of his name with Harry's makes it overwhelmingly likely that Harry, too, had been left behind in Épinal, not to join in its gamely hopeless defence, at risk of peremptory execution, but because he was already severely injured. Not atypically, the impression he made on those who remembered him there caused one of them to recall him years after as having been 'un neveu de lord Palmerston'.

Upon the surrender of Napoleon III at Sedan, Garibaldi had written at once to offer his services to the new Republic. Given the extremes of political difference among the French forces still in the field, this was a double-edged proposal: Garibaldi would inevitably be a divisive figure in their ranks. But, against advice, Gambetta invited him to come. Moreover, in part to facilitate this move, he also lifted existing restrictions on how far and how fast foreigners could be promoted within the French ranks. With General Cambriels continuing to fall back to the south, Gambetta now offered Garibaldi the command of some few thousand irregular fighters in a newly reconstituted Army of the Vosges. Cambriels, who was a devout Catholic, proved barely willing to cooperate with a man he considered a disgraceful freethinker. But nearer to ground level, Harry would have had no such qualms. He later indicated that he had fought with Garibaldi, and at a minimum, this would have been loosely true. But then, separated from *Les Gris*, and as a foreigner himself, he may also briefly have taken Garibaldi's direct command.

The French military in Metz, under Prussian siege since 19 August, had long since eaten their horses, and the troops there, roughly 180,000 men, were by now starving, as were the civilians trapped with them. Epidemic diseases were rife too, including cholera and smallpox, and on 27 October, in another terrific blow for the French cause, the city surrendered. Four days later General Werder seized Dijon in the east, while the Alsace garrison town of Belfort was put to enemy siege. After this, Dijon was captured and abandoned by opposing forces more than once. And if Harry did fight temporarily with Garibaldi's new Army of the Vosges, then it would have been here that he was caught up, principally in night movements, skirmishing in the surrounding countryside in the greater battle for the advantage of occupying this critical city. One of his old friends certainly operated in this sphere. It was now, to Garibaldi, 'Illustre citoyen', that an anonymous letter was sent denouncing Draskowitsch as a spurious aristocrat and an enemy spy.

On 8 November, Cambriels, increasingly troubled by his Sedan wound, resigned his command, to be replaced in quick succession by two further generals. As France's position grew ever more hopeless, Gambetta reorganised the country's irregulars into a new, combined *armée auxiliaire*, largely ill-trained or untrained men on whom he pinned his plans for the relief of Paris. One of the new formations he created was the 20th Corps, which absorbed the majority of the remaining members of *Les Gris*, including Girard and M. de Verdier.

A month after this, Harry passed into the regular army at last. On 14 December, Decree no. 683, issued from Tours, announced that 'M. HARRY LARKYNS' was to be 'chef d'escadron d'état-major, au titre de l'armée auxiliaire'. And rather than the 20th, he was assigned to the new 24th Corps, under General Bressoles. A French squadron leader, staff corps, was the equivalent of a British major. At twenty-seven, that is, Harry had been raised to the rank not achieved by his father until almost the age of fifty. Even granting what was by this point a catastrophic shortfall in the French officer class, this was a vertiginous promotion. To have overleapt a captaincy, Harry must have demonstrated real mettle under fire, as well as a capacity to lead other men. For all these reasons, his rank would impart to him a certain glamour from this point on, where it was not dismissed, in the wider world, as a bogus affectation.

Command of the 110,000 men of the auxiliary army, soon dubbed the Army of the East, was given to General Charles Bourbaki, considered dashing by some, but an unfortunately spiritless figure. In fact his anticipatory defeatism as leader of the Imperial Guard had contributed to the French collapse at Metz the previous August. The starving inhabitants of Paris had now eaten even their zoo animals, and from 5 January, to hasten their surrender, the Prussians began subjecting the city to bombardment. Even so, Gambetta reluctantly accepted that it was impracticable for Bourbaki to attempt the relief of Paris head on. He therefore asked him to make a decisive attack on the vulnerable eastern end of the enemy's overstretched supply lines, in order to cut adrift the Prussian forces now concentrated on the capital.

As his opening move, Bourbaki chose to attempt to relieve Belfort, in the south of Alsace, also under siege and, remarkably, still holding out. On the Prussian side, General Werder was ordered to counter-attack, though he was vastly outnumbered with only about 40,000 men. After inconclusive preliminary clashes in atrocious winter conditions, the turning point would come in mid January 1871, with the Battle of Héricourt, fought along the frozen River Lisaine.

Werder's troops, well disciplined, managed to secure highly advantageous positions. The French, by contrast, travelling in hopelessly disorganised transports, arrived underfed, poorly dressed, worse shod and lacking ammunition. They were forced to bivouac in deep snow, and were ordered not to light any fires for fear of giving away their positions. 'Exposé aux rigueurs d'une température sibérienne', some simply froze to death in their sleep on the eve of battle.

There is a detailed account of what happened on 16 January, the second day of fighting, in the journal of the Comte de Belleval, deputed to help with logistics. He was positioned by the 24th Corps,

The Battle of Héricourt, 16 January 1871

which had spent the night bivouacked in the woods directly in front of the enemy. The fighting, he said, started up furiously at nine in the morning; and at noon, he was ordered to advance with *cacolets*, or mule-drawn stretchers, through snowfall raked with shells, to cart away the wounded. In a field ambulance he watched medics, soaked in blood, as they amputated limb after limb, throwing arms and legs into a heap by the door. On no battlefield had he ever seen anything so frightful, he wrote, and the air rang with lamentations. Each patient had to be removed to make room for the next, and there were so many of them that they could not all be evacuated to safety. Despite this, despite extreme 'dépression physique et morale', and at a cost of several thousand wounded or killed, the French did now compel Werder backwards, giving them the promise of a clear route to Belfort.

An official French record of these clashes contains a line on the three-day 'Bataille d'Héricourt': 'LARKYNS (Harry). Chef d'escadron auxiliaire, *blessé* le 16.' Harry was wounded, *blessé*, amid the very carnage that Belleval described. What happened to him next will have depended on his luck, but in the profound humiliation about to overcome the men of the Army of the East, they were forced to haul numerous convoys of their wounded with them.

Though, with appalling losses, Bourbaki had won the advantage at Héricourt, he doubted the resolution of his soldiers. Not only did he therefore fail to press on towards Belfort, but he actually fell back towards his railway supply line. At this, the cause of the French became finally irrecoverable. Gambetta sent frantic telegrams demanding that he turn round and fight on. But after hesitations and misunderstanding, Bourbaki retreated further, towards Pontarlier on the Swiss border, where he and his wretched army soon found themselves in an enemy trap. In the Comte de Belleval's anguished words, Pontarlier was 'l'abomination de la désolation', and on 26 January Bourbaki shot himself in the head, though as he survived, even this exercise was a failure. To their appalled astonishment, the men of the Army of the East next discovered that, along with Garibaldi's men, they had been left exempted from an armistice that now embraced the rest of France. On 1 February, under the leadership of one of Bourbaki's corps commandants, the 80,000 troops starving and freezing on the border threw down their arms and retreated in an abject and agonising march into internment camps in Switzerland.

On 26 February, peace terms were agreed at Versailles. France finally ceded Alsace, excluding Belfort, and large parts of Lorraine. The Army of the East was repatriated to France in mid March.

A French journal would later report that, rather than being dragged into Switzerland, Harry, having played his 'rôle glorieux' in the war, was transported from Héricourt to Bordeaux, temporary seat of government after Tours, there receiving the Legion d'honneur. The most gratifying of these assertions was true. In April 1871, Decree no. 939, countersigned by the Minister of War, listed 'M. Harry-Larkins' among those appointed 'chevaliers de l'ordre national de la Légion d'honneur'. A second official record provided the clipped summary: 'Harry-Larkins, chef d'escadron de l'armée auxiliaire (24e corps); 1 campagne, 2 blessures.'

True to form, Alice would later provide her own romantic twist on Harry's war wounds, describing how he had been nursed in a hospital in France by Père Hyacinthe, an eloquent, excommunicated, liberal Catholic priest much celebrated by English Anglicans at the time. By her account, Père Hyacinthe sent a letter to Conny to say that Harry 'had fought heroically and that France owed him an eternal dept [*sic*] of gratitude'.

From 18 March, Paris was plunged into a new sort of turmoil under the Commune, then subjected to a second siege, with much destruction, until the Communards were crushed at the end of May. One monument from Harry's past in the city had fallen already when, on 20 January, rioters in numbers too great to be resisted broke into the grim and terrible Mazas to release the political prisoners held within. Now, the Communards attacked the Préfecture de Police and the Palais de Justice, burning both of them to the ground. But if Harry silently cheered the downfall of these particular symbols of oppression, they were not the only ones to fall. He later described how the remains of the Hôtel de Ville formed 'the most beautiful ruin that man's fancy could conceive', and noted sadly that many 'magnificent trees' in the Bois de Boulogne had been chopped down 'to give a clear line for the cannon'. Whenever it was that he passed through the wreckage of Paris, his previous dissolute existence there must have felt to him like a vanished dream.

The Hôtel de Ville in ruins

*

The war in France and its aftermath proved an absorbing topic in England. In April 1871, Lock & Hadwen, still then in business, advertised shilling tickets for 'The Storming of Strasbourg' at the Cremorne Gardens, a 'gigantic work of art' illuminated by 10,000 gas devices, with 5,000 flags, battlefield and cavalry charge, and, after dark, a 'real bombardment' in which buildings appeared to be blown up and destroyed. As a startling indication of local sympathies, this was not presented as a record of the city's fall to the Prussians, but as a fantasy spectacle in which the French could be seen taking Strasbourg back.

Even with this popular mood in sway in London, there was no happy equation by which France's 'dept' of gratitude to Harry balanced out those debts that were all his own. Emily Soldene's salacious memoir provides the very last glimpse of him there: 'Poor fellow, he went to the Franco–German War, got wounded and came back lame', she wrote, adding that, to her astonishment, 'he turned up at my house at Wood Green. We had a long and rather sad talk. He had fallen on evil days.' With this breezy note, Soldene confirmed that, in Cleveland Square at least, Henrietta Coffin remained unappeased. As a cousin dryly expressed it, Harry was not felt to have 'rendered a good return for the care' with which she had brought him up.

After his sad talk with Emily Soldene, there is no further record of Harry for roughly a year, though Alice did later leave a typically undependable line to explain how he had departed England, never to return. 'When in France he appears to have become great friends with the Count and Countess Monsouilly', she said, not that the name was real, 'who became so attached to him that they insisted upon his taking charge of their son during a voyage round the world.'

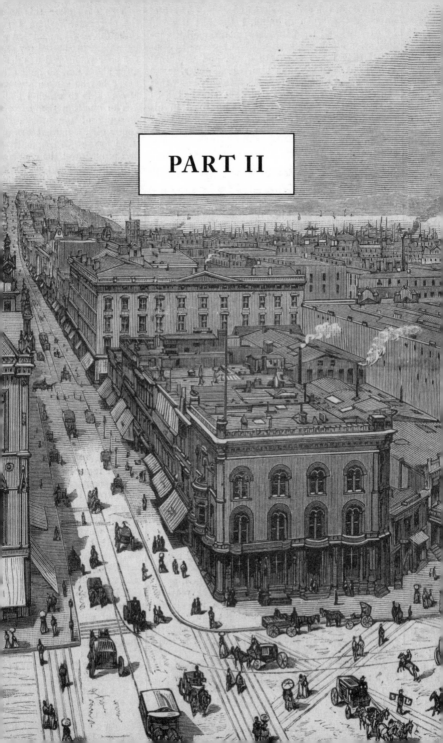

PART II

Previous page:
Montgomery Street, San Francisco, stretching away uphill, 1878

9: America

Harry next washed up in America, and was certainly there by the summer of 1872. From this point on he would be described by pressmen who encountered him as coming from 'a respectable and wealthy family' in England. At the same time, they understood that he had become estranged from his relatives 'in consequence of his reckless and spendthrift propensities', leaving him 'thrown upon his wits for a livelihood'. He was, of course, adept at finding circles in which his sheer charm functioned as a currency in itself. But he still had to eat.

According to one report, on arrival in New York Harry successfully 'sparred his way' at various fancy hotels. But if so, he was soon drifting overland west. The transcontinental railroad had recently been completed. Five years later, Robert Louis Stevenson would describe riding it all the way to San Francisco, sometimes perched atop a 'dirty and insecure' wagon. One day all he saw was 'Desolate flat prairie'; the next, 'ghostly deserts, sage brush and alkali, and rocks without form or colour, a sad corner of the world'. Stevenson lived with 'a tin wash-bowl among four', wearing nothing but trousers and an unbuttoned shirt, and it was a 'strange vicissitude', he remarked, that had brought him 'from the Savile club to this'.

When Harry reached the sagebrush of Nevada, he stopped for a while. The immediate and enormous popularity of Mark Twain's *Roughing It*, published at the start of 1872, may well have contributed to an idea of trying his luck in the silver mines there, though this was a world Twain filled with desperadoes and vigilantes, such as J. A. Slade, the 'matchless marksman', who, unable to abide an insult, could clip a button with 'a good twenty-yard shot'; or Buck Fanshaw, who one day stopped a riot, 'a spanner in one hand and a trumpet in the other, and sent fourteen men home on a shutter in less than three minutes'.

'Variegated vagabondizing' had brought Twain to Nevada in 1860, where the discovery two years earlier of huge silver lodes had led to a rush. In particular, the 'great "Comstock Lode" stretched its opulent length' underneath Virginia City. Twain, temporarily cursed with 'silver-mining fever', set about shattering searches for profitable claims, led by dreams built on hope, lunacy and twinkling pebbles. But these dreams were a 'beggars' revel' in the end. To profit from silver required blasting tons of rock out of the mountains, to be hauled to giant crushing mills where the metal was extracted. Other than by selling an unproven claim to demented speculators, a poor man had no way to realise this wealth on his own.

In 1862, Joe Goodman, the youthful owner and editor of the Virginia City *Territorial Enterprise*, whimsically offered a down-at-heel miner, Samuel Clemens, the job of his paper's city editor, and so began the writing career of 'Mark Twain'. To start with, Twain 'let fancy get the upper hand of fact too often when there was a dearth of news', only later, he suggested, growing more truthful. And after all, Virginia City itself thrummed with swindlers, as well as the self-deceived. To his descriptions of their excitable society Twain added accounts of entertaining hoaxes, accounts that themselves appeared to be entertaining hoaxes. A typical caveat in *Roughing It* read: 'I have scarcely exaggerated a detail of this curious and absurd adventure. It occurred almost exactly as I have stated it.'

A Virginia City stalwart described how 'Adventurers, with keen wits and empty pockets, were drawn there as naturally as gamblers seek a faro room', and added that, in an atmosphere of indigent hopefulness, 'Everybody was rated for what he was, not for what he had', so that 'men most distinguished for ability were the best fellows, the heartiest roysterers, the most democratic'. An unsigned literary snapshot of Harry on the Comstock Lode suggests that this was an atmosphere in which he thrived, as though he had stepped from the pages of *Roughing It* himself:

He came to Virginia City from England, and for a few brief months charmed all with whom he came in contact. He flitted in with an opera company, and during the theatrical engagement had such a royal good time that he chose to remain. Larkins was over six feet tall, straight as a lance, and had a gift of spreading a ripple of sunshine wherever he went. His wit and clever stories, and general affability won him a legion of friends. He was every inch the Bohemian, and debonair man of the world. He spoke diverse tongues, all equally well as he did English. Some placed the languages of which he was master at 17, with several dialects to be added. He had been everywhere and seen everything. He had roamed the world, and being a soldier of fortune, writer, poet, musician—the lord only knows what he had not been. He could box like Jem Mace, and fence like Agramonte (which is another story), and he could outfoot them all in a race. He could hit more bottlenecks with a pistol at 20 paces than anyone else, and he never sent his right, or left, into a bully's face but that the bully was carried away on a shutter. Larkins was a scientist, chemist and metallurgist, lecturer—a veritable what-not. No one can mention anything that he could not do better than anybody else, and when it came to cooking a delicacy in a chafing dish, Delmonico was simply not in it. A sniff and a shrug of the shoulders from him would put any brand of wine out of commission with the epicures of the Comstock. One day he got a chance to play the organ in the Bishop's church. I shall never forget the enrapturing melody he wove from the keys. It was an improvisation, but it kept the congregation glued to the seats at the time when the music was expected to play the attendants at the service out of the church.

Even if every last assertion here were untrue, this portrait could be read as a whimsical celebration of its subject in the veritable Comstock style. And yet, though cumulatively excessive, these statements are far from wholly false. At twenty-eight, Harry was very well travelled. He had indeed been a soldier of fortune; must have been an excellent shot; spoke several tongues; and was even known for his outdoor cooking. In addition, as one who had been arrested after an evening at that haunt of princes, the Café Anglais in Paris, no doubt he could speak authoritatively on 'brands' of wine. Quite how he occupied himself in Nevada goes unexplained, but talk of metallurgy and chemistry suggests that he at least flirted with Virginia City's governing passion. And here too, having fraternised for weeks with the mining engineers of *Les 40* on a mission to blow up a tunnel in a mountain, presumably Harry was adequately informed about shafts, fuses and blasting powder.

Whether he was actually reduced to labouring in a Nevada mine is another question. The Comstock Lode had come to resemble an underground city, with seemingly miles of streets and thousands of workers. Deep inside the mountain, Twain wrote, was an 'intricate maze of tunnels and drifts, flitting hither and thither under a winking sparkle of lights', while towering above, into the vanishing gloom, like 'some colossal skeleton', a 'vast web of interlocking timbers' kept 'the walls of the gutted Comstock apart'. To work in there was extremely dangerous, and if Harry was able to avoid this kind of graft, he would have been wise to do so.

One detail in his Comstock portrait stands out for being presented as a direct memory: his having improvised an 'enrapturing melody' on the organ in the 'Bishop's church', presumably St Paul's the Prospector. This, too, is believable. His mother had been relentless in urging keyboard practice in her letters; and the memoir of Henry Dickens confirms that there were pianoforte lessons at Brackenbury's. Furthermore, in the winter of 1867, when Harry stayed in the 'prophet's chamber' in Wanstead, Alice was dutifully teaching herself to play the church organ. It is easy enough to imagine that Harry, at loose ends in a suburban villa, might have amused himself by improving his facility too.

More than anything, though, he surely was affable and amusing, and, where possible, debonair. If he divulged even the least truth about *la fée aux giffles*, and stealing diamonds in Paris, along with his awful time in Mazas; if he described border skirmishing in India, or his exploits as a *franc-tireur* and spy, and his battle wounds in France, well, no wonder he 'charmed all'. His best anecdotes would have been just the thing over a brandy toddy in a Virginia City bar, let alone out prospecting with a canteen, slouch hat and blanket, 'yarn-spinning' round a little sagebrush fire, on a frosty night under the stars.

Of the close of his Nevada sojourn, the Comstock portrait says nothing beyond the fact that 'One day Larkins drifted away from the Lode, and the next heard of him he was in San Francisco.' By this, though, the writer missed out an ill-fated step on the way.

First, Harry got himself to the Mormon capital of Salt Lake City, or Polygamopolis as it was waggishly known. And there, in a hotel bar in late October, he ran into an acquaintance from one of his spells in London. To Harry, a penniless wanderer once again, this chance encounter opened up an irresistible prospect. Because, unfortunately, the acquaintance, Arthur Neil, was needy, directionless and rich.

Neil was the sixth of seven children, from a family wealthy enough to provide amply for them all. Each of his three older brothers became a Church of England clergyman; but in August 1864, aged eighteen, Neil himself went as a cadet to Sandhurst. His entrance papers unforgivingly record that he was five foot four inches and four-tenths. Nor did he stand tall in other respects, ranking in the middle of a cohort of 103 entrants, and going on to achieve a generalised grade 'B' with no awards of merit. His 'conduct in study' declined from 'Mod' to 'Irreg.', and 'conduct out of study', from 'Indif.' to 'V. Irreg.' Happily for him, however, there were those who still thought it more gentlemanly to buy your way into the British Army than to earn your rank by competition. In January 1868, therefore, courtesy of the family purse, he gained a commission by purchase. Two years later, however, in December 1869, with no recorded explanation, he was 'permitted to retire from the service'. Aged twenty-three, that is, he sold out.

It must have been after this that he became acquainted with Harry. By Neil's account, they met at a club in London. He felt that he and Harry 'liked each other, and had a good time', and even 'got quite intimate'. And, blind to the mechanics of 'a Bohemianism of eternal hardupishness and eternal squandering of money', Neil took it that Harry had means. But that was it: after no more than 'a few days', they separated again.

In 1872, Neil was meandering round America. He was mysteriously unwell, and would in fact remain so for the rest of his life. He stopped in Salt Lake City 'to look at some mining property there, with a view to investment'. Naturally he and Harry were very surprised to meet, he said. But they happily 'renewed their friendship', and agreed 'to come together to San Francisco, whither both parties were bound'. That was the start of it, according to Neil.

*

It took five months of companionship before Neil sought a warrant for Harry's arrest, on the old charge of gaining money by false pretences. At sundown on 13 March 1873, Harry found himself slung into a San Francisco jail. That same evening, elsewhere in the city, Neil poured out his story to a press reporter in excruciating detail. Pre-empting the judgement of the court, due the next morning, whatever that might prove to be, he sought to destroy Harry's reputation for ever.

The newspaper Neil turned to was the *San Francisco Chronicle*, which had been launched in 1865 by the De Young brothers, still adolescents at the time. They made it deliberately 'spicy', with 'a great deal of dramatic news'; and on this basis it had flourished so quickly that, within a year or so, the capitalist Aleck Badlam offered them, unsuccessfully, $50,000 for a half-interest in the business. Once the *Chronicle*'s editors understood quite what Neil was offering them, they hurriedly dispatched a second reporter into the gathering night to snatch a glimpse of the malefactor, Harry Larkyns, as he languished in his underground cell.

The following morning, the paper published an enormous article on the case under mocking headlines, beginning: 'FINANCIAL GENIUS. The Prince of Confidence Men in Limbo. MAJ. HARRY LARKYNS ARRESTED FOR SWINDLING.' Further: 'Three Thousand Dollars from One Confiding Victim. Hotel Bills that Would Make a Millionaire Shudder. BOGUS DRAFTS ON EAST INDIA HOUSES', and 'The Coolest and Most Impudent Letter Ever Written.' Nor was the article itself any less mocking: 'Major Harry Larkyns, late of the East Indian Army, late of H. B. M. Seventy-third Regiment of Infantry, late of the staff of General Bourbaki of the French Army, late of the Grand Hotel, Jardin Mabille, Palais Royal and Bois d'Boulogne, Paris; late of the Cremorne Garden, Argyle Rooms, and all of the Clubs in London', and so on, 'late of everywhere on the known globe', it said helplessly, rendering suspect by satire what was actually a pretty accurate list: 'Hurrah! for Major Harry Larkyns. He has done well. The Major is a brick! He is likewise a fraud', it said. It added that he was 'about 39', and claimed to be 'the scion of a noble house', and that, altogether, he had 'pleasing address, gentlemanly manners and a degree of assurance that would astonish a mule'.

The piece went on to describe how Neil had spent 'several months' with Harry in Paris, 'just after the close of the Franco–Prussian war', where they dined at the Palais Royal and 'wined with Schneider and the famed Markowitz', and were 'one and inseparable', until 'each believed that the sun rose and set in the other'. Evidently Harry had described aspects of this life to Neil. However, when Harry really was 'up to everything' in Paris, Neil was still in the army; while at the close of the war, Harry had returned injured to London. Moreover, if Neil had really run with Harry in Paris, he could not subsequently have become his innocent dupe. But the *Chronicle* reporter, not knowing this, invented a previous closeness between the two, apparently to make more explicable Neil's faith in a leech and blackguard, and to make Harry's betrayal of his boon companion the greater disgrace.

Had Neil known anything, he would have laughed in Salt Lake City at the line Harry shot him, asking to borrow money. Through some 'blundering mistake' on the railways, his baggage, ready funds and letters of credit had all been sent ahead to San Francisco, he said. And he explained that he was 'on his way to Yokohama', sent by 'his friends in London to avoid scandal on account of a disagreeable scrape he had gotten into in Paris'. In the *Chronicle*'s dime-novel prose, Neil replied: 'My purse, Major, is at your disposal', and even bought Harry new clothes. Meanwhile, as he had with the jeweller Kramer, Harry flourished a letter from his brother-in-law, 'Dr. Cutter' or 'Cutler', stating that £1,000 awaited him in the London and San Francisco Bank. 'The letter was so plausible, and the Major so old an acquaintance of Mr. Niel's [*sic*],' wrote the *Chronicle*, 'that he never for an instant suspected anything wrong.'

Neil 'very willingly acceded' to a proposal that the two should travel together, and on 22 November 1872, they signed in at San Francisco's magnificent Occidental Hotel. Soon, though, Neil began to agitate for Harry to square the 'several hundred' dollars he owed him. Harry returned from a trip to the bank with provoking news of a new letter from Edward Cutler about the £1,000 credit note: 'They are afraid I will spend it here, and so you see they have

The Occidental Hotel, Montgomery Street

provided for me in Japan by sending the money all to Yokohama.'
Neil, again, 'did not for a moment suspect him'. Nor, it seems, did
he baulk at the idea of subverting an attempt by Harry's family to
save him from himself. He simply took Harry's 'word of honor as
a gentleman' that he would pay up once he reached Japan.

Here the *Chronicle* reporter could not contain himself. Harry had
pursued 'a riotous, extravagant course' in San Francisco, including
'champagne dinners at the Occidental, to which he invited Mr.
Neil (the man who paid for them) and dozens of other friends'.
He chased a 'notorious' lady, 'Fanny —', sending her flowers, carriages and opera boxes. He even shiftily offered to help Neil send
a Christmas present to a lady in Brussels: Neil gave Harry the
amount in gold; Harry gave Neil a draft for the sum, drawn on a
Brussels bank; and Neil sent the piece of paper, later learning that
the draft had proved useless. The *Chronicle* set this fraud alone at
an implausible £100, roughly equivalent today to £8,500.

On 5 December, Neil abruptly announced that he was leaving
the next day for Honolulu, departing on the steamship *Dakota*.
He consented 'willingly enough' that Harry should accompany

him, Honolulu being on the way to Japan, and they saw their bags stowed on board ship. Then Neil insisted on further hasty steps to untangle their finances. He wanted a draft against Harry's letter of credit in Yokohama, and requested that his loan should be redeemed through the services of Mr Milton S. Latham of the London and San Francisco Bank. Latham was a substantial figure at the time. In 1860, through a curious political rigamarole, he had won and then lost, within a week, the office of Governor of California. Quitting what he then chose to call 'the filthy pool of politics', he next became a banker, making himself one of California's railroad barons. Harry forgot to bring his letter from Edward Cutler to their interview. Nor did Latham recognise the name of Harry's bank in Yokohama, rendered in the *Chronicle* account as the 'Bank of China, India and Japan'. Nevertheless, Latham agreed to take instruction.

Neil now demanded to see Harry's letter himself. Back on board the *Dakota*, Harry rummaged through his bags, but was unable to find it. Nothing daunted, he found a reputable shipping merchant ready to vouch for the existence of the bank, relaying this information to Neil himself, who failed to check whether it was true. The next morning, in the hours before they sailed, Harry drew up all the necessary paperwork, mentioning the Hongkong and Shanghai Banking Corporation and others, and requesting that his entire expectation of £1,000 be transferred from Japan into an account in his name in Latham's bank. Further, he directed that once the money arrived, he should be informed in Honolulu, and that Latham should make over to Neil a sum that the *Chronicle* set at $2,500.

Neil's case, in the press, essentially boiled down to saying that he had innocently fronted Harry a large amount of money, and had been deceived into believing, almost to the last, that Harry both could and would repay him. Perhaps the best that can be made of this is that, remembering the figure Harry had cut in London, then glamorised anew by this spreader of ripples of sunshine, Neil had wanted to believe what he was hearing, despite, or even because of, a hint of danger that Harry conveyed. After all, Neil was five foot four inches and four-tenths, sickly, and with an aborted military career, while Harry was tall, handsome and compulsively affable, and trailed a heroic record as a soldier of fortune. Money might have given Neil the whip hand, but it was not a form of power he was well equipped to wield.

The *Dakota* arrived in Honolulu on 15 December, and in the *Chronicle*'s telling, 'Mr. Neil, not being well, at once rented a house there and set up a splendid establishment. He had his servants, cooks, etc., and of course invited the Major to live with him.' For his part, Harry supposedly once more gave 'splendid dinners' and 'spent money like a millionaire'. But after a week or so, Neil, fired up by 'the English and French Consuls and others', at last suspected 'that his friend was a beat of the first water', and that he himself had been 'badly sold'. He started to 'despise the man whose victim he had been', and there followed several days of 'coolness' and 'wrangling'. For his part, Harry chafed under Neil's direct insults, and was dismayed to discover that he was being spoken of as a dastardly limpet and probable thief.

Harry, with his various shams and valueless arrangements, was now racing ahead of a storm well past the point where he could easily escape. He did, though, on 31 December, attempt to save himself by sending Neil a letter. In it, he boldly suggested that Neil was more indebted to him than the other way round. 'Things cannot continue as they have been going on for the last week', he said. 'There are, doubtless, faults on both sides, but unless you care to take your part in remedying these, our connection must cease.' In Salt Lake City, Neil's doctor had informed him, about Neil, he said, 'that unless your health mended at once and rapidly, your illness *must* speedily terminate in death or idiocy'. Better than any medicine would be a friend, 'who would keep your mind working and prevent your falling into a morbid state'. Harry had set aside his trip to Japan in order to save Neil. And 'You, yourself,' he wrote, 'in those days, seemed to share the idea.'

Wily as this seems, as Harry was addressing Neil himself, he cannot have pulled this argument out of thin air. He continued that it was only in San Francisco that matters between them had darkened. There, '*your own* friends, not mine, remarked that I must find it very hard to put up with you sometimes. I answered that a sick man was always irritable, that it was your manner, and that you meant nothing.' Harry had wished, above all, 'to set you on your legs again'. And, 'I leave it to you to judge if I was *ever* otherwise than perfectly even-tempered.' By contrast, Neil's behaviour had grown worse, with 'insolent airs and speeches', culminating in his recent accusations of bad faith. 'I am using your money? Why?' asked Harry rhetorically. The money was spent on good cheer for Neil. To Harry himself it was a nothing, he said. He had sought 'no better return than to see you recover, and of course, to enjoy that friendly intercourse which should exist between two gentlemen, and here's the result!' Sounding genuinely stung, he accused Neil of 'that misplaced pride and stubborn obstinacy which you glory in'. They might start afresh, but equally, if Neil wished it, Harry was ready to 'go quietly to the hotel' and to return from there to San Francisco by the next boat.

The *Chronicle* published Harry's letter with a string of asterisks in the middle, apparently obscuring more specific and worse allegations against Neil by Harry. Neil himself explained that the letter had caused him to throw Harry out, though he still made himself responsible for Harry's hotel bills. Then, on 10 January 1873, the steamship *Nevada* had sailed for San Francisco.

Setting aside the *Chronicle*'s verdict that Harry's letter was one 'which for unblushing effrontery, sublime cheek and exasperating insolence we have never seen equalled', and reading carefully through even the mutilated version, it would appear that, having been made to sing so wearyingly for his supper, Harry was able to persuade himself that he should not then also be asked to pay for it. Equally, it seems that Neil had half recognised for quite a while what a mess he was in with his charismatic companion, becoming at times restive and resentful, but remaining half seduced.

It is impossible to tell in how many ways the *Chronicle* article misrepresented the truth. But it certainly cut the amount of time over which Neil had funded them both, lessening the duration of his supposed wide-eyed faith in Harry, while making Harry seem to rack up his bills reprehensibly faster. The piece implied that they had been together in Salt Lake City for just a few days;

but it was a month. And it put them together in Honolulu for a little over a fortnight; but it was six weeks: the *Nevada* actually set sail on 27 January. And initially Harry and Neil embarked for San Francisco together. Only when the steamship turned back to Honolulu to take on more coal, having stalled in shocking weather, did Neil disembark again. He followed on the *Moses Taylor* two weeks later.

There could hardly have been a more propitious time for Harry to go on the run than when he arrived back into San Francisco alone, especially with Milton S. Latham awaiting letters from abroad that would discredit Harry completely. Yet rather than skip town, he went back to the Occidental Hotel where, again by the *Chronicle's* account, he 'splurged out in the wildest extravagance on the credit his former payment of his bills (at Mr. Neil's expense) had given him'. Quite how Harry managed this was a mystery to the reporter, 'for no matter how much he obtained on credit, he certainly must have required some money'. Nevertheless, Harry rioted on until Neil's return, and for a couple of weeks afterwards too. Finally, though, Neil and 'some friends' had sought a warrant for Harry's arrest, and a few hours later Harry was 'breathing the pure air of the City Prison'.

This last observation was a bleak jest. San Francisco's remand prison sat in the basement of City Hall. According to Benjamin Lloyd's 1876 guide to the city, a person walking past this unremarkable building was liable to be assaulted by an 'unwholesome odor' emanating 'from the small barred windows 'neath the side-walk'. The older cells down there, often woefully overcrowded, were dark, badly ventilated and 'very foul'. If the cut of a man's clothes and the 'caste' of his crime gave him status, he might be treated with relative courtesy, but the atmosphere, in all senses, remained profoundly unpleasant. The guards were often brutal, and if you wished to contact your lawyer they required bribes.

Right at the end of the *Chronicle's* immense article of 14 March came an added paragraph by a second reporter, sent to find Harry in these cells. After numerous column inches treating him with unrelenting scorn, the final note was very different:

Last evening a CHRONICLE reporter called at the city prison and saw the gallant Major. He is a young man, not over thirty, with a quiet, aristocratic air that rather impresses one. He was dressed in the height of fashion, having on a nobby suit of clothes and an English hat with a peacock feather, such as Mr. Latham wears to the races. He said he had nothing to say about his case, except that Mr. Neil had acted rather hastily. He would tell a story to-day that might put a different complexion on the whole matter.

Little can Harry have guessed how far his restraint in this simple statement was going to contrast with the deluge of hostile paragraphs about him that preceded it.

The 'to-day' of the printing of the entire article was the day of the hearing in 'Judge Louderback's mill of justice'. Harry, once one of 'the dashingest young men in Paris', appeared there as 'a pale-faced young man in fashionable attire, but with unkempt hair and a sorrowful countenance', reported the *Chronicle*, his dress disordered, shirt dirty and eyes 'sodden and bloodshot'. And yet, though he 'seemed to take but little interest in what was going on around him', nevertheless he 'sat against the wall and looked about him unabashed', meeting the gaze of those who stared at him 'with a *sang froid* that was refreshing'.

The court was packed. Neil had lined up a lawyer named Campbell, as well as the witnesses Milton S. Latham, Mr Macondray, the shipping merchant supposed to have verified the existence of Harry's Yokohama bank, and 'another of the Major's victims', a young man called Baines whom Harry had apparently also bilked 'in a small way'. Also present were 'several fashionably dressed young gentlemen' whom Harry had wined and dined at Neil's expense.

When his case came up, he bowed to Louderback 'with the air of an English Earl', and 'with a dignified yet slightly injured tone' gave a plea of 'Not guilty, sir, of course.' He asked for continuance of a day because his counsel had not appeared. Here Neil's lawyer helpfully intervened. 'Mr. Larkyns had not, I believe, secured his services in the usual manner', he said, failing to provide 'the customary fee'. Louderback grumbled that it was 'a bad precedent to establish to postpone a case because the defendant had no counsel'. Nevertheless, he granted Harry another day.

The *Chronicle*, left hanging, scraped up for its readers 'Additional Particulars of His Brilliant Career.' Best of these was the matter of Orr & Atkins, 'undershirt men', with whom, the day before leaving for Honolulu, Harry had supposedly spent a colossal $200. 'With the air of a quintuple millionaire' he had handed them a cheque on Latham's bank, postdated to after the *Dakota* sailed, a cheque later marked 'No funds', leaving the undershirt clerk to depart the bank 'with the odor of a mouse's tail filling both his nostrils'. On Harry's return, faced with this 'confounded' muddle, he had turned to a young Englishman called Hughes, whom he had befriended on the *Nevada*. Hughes lent Harry his watch and chain as security against the debt; and that watch remained with Orr unredeemed. The *Chronicle* told a jumble of such stories, in particular relishing Harry's duplicitous generosity towards the phantom it called the 'notorious' Fanny, to whom he had supposedly given bouquets, silk dresses, carriages to ride in, opera boxes and, before he left for Honolulu, another of his dud cheques. If this was even half true, it would seem that Harry had been attempting to recreate the greater glories of his lost life in Paris.

When it came to the resumed hearing in court the next day, the *Chronicle* slashed its reporting to a couple of paragraphs, referring indifferently to Harry's attorney without even giving him a name. Other papers, however, recorded that again a 'great crowd of young city bloods' attended court, even as the prisoner sat in the dock 'apparently careless and indifferent', and that Harry had somehow now netted himself two lawyers, Frank M. Pixley and Judge E. D. Sawyer. Both were prominent figures. A couple of days before, Pixley had offered his services to an impoverished young woman called Lizzie Gannon who, in murky circumstances, had shot at a rich admirer; Gannon later attempted to jump bail, successfully shot a different man, and ended up incarcerated in a lunatic asylum. Pixley's decision to take Harry's case might have seemed strange given his own recent unmasking as an editorial writer for the

Chronicle. But as a 'merciless' humorist put it, Pixley was 'furiously sincere', and something of a kangaroo: 'you never know which way he is going to jump'.

Proper legal representation, however it came about, had immediate effect: Neil at once agreed to 'compromise' the matter. The two sides conferred during a recess, reached a settlement, and Louderback dismissed the case. Harry was to sign various papers, and then he could walk free. Reportedly, one was 'somewhat in the nature of a confession' that he had had 'no expectation of remittances or anything else in China or Japan', with, the *Chronicle* hinted darkly, and unverifiably, 'other acknowledgements' too, 'which have not been made public'. The other was 'a certain promise to pay with funds to be received from a wealthy aunt, living in England'. The sum in question was given in different papers as anything from $1,000 to $5,000, with Henrietta Coffin described doubtfully as 'a reputed widow lady of reputed wealth, reputed to reside in England, and reputed to be the aunt of "Major" Larkyns'. The *Chronicle* believed Neil had 'little hope of collecting the draft in London', but helpfully suggested that he might use copies of its own columns to force the issue.

In this way, Harry escaped 'the branding-yard of the law-breakers', but the *Chronicle*, with a circulation of some 40,000, was determined to brand him anyway. In sum, it wrote: 'His career in this city has been brief, but it has been brilliant. He went up like a rocket and has come down like the stick. Let his fate serve as a warning to such young gentlemen among us as may be living on the credit of expected remittances.'

Harry was sufficiently stung by this treatment to write a letter to the paper, which it printed at once under the heading: 'A Card from the Gallant Major—He Says He Has a Great Notion to Hang Himself.'

SIR: My name having been prominently brought before the public in your columns, may I hope that you will allow me to say a few words through the same medium. That you only repeated statements concerning me as they were made to you I have no doubt; but it is no less true that in many points—in fact, in nearly every point—those statements were far from the truth. However, any verbal explanations or contradictions I might make would carry little weight; but deeds avail where words go for nothing. I have to redeem my character in San Francisco—and I will do it. The task is a hard one. Those who only know me by what they have read must despise me; those who do know me and would fain believe well of me, cannot but be biassed against me. 'Give a dog a bad name, and hang him.' God knows that in the bitterness of the last few days I've been tempted to wish I were coward enough to hang myself. I start with everything against me; but if it takes me the rest of my life to do it, I will make this city my home until I can claim the respect and esteem of those who are now perhaps the first to condemn me.

He signed the letter 'Harry Larkyns, Chevalier of the Legion of Honor and late Major of Headquarters' Staff, Twenty-fourth Corps of the French army.'

One of Harry's friends later summed up indignantly that although Neil agreed terms, and 'this ended the case', as he had caused Harry to be 'written up in the *Chronicle* at full length as a confidence man', Harry was left in 'dire straits' and was 'irretrievably disgraced'. Neil himself, meanwhile, was portrayed by the more sympathetic papers as a rich but 'soft-headed young Englishman'. But this picture of foolish innocence scarcely tallies with the will drawn up two years later by his father, when the old man was eighty-two. James Neil noted to the penny the sums he had so far advanced to his seven offspring. Neil, at twenty-nine, still with no fixed profession, far outstripped the rest, having run through £10,210, nineteen shillings and ten pence: in the order of a million pounds today. The most extreme guess anywhere set Harry's debt to Neil at about £500. Even if Neil never recovered any money from Henrietta Coffin, what he had drawn from his father would equate to a further nineteen similarly expensive escapades, or disasters; and this really did 'make a millionaire shudder'. James Neil's will stipulated that his three clergymen sons were to have permanent 'uncontrolled discretion' over Neil's inheritance, including the right to reinvest all the interest it generated, handing their brother not a penny.

Ploughing through the cold legal language in which this is explained, questions arise once more about the exact relations between Harry and Arthur Neil: quite what each was seduced into believing about the other, and for how long Neil, a prolific spender, ever was truly misled. In 1876, casting himself as a 'retired military officer', he went into exile on the Isle of Man, and lived there for the rest of his life as a bachelor in humble boarding houses. He became a member of the Plymouth Brethren, made efforts to redeem various young men, and the unfortunate more generally, and died in pinched circumstances in 1923.

Harry's unwanted fame won him mocking notice in a journal called the *California Mail Bag*. On its pages, a ditty, 'A Reporter from Hades in San Francisco', included the lines:

> There's been a nice addition to the sharp young men in town,
> Our young friend, Major Larkyns, from the Islands has come
>   down;
> He played his game of confidence right well, I must confess,
> But if he plays the same game here he won't be a success.

The interest of Hades had been piqued.

10: Bohemia

True to form, Harry managed to walk away from his latest legal entanglement. But the *Chronicle* continued to hound him, and reported that he had 'a stunning bill at the Occidental unliquidated', and that the hotel had seized his baggage in lieu. If true, then he now possessed not much more than a crumpled suit, and a hat with the eye of a peacock feather tucked in its brim. He was offered help to leave town by Isaiah Lees, Captain of Police, and by a visiting French gentleman who, knowing Harry to have been a gallant servant of France, 'desired to assist him in his emergency'. But Harry 'declined the tender of a passage to China', or anywhere else. He had decided to stay and fight, whether through exhaustion, anger, or a sense, perhaps, that in the glittering roil of San Francisco he might still get by. The press raised an eyebrow: 'so the Major is to remain with us, after all that has been said and done'. But some interpreted his decision as an argument in his defence. He could hardly be 'the scoundrel that men sometimes spoke of him as', for, as the 'dullest fool' could see, 'no successful plan of rascality could be carried out by a man so well known as he', and 'to be successful in that way, he must go to new fields'.

There was some truth to this, viewed as a prediction.

Harry was now reduced to 'positive want'. He tried, 'with discouraging success', the job of canvassing, going door to door hustling for subscribers for almanacs, encyclopaedias, directories and the like. But perhaps failing at this was no bad thing. The unsavoury side of the trade was laid bare in an 1879 exposé, *How 'Tis Done. A Thorough Ventilation of the Numerous Schemes Conducted by Wandering Canvassers Together with the Various Advertising Dodges for the Swindling of the Public*. That said, sinking even lower than this forced him to risk life and limb simply to eat.

A family heritage of running ships for the East India Company was dramatically upended when Harry, at 'the foot of the ladder', as he put it, began working at the city docks. He secured coarse clothing, and sought day labour hauling freight among the stevedores. The contemptuous label 'wharf rat' implied opportunistic thievery, yet the work imperilled more than a man's reputation. Newspapers regularly carried three-line stories of stevedores brutally injured or killed by unsecured freight, or drowned when they fell in the water. Harry later wrote of how, in this period, after 'undeserved disgrace', he abruptly dropped from associating on terms with anybody at all 'to the level—at least in the eyes of others—of riff-raff scum'.

He survived like this for several weeks, no doubt aided by his physical strength and bonhomie, before at last being 'discovered by a well known Bohemian', who got him a position working for the idiosyncratic Hubert Howe Bancroft. The press would dismiss this as 'odd jobs at translating'. Yet Harry was about to play a part for which he might have been specially formed by his roving, rackety life, and now contributed his tuppence worth to a vast intellectual venture.

Bancroft had established himself in San Francisco in 1856 as a seller of books, maps, charts, general stationery and more. In time he came to publish books too. In 1868, for example, seeking to exploit a growing tourist boom, he brought out a guide, *Yosemite: Its Wonders and Beauties* by John S. Hittell, historian and long-time editorial writer on the newspaper the *Alta*. As well as offering 'information adapted to the wants of tourists', the book cannily contained 'Twenty Photographic Views taken by "Helios,"' the prints hand-pasted into every copy. Through his drive and enterprise, Bancroft became 'Master, happily, of a handsome fortune'. He set about a remarkable programme of buying books, manuscripts, journals and whole archives about the territories of the American West, in numerous languages, from sellers around the world. In 1869, he made over the running of Bancroft & Co. to his younger brother, at the same time building a huge new brick premises for the business on Market Street, 'queerly decorated at the top with fantastic images or gargoyles'. The top floor he took for his own, housing his library there, 'some sixteen hundred bound volumes of

*The Bancroft building, with its literary factory
on the fifth floor: photograph by Muybridge*

all kinds'. But he also turned the space into a 'literary workshop',
and the focus of what would be the dominating project of his life.

Bancroft's slowly developed idea was to write a comprehensive
history of the North American West. He aimed to digest his
ever-expanding library so as to generate 'records of a vast territory
founded on original data'. The eventual result would be thirty-nine
hefty volumes, published between 1875 and 1891, not a feat he
could accomplish alone. He employed numerous others to index
his library, page by page, and to extract pertinent material from what
seemed otherwise a 'trackless sea of erudition'. They assembled up
to 1,000 paper snippets per topic, stuffed into labelled paper bags,
in theory leaving Bancroft to synthesise each packaged blizzard of
information, and compose the final text.

In the thirty-ninth volume, *Literary Industries*, Bancroft purported to describe his working practices, devoting one chapter to
his various assistants across time: not the 'army' of 'no less than
six hundred different persons' whom he had employed to do basic
tasks, but the select few, some 'twenty in all', who had aided him

in his 'more responsible labors'. They had represented a 'wonderful variety of nationality and talent', he said, highly educated, cosmopolitan and literary; but, typically, had been driven from home by failure, waywardness and debt, so that, winding up in California, they were ready to accept his very low rates of pay. One was a multilingual Swede operating under the nom de plume 'William Nemos'. Another, Henry Lebbeus Oak, had been in his time a 'sick and destitute wanderer'. Thomas Arundel Harcourt 'claimed to be a scion of the English aristocracy'. As for Walter Mulrea Fisher: 'Old-time ways by rule and rote he could neither profess, preach, nor practise.' So Bancroft went on, including a description of 'Harry Larkin', whom he called 'an English adventurer of good abilities, many accomplishments, and an adventurous career'.

The 'more responsible' work of the best assistants was essentially to write Bancroft's books for him. In 1893, Henry Oak asserted bitterly that Walter Fisher had written half an early volume before leaving the company; Frances Fuller Victor, the sole woman among them, four volumes; Nemos, five; Oak himself, he said, ten. Bancroft, Oak credited with writing no more than about four and a half,

Bancroft satirised as 'The Boss Historian'

despite his name being on them all, and hostile reviewers agreed that the project was 'open to the charge of unfairness'. Oak ended his painful accounting with a final 'few others' probably responsible, he thought, in aggregate, for one whole volume, their digests and translations absorbed into the finished texts verbatim. And though Harry was gone again before even the first volume was published, the implication remains that, via the paper bags, he too contributed to that aggregated volume.

Walter Fisher wrote that the position of the assistants 'was somewhat peculiar, isolated as they were by many thousand miles from outer help or sympathy. The mildest popular local theory about them was that they were touched with some harmless craze.' Still, he said, 'They had a little *salon* of their own', with 'its keen glad nights of conversation' during which Thomas Harcourt, in particular, was 'a very berserkr of argument', making him 'the fire of our councils, the splendour of our festivals'. But there were also 'days of utter lassitude of mind and body, days of intense discouragement' in their 'struggle with Dryasdust', as well as times when 'petty disputes divided the little band of brothers'.

Three members of this band, all of them Irish, became Harry's definite friends. One, William Paton, was 'an Irish captain' who 'possessed decided talents in some directions'. Another was an explosive young man called Gerald Darcy. The third was Walter Fisher himself, taken to be 'of great promise in a literary way'. But all must have been Harry's fast companions while he was there, not least the fiery Thomas Arundel Harcourt. Harry laboured 'principally at translations of French, German and Spanish works'. And all the while he was recovering a demeanour that soon led to his being described once more as 'gay, dashing and handsome', and someone who, 'From making a translation or writing an original article to fencing, boxing or jumping over a pile of tables', could 'do almost everything and do it well'. Even with his sympathetic new band of brothers, however, the 'Dryasdust' pursuits of the literary factory were hardly calculated to keep Harry in their thrall, and as soon as he could talk himself into a better job, he was on his way.

*

In mid June, Harry began writing for the *Daily Evening Post*, based at 605 Montgomery, and edited by the combative reform advocate Henry George. It is possible Harry had experience in this line already, if he did try to earn some pennies on his return to England from India. Being a gentleman scribbler in Grub Street was one of the more desirable straws at which London's upper impecunious classes tended to clutch; and the calling was veiled by anonymity. Only rare luminaries, such as 'Boz' or 'Mark Twain', saw their identities become a worldwide open secret. Then again, if Henry George knowingly took a chance on an outright novice, he may have been spurred by contempt for the machinations of the *Chronicle*, which he viewed as a sink of 'literary filth'.

Through his seminal work of 1879, *Progress and Poverty*, George would become internationally famous himself as a political economist and advocate for social change. But he made his mark in California before this, not least with an 1868 essay, published in Bret Harte's *Overland Monthly*, 'What the Railroads Will Bring Us'. In it George predicted that the transcontinental railroad, soon to be completed with a hammer blow from the politician and railway baron Leland Stanford, would bring about a vast access of wealth in the state, facilitating business and greatly aiding immigration into California. But he also foresaw that, with monopolisation of land and natural resources by the increasingly wealthy few, and the driving-down of wages through increased competition for work, the railroad was set to benefit 'only a portion', creating a dark mirror of poverty among the growing masses. All in all, the effect of the transcontinental railroad would be this: 'those who *have*, it will make wealthier; for those who *have not*, it will make it difficult to get'.

George co-founded his 'bold, fearless, reform paper', the *Evening Post*, in December 1871, when he was thirty-two. And there, as editor, he pressed on with what a competitor called his 'fearful eruptions of socialism'. He pulled no punches: 'we should make the rich poorer and the poor richer', he said. And his hiring was singular. On board from the start was Dan O'Connell, one-time Greek scholar, indigent bon viveur, prolific journalist, all round man of letters, and also a great-nephew of the leading Irish patriot of the same name.

But George soon also employed Caroline M. Parker. In 1851, as a young widow with three children to support, she had opened a school for girls on Vallejo Street. Two decades on, she appeared as one of twenty-two San Francisco representatives at the Women's Rights State Convention. And by March of 1873, now in her forties, Parker had her position on the *Post*, not as a 'lady correspondent', but as a reporter, the sole woman with this job title alongside fifty-odd men in that year's San Francisco directory. The *Post* also employed a woman printer, Miss Annie Edwards, while another labourer in the print works was the youthful and ardently scholarly Charles H. Hinton. On 15 June 1873, he composed a long letter to Charles Darwin discussing Darwin's recent book, *The Expression of the Emotions in Man and Animals*. After quaintly theorising about dog smiles, and the 'stiff upper lip', Hinton explained that he could vouch for earthquakes providing 'unusually good opportunities' for observing 'the most violent expressions of terror'. He added hopefully, 'I will engage to keep very cool at the next "shake" and send you my observations, if you wish it.'

Throughout his editorship of the *Post*, Henry George 'kept busy with fights of one kind or another'. When he saw evils 'he did not hesitate to oppose them', wielding 'a whip of scorpions' as he campaigned against monopolies, unfair land taxes, corruption and other ills. He was sometimes threatened in reply. A month before employing Harry, as he dawdled with Dan O'Connell in the Mint Saloon on Commercial Street, he was violently assaulted and nearly shot by an ex-detective aggrieved that he had questioned the probity of the city's Chief of Police.

Harry took on the role of the paper's new dramatic critic. His predecessor had routinely described individual performances as 'creditable' or 'well sustained', with whole plays summed up as having 'passed off pleasantly'. Even Shakespeare roused no stronger response from this deathless contributor than to comment that the Bard's efforts were 'always palatable'. Harry's verbal panache could not have been more immediately different, as when he called one production 'an absurd mixture of pistols, profanity, poker and lynch law, without a particle of literary merit'. He was an unabashed lover of the theatre, too: 'Surely, if the drama has a mission, it is to humanize and soften the human heart,' he wrote, 'so apt to become callous by contact with this hard, workaday world'. Harry often mitigated his criticisms of actors and singers by saying that they had been overstrained, or miscast, or were ill served by their material. Of a saucy beginner who had faltered, he remarked genially: 'we will make our mention of her as short as her own petticoats'. When it came, though, his admiration could be unstinting. Bella Pateman, an actress new to San Francisco, left other critics unsure when she played the part of a reformed prostitute in *The New Magdalen* by Wilkie Collins. But Harry, noting women in the audience with 'up-lifted noses and down-drawn lips', described Patemen's acting as 'unspoilt by florid exaggeration' and 'beyond praise'. And when Madame Anna Bishop came to town, the singer who had so entranced him as a boy, he urged his readers to experience for themselves a 'musical marvel'.

As was standard, the *Post* permitted Harry to review only those productions that were being advertised on its pages. This lent his 'Amusements' column a see-saw dynamic, in which a thoughtful response to Verdi or Donizetti at Platt's Hall on Montgomery Street might be followed by an amiable review of the entertainments at the Woodward's or City Gardens: an attempt by 'Jack Sheppard' to walk 1,000 miles in 1,000 hours, perhaps, or the wonder of 'Natator, the London Man Fish', who smoked 'with the utmost nonchalance' underwater. Happily, the *Post*'s advertising also dictated that Harry should repair often to the California Theatre. This tremendous edifice on Bush Street, completed in 1869, had been built principally by William C. Ralston, manager of the Bank of California, who had a personal Comstock fortune at his disposal. It was the sole venue in the city to encompass 'legitimate' drama: blank verse, five acts; and it boasted a dress circle, gallery and *trompe l'oeil* boxes down the sides. Even the drop curtain had been beautifully designed by the renowned Nahl brothers, Arthur and Charles, artists with a gallery on Montgomery Street. Amid countless scrolls, they featured a view of the Golden Gate, an image of Yosemite, a grove of Mammoth Trees, '*vaquero* lassoing wild cattle', Shakespeare being crowned by the muses, and 'the first train on the Pacific Railroad crossing the Sierra Nevada'. Many great figures would tread the boards here, switching from the 'ecstacy of assumed rage' to 'boundless joy' and back.

Harry's position came with highly congenial benefits: free tickets to share, and introductions to all the city's actors and actresses, as well as to the travelling stars who blew into town. And after all, as George Moore put it, 'The dramatic profession has been, is, and always must be, a profession for those to whom social restraints are irksome, and who would lead the life their instinct dictates.' Harry's fledgling daily 'Amusements' column reveals that his new life often involved taking in an afternoon show, such as the 'menagerie circus' then in town, followed by the theatre, or an evening lecture or concert. And in between he was mugging up information for much longer articles under the title 'Dramatic Sketches'. In these, with his own amusing sidelights, he would give an account of a play currently in performance. After trawling other sources, he would serve up ancient chatter about the playwright, and outstanding performers in important roles down the years, before then dissecting the current production with added gossip about its stars.

Consuming as this clearly was, the role of dramatic critic was far from the whole of Harry's newspaper job. After two years in circulation, the *Post* had an earnestness that Henry George apparently wished to leaven, and his pages were heavily dependent on stories cut out and pasted in from other newspapers across America and the world. In Harry he found a witty and cosmopolitan exemplar of the family Smorltork, as conjured up by Dickens. George therefore also set him a hectic schedule as a literary raconteur.

Within a fortnight, Harry was writing urbane front-page articles for the *Post* at a rate of two, three, four, even five a week. Two early pieces he called 'chat about circuses'. The first was an essay on bareback riding, which he considered 'the most daring and attractive feat in circus entertainment'. Training started at age three, and maintaining a child's confidence was vital, with juggling and jumping through hoops added only after several years. The second, with a less cheerful tone, was on lion-taming, how cubs were 'broken in' by ruthless whipping, and with a heated iron bar used as 'a settler' to shock any animal that bit. Lions cost $7,000 each, and were principally supplied by the London Zoological Gardens. Harry

Bareback training illustrated in 1877 with an infeasible horse

also wrote a lengthy piece on costume. He rued the prevalence of black in men's clothing, recalling a fad inspired by the Prince of Wales for jackets of lilac velvet. He then discussed the fashion plates of Adolphe Goubaud and Frank Leslie; and how Worth had terrorised duchesses in his salon on rue de la Paix; and described the special dressing machine by which Empress Eugénie had managed her thrice-daily costume changes, 'before evil days came on France'. Chivalrously, Harry ended this piece by remarking that San Francisco's women dressed 'emphatically well'. In further amusing and informative articles he wrote on duelling, and also on forms of 'street locomotion', when he pondered the growlers, hansoms and fiacres of London and Paris, before calling San Francisco, with its street cars, the 'most favored of all'. On 23 July he turned out an article on spiritualism. At a typical performance, 'I was', he wrote, 'shocked by a solecism committed by George Washington.' The horror: 'How could I be happy in a sphere where grammar was unknown—I, to whom philology was as dear as electro-biology, and who believed as implicitly in the souls of words as in the souls of human beings, or even a little more!' The medium, under challenge, had offered him the brilliant explanation that premier spirits were too busy to fulfil all engagements, so that less educated spirits were compelled to masquerade as their superiors, speaking ungrammatically on their behalf.

There is no knowing quite the full extent of what Harry wrote. But he was clearly also sometimes the author of a new *Post* column 'Our London Letter', his pen name there seemingly 'Aladdin'. He also provided regular 'Parisian Gossip' in another faked foreign correspondence; one piece started, 'Ouf! How hot it is!' And for this column he used the telling name 'Ishmaelite', meaning 'outcast'. The London letters were often simple rehashes from the British press. One, taken almost wholesale from *The Times*, concerned a debate in Parliament on how to curb the depredations of man-eating tigers in India; to this Harry added a funny story of his own about a Bengal tiger that had gorged on postal carriers. But he entered far more into his news from Paris, explaining how the city was agog at a visit by 'the Shah, the whole Shah, and nothing but the Shah', who had recently been at Longchamp riding his 'beautiful flea-bitten gray arab', its caparison 'blazing with jewels' as he paraded before a military barely recovered from recent 'crushing disasters'. Then, commenting on the withdrawal of the last Prussian troops from France, Harry described the 'longing for revenge' left by the enemy in its wake, and the 'cherishing of every feeling likely to render another tremendous war with Germany inevitable'. Turning on a sixpence, he also discussed an imminent Offenbach opening night, bound to be 'a brilliant spectacle', attracting 'all the leading celebrities, from Countesses to courtesans', women whose diamonds made 'the flashing drops of the cut-glass chandeliers pale'. He threw in risqué jokes as well, as when he made himself the witness, on a bench under the trees, to an exchange between a Parisian husband and his wife. With angry looks, the husband had explained how he had almost been provoked into a duel by the effrontery of a third party, who declared that 'of all the husbands on our street, only one could boast a faithful wife'. 'Que diable', exclaimed the wife, 'I should very much like to know which.' In another funny story, about an upper-class English pickpocket, Harry sailed close to the wind in a different way, describing the fellow being locked up in Mazas, 'an immense prison on the solitary system, across the Seine'. French courts were 'avowedly more severe on foreign transgressors', he explained, as they wished to 'discourage the imported article'. And yet extenuating circumstances were viewed tenderly, such as the plea, for example, 'Remember that I am a poor orphan, a double orphan, without either father or mother.'

Harry began to make many more friends now, several of them well-known figures in San Francisco and beyond. Dear among them was Harry Edwards, with whom he formed a bond of 'close intimacy'. Edwards, originally English, was a founding member of the California Theatre's stock acting company, especially admired for his comic roles. But he was also a leading entomologist, and a prominent member of the California Academy of Sciences and the Microscopical Society of San Francisco. Over his lifetime he collected roughly a quarter of a million butterflies, preserved to this day in the Museum of Natural History in New York. Unsurprisingly, another widely loved character to embrace Harry was Dan O'Connell, who was responsible for saying of Harry that 'Few more brilliant waifs from other lands ever drifted to this coast.' But perhaps the most ardent of his new friends to leave a record of the fact was the 'happy-go-lucky' young writer Samuel Post Davis. Sam Davis, also cutting his teeth as a journalist in San Francisco, was destined to move on to Nevada in 1875, where he soon became editor of the *Carson Appeal*.

To be close to a few toiling writers in San Francisco inevitably meant you half-knew most of the rest as well. Thus Dan O'Connell was a regular contributor to the *Overland Monthly* along with the Bancroft literary-factory assistant Frances Fuller Victor, even as the *Overland* was taking odd articles from Harry Edwards, John S. Hittell, author of Bancroft's guide to Yosemite, and so on. And when in 1877 Frank M. Pixley, Harry's defence counsel in the police court, started a paper called the *Argonaut*, among its numerous contributors were, again, Dan O'Connell, but also Sam Davis, Joe Goodman, who had launched Mark Twain's career, and Harry's Bancroft companion, the 'berserkr' Thomas Arundel Harcourt.

San Francisco's 'quill-drivers' of the 1870s mixed off the page as well. At the start of the decade, journalists spilling out of their offices after their midnight deadlines habitually resorted to one or other of the city's popular restaurants, seeking out actors, singers and other friends of the after-hours classes, along with a sustaining glass and a bite. But these meetings were chancy, and so on 5 February 1872, in the editorial rooms of the *Examiner*, five or six reporters, including Dan O'Connell, hatched a plan to open a club of their own. This alliance of jolly fellows, 'children of the night and minions of the San Francisco Gas Light Company', put out feelers to 'all journalists of any standing', with suitable sympathisers to be considered as honorary members, hoping to promote 'social and intellectual intercourse between journalists and other writers, artists, actors and musicians'. The owl was to be the club's 'tutelary deity', as a nocturnal symbol and an 'ancient bird of wisdom', while the club motto, 'Weaving spiders come not here', took aim at the 'dull plodder' who cared for nothing but 'money-getting'. The initiation fee was to be $10; monthly dues, $2.50.

Choosing a name proved a 'storm-center', with the 'Bohemian Club' said by opponents to invoke a shameful picture of 'a fellow who buttoned his seedy coat to conceal his lack of clean linen', a 'long-haired, impecunious person', who might have talent, but who lived in 'frosty attics' and starved in cheap restaurants; perhaps even a 'predatory disreputable character who devoted his cleverness to borrowing money from his friends which he never repaid'. Dan O'Connell shouted this down, not because it was untrue but because it was wrong-headed. 'Are we to truckle at the very outset of our career to the ogre Respectability?' he demanded. 'Are we to button our pockets against our friends, smooth our faces into a smug semblance of a well-to-do shopkeeper?' After further resistance, 'the exponents of respectability withdrew in withering silence', and on 14 April 1872, the convivialities began.

The club was soon able to rent first-floor rooms on Sacramento Street from a landlady feelingly referred to as 'Mrs. MacStinger', in a brownstone corner building opposite a 'dear old coffin shop'. With second-hand carpet, a motley array of old chairs, a sustaining sideboard and a caged owl in the window, they were up and cracking, the walls soon transformed with anything from caricatures to landscape oils by artist members including Jules Tavernier and Virgil Williams.

Much of the club's early history would end up 'lost in the obscurity of the past'. But among the hotchpotch of recorded original members were Ambrose Bierce, best known today for his *Devil's Dictionary*, though he left for England almost at once, and the philosopher and naturalist John Muir, who dropped by when he was in town. Frank Pixley and John S. Hittell were members too, along with John McCullough and Barton Hill, who were lessee and acting manager of the California Theatre. Walter Fisher, Bancroft's assistant of literary promise, wrote that he spent 'many a pleasant evening' there. And for all of Harry's time as a San Francisco journalist, the president of the Bohemian Club was Harry Edwards.

Edwards said of Harry that he was 'a brilliant writer, to whom no theme appeared to come amiss,—a musician of culture,—an artist of refined and polished taste' and, with this, a conversationalist who was 'rarely excelled', an accolade that must in part have been won opposite the coffin shop on Sacramento Street. Presumably many of Harry's other alliances, too, were cemented over a nocturnal drink in the club's dilapidated upstairs rooms, where 'the froth of the cheap and ever pleasant beer' stood 'thick upon moustaches'. Indeed, given that Henry George was an original trustee, it is possible that he first encountered Harry at the club and took him on after falling for his entertaining stories.

As the club's bills mounted, the initiation fee rapidly rose to $50, with monthly dues of $3. But it was 'no easy task' to collect money from true Bohemians, more willing to supply wit, art, song and gossip. And so club officials cast their net a little wider, to catch those with 'the coin to pay for it all'. Word was out that 'a nicer little spot to chat with brilliant minds, and sip number one drinks, isn't found on this coast', so there was no shortage of stuffy applicants. In one of his *Post* columns, Harry took an irresistible swipe at an old adversary whose sheer overdose of money was not enough to get him in: 'Start a club, call it Bohemian,' he wrote, 'and even all-potent bankers rush to seek admittance (Mr. Milton S. Latham will kindly understand that no personality is meant).' William C. Ralston, who had built the California Theatre, was allowed to join, but was only briefly the sympathetic standard-bearer for the banking class. After suffering extreme financial reverses, he drowned in 1875, possibly on purpose, while taking an 'ocean bath' in the Bay.

Harry's own finances remained perpetually insecure. Harry Edwards noted about him ruefully that, for all his élan, 'Poverty always hung like a gaunt spectre about his footsteps.' And as one spendthrift to another, Dan O'Connell called Harry 'Reckless beyond redemption.' A colleague on the *Post* explained that Harry coupled supposed family 'expectations' with having 'no idea of the value of money', and, lacking 'commercial honour', borrowed from anyone foolish enough to trust him. Equally, though, all recognised that when he did have money, Harry was absurdly and touchingly generous. In fact, Harry Edwards wrote, 'his generosity led him often far beyond the bounds of prudence. Many a story of his kindness to those in want is well known to his associates.' Sam Davis went further and described how Harry 'never seemed to own anything that he considered his'. There was 'hardly a Sunday morning that some wandering Bohemian did not come up to his apartments' and 'help himself to shirts, underwear, neckties and, in fact, anything in sight'. One evening, Davis recalled, when the two of them were both hungry and penniless, Harry offered to 'fix it' by pawning a small bronze statuette. He returned delightedly some time later saying he had raised $5. Then, just as they reached Campi's restaurant, Harry 'remarked that he was still broke'. He had given $2 to one of the Kearny Street begging women whom, he said, 'I can never pass', had lent $2 to Dan O'Connell, 'which, of course, is gone forever', and, happening to see the names of two congenial ladies in the register of the Occidental Hotel, had spent his last $1 on sending up flowers. In the balance of this tale, the pair of them order a meal in Campi's anyway, and while they eat Harry relates half of a story so tense and funny that a departing eavesdropper at the next table, successfully begging to have the denouement whispered to him, voluntarily pays their bill on his way out. Sam Davis was a compulsive yarn-spinner himself. Still, the nature of this tribute is revealing.

It was no accident that Davis set his story inside Campi's restaurant. Benjamin Lloyd, in his guide to the city, wrote about coffee houses, oyster 'grottoes' and lunch rooms in 'bewildering abundance', explaining that the sign 'Furnished Rooms to Rent' was aimed at 'restaurant-livers' of 'the "shabby genteel" class', whose own 'worldly effects' were 'nothing but the clothes they have on their backs. The cheap restaurant feeds them.' As for Campi's, it had 'high repute' in struggling circles, with charges 'a little higher' than elsewhere, and was especially known for its macaroni.

Lloyd's picture, applicable to Harry and Sam Davis, would be confirmed by Robert Louis Stevenson. The 'strange vicissitude' that brought him to the city in 1880 was that of having fallen in love with a married American, Fanny Osbourne. Stevenson's father cut him off in dismay, leaving Stevenson to become for some time one of the city's impoverished writers, so unwell that he actively hoped not to die before Fanny's divorce was completed, in order that they might still marry. In letters to friends at home, he described barely managing just the sort of shabby existence Lloyd detailed, in furnished rooms on Bush Street. For ten cents Stevenson breakfasted at the Pine Street Coffee House on a bread roll, a scrape of butter and a cup of coffee. At midday he ate a fifty-cent meal at Donadieu, with a half-bottle of wine, coffee and brandy. Then, at about six, he repeated his breakfast. To feed the fire in his room, he split sticks and lumps of coal on his windowsill using a little hatchet. It was a great mercy that food in San Francisco was so cheap, he wrote; and it must have seemed even more so when he was forced to reduce his outlay on his main meal by half. He was welcomed at the Bohemian Club, but was disappointed to find that drink had become 'more the order of the day than wit'.

A particular instance of Harry's kindness in poverty was the hand he held out to an unattractive Englishman with journalistic pretensions, Edward Ellis, described by one newspaper as 'a heavy-set, black-whiskered, pale, nervous person, with a manner of usually elaborate and distressing civility, bordering close on servility'. San Francisco was 'a bad location for Bohemians who do not pack their own blankets and steal chickens', and when Ellis was comparatively on his beam ends, labouring in a restaurant, Harry offered him quarter in his lodgings and even shared a few dimes with him in return for help with drudge work on an early 'London Letter' for the *Post*. Soon enough, though, Ellis struck lucky and secured his own job as a dramatic critic on the *Chronicle*.

*

Harry never would shake his 'discreditable notoriety' in San Francisco. But as the weeks passed, he must have felt encouraged in his project of redeeming himself, at least among his Bohemian friends. Many of them came to accept that Neil's fraud charge had itself been a fraud: that Neil had initially 'furnished the money of his own free will, and to secure the companionship of Larkyns', only later refiguring this as a debt. Furthermore, some wrongly but conveniently understood Neil's intemperate vendetta against Harry to be the cause of Harry's current pennilessness, believing that because Neil had 'brought all this trouble on him, his family were completely estranged from him'. Some accounts also later concurred in giving as a suppressed reason for the pair's ruinous breach that Neil had pursued a young woman in Honolulu while 'suffering from an incurable desease [*sic*]'. Harry had denounced him 'for his course towards the young lady', and it was this that caused their 'serious quarrel'. Sam Davis put this even more strongly, stating that Harry had intervened, recognising that for Neil 'to seek to mate with any woman' would be a 'terrible outrage against humanity'. A suggestion of, it seems, syphilis, is as close as the record ever gets to filling in the ellipsis left by the *Chronicle* in its printing of Harry's stinging letter to Neil. Meanwhile, it had been contempt, Davis added, with charming faith, that had prompted Harry to offer Neil financial restitution, courtesy of Henrietta Coffin, as he 'did not wish to be under any manner of obligation to the creature'.

Whatever veils Harry now draped over his past, after his 'stormy introduction' to San Francisco he did manage to establish himself with exemplary speed as a working writer on one of the city's most interesting newspapers. Because the *Post* was an evening title, copy deadlines fell in the afternoons. A typical day for him would therefore have embraced a stint of writing, a cheap lunch in one of the city's countless coffee houses and restaurants, the occasional popular entertainment in the afternoon, free entry to one of the city's theatres almost every evening, and often, no doubt, a glass at the Bohemian Club in the small hours, where, blessedly, being poor was almost fashionable. At the weekends, too, Harry sometimes went to the Recreation Ground for a practice session of cricket. He was described in this period as 'Warm-hearted, impulsive, sorely tried and hard-working'. And if his reputation remained raggedy with some, at least in San Francisco this in a measure protected him from any temptation to venture on a sustained 'plan of rascality' once again.

There was, however, a different form of misappropriation that remained open to Harry, as property then tended to be understood: a desire to have and to hold that he could not bring himself to resist. By high summer of 1873, he had fallen precipitously in love with a young woman who was, at the same time, another man's wife.

11: Flora

Flora Muybridge was described by the press as 'a handsome woman of petite but plump figure', with 'large, tender blue eyes and a profusion of beautiful wavy brown hair'; and again as 'petite, but voluptuous, with a sweet face and large, lustrous eyes'. She was also credited with 'more than average intelligence' and a 'fascinating manner'. One garbled account of her childhood said that she was from a 'good Kentucky family', but lost her mother 'very early in life'; and that she was thereafter 'reared' for some years by a stepmother, before, aged thirteen, being brought to California by an uncle, 'Capt. T. J. Stumpf', and left with an aunt, Mrs Downs, who placed her in Mills Seminary in Oakland. A later account suggested that she had been fostered by a Captain Shallcross.

In 1860, Thomas J. Stump and William D. Shallcross, aged twenty-six and thirty-two, rented adjacent dwellings in Sacramento. They were adequately well-to-do, with personal wealth of $2,000 each. Both were river pilots, or 'steamboatmen'. Shallcross had survived a disaster in 1856, piloting the *Belle* on the Sacramento River, when the boiler exploded, causing the vessel to sink with the loss of some thirty lives. Both men were married, Stump with two small children. And their wives, Flora Stump and Sarah Shallcross, both from Ohio, shared the maiden name 'Frazier'.

Among the designated 'Passengers for California' arriving into San Francisco on the *Constitution* in February 1863, was 'Flora E. Downs', born in Ohio and a month off turning thirteen. As she later called the Stumps her uncle and aunt, and was herself described as 'the niece of the wife of Captain Shallcross', presumably Mrs Stump, Mrs Shallcross and Flora's deceased mother were all three Frazier sisters. It was the Shallcrosses who now took the young girl in. William Shallcross spent almost the whole of the 1860s working as a captain for the California Steam Navigation Company, 'plying both between Marysville and Sacramento, and

San Francisco'. Stump, though, by 1862 was plying north, between Redding and Red Bluff, and by 1865 had moved further north again, to Oregon.

Flora became known for a while as Lily Shallcross. But nowhere does she appear in the records of the institution shortly to become Mills Seminary in Oakland. Any schooling she received was therefore humbler. And soon enough, anyway, she left the immediate orbit of the Shallcrosses for the bright lights of San Francisco. There, aged sixteen, she landed a job as a clerk selling fancy goods in Ackerman's at 123 Kearny Street, a dollar store advertised as a 'Grand Central Variety Establishment' with 'thousands of beautiful articles'. At night, until the clock struck ten, Kearny was 'a brilliant scene of gayety and life', twinkling with 'thousands of burners and reflectors in the windows of the shops and stores'. It was also a resort for 'glances of recognition' and 'casual meetings', and had its 'higher-class houses of prostitution'. The song 'Clementina Moore', issued in 1869 by the music publisher Matthias Gray, conveys the default idea of 'The Girl in the Dollar Store'. A mere glimpse of her causes a young man to go weak at the knees, and he walks in: 'Just at this point the boss came up. He thought I was a thief, / or else had come to swindle her was surely his belief', etc. The 'Lady Correspondent' of a Marysville paper gave a less winking picture of these social perils. San Francisco was 'filled with a set of dissipated, no-principled young men', she wrote, who did not scruple to accost young women with improprieties. They were 'the terror of lonely females and the aversion of all'.

Flora did not sit still amid the commercial glitter and the glances. Whether she sought greater security, new excitements, or perhaps both, in the summer of 1867 she stepped back out from behind her shop counter to marry. A line in the press noted: 'In this city, July 11th, at the residence of Capt. W. P. Bromley, by the Rev. H. A. Sawtelle, Lucius E. Stone to Flora E. Downs, both of San Francisco.' She was still only sixteen. Lucius was twenty-four.

It is possible Flora had been lodging with Captain Bromley, his wife and daughter. At any rate, as Bromley shared the profession of her uncles, it does seem she had a confederacy of steamboatmen looking out for her. And on paper her marriage was a coup.

Lucius's father, Rockwell, had started out in a saddlery business in Sacramento, but moved his family to San Francisco in 1864, Lucius immediately going to work for him as a clerk or salesman. In 1870, as an 'importer hardware', Rockwell's wealth would be recorded in the census at $110,000. Lucius was simultaneously registered as having no money, but by any ordinary measure the Stone family was already rich; and it was getting richer fast. On Rockwell's death in 1883, Lucius and his mother, Sophia, would find themselves joint inheritors of well over half a million dollars.

The Stones were flourishing even in 1867, when Flora and Lucius wed. However, as a 'lady friend' later divulged to the press, the pair of them 'lived very unhappily and soon separated'. Intriguingly, they are missing from the two editions of the city directory that span their time together. Lucius then reappears in the edition of December 1869, once more working for his father, and back living with his parents in their new home at 713 California. It would have been a strong gesture for him to move out of the family home. After splitting from Flora, he lived back with his parents for over a decade.

Flora, her 'lady friend' continued, supported herself through 1869 and 1870 working in the successive Montgomery Street galleries of the artists and photographers, the Nahl brothers. She was employed behind the scenes as a retoucher, no doubt hunched over a plate stand with a fine paintbrush and a magnifying glass. At the most basic level this job required dotting out, on a varnished, glass-plate negative, the dust flecks and chemical splotches that would otherwise mar a developing image. There was also the delicate job, on request, of tinting black-and-white prints with colour. In a good establishment, a hierarchy of such backstage workers was topped by trained artists, all with their tricks of the trade. Ground cuttlefish bone and other powders were used to lift varnish and chemicals from a plate; and lead pencil, or finely painted inks and reds, were applied to give finer gradations of shade. Meagre tresses could be plumped, battered complexions smoothed, portly figures slimmed and more. The Nahls, both classically trained painters themselves, solicited 'any kind of Artist Work', including 'Copying from small faded pictures'. And they were praised for 're-touched and coloured photographs' that were 'second to none'. Flora could hardly have learnt her new skills anywhere better. And so it was, after roughly a year, that she came to be entrusted with 'painting photographs' for a new business associate of the Nahls, Edward James Muybridge.

Muybridge had first attempted to make a life for himself in San Francisco in 1855, in his mid twenties, under the name 'Muygridge'. He was originally from Kingston upon Thames in England, and had tried his luck selling books in New York, before he brought his business to an upstairs address at 113 Montgomery Street. Advertisements from the time show him soliciting subscriptions for the complete works of Shakespeare, a multi-volume *New American Cyclopedia*, a history of the Indian Mutiny, and so on. For a holiday promotion at the end of 1857, he boasted of having the finest books 'ever offered for sale in California', smartly bound and 'admirably adapted for placing on the center table'. Muygridge also acted as a moneylender on the side, in which capacity he was cited that same year as an innocent contributor to the suicide of Joseph Washington Finley. Finley, a 'very amiable' man, to mitigate a $50 fine for assault and battery, asked a friend called Hampton to borrow $30 on his behalf from Muygridge. When Finley failed to repay Hampton the $30 as agreed, Hampton wrote to him urgently: 'Mr. Muygridge will sue me if your note is not paid to-morrow, and I don't wish to believe that you will suffer this.' In reply, Finley, 'laboring under great depression of spirits', cried out, 'Damn Hampton', and shot himself in the head, leaving his brains 'scattered around the room'.

In 1858, Muygridge moved his business to 163 Clay Street, where a friend from New York, Silas Selleck, had set up as a 'daguerreian artist' with his own photographic gallery. Where Muygridge battled among throngs of advertisers to promote his 'beautifully embellished' books, he found himself receiving free publicity in the press when he sold a 'very beautiful photograph' of the Golden Gate by the landscape photographer Carleton Watkins, said to be the only shot to give 'a perfect delineation of the beautiful passage-way that connects San Francisco harbour with the ocean', and therefore recommended to all who 'procure views in California for preservation'.

Muygridge had entered the San Francisco book market at exactly the same time, and on the same street, as Hubert Howe Bancroft, whose 'Wholesale Book Store, Stationery and Publishing House' soon took over 151 Montgomery top to bottom: 'dark, uneven, with stairs in the most unexpected places, cut up by shelves running in all directions, and every inch of space utilized—the whole establishment as busy and orderly as a beehive'. It was when Bancroft's business burst these bounds that he constructed his edifice on Market Street, with its literary factory on the fifth floor. Comparatively, Muygridge remained a commercial minnow. In 1859 he had the satisfaction of being voted one of nine directors of the city's Mercantile Library Association; but at about the same time he began extracting himself from various obligations. Before long, the music dealer Matthias Gray 'took his store', and in the summer of 1860 Muygridge quit San Francisco to return to England.

In Texas, as Muygridge travelled overland east, the mustangs drawing his stagecoach ran out of control, hit a stump and capsized the vehicle. All the passengers were badly injured, and two died. After nine days in a coma, Muygridge emerged with symptoms of brain impairment. Everything, he later said, 'was to my vision two'. He had 'no taste, no smell, and was very deaf; had a scab upon my head; was troubled with a bad headache'. He made his way to London, where for a year he sought treatment from William Gull, later knighted as physician to Queen Victoria. Muygridge instituted legal proceedings against the stage company for $10,000, eventually settling for a quarter of that sum, nevertheless a useful pot of money to sustain him.

Though his family name was actually Muggeridge, back in England he initially stuck to 'Muygridge'. Under this name, for example, on 1 August 1861, he patented 'machinery or apparatus for washing clothes and other textile articles'. To no great effect, he took out a second patent in Paris, and exhibited the device in an industrial annexe of the 1862 International Exhibition in Kensington: the 'Albertopolis'. Muygridge was an aspiring capitalist too. So it was, in June 1865, apparently for the first time, that he became 'Edward J. Muybridge, Esq. (late of California)', a director of the brand-new Austin Consolidated Silver Mines Company, under the chairmanship of Freeman Harlow Morse; Morse, US

Consul in London, had had a mandate from Lincoln throughout the Civil War to oversee vital foreign surveillance and espionage. Austin Consolidated promoted ten-shilling shares to speculators to help fund crushing mills for prospective finds of ore. In November that same year, 'Edward J Muybridge, Esq.' was listed again, this time as one of nine directors soliciting capital via the Ottoman Company for a new 'Bank of Turkey'. The timing, however, was unfortunate. This was exactly the period of financial turbulence that culminated in the collapse of Overend Gurney, and none of these ventures thrived.

Muybridge himself much later summed up this spell by saying that 'all of the time since 1860' he had been 'diligently, and at the same time studiously, engaged in photography'.

Muybridge arrived back in San Francisco on the Pacific Mail steamship *Golden City* on 13 February 1867, appearing on the passenger list as 'Mr. Maybridge'. For years to come, the first syllable of his refashioned surname would be misspelt 'May', 'Moy' and 'My'. But then, in its own way, a name that was overthought and awkward was fitting. In 1882, he would adopt a new spelling for his first name as well, 'Eadweard', causing the joke to ripple out across the press, as far as Derry in Ireland, that this Anglo-Saxon affectation was evidently 'an eadvertisement'.

On his return to San Francisco, now aged thirty-six, Muybridge's friends, including Silas Selleck and Matthias Gray, found him noticeably grey-haired, newly eccentric, irritable, careless of dress and undependable in business, changes they ascribed to his stage-coach accident seven years earlier. He simply did not seem 'the same man in any respect since'. He brought back with him photographic goods for sale worth some three or four thousand dollars, though he insisted on giving Selleck whatever he wanted. At the same time, he planned to follow in the footsteps of the photographer Carleton Watkins and to travel to Yosemite. And indeed, come October, a roving press reporter noted that 'Mr. Maybridge, of San Francisco, is here, taking photographs of the Valley and its surroundings, and has a fine collection of negatives.'

The following spring, Muybridge advertised that Yosemite views by 'Helios' were soon to be available from Muybridge at Silas Selleck's gallery, now relocated to 415 Montgomery. 'Helios', Greek for 'sun', was used as a business name by photographers right around the world at a time when photographs were still referred to as 'sun pictures'. Among subscribers for the prints were, Muybridge wrote in his advertisement, 'all the eminent artists, and most of the gentlemen distinguished for their cultivated taste in this city, who pronounce them to be the most wonderful and artistic photographs ever taken on this coast'. Gratifyingly, a jury of his photographic peers on the East Coast agreed that, 'indefatigable and untiring', he had 'outdone all competitors'. Closer to home, the *Alta* found that some of his work showed 'just such cloud effects as we see in nature or oil painting, but almost never in a photograph', the 'peculiar atmospheric effects' of 'floating clouds' and 'low-hanging mists' revealing 'the devotion of a true artist'. After this, Muybridge let his guard down so far as to advertise himself as '"Helios" working through the mediumship of Edward J. Muybridge'.

The artistic value of even an outstanding photograph was much disputed in this period, so that after praising Muybridge's work the *Alta* concluded bathetically that his Yosemite images should inspire 'meritorious home art'. It was a month after this, in March of 1868, that Bancroft published *Yosemite: Its Wonders and Beauties*, by the *Alta* writer John S. Hittell, with twenty Yosemite views by 'Helios'. In the preface Hittell explained that photographs were included, 'because no engravings could do justice to the scenes, or convey perfect confidence in the accuracy of the drawing of such immense elevations'. This paean to photographic accuracy did not mean that Muybridge scrupled to manipulate his images. He created, for example, many 'Moonlight Effect' pictures taken during the day. And as the exposure times for darker landscapes and bright skies were liable to be very different, he often also spliced separate shots of the two, creating a composite. The writer Helen Hunt Jackson was impressed, calling the result 'true', Muybridge having eliminated 'the usual ghastly, lifeless, pallid, stippled sky'. Popular painting styles were currently going to another extreme, leading Mark Twain to rebuke the renowned painter Albert Bierstadt, also in the *Alta*, for Yosemite images 'altogether too gorgeous', with 'more the atmosphere of Kingdom-Come than of California'. Muybridge presented some of his Yosemite prints to the directors of the Mercantile Library, along with a Uriah Heep-ish letter that ended, 'Your worthy ex President whom I believe to be considerable of a connoisseur expressed a desire to have them framed and placed in some desirable place in the new building, should this be concurred in by the rest of the board I shall feel highly flattered.'

In September 1868, Muybridge accompanied a government expedition to the recently acquired territory of Alaska. Under the heading 'Helios Rampant', a journalist described how, with 'shirt-sleeves rolled up, and hair on end, he trotted his flying studio through town while the daylight lasted', capturing images later deemed to be better than 'any written description'. In both portfolio and stereoscopic form, by which paired pictures appeared three-dimensional, seen through a special viewer, Muybridge's work was sold by Bradley & Co. on Clay Street, the address from which Henry Bradley sold photographic and ambrotype materials. Next month, the press noted that 'A Gensoul, on Montgomery Street, has published a number of interesting photographs, by "Helios," of buildings most damaged by the great earthquake.' But for all this, Muybridge remained primarily located with Silas Selleck. His advertising stated that 'HELIOS is prepared to accept commissions to photograph Private Residences, Ranches, Mills, Views, Animals, Ships, etc., anywhere in the city, or any portion of the Pacific Coast.' He also offered to copy the drawings of engineers, surveyors and architects, and to make 'Photographic copies of Paintings and Works of Art'. In March 1869, he snatched an image of the notorious and much-loved San Francisco character Emperor Norton, or 'Norton I, Emperor of California and Protector of Mexico, *Dei Gratia*', as he rode a bicycle at a Velocipedestrian School. Emperor Norton exercised a shadow rule over the city in which the populace cheerfully conspired, his face 'a free ticket for him' anywhere he wished to go. Yet when 'his Imperial Majesty', thoroughly displeased, 'issued a decree prohibiting the sale of the photographs', Muybridge ignored him and sold them anyway. Perhaps Muybridge paid more attention when he came up as 'delinquent' regarding land stocks of $122.50 in a 'Homestead Association', a business listed at Silas Selleck's 415

Emperor Norton: photograph by Muybridge

Montgomery address. Soon afterwards, he shifted his trade down the road to 121 Montgomery instead. He had decided to take his business to the Nahls.

In the 1870 census, Flora gave her profession as 'Artist'. She formed a household of one, and was supposedly aged twenty-one, with personal wealth of $700. As she was actually nineteen, she perhaps also exaggerated her nest egg, claiming roughly a year's wages to give herself extra status. Then again, it is also possible that the Stones had paid her off, or wished to keep her from falling too low. After all, on paper she remained Lucius's wife.

Flora had had an extremely unstable life so far. By the age of thirteen she had been bereaved or permanently deprived of her mother, father and stepmother. Four years later, plumb in the middle of her marital turbulence with Lucius, her aunt and proxy mother, Sarah Shallcross, died. A year after that, for good or ill, Flora lost Rockwell and Sophia Stone as functional parents-in-law too. The nearest parental figure she had still standing in 1870 was therefore William Shallcross. In January that year, he opted for his own fresh start, marrying a Miss Lucy C. Baldwin, the thirty-four-year-old daughter of a Marysville jeweller. But nine months later he succumbed to 'ulceration of the bowels', and he too died. This left the Stumps, away in Oregon, as Flora's closest adult relatives.

Towards the end of 1870, Flora gave her boarding-house address to a canvasser who was gathering information for Langley's city directory, due out in April 1871. She would appear there as 'Stone Flora Mrs., dwl 6 Montgomery', with Lucius listed a few entries below, back with his parents at 713 California, in a neighbourhood of bankers, stockbrokers and wine merchants. Six Montgomery, by contrast, was a commercial building on the same great thoroughfare as Flora's workplace, with a few furnished rooms in the attics. Her neighbours up there included two carpenters, a boiler-maker and a hairdresser, while lower down, among others, Olney & Co. plied their trade as auctioneers, Horace E. Pope dealt in postage stamps, and Grover & Baker dispatched agents to promote their elastic shuttle-stitch sewing machines. Montgomery, like Kearny, was a fancy shopping street, 'resplendent with gaudy displays'. It was also the address of many of the city's foremost hotels, and gave access to the best theatres. But, unlike Kearny, once the gas was lit at night it was 'almost deserted'.

As a fresh expression of her independence, in December 1870, Flora secured a divorce from Lucius. Legitimate grounds for this in San Francisco's court system included adultery, desertion, and the frequently asserted catch-all, 'extreme cruelty'. A strong, adversarial case was imperative. In 1869, a California newspaper reported with derision an attempt in a Michigan court to present an application jointly, 'whereas my wife being Entirely Repugnant to my mind, and whereas I am entirely Repugnant to her mind'. Henry George reported that, nevertheless, there was 'one divorce granted in San Francisco for every three marriages', those divorces often 'got in a single day': too easy, he thought. 'If I ever had any leaning to the modern doctrine in this matter I have entirely got over it.' When Walter Fisher mused on the same topic, he wrote of San Francisco as the home of a type, the 'mysteriously' respectable woman, 'nothing coarse, nothing depraved about her', who nevertheless acted as a 'Venus's fly-trap'. Given 'the fewness of her sex and the laxness of the law', she was able to 'glide from divorce court to divorce court, sucking husband after husband dry', discarding each in turn to 'gain a higher place'. This woman, wrote Fisher, was 'something to chill the blood of an octopus'.

Beyond a default charge of 'extreme cruelty', the only information on Flora's divorce would come much later, from Muybridge: 'She told me that the trouble between her and Stone was inequality of age', along with 'incompatibility of temper and cruel treatment of her by him and his mother'. But something more than this is hinted at by Lucius's behaviour after his father died. Lucius then inherited $300,000, half of Rockwell's wealth, and with his mother became manager and joint owner of Rockwell's businesses. Yet within five years, the 'odor' of trade proved too 'common' for him, and Lucius sold out. After this, incredibly, in two years flat, he burned through half a million dollars. As well as vast sums lost in land speculation, he threw away money on carpets, jewellery, furs, pictures, carriages, pianos, not to mention a steam launch. He even bought his way into the Bohemian Club, now heavily overloaded with 'weaving spiders,' so that many original members had quit; Oscar Wilde reputedly quipped after a fleeting visit that he had never seen 'so many well-dressed, well-fed, business-looking Bohemians' in his life. Lucius had got himself 'in the lurch all along the line', and filed for insolvency without warning, leaving financial wreckage behind him 'singularly complete, total and entire'. In light of this catastrophe, his union with Flora looks like a foreshadowing of a greater rebellion to come.

Within three months of his divorce from Flora, on 29 March 1871, Lucius remarried. His new bride, Miss Idelia Baker, twenty-two, had previously kept house for her widowed father, a retired merchant. The speed of this new match makes it highly unlikely that the Stone family had put up barriers to the divorce. Idelia moved in with Lucius and his parents, and they remained like this, as a joint household, for the next ten years.

Muybridge later defensively disputed the idea that he had had 'any agency' in securing Flora's divorce from Lucius: 'I never counselled her to get it, and did not assist her in it in any way.' She had been employed 'by him in his gallery to retouch photographs', he suggested, but that was all: 'I was acquainted with her in this way, but not intimately.' The *Post* was more jaundiced when it wrote that

Flora was 'just the woman to make an impression on a cynic like Muybridge', being 'petite but voluptuous looking', with 'a wealth of dark brown hair' and 'a sweet, winning face and large eyes of tender blue'. Rather more pragmatically, Muybridge may well have been drawn to the idea of folding an accomplished young wife into the exacting process of perfecting his finished prints. As he himself noted, retouching was customary with 'all first-class photographic work', to give 'a better effect to the details'.

Flora's own retrospective account of her early transactions with Muybridge would prove to be very different, and her details have the force of being oddly specific. As summarised by a press reporter: 'shortly after they were engaged to be married he appeared devoted to her and employed counsel to procure a divorce from her husband, and said he would pay the expenses'. Then:

> the day after the divorce he gave her $30 to purchase clothing, etc. She refused to spend it according to his capricious wishes, and the day following he abused her and demanded the money back. She returned it to him, and all matters between them were at an end. He renewed his attentions again, and threatened that if she did not marry him he would be revenged upon her. She was in his employment, and depended upon him for a living, and so consented to marry him.

This scarcely conforms to the San Francisco cliché of the 'Venus's fly-trap', trading husbands in order to 'gain a higher place'. One small clue, at least, suggests that Flora did indeed arrive late at her final decision to wed Muybridge. After its annual canvass, Langley's city directory always flooded the press with calls for last-minute corrections. And in 1871, the last appeal for emendations appeared on 19 March. 'Stone Flora Mrs., dwl 6 Montgomery' was destined to become redundant exactly nine weeks later. But Flora allowed the entry to stand.

On 22 March, after a 101-gun salute, a grand 'Peace Celebration by the German Citizens of San Francisco', with the Nahl brothers prominent among them, marked the end of the Franco–Prussian War. A parade followed, with bands, buglers and mounted Uhlans, the terror of France's *francs-tireurs* in the Vosges, as well as three 'triumphal wagons' designed by Charles Nahl. Then in April the brothers removed their gallery to 12 Montgomery Street, where they advertised 'Skylights built after new and approved rules' for photography, and 'all other improvements latest discoveries have applied to the art'. Muybridge moved his business with them. And Flora's account implies that it was his patronage that ensured she now kept her job too. What is indisputable is that it was just a month after the move that the two of them actually wed.

Press announcements of their marriage, with slightly differing dates and spellings, declared: 'In San Francisco, May 30th, Edward J. Maybridge to Flora E. Downs', and 'in this city, May 20, by the Rev. Mr. Sawtelle, Edward J. Muybridge to Flora E. Downs'. Flora had recently turned twenty; Muybridge was now forty-one. It seems he found inequality of age in his own marriage no concern. Strikingly, Sawtelle, who had officiated when Flora married Lucius four years earlier, presided over her nuptials a second time. He was a kindly Baptist who preferred to be on 'liberal terms of communion and fellowship' with all his Christian brethren, and can only have thought that, after all the chaos in her life, this new marriage would set her up for good.

Muybridge had now been selling his prints through the Nahl brothers for a year. Between more ambitious projects, he still sought work in something of a jobbing capacity, and also advertised his 'flying studio' for hire to any photographer interested in 'open air work'. Among San Francisco subjects, he was selling pictures of Woodward's Gardens and other popular attractions; from further afield, railroad views. But a recent press notice calling his pictures 'beautiful specimens of the sun painter's art' scarcely matched the praise for his work in Yosemite, and in November the *Philadelphia Photographer* reported: '"Helios" hopes to go to the Valley again some time soon, when he promises to secure us some more splendid subjects.' It was a fine ambition, but for this Muybridge needed substantial new backing.

At some point during that autumn, Flora endured the woe of a stillbirth. And she would suffer a second in the months that

Muybridge's business card for 121 Montgomery

followed. These distressing deliveries were later revealed to the press by the nurse who attended her, Susan Smith, and they raise the small thought that Flora's marriage to Lucius might have involved a failed pregnancy too.

Muybridge continued to wish, or wished to continue, as he saw it, to eclipse all other landscape photographers, and in early spring 1872, produced a series of pictures of the Buena Vista vineyard in Sonoma County. He also advertised the fact that he had been 'employed by the Lighthouse Board and the Treasury and War Departments in executing numerous photographs required by them upon this coast'. Meanwhile, he pressed on with a prospectus seeking new Yosemite subscribers at $100 each: 'At the suggestion of several artists and patrons of Art', he wrote, and bearing in mind 'improvement in the science of photographic manipulation', his aim was to return there and to devote 'the approaching season to the production of a series of large-size photographic negatives'. This was an enormous undertaking at a time when 'Every photographer was, in great measure, his own chemist; he prepared his own dipping baths, made his own collodion, coated and developed his own plates, and frequently manufactured the chemicals necessary for his work.' Photographing outdoors and away from civilisation required mules, tents, large cameras, chemicals, food, ropes, assistants, a gun.

Muybridge and Flora had initially 'commenced housekeeping' together. But as his 'business and habits' militated against this respectable style of living, when at last he had enough Yosemite backers, Muybridge, in the true San Francisco style, shifted their household into a set of furnished rooms at 32 Fourth Street. And presumably he had already disappeared into the soaring wilderness when Wilson, Hood & Co. commenced suit against him to recover $762.28 for goods sold and delivered in April. Flora now carried on alone, living in a boarding house also occupied by a bookkeeper, an attorney, a ship's joiner, a plumber and the like. Nor would this remain her home for very long. The following year, she and Muybridge would shift again to rooms on Howard; and the year after that, to 112 Fourth, living above Hartshorn & McPhun, specialists in 'upholstery, paperhanging and window shades'.

Presumably Flora read a piece in the *Alta* early in November under the title 'Industrial Condition of the Slope', reporting on a kind of picture rush in Yosemite. Various painters, Albert Bierstadt among them, were out capturing 'the disposition of effect and color'. And notwithstanding a 'multitude' of existing photographs, 'Mr. Muybridge is now there, and Mr. Watkins will start in a few days.' A second *Alta* article explained how, 'sparing no pains' to achieve the best views, Muybridge 'cut down trees by the score that interfered with the camera from the best point of sight', and sometimes lugged his equipment himself, going 'where his packers refused to follow him', or had himself 'lowered by ropes down precipices'. He also determinedly waited 'several days' if need be 'to get the proper conditions of atmosphere'. His friends at the *Philadelphia*

Photographer wrote more poetically that capturing Yosemite was 'not ordinary work', and 'aye a year would not do it all'. For a photographer entering the valley, 'oh! how overwhelming the sight! First he totters with fright at the task before him. The sublimity, the awful loneliness and desolation, the marvellousness', not to mention the 'excruciating' expectations. 'Oh! what a privilege to be in such a place with a camera. There is everlasting food for it there.' Everlasting maybe: Muybridge returned home in late November with 800 negatives.

Once back, Muybridge shifted his business yet again, this time up Montgomery Street to the establishment of Henry Bradley and William Herman Rulofson at number 429. Bradley may have been the city's largest importer of photographic materials, but the

BRADLEY & RULOFSON'S
CELEBRATED PHOTOGRAPH GALLERY,
CORNER SACRAMENTO & MONTGOMERY STREETS, ENTRANCE 429 MONTGOMERY, SAN FRANCISCO.

reputation of the gallery was acknowledged to be 'more particularly due to the ernest enterprise of Mr. Rulofson'. They had recently knocked through from 429 into the next-door building to create a 'palace of art', with reception rooms, 'operating rooms' or studios, and 'dressing boudoirs for the ladies', as well as finishing rooms, including printing and 'bath-rooms'. In built-up cities, photographers were driven to work on the top floors, in pursuit of the best light. Rulofson claimed enticingly that 'the higher you get, the purer the rays of the sun'. But this left flights of stairs as a penalty for a weary customer; and so, from 1872, Bradley & Rulofson also trumpeted the wonderful boast on its backstamps that it had 'The only Elevator connected with Photography in the World'.

The gallery was best known for its portraits, offering, comparatively, 'tone better, attitudes more graceful, less of a studied effect and more of natural ease'. In the inarticulate praise of one rural newspaper, the results manifested 'merits of which we cannot even refer to'. Sitters were kept motionless with hidden 'hooks, prongs and sticks, set behind', and Rulofson, having 'exploded' the truism that a subject must not sit in front of a light source, sought 'the softest and most satisfactory effects'. His top-tier 'corps of assistants', each 'an artist in his own speciality', was presided over by Max Bachert, who ruled the operating rooms and determined 'the *pose* of the subject to be pencilled in by the sun's ray'. Then the pictures were finished somewhere in the 'upper regions' of 429. There the plates themselves were retouched, 'in small rooms from which the light is excluded except from a small opening exactly the size of the negative'. With every defect thus illuminated, and using 'fine camel's hair', it was possible to 'tone down' infelicities: a furrowed brow could be 'relieved of wrinkles', and a cheek 'made plump and rounded'. By 1873, Bradley & Rulofson employed over thirty artists, and offered 'Retouched Bust Photographs', 'Crayon Photographs In Delicate Velvet Frames', 'Ivory Miniatures' for lockets, and so on. A portrait of Emily Soldene from 1877 shows just how accomplished the work was. British photographs did little to conceal what she herself called her 'beefy' figure. At Bradley & Rulofson, age and excess were dusted away.

Muybridge shifted his operations there in part to make use of the company's superior finishing and printing processes. Rulofson, meanwhile, who had subscribed to both of Muybridge's Yosemite expeditions, clearly wished to expand his stake in the prestigious landscape market. Though Muybridge was on the up, and might have wanted his wife respectably 'keeping house', in fact he brought Flora with him again. She continued on as a retoucher at Bradley &

Emily Soldene photographed in London, mid 1870s

Soldene by Bradley & Rulofson, 1877

Rulofson part time, and may well have relished the change herself, not least as just about every celebrity who visited San Francisco left a 'shadow behind in this world renowned art gallery'.

Over Christmas 1872, the California Theatre put on a spectacular version of 'Aladdin's Lamp', somehow rendered Chinese. Audiences crushed in to see enchanting scenery, illuminated fountains, child acrobats, 'gorgeous dresses', the pantomime itself, and altogether bewildering loveliness, capped off by the gracefully amazing 'premiere danseuses', Emily and Betty Rigl. Once Emily Rigl had been to sit for Bradley & Rulofson, Flora picked out three bold portraits of her to keep.

It took until April 1873 for Muybridge to produce the first sets of his Yosemite prints, 'eight hundred of the most perfect photographs ever offered for public inspection—some of them gems of art', according to the *Alta*. The best of them, it added, 'should be taken as the subject for a great painting, and probably will be by Mr. Bierstadt'. But it would be a while before the general public might buy any, according to another review, 'as Mr. Moybridge will be weeks engaged in getting ready for delivery the copies already subscribed for'. A Bradley & Rulofson catalogue claimed that those subscribers, at $100 for thirty prints, had between them put up more than $20,000. In a later, anonymous assessment of his second Yosemite venture, Muybridge gave his photographs the credit of imparting to the world 'a realizing sense of the wonders of California scenery'.

Among the more prosaic commissions Muybridge had taken the year before, or so it may have seemed at the time, was the job of photographing the private residence of Leland Stanford, one of the figures excoriated by Henry George as an exploitative railway baron. Muybridge saw Stanford differently, explaining how, 'in the eternal fitness of things', he had been 'rewarded with fabulous wealth for the splendid and romantic daring that had built a railroad', across 'mighty mountain ranges' and through the hunting grounds of the 'savage red man', for ever uniting 'the civilized world with its dauntless vanguard on the Pacific slope'. With this great wealth Stanford 'determined to essay a very remarkable discovery', for which he needed the help of a photographer; and given that 'Mr. Muybridge had obtained such undisputed pre-eminence,' noted Muybridge later, 'it was to him that Mr. Stanford appealed'. Nearer to the time, it has to be said, Muybridge explained that the *Alta* editors had recommended him. In a further account, Muybridge spoke about how the motivating impulse had been to prove whether a horse at speed ever had all four feet 'simultaneously free from contact with the ground'. Stanford wished to solve this puzzle using his own racehorse, Occident, as the model. One journalist wrote about this creature: 'anti-railroad organs tell us that Occident is as big a fraud as old Stanford himself, and, like his master, is only useful in deceiving the people and beating them out of their money'. Others, though, celebrated Occident as expressing 'the very poetry of motion'.

According to press reports, Muybridge believed Stanford's challenge to be 'impossible'. All but the most experimental photographs still required their subject to be static; the rapids in Muybridge's own Yosemite pictures, for example, came out as a white blur. But his interest was piqued, and so he 'would make the effort'. After all, photography was a 'swiftly progressive art', with fierce competition to manufacture ever-faster cameras. In fact, so keen was the focus on speed that a new term for supposedly instantaneous exposures was the 'pistolgram'. But it was not until April 1873, while Muybridge's Yosemite prints were being manufactured in large numbers, that he was reported to have devised, finally, 'some special exposing apparatus' to meet Stanford's challenge. A story in the *Examiner* on the 7th explained that 'A few days ago he announced to the owner of "Occident" that he believed he could take the picture.' According to this article, 'Mr. Muybridge, the artist with the travelling studio', had 'expressed his doubts that it could be done', but 'began experimenting', and 'after a while was able to catch objects on the wing with great success'. Occident was trained to trot over numerous white sheets, arranged as a background, and after three days of trials and refinements Muybridge brilliantly 'secured a negative that shows "Occident" in full motion—a perfect likeness of the horse'. The picture, 'one atom of time', was, Muybridge later conceded, Occident merely in 'hazy outlines'. Yet the result was sufficiently clear to settle the question 'for once and for all time in favour of those who argued for a period of unsupported transit'. Under the jaunty title 'Quick Work', the *Alta* described this result as 'a great triumph as a curiosity in photography': 'a horse's picture taken while going thirty-eight feet in a second!' And the *Examiner* called it 'probably the most wonderful success in photographing ever yet achieved'.

Muybridge's hazy first result, which has not survived, remained a curiosity for some time to come. Not until 1877, after he and Stanford substantially extended and refined their experiments, would they win international fame for freezing the gait of horses. Nevertheless, the excitement of that first image is conveyed by Muybridge's later reflections, where he credits it with prompting further results 'probably more important to art than any other of the century'. He had to fight to get anything like general agreement for this immodest conclusion. Where his Yosemite pictures were often devalued as mere prompts for true artists, his horses in motion were for years devalued as aesthetically repellent. As one writer put it, although these 'singular' images might be valuable to science, Muybridge had proved that the '"poetry of motion" does not apply to that which has no motion'. In 1879, the *Illustrated London News* concurred. Though 'astonishing' and 'literally realistic',

Muybridge's revolutionary images showed how 'nearly every attitude of the galloping horse is grotesquely awkward and ungainly' and 'not pictorial'. An aghast English cavalry officer went so far as to denounce 'Professor Mybridge' for giving his beautiful subjects the look of 'so many lame cockroaches'.

Days after his groundbreaking shot of Occident, Muybridge was off again, this time under the aegis of the US War Department. On 25 April he passed through Marysville on his way to photograph one of the period's 'Indian Wars', when a small band of Modocs held out against the appropriation of their land. In his usual contorted style, Muybridge later explained that 'as such Government photographer Mr. Muybridge was dispatched to the front during the Modoc war, and the wide spread and accurate knowledge of the topography of the memorable Lava Beds and the country roundabout, and of the bravery of the few Indians who, with the bravery at least of the classic three hundred, defied and fought the Union, is due chiefly to the innumerable and valuable photographs taken by him'. He returned three weeks later and must have plunged straight back into the processing rooms at Bradley & Rulofson, as a week after that, and three days after his second wedding anniversary, the gallery was advertising his latest Modoc stereocards. Also on offer was a giant back catalogue of Muybridge's other work, including his Yosemite pictures, the Pacific Coast views, Alaska, Mammoth Trees, Geysers, and so on.

While Muybridge was busy with these endeavours, Orson Squire Fowler, leading phrenologist, women's rights advocate and the first publisher of Walt Whitman's *Leaves of Grass*, was delivering free lectures in San Francisco; on 'Female Health and Beauty' to ladies only, and to gentlemen on 'Manliness'. Fowler had recently produced his own book, *Sexual Science*, a near thousand-page work in which he argued that it was imperative to cultivate both male and female sexual fulfilment as 'the grand motor wheel of everything human'. His theories galvanised San Francisco audiences in general, and those under the roof at Bradley & Rulofson in particular, where, beyond merely photographing Fowler, Max Bachert was soon inspired to set up as his business manager.

*

It was some time during this same period, the early summer of 1873, that Harry made the shift from wharf rat to assistant in Bancroft's literary factory, establishing himself there as a charming, accomplished, indigent Bohemian; and a couple of months after that, that he became the theatre critic on the *Post*. Along the way, Harry's circle and that of the Muybridges began to overlap. Bancroft and Muybridge had been early rivals in the book trade, Bancroft then publishing photographs by 'Helios'. Harry Edwards, president of the Bohemian Club, knew Muybridge 'tolerably intimately' too. William Rulofson, meanwhile, himself a member of the Bohemian Club, and whose business photographed almost every theatrical celebrity to pass through town, ran a gallery that lured in everyone else who wished to see or buy the resulting prints. In an early review, Harry can be found musing directly on a Bradley & Rulofson portrait of Madame Anna Bishop, as taken by Max Bachert: Madame, now somewhere in her sixties, was ecstatic at a 'work of art', Harry revealed, that gave 'the impression of representing a lady of thirty-five at most'. And then, in and out upstairs, working in the printing rooms and darkrooms, according to their own erratic timetables, there were the Muybridges.

With, no doubt, many more connections than just these, Harry and Flora could have met in any number of ways. A *Post* colleague recorded straightforwardly that Harry was taken by a mutual acquaintance to the home of the Muybridges, where, with his 'fine personal appearance and varied acquirements', he made a 'decided impression upon both', becoming a 'constant visitor at their rooms'. To this thought must be added the rubric from Muybridge's advertising: he expected to be away for much of that summer season, 'constantly making additions to his superb and comprehensive collection of negatives'.

Rather than how or where exactly Harry and Flora first met, the more loaded question becomes when. It is, in fact, perfectly possible that he met her while he was still working at the literary factory: Thomas Arundel Harcourt, the fiery Bancroft assistant, would shortly marry Rulofson's daughter Fannie, and their courtship may well have been under way even as Harry was slaving among the 'little band of brothers'. But his own earliest recorded mention of

Flora's workplace was on 7 July. Writing about the singer Jule de Ryther, Harry remarked that he 'never saw a more perfect specimen of photography than a large portrait of her by Messrs. Bradley & Rulofson', being 'the ne plus ultra of photographic art'. In the end, though, whether or not he and Flora met before he took his *Post* job, it remains that the two of them must have fallen for each other extraordinarily fast. In the summer of 1873, possibly as early as mid July, Flora once more became pregnant. And, disastrously, Harry, no less than Muybridge, believed the child to be his.

12: Amusements

Harry's San Francisco friends overlooked his 'lamentable poverty of principle as well as purse' because to them his wit and grace stood for more. To them, he would never not be a 'true gentleman' either, as the term was then understood. Even eking out a precarious existence on Montgomery Street he radiated refinement and *savoir faire*, giving him 'easy access wherever his purposes directed him'. Flora must have seen at once that this put him in a different class from both of her husbands: Lucius Stone, on a path that would see him eventually capsize a family fortune to obliterate his decades as a clerk; and Edward Muggeridge, or Muygridge, or Muybridge, the eccentric, irritable and intensely driven son of a corn and small-coal merchant, whose family ran barges on the Thames. She must rapidly have discovered, too, that whatever the press chose to imply, Harry's war stories and battle scars were both literal and genuine. He really had served the Queen in India; really had been awarded the Legion d'honneur; and really was wounded while valorously serving France. On a more frivolous front, he had a madcap way of showering gifts on a woman he admired. And his Bohemian proclivities offered Flora a bridge into the intoxicating backstage world of San Francisco's theatres.

Flora was evidently no less enchanting herself. She was seven years younger than Harry, but cannot have been all that naïve, and would hardly have appealed to him if she were. However, where Harry's past pursuit of notorious women had been, in part, a social performance, to chase Flora conferred no cachet on her admirer. Harry's friends did not approve of her, and soon warned him to let her go. By falling in love, that is, the two of them defied everybody.

Beyond their raw attractiveness, what they shared may not have been apparent to outsiders. In particular, both had endured chaotic childhoods, suffering abandonment and orphanhood, finding themselves passed between aunts and other guardians, and transported

thousands of miles between states, countries and continents, staying nowhere very long. At just sixteen, Harry had parted from his
remaining relatives and embarked for India as a cadet, prospectively
committing himself there to a lifetime of military service. In the
end, he had fallen foul of the haphazard discipline applied to this
haphazard existence, but not before his unsteady Indian years had
set the pattern for a wandering, impetuous and sometimes shady
life thereafter. Flora, also at sixteen, had likewise left her remaining
family guardians, going to find work in San Francisco, entering
almost at once on a disastrous marriage, soon separating again, and
then divorcing; only to follow this with a second hasty marriage,
equally ill assorted. On their winding paths, the two of them had
certainly manifested grit. But both were also unguarded in their
desire for pleasure, leaving them vulnerable to the lure of wealthier
men, so that by the time they met, each was compromised in the
eyes of respectability. Despite this, both had so far survived the
trouble they had provoked, as well as the trouble that had come
to find them. Superficially, their backgrounds could hardly have
seemed more different, and yet they shared much to draw them
powerfully together. Whether their similarities made them a good
match – that was another question entirely.

In his public guise, Harry had taken to his reviewing work with
aplomb. And in addition to the free tickets he could now offer to
his friends, he soon found another way to capitalise on the access it
gave him. From early August, the stage at the California Theatre was
ruled by the actress Charlotte Thompson, who had been causing a
'furore' across America with her own version of *Jane Eyre*. Charlotte
Brontë, after failing to secure a publisher for her Brussels novel *The
Professor*, stooped to giving her next manuscript lurid touches, and
later wrote about Mrs Rochester with remorse: 'I have erred in
making <u>horror</u> too predominant.' But Thompson took *The New Jane
Eyre* to further extremes, dragging the story fully into the popular
realm of accidents, secrets, comedy servants and dubious aristocrats,
'Lord' Rochester included. Without compromising himself, Harry
tried to admire these efforts in his *Post* columns, asking generously
of Thompson, 'who would criticise the setting when the gem is

faultless'. When it came to her greatest San Francisco success, however, an extravaganza called *The Sea of Ice*, all he really praised was the staging: a 'magnificent triumph of scenic art', with the Aurora Borealis created by gas and magnesium lights behind painted gauze, and cold air pumped through the theatre. Thompson's Juliet also left him unmoved; and her farewell benefit, opposite Harry Edwards in Sheridan's *The School for Scandal*, drew from Harry the subtly equivocal remark that she had performed 'in a manner to elicit the highest praise'. Despite his doubts, backstage Harry was seeking to impress Thompson, and as she left town various newspapers reported that he had sold her a play for $500 called *Lenore the Loveless; or, The Moral of a Dream*. 'It took the versatile Major just two weeks to accomplish the work' and 'he is much elated at its success', wrote the gossip columns. The play was said to be destined for New York, but there is no evidence that Thompson ever did give the world her Lenore. Still, $500 would have been reason enough to celebrate.

Muybridge was away again in the middle of October. On the 16th, the *Marin Journal* noted that 'the justly celebrated photographer' was in town, with plans to capture views of Mount Tamalpais and San Rafael, adding that his work sold through Bradley & Rulofson where, amusingly, you could 'sit down to go up stairs'. His fresh absence coincided with a brief engagement at the California Theatre of the actress May Howard. Howard found herself facing ungallant press whispers that her success derived principally from her stupendous costumes, though Harry merely observed that she was 'ventilating her magnificent wardrobe by means of photographs in the windows of Montgomery and Kearny streets.' Determined to prove her detractors wrong, on 18 October, the night of Harry's birthday, she performed as the poorly clad Nancy in *Oliver Twist*. But her effort was a disaster, and the city's critics found they preferred her sumptuous. So too, it seems, did Flora, who picked up a Bradley & Rulofson portrait of Howard in a glorious sculpted gown. Nor was this the only photograph Flora collected to mark the entertainments of the autumn. She also saved a copy of the portrait of Madame Anna Bishop looking thirty-five at most, a shot

Top left: *Charlotte Thompson as Jane Eyre*
Top right: *Fay Templeton as Cupid*
Bottom left: *May Howard 'ventilating her wardrobe'*
Bottom right: *Anna Bishop, 'thirty-five at most'*

of Charlotte Thompson, three pictures of Bella Pateman, whom Harry so admired, and another showing the child performer Fay Templeton in a dainty pair of wings. Harry, always tender about children, had written in a review of Templeton's performances that she possessed 'vim and force, and quaint beauty', and displayed 'an abandon and spirit truly wonderful for her age'.

Alongside Harry's numerous reviews, articles and letters, Henry George gave many front-page column inches to his singular reporter Caroline Parker to fight for women's causes. One time, after being patronised by a man who expected her topics to be 'pretty', she responded angrily by asking why a woman's sphere should not be, like a man's, 'unlimited, uncircumscribed, everywhere'. What exactly was the 'woman's sphere' anyway, she wanted to know, when men worked as janitors, dressmakers and salesmen in fancy stores; 'we say nothing', she added sardonically, 'of masculine doctors, who make a speciality of female complaints'. A woman might as well be a blacksmith or a hod-carrier, she wrote. The only relevant questions ought to be 'Can I do it, and will it pay?' On 7 November Parker responded derisively again to the idea of blaming a decline in the popularity of marriage on improved female education. A true union of heart and hand might be desirable, but consider 'marriage as an end, marriage as the lesser of two evils, marriage as an escape from the odium of old maidenhood'. If education got women out of these awful compromises, then only the 'wilfully blind and wilfully wicked can fail to be thankful'.

On his recent birthday Harry had turned thirty. Redemption through labour was all very well, but there was an awful clock ticking down. Flora's pregnancy, now undeniable and growing ever more obvious, must have raised painful questions for them both, whatever understanding they believed they had. Should she stay in a marriage that was not a 'true union', hoping that the baby either was her husband's, or would plausibly pass for being so? Or should she plan to run away with Harry? And if Harry, meanwhile, hoped to claim Flora and the baby as his own, how exactly should he set about this? As his *Post* columns would go on to make clear, his raffish Parisian views on sexual freedom were starting to gain intellectual ballast from the kinds of arguments Parker was making; but any immediate thought of joint flight with Flora left the considerable difficulty of how, then, they were supposed to live. For the time being, and perhaps taking account of her fragile history of stillbirths, the two carried on exactly as they were.

In November, Harry's scope as a dramatic critic temporarily expanded when Thomas Maguire, first among San Francisco's popular impresarios, paid to advertise his productions in the *Post*, punningly referred to by Harry as the 'leg-itimate' theatre. Maguire currently ran two houses. The Alhambra was best known as being the home of the California Minstrels, classed among the higher grade of the era's 'burnt corkites'. But Maguire had also just bought Shiels' Opera House, engaging the Jennie Lee and Susan Galton troupe for a year to perform opera bouffe and comedy there. They embodied, as he put it, 'All that is Truly Artistic and Incomparably Excellent in the World of Art, Talent and Genius!' The troupe promised an ever-changing programme of comedies, operetta and in particular Offenbach, with Jennie Lee's husband, the love of her life, J. P. Burnett, to perform as her leading man.

At the Alhambra, Harry found he enjoyed the dashing male impersonator Ella Wesner. But in one of his longer columns he was soon reflecting that, while it might seem 'strange to lament the decadence of Negro Minstrelsy', when it came to 'the boys disguised in burnt cork' who now sang any random songs, there was a 'lack of fitness' to the whole, and they would be better to 'retain their ordinary hue'. In particular, he picked out for praise the 'excellent singing' outside the minstrel repertoire of the baritone George Russell. At the Opera House, meanwhile, Harry reviewed a staging of *The Grand Duchess*, with Susan Galton in the lead and Jennie Lee as Wanda. To someone he trusted, he could have whispered an amazing tale of how the original Duchess, Hortense Schneider, had tried to help him out of prison in the matter of some rashly appropriated diamonds. Along with thoughts of Paris, Harry must also have been catapulted back to London in 1870, when Jennie Lee, then an adolescent wonder, had been one of the 'landmark' stars in Hervé's *Little Faust* at the Lyceum. Harry thought Galton was 'not up to music written for Schneider's contralto voice', and that she had the 'chic' but not the 'cheek' for the part. But Jennie Lee he adored, calling her a 'truly accomplished artist' who had 'carried London and New York by storm', was 'beyond praise', and even now 'quite eclipsed' everyone else on the stage.

Maguire soon pulled his advertising from the *Post*, and Harry's bouffe reviews therefore ceased. But that would not have stopped him attending the productions privately. When Sam Davis later told Harry's story, he wantonly recombined and exaggerated many elements in the true 'sagebrush' style. After recounting the debacle with

Arthur Neil, for example, he described how, 'Dead broke, Larkins went to work as a stevedore, and stuck to it until Jenny Lee chanced across him one day on the waterfront.' At once, 'the leading footlight favourite' embraced the 'common wharf laborer' and covered him 'with tears and kisses', and the next day 'her husband secured for him a position as a translator'. This may have whimsically scrambled chronology and facts, but Davis pointed nevertheless to what was an undoubted affection between Harry and Jennie Lee.

Muybridge's frequent absences gave Flora and Harry considerable latitude in the conduct of their liaison. But he was not always away. On 26 November a row erupted when Thomas Houseworth, a rival photographer, displayed in the window of his own Montgomery Street gallery a conspicuously poor print of one of Muybridge's Yosemite photographs. In the press that evening Bradley & Rulofson crowed about free publicity for their wares, while dismissing the picture itself as 'an old soiled print from a condemned negative of Muybridge's', and calling Houseworth's 'wretched' move a 'fruitless effort to compete in business'. Houseworth replied in the press the next morning, asserting that the shoddy print had been provided, as was, to one of Muybridge's subscribers. This provoked Muybridge to set about composing his own reply in time for that evening's newspaper copy deadlines.

As this unpleasantness was playing out, Flora immersed herself in gaiety. That very night, 27 November, dressed to the nines, she went to the Liederkranz Masquerade in Woodward's Gardens, an event that promised large crowds, a prismatic fountain, 'a grand march led by a giant band of giants' and more.

The next morning, Muybridge's response to Houseworth hit the stands. Aesop, he wrote,

> in one of his fables relates that a miserable little ass, stung with envy at the proud position the lion occupied in the estimation of the forest residents, seized some shadowy pretext of following and braying after him with the object of annoying and insulting him. The lion, turning his head and observing from what a despicable source the noise proceeded, silently pursued his way, intent upon his

own business, without honouring the ass with the slightest notice. Silence and contempt, says Aesop, are the best acknowledgements for the insults of those whom we despise. MUYBRIDGE.

While Muybridge gratified himself with false comparisons, Harry, in the *Post* that evening, was no less unguarded in a review of the Liederkranz Masquerade: 1,500 people had attended, and 1,500 'regretted not having staid at home', he wrote. Even the decorations had been spoilt with advertisements for Nabob Sauce and Pipifax. One lady had dressed 'capitally' as Emperor Norton, and there had been an amusing gentleman Quakeress, but most of the costumes had warranted barely a glance. As for the judges, they could only have hailed from 'some asylum for the blind'. After all, he explained bitterly, 'Mrs. Muybridge, in green satin trimmed with gold, was universally acknowledged to be the most handsomely dressed lady, but it is needless to say that she did not take one of the prizes.' The contrast could hardly be more striking. Harry had been riled into publicly defending Flora's loveliness; Muybridge, into publicly defending himself.

Muybridge, at least, soon had new reason to preen, when the California press belatedly broadcast the fact that his work had been recognised at the Vienna Exposition. Back in February he had submitted 130 stereoscopic and other prints to be considered for a great haul of improving goods to represent California. According to one of Harry's summer columns, Vienna had been an 'unqualified failure', blighted by cholera, bad press, and weariness at a surfeit of international expositions in general. Nevertheless, in early December the San Francisco papers reported the fact that Muybridge had been awarded a 'Medal for Progress' for demonstrating advances using 'new materials and contrivances', a result only slightly less gratifying, presumably, for the fact that Thomas Houseworth had won the same. A few days later Muybridge was off again, down the coast, making giant negatives of the Pigeon Point lighthouse.

As people recalled it afterwards, it was towards the end of 1873 that the 'intimacy sprung up between Mrs. Muybridge and Larkyns' began to be 'generally noted with scandalous comments by those acquainted with the parties'. The *Chronicle* was able to dig out the perfect, jaundiced informant, a 'bright, intelligent lady' who said that Harry and Flora had been 'constantly together at places of amusement, out riding, etc.', inspiring 'remarks from the neighbors'. Flora was taken to be a 'thoughtless, impulsive woman, given to fine dress and flirting'. However, she did not provoke local suspicions of 'serious misconduct'. And what of Muybridge, the *Chronicle* wanted to know: had he been 'given to jealousy'? Indeed so, was the reply. He 'always seemed morose and unhappy when he saw his wife in the company of other gentlemen'. Being 'so much older than she, there was a good deal that was fatherly in his regard, but sometimes he was very unjust and made her very unhappy'. Perhaps it was 'the warmth of his love which caused him to be cruel now and then', said the lady, though adding in mitigation that he suffered from a mild form of brain damage. In the story she had heard: 'About seven years ago he got injured about the head in jumping from a railroad train, and ever since has been more or less eccentric. The least thing would put him out of temper. Although a good-hearted man, I always considered him "grouty".'

This brief but remarkable account made Flora lightweight and flirtatious, and Muybridge, though well intentioned, jealous, 'grouty', and from time to time 'very unjust' to Flora, even 'cruel'. It may be that one or other portrait was exaggerated, or that both were, conjured up with the benefit of hindsight. But the underlying assumption that the Muybridges were unsuited was to prove near-universal.

Harry's Bohemian circles formed their own view of these matters, with fellow newspaper writers later reporting that, across these months, 'Muybridge formed the acquaintance of Larkyns', was 'charmed' by him and 'liked him very much', until a friendship was 'cemented between them'. Even the *Chronicle* understood that Muybridge 'invited him to his house as a friend', and that Harry 'often visited Mr. Muybridge's house', where 'for a long time he was always kindly received'. Simultaneously, it became more or less a truism in the press that Muybridge was neglectful of Flora, and that, caring more for his work than for his wife, he was 'always willing for her to seek amusement with younger men, that he might be relieved of the trouble'.

In a much later interview, Muybridge himself transferred his acquaintance with Harry away from home, to the premises of Bradley & Rulofson:

> he came up into the gallery where I was at work. Mr. Rulofson and Max Burkhardt, who were employed in the gallery, had known him for some time previous to this. He wanted to get some of my views for some purpose he had in view; I do not now remember what. My wife, who sometimes worked in the gallery a little touching up pictures, was present, and she introduced him to me. I had frequently heard her speak of Major Larkyns before, but did not know that she was much acquainted with him.

He continued: 'After his introduction to me he frequently came up to the gallery, and I often gave him points in regard to art matters, which he was then writing about for the *Post*.' In fact, the 'Art Jottings' in the *Post* were extremely limited, so that this explanation looks characteristically self-serving; and yet it is easy enough to imagine Harry soliciting notes from Muybridge as a genial cover for catching sight of Flora too. 'He was under such obligations to me frequently,' explained Muybridge, 'and as a return he was always trying to get me to take passes to the theatre, of which he said he had plenty. I didn't want to accept them from him. In fact, I am not much of a man to take favors from anybody. I seldom go to the theatre, and when I do I am always willing to pay for it.' Once in this groove, Muybridge was unable to stop himself: 'I did not fancy the Major's style of man, and did not feel like placing myself under obligation to him, as I felt that by so doing I should be encouraging a closer acquaintance than I cared to cultivate with him.' But having said this, and seeming to recognise that a complete denial would hardly wash, Muybridge conceded that at least once the mercurial Harry had persuaded him to yield. He 'insisted so often and so strongly that one day I accepted passes from him, and in the evening myself and wife went with him to the California Theatre. After the play, he and I took a drink of whisky together, and he 'accompanied us home.' Muybridge insisted that he had nevertheless remained staunchly frosty. Harry had come to the house 'once', he said, 'on a matter of business, I never invited him to come as a friend, and I had no idea that he ever came in my absence'. In fact, he continued doggedly, 'I did not know or suspect that he was visiting my wife or ever went anywhere with her.'

On 27 December, Harry was had up in the Police Court for vulgar language and assault. He pleaded guilty and received a $10 fine. His accuser was Edward Ellis, the peculiar Englishman he had briefly helped, before, in September, Ellis became the dramatic critic on the *Chronicle*. In his new column, 'Footlight Flashes', Ellis had immediately set about sneering at the offerings of the city's theatre managers, or 'caterers' as he called them, at the same time rashly accusing 'the rest of the San Francisco press' of knowing 'little' about music, and worse. After six weeks of his potshots and insults, a local playwright, Charles Gayler, published a long list of factual errors in Ellis's articles. And the *Alta* pitched in too, writing that it expected Ellis to respond with 'weal solid quiticism' to that 'bloody fool, Gayler, who writes, you know, like a blarsted Yankee', ignorant 'about tha Bwitish dwama, you know'. Ellis responded instead by condemning the *Alta* itself as 'an obscure city contemporary'. Everything, replied the *Alta*, was obscure to Ellis's 'spongy brain'. Casting aspersions on his use of sources, it added: he 'can't even drain an encyclopedia of dramatic news through it successfully'.

Whatever the contretemps between Ellis and Harry, it went beyond mere insults. Reportedly, 'As rival theatrical critics' the two 'quarrelled in the vestibule of the theatre, and Larkyns struck Ellis and threw a cigarette in his face.' The only explanation for this brawl was given by the *Chronicle*, Ellis's own paper. Hearing of Harry's 'questionable transactions' with Arthur Neil, and supposedly feeling 'disappointed' by this, Ellis had written to the *Post*, generally 'exposing a scoundrel' but also divulging how he himself had earlier had a hand in Harry's work. Ever hostile to Harry, the *Chronicle* went on to assert that he had assaulted Ellis because this letter lost him his job writing for Henry George. A third paper, dismissing

Ellis as a 'Flash critic', commented that, in his 'difficulty' with Harry, Ellis 'came off second best'. What is true is that Ellis was left in a state of enmity that Harry's $10 court fine did nothing to assuage.

On 6 January 1874, Henry George accused the Regents of the University of California, under Dr Samuel Merritt, of 'peculation', embezzlement from public funds to the tune of $50,000, during the construction of the new College of Letters building in Berkeley. This cabal of 'moneybags', as George called them, had paid no more attention to the law than they might 'to an edict of Emperor Norton'. His exposé provoked a rancorous and knotty investigation that would last into March, with weeks of testimony on the quality of the building work promised and actually delivered; on expenses claimed versus probable costs; on wooden girders, crest rails, tinning leaders, glass weights, plank widths, attic wall sheathing, and much more. One day the hearing was paused so that a note could be read out. It concerned a remark by Dr Merritt's lawyer suggesting that the *Post*'s reporting 'had been "industriously so worded" as to convey a certain impression. This casts an imputation on me', wrote the journalist, 'which I do not wish to pass unchallenged. I beg to state that throughout this investigation I have faithfully reported what I have heard, neither more nor less. HARRY LARKYNS, "*Post*".' This protest, serendipitously captured in the legal record, reveals that it was Harry knocking out the bogglingly detailed, unsigned columns on the case. Either his brief for the *Post* had expanded even further, or this task was penance exacted by Henry George for Harry's run-in with Edward Ellis. Whatever else, though, it is clear that Harry had not lost his job.

In Harry's reporting on the College of Letters case, he can be traced handing copy to a runner for the paper's afternoon dead-line, then remaining to record the balance of the day's testimony, before repairing to the theatre at night, afterwards turning in an 'Amusements' column as well. He was in this draining work pattern when Dion Boucicault, of 'world-wide renown', arrived to play a short, triumphant season at the California Theatre. Harry acknow-ledged that Boucicault was known not only for his prolific output but also for plagiarism, and generously cited Pope as a form of defence: 'those move easiest who have learned to dance'. He also mocked another, unnamed critic who had criticised Boucicault's 'flavorless' performance in one of his own Irish plays. Harry instead praised Boucicault for restoring 'delicacy of light and shade' to the work, rising above the degraded 'Ragged Pat' stereotype. When this piece came out, Boucicault was accused of having written it himself. He responded wittily and flatteringly: 'I appreciate the compliment too highly to disclaim it.' And yet, Boucicault added, he spurned the 'gross' interpolated 'gags' that the hostile critic had been expecting and had missed, even if 'my reputation is made by appropriating the brainwork of other people'.

Harry must also have dropped in at Maguire's Opera House, where Jennie Lee was having a storming success as the Earl of Leicester in a burlesque adaptation of Sir Walter Scott's novel

Dion Boucicault   *Jennie Lee as the Earl of Leicester*

Kenilworth. George Evans, leader of the orchestra, composed a special dance in her honour, the 'Kenilworth Galop', with the sheet music sold by Muybridge's long-standing friend, the music publisher Matthias Gray. Tipped in on the covers, Gray offered a selection of fifteen different photographs by Bradley & Rulofson of Jennie as Leicester, in a fetching pair of shorts.

When Boucicault was succeeded as the main draw at the

California Theatre by his mistress, Katharine Rogers, Harry took this as the perfect prompt for an essay column. Rogers had played the lead in London in Boucicault's scandalous work _Formosa_, and now starred in his adaptation of Henri Murger's novel _Scénes de la Vie de Bohème_. Harry therefore set about ruminating on Bohemia, and those 'philosophic vagabonds' who elected to 'live long by Art', most of them destined to die unmourned. After noting various penniless geniuses of history, including the Twelve Apostles, who had believed 'heaven will provide', he laid out his own version of his editor's economic argument, that 'we should make the rich poorer and the poor richer'. Harry's financial credo, he wrote, was that no Bohemian ought ever to retain 'more money than he absolutely requires for the necessities of the moment'. Should he find himself miraculously blessed with riches, 'His hands, unaided, are not large enough for him to lavish his wealth, nor are any windows wide enough for him to fling it out of.' It was a paradox, he added feelingly, that it was so expensive to be hard up. For instance, finagling a meal on credit required resorting to a pricey restaurant, as no chophouse would feed you except for cash. Yet although a Bohemian might go in 'loop'd and window'd raggedness', he continued, quoting Lear, still 'His careless open-handedness, if it be a vice, is preferable to some men's virtues.' He finished plangently, 'Reader, will you not think well of them on their up-hill road?'

Romantic vagabondage was all very well; so too was the posture Harry sometimes struck of finding wedlock a 'severe' cost to a young man. Yet one of his Bancroft confrères now succeeded in achieving a kind of happiness that surely looked idyllic. Thomas Arundel Harcourt was becoming known as a San Francisco litterateur; shortly he and Walter Fisher would graduate from the literary factory to become joint editors of the _Overland Monthly_. And on 25 February, Harcourt married the strikingly beautiful Fannie Rulofson.

When John McCullough, manager of the California Theatre, after six months on the road, returned to perform for his home crowd, he opened with _Spartacus_, a huge hit, then turned to Shakespeare. Harry believed that 'as a creator', Shakespeare 'had more divine attributes than any man that ever lived', and condemned McCullough's Hamlet as insensitive, before raging about 'rank sacrilege' when McCullough staged Nahum Tate's 'emasculated' and 'bastardized' version of *Lear*. Harry also took a new side-swipe at Edward Ellis, professing to be amazed that 'so able and careful a writer' could make the 'ludicrous error' of writing that Edgar was usually played by a woman. Ellis sneered back and accused Harry of plagiarising the dramatic authorities he drew on, instead of nicely adapting them.

It appears overwhelmingly likely that part of the rationale for Flora's growing collection of Bradley & Rulofson portraits was a desire to memorialise productions she attended with Harry. From just the first two months of 1874, she saved a large profile shot of Boucicault, hiding his bald pate under a decorated cap, multiple shots of Jennie Lee as the Earl of Leicester, and a splendid image of John McCullough as Spartacus. She also kept a print of Fannie Rulofson in her wedding dress, enigmatic, beautiful and wan.

The Muybridges did not remain long above the upholstery shop on Fourth, but moved yet again, to an address on the corner of Howard and Third, 'a fashionable boarding house in the vicinity of South Park'. Harry remained a 'frequent visitor', according to his friends, with Muybridge 'perfectly aware' of the attentions he 'lavished' on

Fannie Rulofson

Flora. Indeed, to some Muybridge 'seemed to encourage them'. When he went away the pair 'were frequently together, visited the theaters, and generally dined at a small French rotisserie on Pacific above Dupont'. Most San Francisco restaurants offered 'cozy alcoves or stalls', and even the cheapest often hung out signs reading 'Private rooms for suppers—open all night', a great resource for the city's 'after-dark patrons'. The liaison between Harry and Flora, a matter of 'common notoriety among his friends', was worrying to those who cared about him most, and they began to warn him of a 'terrible reckoning' if he did not bring it to a close.

13: Utterly miserable without you

'As related to the writer by Larkyns', noted a reporter, a huge row was sparked after two of Harry's friends, eating in Campi's, were overheard discussing his attentions to Flora. Informants told Muybridge that his wife's behaviour had become 'table talk in public restaurants', and Muybridge sent Harry a letter demanding that his visits to Flora now cease. Harry, adhering to gentlemanly code, wrote by return demanding to know why. But he received no answer. And though he became more careful after this, during Muybridge's further absences he and Flora remained 'almost inseparable'. Then, one night, Flora could not resist going with Harry to the theatre. After all, 'Neilson was playing her engagement' in the city, and Muybridge was away photographing in Alameda.

Adelaide Neilson, an English actress and a huge star, held audiences spellbound at the California Theatre through the second half of March. Harry had finally been liberated from the grind of the College of Letters hearing, the *Post* vindicated in its lengthy campaign, and he reviewed Neilson rapturously. She was entrancing as Rosalind in *As You Like It*; and as for her Juliet, delivering Shakespeare's words unadulterated, she was 'without a peer', he said, and left audiences 'infatuated'. Her run coincided with Flora's twenty-third birthday, and it is tempting to read a review by Harry, printed the day before, as a circumspect tribute to Flora, when he wrote that the California Theatre had been graced by a distracting array of 'bright angels', creating a beautiful '"balcony scene" on either side of the footlights'. Flora herself selected four portraits of Neilson to keep, two of them showing her in her costume as Juliet.

Muybridge had said he was going to Alameda for three or four days. Unexpectedly, he returned sooner, to find Flora missing. When she arrived home late in the night, back from seeing Neilson at the theatre, he 'stormed and swore' at her. Flora managed to send an

Neilson as Juliet with her nurse

emergency note to Harry, who, 'although totally devoid of anything like fear', removed 'half a dozen' photographs of Flora from around his room and borrowed a pistol. Muybridge, also armed, went hunting for Harry the next day. 'Nervous and excited', Muybridge called at the offices of the *Post*, where he was observed to have 'a strange light in his eyes'. But only in the afternoon did he corner Harry at home. Harry gave a blameless account of his movements; and Muybridge was unable to disprove it. That, at least, was one version of events. A second stated that 'Muybridge forbid Larkyns coming to his house and after high words had passed, Muybridge struck the Major, who, although much more than a match for his opponent in physical strength, did not return the blow.'

What no one writing about this mentioned was that Flora was by now heavily pregnant. With at least two warnings from Muybridge, and an atmosphere of violence, Harry's safest course would have been to abandon his mistress to her husband's mercies, such as they were. But he believed the child was his. And he loved Flora passionately, and found parting from her unbearable.

*

In April, Maguire made over the Opera House to the immensely popular English performers, the 'Great Lingard Combination'. William Horace Lingard was one of the most successful comic actors of the day, cherished as Captain Jinks of the Horse Marines – 'I often live beyond my means' – but also as a singing lady impersonator: 'We marched up to the minister, Papa gave me away, / And how I felt (although I know), I shouldn't like to say', etc. The troupe

Horace Lingard

included his wife, Alice Dunning Lingard, and his sister-in-law, Dickie. They opened their season with *La Tentation*, a burlesque on the novel by Octave Feuillet, putting them in satirical competition with the California Theatre, which was staging *Led Astray*, an adaptation by Boucicault of the very same work. It concerned the triangle of a neglectful older husband, his sensitive, lovely, much younger second wife, and the 'inspired scoundrel' who slightly shakes her virtue. Boucicault's version incensed Harry. Its morality, he wrote, was summed up in the line, 'What is only folly in man, in woman becomes a crime.' Why, he wanted to know, did those women in the audience who 'professed to stand up so energetically for their rights', by implication their sexual rights, not 'hiss such a vile maxim every night it was uttered'?

For some days, Harry virtually stopped reviewing performances at the California, and instead hid out at the circus. John Wilson, 'the Barnum of California' in Harry's view, had recently opened his brand-new Palace Amphitheater on the corner of New Montgomery and Mission Streets, an elegant building that had cost \$30,000, held 2,000 spectators and was altogether astonishing, with countless dazzling gas jets and private boxes like 'regular little nests'. Wilson advertised assiduously in the *Post*; and Harry, who anyway loved the circus, assiduously reviewed the dog acts, comic mules, 'boneless boys', trapeze artists, a thirty-inch clown, a 'sagacious' forty-inch, tightrope-walking baby elephant, and much more. 'All the artists are stars', he wrote. Even the band was exceptional. But Harry's respect went above all to the ring rider Omar Kingsley, who ruled his horses 'by love and not by fear', and performed incredible stunts with the utmost grace, receiving bouquets 'as though he were a prima donna'. After Wilson's colossal outlay, and given his determination to provide pleasure, it was almost a 'duty', wrote Harry, to repay him by visiting his circus.

On Monday, 13 April, eschewing an opening night at the California Theatre, Harry went to Platt's Hall to hear the English Christian Socialist Gerald Massey give the first of three lectures, introduced by his 'old friend of twenty years' Harry Edwards. The event, wrote Harry, drew 'most members of the community who belong—or who aspire to belong—to the world of letters', and Massey spoke with 'dry humor' on Shakespeare the man, and on how 'intensely human' he was. Only on Tuesday did Harry go to the California Theatre to see *The Wicked World* by W. S. Gilbert. Afterwards, late in the night, with Muybridge away in Oakland, Harry took Flora to the Cliff House, a fashionable resort on the edge of town. One of the main routes there passed by Lone Mountain, its peak 'surmounted by an immense cross visible for miles around', and with the city's clustered cemeteries nestled beneath. In his San Francisco guide, Benjamin Lloyd described the Cliff House as an attraction 'for all the first families of the city'. It offered 'palate-tempting' cuisine, accompanied by the 'guttural cacklings' of sea birds and the 'weird half howl, half bark' of seals on the rocks below. Best of all, the balconies gave views of the 'immensity of the ocean, its mysterious depths, its restless life, together with the illimitable expanse of the overarching heavens—at night studded with flashing stars'.

'Moonlight Effect, Seal Rocks, from the Cliff House': photograph by Muybridge

Well into the small hours of Wednesday morning, 15 April, Mrs Smith, the same nurse who had attended Flora in her previous pregnancies, found herself roused at her home, 2116 Powell Street, by a carriage rattling up to the door and 'a furious ringing of the bell'. A figure unknown to her, 'a tall gentleman, with a high white hat', told her that Mrs Muybridge wanted her immediately. Mrs Smith, who knew Flora's 'condition', said she would dress, but the man 'cried out' that Flora was in the carriage. He refused to bring her in; 'said no, and half lifted me across the sidewalk'. Mrs Smith found Flora lying in the carriage, 'suffering in the first stages of labor'. As they drove rapidly to her address, the man 'held her in his arms, with his coat around her', and when they arrived he 'carried her up stairs, and then went for a doctor'. On his return, the man was 'pale as death'. He leant over Flora 'and kissed her', and said, 'Keep up good heart baby, you'll be all right in a little while.' But, Mrs Smith explained later, he 'only staid about three minutes' before leaving again.

At about four in the afternoon, after a labour of more than twelve hours, Flora gave birth to a scrap of a baby boy. Mrs Smith sent Muybridge a telegram and he returned to San Francisco, staying 'for a week or ten days, until all danger was past'. Mrs Smith had nothing to say about him in the role of father, except that, when she asked him what the baby was to be called, he replied, 'Never mind, I will find a name for him by-and-by that he will not be ashamed to own when a man.' For months afterwards, though, said Mrs Smith, he never did supply one.

Harry necessarily kept away. The evening of the 15th, hours after the baby had been born, he was compelled to attend the second Gerald Massey lecture, 'Why Does Not God Kill the Devil?' Then the next night it was the event of the Easter season, at Union Hall, on Howard between Third and Fourth. Harry was forced to endure, and report on, a 'Dickens Ball', which acted surreally to bring together his extremely disparate San Francisco connections, even as Flora and the baby were a mere two-minute walk away. Amid bunting and an 'artistic profusion' of flowers, various of the city's elites paraded: Harry Edwards as Peggotty, Dan O'Connell as Silas Wegg and Jennie Lee as the Artful Dodger; but also Frank Pixley dressed pointedly as a knife-swallower, and Mr Smith of the Occidental Hotel portraying the bounder Mantalini. Dr Merritt, of the College of Letters scandal, had the nerve to come as Mr Bumble, while Leland Stanford flattered himself, more or less, by dressing as Tony Weller. Thomas Maguire attended too, in the person of actor-manager Vincent Crummles, and even John Wilson, the circus supremo, came. Their presence inspired a barbed joke in Harry's write-up, concerning two of the enormously wealthy bankers also present, one his old nemesis: 'Tom tried all his blandishments on W. C. Ralston and Milton S. Latham, whom he is very anxious to get for a side show, but John Wilson, as Sleary, prince of circus men, secured their services as "Bounding Brothers".'The gas lights were not extinguished until two in the morning.

The next day, Harry churned out his piece for the *Post*'s afternoon deadline, then proceeded to the final Massey lecture, a talk on 'The Coming Religion', which he found to be 'replete with brilliant and telling passages'. Massey believed that the 'desire to accumulate wealth' was 'insane', and that true Christians did not 'amass large fortunes', even to give away, but instead worked to prevent 'unequal social conditions' in the first place. He doubted the rich would recognise Christ if he came among them, given how they cruci-fied the bodies of their workers. Instead, perhaps 'Communists and Internationalists were the chosen instruments to do his work.' Harry dismissed views Massey then ventured on spiritualism, but did write up his rousing theme, as Harry himself put it, of 'the great movement going on, in so many different ways, which showed that womankind was coming forward to take her proper place in the world—no longer the abject slave, but the equal, of man'.

Harry's open-mindedness found another expression in his deep respect for the ring rider and 'perfection of horsemen' Omar Kingsley, who was soon to receive his benefit show at Wilson's circus in recognition, as the advertising heavily expressed it, of his 'artistic excellence and manly qualities'. It was only now that Kingsley stood revealed to the public as being the more famous Ella Zoyara, the female guise he had adopted for a large part of his career, and he promised to appear for his benefit performance in a tutu. This 'bright particular star', wrote Harry, 'challenges, invites and defies criticism'. And certainly he had none of his own. In the event, he found, 'the deception is perfect; as astonishing as it is graceful', and he laughed at the 'larger portion' of the crowd, who insisted that Ella Zoyara must be Omar Kingsley's sister.

Two days later, a small announcement appeared in the California press: 'San Francisco, April 15—Wife of — Muybridge, a son.' Muybridge, feeling free to leave again, went to Belmont, south of San Francisco, where he photographed the estate of William C. Ralston, about whom Harry had jibed in the press. And soon afterwards Muybridge also visited Berkeley, where, among other edifices, he photographed the contested College of Letters building.

Mrs Smith worked for seven weeks in the Muybridge household, later reporting that, the minute it became possible, Flora enjoined her to carry a letter to Harry at the offices of the *Post*. From this point on, said Mrs Smith, Harry 'called frequently', seeming 'very fond of the baby'. She also spoke of being 'sent from the room' when he came, or so the *Chronicle* had it. When Muybridge returned home again after about a month, Mrs Smith continued, he 'always seemed affectionate and attentive' with Flora and the baby. Yet, turning anecdotal, she gave the lie to this platitude at once. Flora had asked her to carry another letter to Harry, and 'While we were standing in the doorway of the office of the *Post*, Mr. Muybridge passed.' That evening Muybridge 'came into his wife's room' and asked Mrs Smith point-blank whether she had earlier seen Harry. Flora, 'white as death', secretly held up a warning finger, and so Mrs Smith 'passed it off' as a chance meeting: she had been there to place an advertisement. Muybridge looked 'hard' at Mrs Smith before producing an anonymous letter from his pocket. He asked Flora if 'the Major' had sent it. When Flora 'said quite boldly that he had not', Muybridge tossed it to her, asking, 'Then what do you make of that?' Flora apparently 'laughed and declared that it was all a joke'. And now Muybridge turned pale, saying he 'hoped to God that what she said was true, and asked her to swear to it'. He 'seemed very much excited', said Mrs Smith. But at this point she had left the room. 'I saw it was no place for me.'

While Flora was navigating these dangerous waters, the entertainment season was drawing to a close. Maguire once more took advertising briefly in the *Post* to promote the benefit performance of William Horace Lingard. Harry duly vamped Lingard's 'inimitable sketches', of 'world-wide fame'. More feelingly, though, he also pressed *Post* readers to visit the circus before Wilson packed up for the summer and went on the road. 'Very soon,' he wrote, 'John and his magnificent troupe will be astonishing the natives in the provinces.' Even now, Harry remained testy about the California Theatre, its productions, he said, still being 'pitch-forked on anyhow'. Its new 'leg play', Charles Webb's *Belphegor the Mountebank*, was choked in 'trash', with the 'charming danseuse'

Maria Bonfanti swamped by the 'elephantine gambols' of the other dancers. Harry only relented when the California invited Jennie Lee and her husband Burnett to feature in a benefit performance for one of its departing stars. Burnett was excellent. Harry Edwards played 'just the man his wife would adore'. And Jennie represented 'the exuberant Polly with an overflow of life and animal spirits that quickly made its contagion felt among the audience'. Harry added hearty congratulations to this notice. It was the close of her contract with Maguire, and the California Theatre had stepped in to secure Jennie and Burnett for the next year.

About now, the informal practice sessions at the Recreation Ground inspired the revival of a lapsed California Cricket Club. Under the presidency of William Lane Booker, Her Britannic Majesty's Consul in San Francisco, fifty members immediately signed up, and on Wednesday, 6 May Henry George gave Harry a page-one column in which to explain what cricket was. For a start, it was 'more than a game', wrote Harry: it was 'a national institution'. Englishmen, 'rich or poor', played it just about everywhere, even under the beating sun in India, marking them out across the world as 'cricket mad'. And as it was played 'for pure love', cricketers were 'the most harmonious antagonists in the world', he said. This was put to the test three days later, on a windy, dusty Saturday afternoon, in a match between the club's own members. Harry captained the Blues against the Reds. The players were rusty, but many 'showed good stuff', with the true winner, according to a sports report, a 'thorough love of the game'. Against the odds, too, the Blues beat the Reds by a slender four runs.

Harry may not have known it out there on the dusty Recreation Ground, but he really was now about to lose his job, with that morning's Saturday column set to be his last. In a matter of days a new critical voice would rule over the drama columns in the *Post*, where Marie Aimée, a visiting queen of opera bouffe, was now derided as 'decidedly Frenchy', an expression that would have made Harry flinch. Reporters on other papers had little more to say about his downfall than, simply, that he 'ceased his connection' with the *Post*. But given the desperate circumstances in which this left him, it seems more likely that his tangled love life, fecklessness and general lack of moral compass had become too much for Henry George. Even Dan O'Connell, ever reliant himself on 'the providential impulses of his friends', said affectionately of Harry that 'the axiom, "once a spendthrift, always a spendthrift," was perfectly illustrated in the major', so that 'The Post editorial rooms were every day thronged with the major's duns. The people in the business office were distracted every moment by demands for the whereabouts of Major Larkyns.' Whatever the real reasons, the timing of this disaster could hardly have been worse. And apart from needing money simply to live, Harry must now have felt utterly defeated by wondering how he would ever provide for the little family that he wished to claim as his own.

The edition of Langley's city directory issued in April 1874 gave Harry's dwelling as '605 Montgomery', the same address as the *Post*. If he really had sleeping quarters there, they were his no longer. It was Caroline Parker, his fellow *Post* reporter, who pointed him towards a final foothold in the city. Some months before, she had herself moved to a large boarding house at 1010 Montgomery. Fellow residents included a 'stovemounter', a lady grocer and a fireman on the steam tug *Water Witch*, as well as a lithographer and several clerks. Harry moved to a room there, and at least two of the clerks, Charles Pring and Alfred Bulch, became firm friends.

Caroline Parker had recently been helping to nurse a well-known 'trance and seeing medium', Ellen Violetta 'Harmony' Post, who was nearing death from cancer. And she gave the funeral address when Harmony Post soon died. Parker's words were written up in a new San Francisco journal, *Common Sense*, dedicated to addressing, as naturally aligned topics, 'SPIRITUALISM, ITS PHENOMENA AND PHILOSOPHY, SOCIAL REFORM, WOMAN SUFFRAGE, ETC.'

Spiritualism allowed serious women moral standing denied them by the Church; and Parker explained that the 'communications' relayed by Harmony Post 'were seldom in reference to material things; they generally related to principles, and came with a power that clothed them with authority'. But Parker was not immune to the lure of the ghostly too: 'The spirit world will seem nearer to us, now that Harmony Post has entered it.' *Common Sense* went further, reporting as fact that 'Mrs. Post was present during the services, being distinctly seen by several mediums.'

At the end of May, Wilson put the Palace Amphitheater out to rent for the summer, had his travelling troupe pack up, and prepared to take his pavilion tent on the road. He also stepped in to rescue his faithful advocate, offering Harry a job as his agent. This would require him to become the humblest of peripatetic performers himself, drumming up business as they wound their way between Marysville, Napa, Red Bluff, Tehama and all over. And as Harry's immediate choices were few, he agreed to run away with the circus.

As they set off, one of the great convulsive performances of the year hit San Francisco, delivered by Victoria Woodhull, a complex proponent of revolutionary ideas. Harry had previously kept tabs on her in his *Post* columns, most recently noting when Gerald Massey characterised her as defending Christ 'from a man who claimed to preach his religion' – a reference to Henry Ward Beecher, prominent pastor, abolitionist and brother of Harriet Beecher Stowe, whom Woodhull had publicly unmasked as a sexual hypocrite.

Woodhull herself, after divorcing her first husband, had hitched up with a Unionist army officer, Colonel James Blood. She worked for a time as a spiritualist before, in 1870, she and her sister, Tennessee Claflin, became the first women to run a Wall Street brokerage firm. The two of them funnelled the profits into a newspaper in which they promoted women's rights and free love, also printing the first English translation in America of *The Communist Manifesto* by Engels and Marx. Then in 1872, Woodhull militantly stood as the first woman candidate for United States President, as well as publishing her allegation against Beecher of double standards. Though married, and a preacher against free love, he was embroiled in an affair with one of his parishioners, Elizabeth Tilton, the wife of his friend Theodore Tilton. Woodhull's actions landed her in prison on the criminal charge of sending obscene materials through the post. She was freed after a month on a technicality.

By the summer of 1874, with legalities in the Beecher–Tilton case at a pitch, there was intense interest in San Francisco when Woodhull announced that she would appear at Platt's Hall on

1 June. Tennie Claflin was on the door. Colonel Blood sold photographs of Woodhull and copies of her speeches. Her daughter, Zulu Maude Woodhull, aged about thirteen, opened proceedings by reciting a lengthy poem. 'Rather a stout girl', wrote a hostile paper, with a 'very self-possessed manner'. Woodhull then stood up to argue that, despite abolition, 'subtle slaveries' persisted in America:

Victoria Woodhull

'the Government has degenerated into a mere machine, used by the unscrupulous to systematically plunder the people'. Moreover the president, 'Useless S. Grant', was so corrupt that 'if Jesus Christ had been running against this man, He'd have been defeated'. After an hour of this, Woodhull laid down her papers and began to deliver *extempore* her 'ultra views' on love and marriage. She denounced those who expressed 'abhorrence' at free love as 'preferring free lust to true love': her idea of marriage as then commonly understood and practised. 'I curse it; I abhor it; there is nothing my tongue can utter that is bitter enough to describe it in its real colours', she said. Legal marriage was 'enforced prostitution'.

Predictably, Woodhull's lecture was condemned by the press in the strongest terms. 'Everything that We Hold Sacred Denounced', said one headline: 'the sentiments and language, generally, falling from the lips of a woman before a public audience, were disgusting in the extreme'. There was levity too, when a reporter wrote that Woodhull had made him blush: a joke went round that he had been 'promptly discharged' from his job for 'conduct unbecoming a journalist'. *Common Sense*, by contrast, called Woodhull magnificent, an 'inspired Pythoness' and a 'great Apostle of Liberty', who had demonstrated 'heroic courage in proclaiming unwelcome truths'. But most of San Francisco's citizens would have had to extract Woodhull's views from hostile reporting. The critical burden of her message appeared in the city newspapers from 2 June.

The opening engagement of Wilson's travelling circus took place on 4 June in Oakland. Harry slipped back to San Francisco two days later for a last cricket match, for which he was relegated to the role of umpire. This was followed by a banquet at the Overland House, a cheaply gigantic hotel, and 'wine, wit and wisdom, song and sentiment ruled unburdened'. By the time Wilson opened in Sacramento two days after that, the show was a sure-fire success. A Vallejo paper later dredged up a thin image of Harry as publicist: 'In that capacity he made a number of acquaintances during his visit here.' And on 13 June the *Carson Daily Appeal* reported that 'A letter received yesterday from Mr. Harry Larkyns, agent for John Wilson's "Palace Amphitheater Circus," informs us that the entertainment will shortly come to Carson.' He had forwarded a rapturous review in the *Sacramento Daily Union*, praising, in particular, 'Fred O'Brien, in his unparalleled act of throwing a double somersault over ten horses with a pyramid of men upon their backs'. And the show, with its trapeze artists and India-rubber men, would more than fulfil Carson's expectations. An account of the audience there stated quaintly: 'We infer that certain young gentlemen and ladies with due regard for spangles and calico ponies and the likes, have been hoarding up their small means for this tempting occasion.'

Mrs Smith later stated that Flora asked her to take care of the baby 'while she and Larkyns traveled together with Wilson's Circus'. Had Flora actually taken this step, going on the run with Harry, it would have been an act of irreversible boldness, openly enacting free love, and estranging her for ever from her husband. But in telling this particular story, Mrs Smith added that she had declined to help.

Out on the road, Harry paid for a secret message to be printed in the front page 'Personals' column of the *Chronicle*. It appeared on 12 June: 'F.— PINING FOR SUNSHINE. EVER yours. T.' Given the baking weather at the time, 'sunshine' was either metaphorical or a code word. 'T', meanwhile, presumably stood for Harry's second name, Thomas. As for 'pining', and 'ever yours': this seems clear enough.

A day or two later, Flora left town in a hurry taking the baby with her. She caught the Portland steamer and went to stay with Flora and Thomas Stump, her aunt and uncle in Oregon. Stump was by now a 'well known upper Columbia river steamboatman', and the family lived in The Dalles, a riverside town at the inland end of his run. How well Flora knew them is not at all clear, but they seem to have been happy enough to take her in. She departed San Francisco at the same time, and possibly on the same vessel, as Maguire's California Minstrels, who had a fortnight's engagement at the Oro Fino Theatre in Portland, starting on 17 June.

Asked later why Flora had left like this, Muybridge gave a benign explanation. By mid June, he had been negotiating for 'several months' with the Pacific Mail Steamship Company, he said, to take a trip on one of their vessels, in order 'to photograph the coast'. He expected to be gone for five or six months. 'My wife had no relatives in the city, and I did not like to leave her here alone with her baby.' Thus, 'I told her I would send her up to Oregon to her uncle.' He had offered, he said, to 'give her money to pay her expenses there while I was away if she would go. She consented and I gave her the money.' That is: 'I told her that I would allow her $50 per month', a sum he thought 'sufficient', and if she wanted more she could 'easily earn as much as that' again by working as a photographic retoucher.

This arrangement, a monthly stipend, and go to work if you want more, may well have been the deal the two of them had already. Yet there was a hint of pressure in the wording: he had offered the money 'if she would go', and she had 'consented'. Nor does his account sit easily with all the facts. In particular, why this last-minute arrangement with Flora, when he had been planning his absence for months? Other evidence suggests that the Oregon trip was decided on in haste, through anger on Muybridge's part, fear of that anger on Flora's, or a combination of the two. The press later drew its own conclusions, one report stating bluntly that Muybridge, knowing of Flora's fondness for Harry, 'sent his wife on a visit to a relative' in the hope of 'finally interrupting' the 'scandalous intrigue'.

Whatever the truth of this, Flora's departure caught Harry completely off guard. And any message she sent in explanation while he travelled, he missed. On 23 June, in despair at her seeming silence, he placed a second message in the *Chronicle*'s 'Personals' column: 'F. DO WRITE TO ME. I AM UTTERLY miserable without you. Your devoted T.' The next day, in a desperate letter to Mrs Smith, he mentioned this secret message, and quoted another, less circumspect, that he had placed in the Portland press. The fullest copy of his letter survives in a box of court documents. It has been transcribed, with a few hurried errors, and who knows what slight alterations, but with what looks like authentic punctuation, at least.

'Calistoga Wednesday night'

Dear Mrs. Smith. You'll be surprised to hear from me so soon after I left the city, but I have been so uneasy and worried about that poor girl that I cannot rest, and it is a relief to talk and write about her.—I think you have a sufficiently friendly feeling towards me to grant me a favor, rest assured I will find means to do you a good turn before long. I want you and your girls to be perfectly frank, open and honest with me. If you hear anything of that little lady, no matter what, tell me right out. She may return to the city, and beg you not to let me know, but do ~~not~~ pray not listen to her. Do not be afraid that I shall get angry with her, I will never say a harsh word to her, and even if things turn out as badly as possible and I find she has been deceiving me all along, I can only be very very grieved and sorry, but will never be angry with her. I ascertained to-day that all the minstrels will return from Portland on the next steamer, which will arrive on Tuesday next. I cannot and will not believe anything so bad as that rumor, but I almost believe she will come back, or she would have sent for her clothes.

I have written to the morning and evening papers in Portland today, and advertised in the personals so—

'Flora and Georgie, If you have a heart you will write to H. Have you forgotten that april night when we were both so pale'

She will understand this, I have also put a personal in the Chronicle.—Mrs. Smith I assure you I am sick with anxiety and doubt, the whole thing is so incomprehensible and I am so helpless. I fear my business will not let me go to Portland and I see no other way of hearing of her.—If an angel had come and told me she was false to me, I would not have believed it.—I cannot attend to my work, I cannot sleep, and the longer matters stay like this the more I suffer, besides even if she does write me now, I shall not know what to believe. I cannot help thinking of that speech of hers to you the day before she left, when she begged you not to think ill of her, whatever you might hear, it almost looks as if she had already settled some plan in her head that she knew you would disapprove of. And yet Mrs. Smith after all that has come and gone, *could* she be so utterly untrue to me, so horribly false? It seems impossible, and yet I rack my brain to try and find out some excuse, and cannot do it, if she had nothing to conceal why has she not written? If I go to Portland I must give up my situation, but I think unless we hear I shall go. I shall be in the city about Thursday next, tell the girls to look out for the next steamer, and find out if Flo comes down.

Mrs. Smith, again I beg you to be open and candid and conceal nothing from me. With many thanks for all the kindnesses you have shown Flo.

Yours very truly,

Harry Larkyns.

Evidently, Harry had had an account from Mrs Smith of Flora's nervous demeanour the day before she vanished. Evidently too, Mrs Smith had given no reassuring picture of Muybridge thoughtfully arranging for Flora and the baby to be cared for in Oregon. On the contrary, Harry clearly believed that Flora, of her own volition, had more or less run away, possibly with someone else. In March, reviewing John McCullough's *Othello*, Harry had written of 'the cry wrung from a doubting tortured heart' when Desdemona's father, believing himself betrayed by her love for Othello, says corrosively to Othello himself: 'Look to her, Moor, if thou hast eyes to see: / She has deceived her father, and may thee.' And it seems Harry's friends had played the same card, provoking a no less tortured cry, Harry given his pick of a bogeyman rival: any of Maguire's California Minstrels, now back in San Francisco with their uproarious new turn, the 'Wood-haul lecture'. Flora's abrupt departure, going without spare clothes; the fear that she might unbelievably have left with another man; her own fear of what might be said about her once she was gone; and her inexplicable failure to write to Harry: these elements left him torn between horrible anxiety for her, defiant faith in their love, and crushing doubt. But he would never respond with anger, he said; by implication, unlike Muybridge. And he simply remained sleepless, suffering, anguished.

His 'personal' in the Portland papers was, meanwhile, quietly revelatory: 'Flora and Georgie, If you have a heart you will write to H. Have you forgotten that april night when we were both so pale.' This provides the earliest record of a name for the baby. 'George' might serve as a gesture to Harry's murdered father; but 'Georgie' was the name of his one true brother, also murdered, the 'jolly dog' and little prankster whom he had never met. No wonder he gave way to an anguished cry: 'If an angel had come and told me she was false to me, I would not have believed it.'

Mrs Smith subsequently related that Harry planned to take Flora back to London with him 'and present her as his wife, and the baby as his child'. And Harry Edwards confirmed, in his own ornate language, that Harry's great wish was to return to his family and say: 'I bring you back the honor you bestowed upon me unstained as when it left your hands, and claim, in common justice to my nature, a full oblivion of the past.' Having reached the age of thirty, helplessly in love, and with a tiny child he believed to be his son, Harry's dearest wish, it seems, was to begin life again with Flora and Georgie in England. But the odds against this remained daunting, and he needed to hold his nerve.

*

As June progressed, Wilson took his troupe zigzagging between Yolo, Tehama, Red Bluff and Marysville, then into Nevada, and in July, on to Colorado and Nebraska. However, Harry's letter to Mrs Smith, sent from the Geyser region of Calistoga, suggests that he had parted ways with the circus in California and was already scrabbling after a livelihood by different means.

One of the many friends Harry had made in San Francisco was Richard Wheeler, printer, bookbinder and editor, whose offices sat opposite the rooms of the Bohemian Club. With 'indomitable vim and perseverance', Wheeler ran his own newspaper, the *Stock Report*, keeping track of the expanding business of the San Francisco Stock Board and battling the 'schemers' who attempted to manipulate the market. He knew perfectly well that Harry was spoken of as 'a felon, a confidence operator: one whom it was not safe for men to deal with'. But Wheeler blamed this on the 'infamous trick' of Arthur Neil's *Chronicle* interview, which had put matters in the 'worst possible light' and was written up by an 'irresponsible scribbler' in a 'highly sensational' manner. Wheeler instead found Harry to be 'wonderfully gifted' and impressively versatile, and went so far as to say that 'no better newspaper man worked on the papers of the city'. The 'frightfully uphill work' Harry continued to face in establishing his character was never more 'touchingly shown', wrote Wheeler, than in the way he thanked those 'who cheered him at all, by their words or acts'. And he would know this, as, like John Wilson before him, Wheeler now stepped in, proposing that Harry work for him as a correspondent in the local mining regions.

Harry had a chancier second project up his sleeve, compatible with the bread-and-butter work Wheeler was offering him. He hoped to produce 'an elaborate map of the quicksilver region' around Mount St Helena. He went on an initial 'prospecting tour' and settled on a vast tract between 'Calistoga and the head of Clear Lake, north and south, and Colusa and Healdsburg, east and west', including 'the locations of all mines actually worked' and 'every road, trail, mountain, and creek'. This enormous venture would be a speculative adjunct to the speculative mining business, and Harry needed to persuade financial backers that he had the 'many special qualifications' for the job. But then, if he could get past a reputation for being 'not safe to deal with', he could legitimately explain that army training in India encompassed skills in military drawing, surveying and making 'topological delineations'. Success with a map on this scale held out the promise of 'a substantial start in the world', though he would need immense willpower to get it done.

Before Flora managed to write directly to Harry, she got a letter to Mrs Smith, who acted to some extent as a postal go-between for the pair. Mrs Smith later half remembered a quotation from a second letter that Harry sent about Flora, too: 'If the poor girl is in distressed [*sic*] write and let me know, and I shall go and fetch her down or send her money to come.' And if this was roughly accurate, then it seems Harry remained ready to throw caution to the winds, if ever matters got truly out of hand.

The sole surviving example of a letter by Flora, also transcribed and preserved in court documents, was one she wrote to one of the Smith daughters, Sarah, on 11 July. It suggests that Flora viewed the Smiths as proxy family of a sort, starting: 'Yours of the 3d has just come to hand I had begun to think you had all forgotten me.' Flora's writing style is mildly disjointed, but she had forceful points on her mind. In particular, she was not impressed that Harry had been tormented with suspicions, though her high words soon slipped into practicalities: 'I received such a letter from H. L. saying that he heard I had not gone any further than Portland. I was so provoked that I wrote him a letter and sent it to the Geysers, and which if he receives it will not make him very happy. He ought to know me better than to accuse me of such a thing but I may forgive him.'

After almost a month, no $50 stipend had arrived in The Dalles from Muybridge, negligence of a kind to justify a knowing quip in the *Post* about the 'unremitting love' of absent husbands. Flora confided in Sarah Smith that, 'I have not heard from Mr. Sawyer or Muybridge since I came here I wrote to M last week don't think he will answer my letter.' Presumably Sawyer, Muybridge's legal man, oversaw her allowance. She added: 'I will send you the money to get my clothes from the Chinaman and from the Laundry just as soon as it is sent to me, it is over due now.' And it seems she was talking about money again when she threw in: 'I am so sorry for your poor mother having so much trouble and feel so bad not being able to have helped her before I left but tell her to keep up a good heart and it will come soon.' Mrs Smith had not yet received her pay for attending Flora, her nursing rate also being $50 a month.

The length of Flora's absence was evidently not fixed. 'About coming to San F you will see me back before you know it', she added, though also noting, 'I may stay until the first of September here.' Apparently The Dalles held few attractions for her. 'I do not like this place at all, they have a great deal of Company and try to make me go out, but I care for no one here and never shall.' She conceded, though: 'made a trip to the Columbia River with my Aunt on my Uncles Boat the scenery is perfectly lovely'. Her most unaffected pleasure was in her baby, now thriving: 'you cannot imagine how much my little darling has improved he is getting just as fat as a Pig and looking so pretty you would not know him to be the same baby. He notices everything and laughs when you tickle him under the chin to the delight of all. I do wish you could all see him. Tell Mary he will be able to sing to her when he comes back.'

Flora's mood switched back and forth as she poured out her feelings. Financial unease, isolation and her uncertain future were reason enough to brood. 'I have often thought of our good times', she wrote, wondering wistfully whether such happiness would ever return. 'I wish I had a nice little house with you know who, and your mother and all of you near me.' Then again, 'I would be so happy to get away from California', she said, and especially 'from all my pretended friends such for instance as Mrs. Gross', who had been spreading 'a pack of lies'. Flora planned, on her return, to 'tell her what I think of her'. Mrs Gross 'or anyone else can talk about Harry all they please, I am not ashamed to say I love him better than any one else on this Earth and no one can change my mind unless it is with his own lips he tells me that he does not care for me any more'.

Flora added that she had written to Rulofson 'for some of my photos'. Possibly these were personal. Possibly, though, given the parlous state of her finances, and following Muybridge's suggestion that she should find herself work, she had asked for prints to validate her abilities as a retoucher. If so, this could help to explain the strange assemblages in a scrapbook album she created. As well as featuring her collection of celebrity portraits, she filled it with an oversupply of Muybridge's photographs dating back at least as far as their time together at the Nahl gallery. Many of these were stereo images cut down the middle and stuck into the album twice, often with the same subject carelessly repeated on different pages. As for the album's forty-odd portraits, over half can be readily identified. Those showing performers recently on stage in San Francisco she arranged with no reference to their order of appearance in the city, a jumbled chronology that strongly indicates Flora had hoarded her portrait collection, and pasted the pictures pell-mell into the album after she left town. Besides Bonfanti, the ballerina, and, twice, Charles Vivian, 'serio-comic vocalist' at Maguire's Opera House, Flora featured the Lingards six times between them, including a shot of Horace in drag, as well as Jennie Lee in two beautiful portrait studies, offsetting all her comic poses. Another luminary to appear repeatedly was Marie Aimée, bouffe queen, four times across three pages. Taking a different tack, Flora also incorporated a photograph of the sexual theorist Orson Squire Fowler. And in her most suggestive choice, she included portraits side by side of Zulu Woodhull, and of her mother, Victoria Woodhull, the 'inspired Pythoness' who had publicly denounced marriage as enforced prostitution.

It seems no less telling that Flora casually trimmed many of the smaller Muybridge prints, treating them as frames around the portraits. However, these images cannot have been, to her, wholly negligible. His building interiors and outdoor vistas were by definition visual records. Yet, for Flora, each fleeting moment that he captured in a print represented its own secret negative: the block of hours, days, weeks or even months in which Muybridge had disappeared to secure it. Thus, among the most recent of his pictures that she included in the album were images of the new university buildings in Berkeley, pictures that for Flora marked the pitifully brief constellation of hours when it had been possible for her and Harry and the baby to be united.

*

Jennie Lee framed by Muybridge photographs

Flora's bold declaration of her love for Harry, though made in a private letter, was tempered by the frets of all the constraints on her in The Dalles, as well as the pain of being divided from almost everyone she cared for or loved. 'Have you seen or heard of Harry. How I wish I was with you all today, it is Sunday, and the wind is blowing a perfect gale, it does nothing else but blow ever since I have been here', she wrote. But then, 'I don't want Harry to come up here, as much as I would like to see him, for this is a small place, and people cannot hold their tongues.' She finished, 'Now Sarah write to me often and tell me all the news, look after the birds and tell Nora I am going to write today to her, I have not forgotten her, give my love to all the children, Mary, your mother and yourself. I remain ever your friend. Mrs. Muybridge.'

As an afterthought, Flora added, 'Destroy my letters after reading them, for you might lose ~~them~~ one, and it might get picked up. Flo.' But manifestly this was an instruction that Sarah Smith failed to fulfil.

14: Murder

Flora and the baby did not return to San Francisco 'before you know it', but instead stayed put in Oregon. Harry, by contrast, was continually on the move. He found it hard to subsist on his combined income from the *Stock Report* and the map subscriptions, but at least the two pursuits dovetailed. Wheeler had made him special correspondent for the 'Quicksilver Region', tracking investment possibilities in the 'vast mineral resources' around Mount St Helena. As well as hard information on assays, contested claims and dollar yields, Harry was to provide geological sketches, in the language of drifts, dumps, seams, croppings, ledges, leads and loads, the whole to be ameliorated here and there with jokes and stories in the style made popular by Mark Twain.

Harry's first dispatch was published on 28 August. He had set off from San Francisco, he said, 'specially commended to the good offices of Alex. Badlam', the same Badlam, that is, who had once tried to buy a half-interest in the *Chronicle*; indeed, the same Badlam whom Twain had mischievously accused of tipping sharks into San Francisco Bay to encourage backing for a new venture building a gigantic warm swimming bath. Badlam remained a prominent capitalist, and with the Calistoga Mine, in which he had a huge investment, now starting to yield 'pay ore', he was happy for Harry to promote the business to readers of the *Stock Report*. The pair took the 4 p.m. steamer, the *New World*, from the Vallejo Wharf, Badlam's hand on Harry's shoulder, Harry wrote, while Wheeler 'waved a last adieu to us from the dock and shouted a parting injunction to "do the trip in style".' From Vallejo they took the railroad that snaked down the Napa Valley. They reached the last stop, Calistoga, at around nine.

Harry was up betimes the next morning to visit the Calistoga Mine, hard work to reach, he said, 'But what a walk after months of work in the dusty city. The air was fragrant with the scent of azalias, great clusters of their white and lemon colored blossoms lit up the woods on every side.' And as he passed along, 'striped tiger lilies nodded a welcome', their 'gaudy glories made doubly prominent by the deep glossy green of the spikenard plant and Solomon's seal'. The region was known for its geysers and healing mineral springs; and cinnabar, containing quicksilver, or mercury, had long been recognised there too. But 'the real enchanter's wand', capital, had flowed in only when Spanish imports were interrupted by faraway political upheavals, Harry explained. Quicksilver trebled in value, and all at once the deer on the woody slopes of Mount St Helena found themselves startled by the sound of axes. Then 'furnaces blazed, and soon steam whistles woke the astonished echoes'. This rapid advance had been aided by improvements in the capture of mercury vapour, making it worthwhile to work even poor-quality ore, while preserving wary labourers from being poisoned. Here Harry threw in an old story that, in the early days, workers had exhaled so much mercury vapour in their sleep that in the mornings they found their bunkhouse windows turned into mirrors.

The further he crept down the tunnels of the Calistoga Mine, Harry wrote, the richer the walls before his eyes, showing gold and silver in sulphuret form, but also free gold. It was silver in particular, though, that was creating a local craze. 'St. Helena mountain must have been worn down several inches during the past week by the hundreds of feet which have tramped over every rod of it', he remarked. In fact, 'Judge Palmer, the Recorder, has been kept busy, and his books show a record of no less than one hundred and forty-three claims, within an area of two or three square miles.' Sometimes a breathless prospector tumbled Palmer out of bed in the night, and 'planked down' a ludicrous fee to have him come out at once and survey a claim by lantern light. Most proved useless, but richer men were gambling fortunes in the region.

For his second letter, published a week later, Harry visited the quicksilver mines in Knight's Valley, owned by Messrs Stuart & Co. and run by a local favourite, Mr Sarles. The Yellow Jacket Mine owed its name 'to a colony of wasps that ran tunnels on the lead for years, until their claims were jumped'. Dispossessing those wasps, William Stuart had recently discovered that 'All the hill side on this location yields pay dirt.' With the twin power sources of trees to burn and a strong river flowing through the land, work there was 'being pushed very rapidly, and for several weeks a night shift has been employed'. At the nearby Ida Clayton Mine, Harry found that 'The Ida ore is very attractive to the eye, every blast exposes beautifully crystallized quartz, while the presence of arsenic tints the rock with bright green streaks that bring the blood red patches of cinnabar into brilliant relief.' He closed by describing how, 'High up on the spurs which run from Mt. St. Helena, we get from either mine a view over the whole of Knight's Valley and far beyond;

Mount St Helena viewed from Calistoga Springs:
photograph by Muybridge

water is abundant, and on one of the creeks is a most picturesque spot, known as Acacia Falls, which has been immortalized by Virgil Williams and other of our artists.'

Never mind the lyrical touches, for these *Stock Report* pieces Harry had revived his plaintive nom de plume 'Ishmaelite'. His choice brings to mind the letter written by Ray Pelly to Alice in 1867, asking whether Harry 'must be driven out like poor Hagar into the Wilderness' – Hagar, the mother of Ishmael. While her son is in the womb, an angel foretells that he will be an outcast, 'a wild man; his hand *will be* against every man, and every man's hand against him'. The woe implicit in the name ran unabated through a private letter Harry wrote on 29 August, later reproduced, with slightly varied wording, by the *Chronicle* and the *Post*. It was sent from Pine Flat, a small mining town near Calistoga. To someone given as 'Dear Old L—,' he wrote: 'The weather is hot, and if I only had a companion I might have a very pleasant trip, but I'm as blue as the sky and lakes. This asthma sticks to me tighter than poverty. Sleep and I are strangers, and if I could get along without eating I'd prefer it, for feeding is hard labor.' The work was endless and exhausting. 'Up in the mountains, toiling away, riding twenty and thirty miles a day, groping along tunnels, clambering up and down shafts; nothing but mines, mines, mines; everybody making money, apparently, except the poor devils who work hardest, myself and the pick-and-hammer men to wit.' The 'map business' was making him 'gray-headed', he said, but he was trapped and had 'gone too far now to draw back', leaving him to 'wrestle for every cent to carry me on from day to day'. He had, he wrote, 'a really good job waiting for me up in Nevada, and I am more than doubtful that I shall lose it, for those interested are urging me to go up there at once, and I cannot get my map-work up here done under a fortnight at least'. Harry now succumbed to a wave of real self-pity, tracing his troubles back to his dealings with Arthur Neil. It was here that he said Neil's actions had dropped him abruptly 'to the level—at least, in the eyes of others—of riff-raff scum'. He continued: 'The fact is, L—, that the last two years have broken me down terribly; the undeserved disgrace where I was unknown, and the up-hill fight ever since have been too much to carry. I laugh off everything, and have the reputation of being the most devil-may-care, jovial cuss; but I feel my position every hour in every day.' He confessed, 'I have to count cents to insure having enough, a thing I seldom have sense enough to do', and added: 'Were it not for yourself and a few more, mainly those whom I have met through your instrumentality, I could not have stood it out.'

Richard Wheeler, who also knew quite how unhappy Harry could get, wrote of the irony that he 'almost became a proverb among the

men of his acquaintance as "lighthearted Harry Larkyns"'. And
Harry Edwards, too, would also describe, in impiously biblical
language, the depression of the 'jovial cuss': 'He walked among
men as if they knew him not, and it was only those few who were
admitted to a close intimacy with him who felt the warmth of that
heart which showed its secrets but so rarely.'

The ninth of September saw huge celebrations to mark California's
'silver wedding': twenty-five years since the arrival of 'the Argonauts
of '49', and twenty-four since California had been admitted as a
state into the Union. San Francisco's grandest buildings were draped
with gigantic decorations. Ships in the bay hung out their flags. A
great procession wound from Montgomery Street to Woodward's
Gardens, for speeches, and, in the event, a terrible balloon accident.
Muybridge, back from his lengthy coastal trip, managed to capture
a photograph of the massed ranks of the First Infantry Regiment.
What he failed to accomplish, though, and perhaps did not even
attempt, was a reunion with his wife and child, the baby last seen by
him at a few weeks, and now fully five months old. Nor did Flora
seize this opportunity to return to San Francisco herself.

Between all the 'mines, mines, mines', Harry did seek occasional
brief spells of respite in the city. And according to Dan O'Connell,
despite having no funds to speak of, Harry somehow 'continued to
give dinner parties to his friends, smoke the best cigars and drink
the best wines in the market'. In an attempt to convey Harry's
charm, O'Connell conjured up a particular evening when he
appeared in the city in early October:

> he invited some half a dozen to dine with him in a snug restaurant
> kept by an old Frenchwoman and her husband. I place the lady
> first, because she had everything to do with the management of
> the establishment. A table had been set aside for the major and his
> friends, and an unusually good dinner, with a profusion of wines,
> was served. At its close the major said in French to the old lady:
> 'Madame, I regret exceedingly that I cannot pay you just at present
> for this dinner. But as proof that my intentions are honorable, I will

sing you two of the latest Parisian songs, which you may consider as interest in advance on the debt.' The grim guardian of the till was taken by storm. The major, with one hand on the counter and the other in the air, rattled off two lively opera bouffe songs, which so delighted the lady that she insisted upon furnishing the singer's guests with a bottle of extra wine to drink success to the house.

At the tail end of this same flying visit, Harry Edwards also caught up with him, and they discussed Harry's map, still wearisomely some way off being finished. Edwards 'clasped hands with him and bade him God-speed'.

Harry must have dreaded his fresh return to redemptive vaga-bonding. On 9 October the *Stock Report* printed a new letter from their 'Napa Reporter' in which Harry made short work of the facts and figures on the Annie Belcher, the Pacific, the Socrates and one or two other mines. He ended on a promise that, after returning to Pine Flat, in his next bulletin he would take his readers north-east. But if he was privately dispirited, prospecting mania continued at full tilt. A local paper wrote that people seemed to have gone 'luny', a lunacy only boosted when William Stuart managed to sell a half-interest in the Ida Clayton and Yellow Jacket Mines for 'one hundred thousand dollars, cash'. If Harry did indeed make it to Pine Flat by 11 October, he would presumably have been invited to the triumphal party that took place that day in the woods on Mount St Helena. To 'a general popping of champagne corks and a drawing of other corks which did not pop', a group headed by 'Stewart [*sic*], of Knight's valley, with a party of ladies, Aleck Badlam and all the upper tendom of Calistoga, with their wives', came together to celebrate the 'new town which is building up in the neighborhood of the Calistoga silver mine'. After 'a few eloquent speeches from the parties most in interest', spades were wielded, 'Ground was broken, songs were sung—amongst others, "Three Black Crows Sat on a Tree," etc. And thus was born Silverado.'

Six years later, after his spell of dire penury in San Francisco, Robert Louis Stevenson found himself able to marry, at last, the newly divorced Fanny Osbourne. Virgil Williams suggested to them that they should spend their honeymoon out in his beloved Napa

Valley. Stevenson was suffering 'cold sweats, prostrating attacks of cough, sinking fits' and worse. He rejected Calistoga and Pine Flat, now little more than a ghost town, and instead went 'right up the mountain', seeking its healthful air and the huge views out over the 'green, intricate country' below. There, given their continuing impoverishment, he and Fanny took the rakish decision to camp in a bunkhouse of what had become the abandoned Silverado mining camp. The incipient town, so merrily christened by the local elite in 1874, had already almost completely vanished, while the mine itself, deep inside which Harry had observed winking gold and silver sulphurets, was a 'rusty and downfalling' ruin. Altogether, Stevenson wrote, this region, 'the back of man's beyond', was the domain of rattlesnakes and 'Poor Whites or Low-downers'. He and Fanny relished their holiday as Silverado squatters, but felt themselves to be 'in the wreck of that great enterprise, like mites in the ruins of a cheese'.

Back in San Francisco, Susan Smith, the nurse, was still lacking $100 of her wages for services provided to the Muybridge household in April and May. On Muybridge's return to the city, Flora wrote to her imploring her not to approach him; but by mid October Mrs Smith had had enough. She secured the services of a debt collector, Samuel Harding, causing Flora to write in panic offering 'more than the $100' if Mrs Smith would withdraw the suit. Mrs Smith, however, her patience exhausted, went ahead. On Tuesday, 13 October, with Harding's help, she 'recovered judgement against Muybridge, in a Justice's Court, for $100 and costs'.

During this hearing, Muybridge produced evidence of having given Flora money to pay the bill, and implied that Mrs Smith was engaged in a racket. Mrs Smith, in turn, brought out 'a letter from her to me acknowledging her indebtedness', a letter that happened also to mention Harry. Muybridge 'said it was strange that his wife should mention Larkyns' name so familiarly', and 'appeared agitated'. The next day, in circumstances unexplained, he asked Mrs Smith whether she had other letters from his wife, and whether she would give them to him. And it appears that this correspondence now became part of a transaction by which Mrs Smith was to secure her payment. She cautiously agreed that, in front of Muybridge, she would hand over various letters to his attorney, Mr Sawyer.

Despite the verdict against him, Muybridge continued to act as though, morally, he did not owe Mrs Smith her $100. But he desperately wanted the letters. And so, on the morning of Thursday, 15 October, when Mrs Smith arrived at Sawyer's office, there was Muybridge outside, 'pacing up and down, and looking wild and excited'. Mrs Smith was clear: 'I have come to see about getting my money.' Muybridge, though, 'wanted to know if I had any proof of his wife's guilt'. Mrs Smith replied, 'I don't know', to which he responded along the lines of, 'Mrs. Smith, if you don't tell me the truth I shall consider you a bad woman.' The two of them went up to Sawyer's office, Muybridge 'pale and haggard', and Mrs Smith handed Sawyer the letters. As she walked from the room, still unpaid, Muybridge seized the letters and began to read them, and 'As I closed the door I heard a scream and a fall.'

The next morning, Friday, 16 October, the *Stock Report* carried Ishmaelite's latest long letter. It opened with a hymn to Will Stuart: by his nurturing of the Knight's Valley mines, Stuart had 'done more for this country than any ten men'. As well as the Yellow Jacket and the Ida Clayton, he owned or part-owned the Missouri, the Kentuck and the Peerless; and with his latest gigantic investments generating new employment, his local popularity was understandable. The greater part of Harry's letter, however, was given to describing Pine Flat, a 'young Mercury-opolis' in 'one of the prettiest gorges imaginable'. Its mining camp was already well provided with hotels, stores, stables, restaurants and saloons, and there was the promise of dance houses to come, and probably trouble with them. Next Harry switched to giving an account of various quicksilver mines thereabouts, including the Rattlesnake, Red Cloud and Flagstaff, before he provided a valiant summary of a mire of contested claims in the Pine Flat area. To end with, he promised that in his next letter he would say something about the Coverdale mines, the 'famous Sulphur Bank' and rich discoveries in Bear Valley. With this workload, his thirty-first birthday, in two days' time, promised to be nothing but hard work.

That same Friday, Muybridge came to Mrs Smith's home late in the evening on the pretext that he 'wished her to give him further time in which to pay the money for which she had obtained judgement'. Once inside, he revealed Sawyer's opinion of the letters she had handed over: they 'did not show anything more than a harmless flirtation'. Muybridge wanted something more: further letters, and 'proof of his wife's guilt'. He was disquieted to find that Mrs Smith had a photograph of his nameless baby, with a name inscribed on the back. Mrs Smith, perhaps reduced to an attitude of 'a plague on both your houses', gave Muybridge the extra correspondence he sought, and he left again, with the material that would decide him.

The next morning, Saturday, 17 October, various Bohemians ran into Muybridge in the rooms of the Art Association, linked to the Bohemian Club and presided over by Virgil Williams. All found him 'perfectly cool and self-possessed'. Then in the early afternoon, Harry Edwards, walking along Montgomery Street, was summoned by Muybridge into the vestibule of Bradley & Rulofson to talk business. Muybridge, according to Edwards, 'had done some work in experimental photography for me, and I spoke to him about it': outside his acting, Edwards, 'a man of much scientific attainment', had recently identified a previously unknown gall wasp, 'Cynips saltatorius, Hy. Edw', but he was largely studying lepidoptera at the time, and in particular was interested in the transformations of butterflies and moths. During these exchanges, Muybridge 'nonchalantly said that he had some business up country, and intended to leave by the afternoon boat'. Next, Muybridge went inside and had a painful interview with Rulofson himself, in which he admitted that he planned to hunt Harry down. Muybridge gave the letters to Rulofson for safe keeping, then left in a hurry to catch the 4 p.m. ferry from the Vallejo Wharf.

From this point on, 'Muybridge subdued his feelings, but did not relax his resolve', though an old friend, J. P. H. Wentworth, who spotted him catching the same ferry, said later that Muybridge had seemed 'very much excited; turned, when on the boat, toward him as if about to speak, and then wheeled around and walked the other way'.

Muybridge took the train from Vallejo to Calistoga, arriving at about 9 p.m., went briefly to a saloon, and then to the local livery stables of Connolly and Foss. He asked for a buggy to take him to Pine Flat, having presumably read Harry's *Stock Report* letter of the day before. But Connolly, who had just spoken to William Stuart, told Muybridge that Stuart was giving Harry a bed for the night at the Yellow Jacket Mine. Connolly tried to persuade Muybridge to wait until morning, when Harry was due in Calistoga, telling him that it was 'a very dark and a bad road, and I didn't like to let the team go there'. Moreover Muybridge seemed to have no luggage or coat, and had had no time to eat. But Muybridge said it was 'imperative' that he should leave at once. Connolly caved in, hiring him a two-horse buggy with a young driver called George Wolfe, and lending him a buggy robe to ward off the chilly night air.

As they set out, Muybridge offered Wolfe $5 if he could get there before William Stuart, but as they were half an hour behind, Wolfe said it was 'no use' even attempting this. Still, he drove 'as rapidly as possible'. Out in the darkness, Muybridge asked about the danger of robbers on the road. Wolfe said that 'such a thing was not thought of', but Muybridge nevertheless asked, 'Would it frighten your horses if I were to fire off my pistol?' And when Wolfe replied that it would not, Muybridge successfully loosed off one of the bullets in his Smith & Wesson six-shooter. Muybridge 'spoke calmly, betraying no excitement or nervousness', even when he asked Wolfe, 'What is Larkyns doing up here?' He revealed that he aimed to 'give him an unexpected meeting'.

The Clayton family, including Ida Clayton herself, lived in a ranch house on the Yellow Jacket property. And to this house proper, extra quarters had been built on for visitors to the mine. The annexe included bedrooms or bunk rooms, a kitchen, a dining room and a large parlour. Stuart arrived at around 10 p.m. and went straight to bed. William Sarles, his mine superintendent, was also there, and also in bed. Mrs Sarles, Ida Clayton and a few others were in the house. And Harry himself was playing cribbage in the annexe with J. M. McArthur, a miner from Alameda County, and with McArthur's wife. Harry told them that the next day was his birthday.

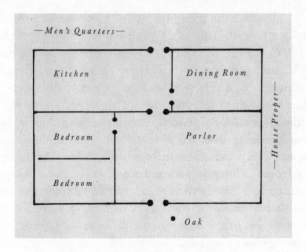

Men's quarters, Yellow Jacket ranch house, back door
opening directly from the kitchen

At about 11 p.m., Benjamin Prickett, the foreman of the Yellow Jacket Mine, and two local farmers, Charles McCrory and Michael Murray, were outside the back door greeting a pair of miners back late from the Missouri Mine. In the darkness, Prickett heard a buggy draw up some twenty feet away. He saw the outline of George Wolfe's passenger, but not his face. The figure got down, came towards them and 'asked for Mr. Larkyn', but when Murray invited the man to walk in 'he said he wanted to see him outside'. Murray and McCrory obligingly stepped in, and 'the boys told Harry he was wanted'.

Harry 'excused himself in a jocular manner' from the card game and went to the back door. By now, the man outside had retreated. Harry ventured out on the back step and, silhouetted against the light, asked who wanted him, adding that it was too dark to see. The figure gave his name, Muybridge, and said, 'I have a message from my wife.' According to Prickett, 'Larkyns stepped down two steps as if to approach him, when there was a report and a flash.' As recounted by all, when the shot rang out Harry 'turned and run through the house'. McCrory saw him 'reel and run'. It was short straight dash from the back to the front door.

At the sound of gunfire, McArthur had slipped into the bedroom for his own weapon. Harry passed before him 'hurriedly, having both hands pressed upon his left breast', followed by Muybridge, 'pistol in hand'. The *Post* later reported that Harry was calling, 'Let me out. Let me out.' He staggered over the front threshold and collapsed at the foot of an adjacent oak tree.

Muybridge, running after him, seemed determined on a second shot, but McArthur prevented this and 'demanded his pistol of him', leading to a brief stand-off before, showing 'considerable hesitancy', Muybridge passed over his cocked weapon. Despite everything, his hand was perfectly steady. McArthur, covering him, told the others to 'look after the Major'.

McCrory and Murray quickly carried Harry back indoors, where 'He groaned slightly for a few minutes' then died – though a more lyrical account had it that, with 'no opportunity to defend himself or to utter a word', he 'ran a few steps and fell a corpse, with a bullet through his heart.'

William Stuart, roused from his bed, now appeared and instructed McArthur to take Muybridge into the parlour. Muybridge began explaining that he had not expected to find genteel company, and he 'made excuses to the ladies and begged their pardon for frightening them as he had done'. Apparently, 'He told them that he considered that this man Larkyns had destroyed his happiness, or something like that.' But then he asked for water, and settled down to read a newspaper 'as though nothing unusual had happened'. If there was even for a moment any 'talk of lynching', then 'through the influence of Mr. Stuart this act of violence was not put into effect'.

Muybridge volunteered to surrender himself to the authorities in Calistoga. But the others demurred, soon hitching up a spring wagon and forming a small party to take him in themselves. Stuart presided. Murray held a lantern. McArthur and Sarles, having roped Muybridge's legs together, acted as an armed guard. On the journey, the back wheel of their wagon missed the edge of a bridge and McArthur was tipped out and quite seriously injured. Nevertheless, they reassembled themselves and completed their journey, Muybridge garrulously justifying himself along the way.

On arrival, before handing him in, they went to a saloon, where Stuart offered drinks all round. McArthur observed Muybridge's hand as he raised his bottle, and 'as a matter of curiosity' saw that it continued 'unusually steady'.

At about 1 a.m., the local constable, Crummel, took Muybridge into custody. He too found Muybridge 'very cool for one who had just killed a man'. Muybridge told him that he had no regrets and predicted that, although it might cost a lot, 'I won't have any trouble to get clear.'

The Yellow Jacket party, meanwhile, returned to the mine with Judge Palmer, from whom Harry had recently gathered statistics and anecdotes about the extraordinary proliferation of mining claims. Samuel J. Reid, a Calistoga medic, also came. He performed a quick post-mortem while Palmer cobbled together a nine-man inquest jury, some of them having been present at the shooting.

The events of the past few hours were now doughtily and consistently described. And Dr Reid confirmed a bullet wound front-on: 'the cause of death was from internal hemorage from the heart and I find an orifice between the fifth and sixth ribs, an inch to the left of the sternum directly over the region of the heart, evidently made by some missel, and passing directly into the heart, which caused his death'. There was hardly a doubt of the verdict. The jury found 'that we believe said Muybridge to be the person by whose act the death of said Harry Larkyns is occasioned'. Two of the jurors signed with crosses. One newspaper, using the property terms that the murderer himself would favour, summed up the entire story thus: 'Edward J. Muybridge, a San Francisco photographer, shot and killed Major Harry Larkyns, a somewhat noted literary and artistic character, in Napa county, last Saturday night, for trespassing on his marital preserves.' Dan O'Connell wrote even more succinctly that 'It was the old story—a faithless wife, a reckless lover, and an avenging husband.'

Word of the murder reached San Francisco by wire the next morning, Sunday. There was soon 'a startling rumour about the city to the effect that a terrible tragedy had taken place near Calistoga'. Harry and Muybridge were both mentioned, but for some hours it was 'not known definitely which was killed'. Only at noon did the *Chronicle* post a definitive dispatch on its bulletin board: Harry had been shot dead. The two men were sufficiently well known that this became the 'all absorbing topic on the streets'. The 'dreadful affair' was not so surprising to those with an idea of the 'real connection' between them, but it came as a 'thunderbolt' to the wider community, who still looked on Harry and Muybridge as 'warm, intimate friends'.

In Calistoga, William Stuart did not stint his murdered guest, paying for a rosewood coffin 'with silver-plated screws and handles', and ensuring that Harry's body would be conveyed that day to San Francisco. Muybridge was reported to be 'very calm and collected, and apparently feeling entirely justifiable in the killing of Larkyns'. Judge Palmer dealt swiftly with the matter of a preliminary examination, and in the evening, Constable Crummel took Muybridge by train to the Napa County jail, where he was incarcerated to await the machinery of the law.

At about the same time, back in San Francisco, William Paton, one of the Irish assistants in Bancroft's literary factory, walked into a beer saloon where he found Edward Ellis and told him of Harry's murder. Ellis, who had 'trembled before the deceased while he lived', replied that this news was too good to be true. He dashed his hat down on the counter, threw his drink over his shoulder, demanded another beer and said that 'he hoped Larkyns hadn't had time to repent, and was then in hell'. He even 'proposed Larkyns' death as a toast'. His drinking companion at the bar, a man called Bridges, was so shocked by Ellis's abuse that he 'could not thereafter recognize him as a friend'.

Ellis soon left, and intercepted a *Chronicle* reporter Charles O. Phelps, volunteering to accompany him on his detail to meet the ferry from Vallejo 'to see if the body of Larkyns arrived'. When the steamer docked, Harry's coffin was duly unloaded, and the driver of the 'dead wagon' informed them that he was headed for the undertakers Lockheart & Porter on Third Street. By the time Phelps and Ellis got there, numbers of pressmen had already gathered to pay their respects. Phelps's news report would state that Harry was dressed in his business suit, and that his face 'looked natural', though 'there were bruises on the forehead and nose, probably occasioned by his fall'. Further, he revealed that Harry's shirt front was bloodstained, and, 'upon opening it, a small bullet-hole was discovered in the region of the heart'. With a degree of verbal handwringing, Phelps added that 'those who knew something of the man could not withhold some tribute of honest regard for him without doing violence to their own natures'. A less contorted account stated that 'more than one who cherished the memory of the deceased stooped to kiss the cold forehead, while some shed tears from a grief that they could not hide'. Both on the way to Lockheart & Porter and leaving again, Phelps was dismayed by Ellis, who repeated that Harry 'had deeply injured him, and he was glad he was dead'. William Paton ran into Ellis a second time that night, and he too felt 'mortified and ashamed', hearing the spiteful relish with which Ellis continued to celebrate Harry's death.

Richard Wheeler, reflecting in the *Stock Report*, observed that the tragedy of the murder, 'from the almost universal popularity of its victim, cast a shadow of gloom over the more Bohemian classes in the city'. Harry had been absurdly generous, 'thinking no time or trouble too much for him to give when he could serve a friend or even a casual acquaintance'. And as he was 'wonderfully gifted both physically and mentally, he stood almost as a representative of that class that now so bitterly mourns for him'. Wheeler did not sanction Harry's liaison with Flora, he wrote; but he ventured that few 'men who are men' could 'find much to say against him'.

On Monday, a fresh influx of mourners came to Lockheart & Porter's to see Harry's remains, including a 'large number of gentlemen connected with the journalistic and theatrical profession'. Sam Davis later suggested that, despite 'big money' now being offered by various papers, a friend went to Harry's rooms and burned Flora's remaining letters. At Bancroft's literary factory William Paton spoke to fellow assistant Gerald Darcy, and described Ellis's disgraceful behaviour of the night before.

The Monday papers were flooded with accounts of the murder, as well as comment on Harry himself, typically that his 'ideas of correct dealing did not stand him well', but that he had had 'good qualities, withal, which won him much indulgence'. Many were expected to 'bestow the touching tribute of "poor devil" on his corpse', and 'His life-history would, no doubt, afford a romantic narrative.' One paper placed him squarely in the tradition of the adventurer, whose fate was often violent death: 'Brave, needy, extravagant and reckless', even their vices added 'a seeming brilliancy to the eccentricity of their characters'. Harry had been a latter-day model of exactly those 'erratic knights of fortune' who, 'banished for their improvidence', became 'citizens of the world' and lived 'precariously by sword or pen'. Some papers sank to tawdry wordplay: 'Poor Larkyns looked into the wrong camera—it had an *obscura* attachment.' But even the *Chronicle* conceded that, as 'a cosmopolitan character', Harry had been 'a man of good parts'. It also gave information strongly suggesting the line Harry had taken in order to conceal his shady past. A lady 'who knew him professionally abroad' had informed the paper that he 'first entered business by putting quite a large sum of money into the Lyceum Theatre'. But the venture failed, incurring such family displeasure 'that with the exception of his sister, they ceased to receive or recognise him'. This tale, of a glamorous gamble gone wrong, would have done very well to explain away his poverty and estrangement, while placing Harry within a world he was fully equipped to describe. The *Chronicle* also reported that Harry had 'volunteered in the service of Garibaldi' and was 'with him in his campaigns', before then fighting on the French side in the Franco–Prussian War. But as even a hostile obituary noted, among Harry's 'erratic traits', he was not, just for the sake of it, given to 'idle boasting and fanciful tales', and so this looks like a straight misunderstanding of the fact that Garibaldi had also fought in France.

As well as writing up Harry's murder, Monday morning's *Chronicle* printed a long interview with Mrs Smith, secured by one of its reporters the day before. She was 'well on in years and proportionately reticent', he wrote, not that that made her a match for his badgering. She earned herself the headline 'An Aged Nurse Tells What She Knows.' Among other details, she gave a partial account of the birth of Flora's baby, and, as relayed by the *Chronicle*, also disclosed incidents 'tending to show' that Harry and Flora had 'kept up a correspondence and intimacy unknown to her husband'. At the same time, Mrs Smith spoke of Muybridge's long-standing, powerful suspicions. She described his surprise, a couple of evenings before, on the Friday night, when he dropped by to request more time to pay her bill, at finding that she had a photograph of his baby, supposedly inscribed 'Little George Harry'. At this, according to the *Chronicle*'s telling, Muybridge 'seemed frenzied and swore he would never pay Mrs. Smith a cent unless she gave him letters of his wife, which he said he knew she must have in her possession. She gave them up. He read one or two of them and then rushed from the house.' The reporter added a note of his own on the perplexing question of why Mrs Smith had kept hold of letters she had been asked to forward, and implied that she had retained them as a form of security against her unpaid bill.

Mrs Smith was sufficiently upset by the *Chronicle* write-up that when a reporter from the *Post* came knocking on Monday she gave a corrective interview, published on its pages that same evening. The idea behind her forwarding letters, she explained, had been to disguise from Flora's relatives that she had a 'gentleman correspondent'. And Mrs Smith had omitted to follow through, not from spite or a desire for profit, but because 'I did not like to get mixed up in their affairs.' When, the previous Friday night, Muybridge had demanded more letters, well, 'I have a family and I must have my money, and so I gave them to him.' But even these new letters contained no 'proof positive of guilt', she said, though they did suggest 'something behind' the words. Contrary to what the *Chronicle* had related, 'He did not read them here, but took them away with him.' Also diverging from the *Chronicle*'s colourful version of her story, Mrs Smith now made no mention of Muybridge being 'frenzied', even in response to the photograph of the baby with a name written on the back when, after all, he 'thought the baby had no name'. Getting into her stride, she explained that it had not been for want of money that Flora 'threw herself away'. Muybridge 'loved the little thing', and often handed her spare change and even twenty-dollar bills. Yet Flora continually ran short, and 'used to come and see me and cry, and wish she had the money to pay me'. Mrs Smith seemed unsure which side to take. She called Flora 'one of the nicest little women I ever saw', but then described how, after Muybridge had gone to Harry's rooms on Montgomery 'and threatened to shoot him', Harry and Flora 'used to laugh about it'. No danger had been enough to keep them apart: 'She told me there was a terrible scene between her husband and the Major just before she went to Oregon', and 'her husband remained away from the house for a week after it. Then he made her promise on her knees that she would never see the Major again.' But within a half-hour, 'the Major was in the house'. The *Post* treated these revelations warily, casting Mrs Smith in sardonic inverted commas as 'A "Mutual Friend"'.

Remarkably, Mrs Smith also attempted to set the record straight in the *Chronicle* itself. Reporting a second interview with her, the paper noted unblushingly that 'The good lady is much disturbed by her sudden and unpleasant notoriety.' In particular, she wished to stress that the letters, 'chiefly those of Mrs. Muybridge and of a very loving character', had 'come into her possession in a legitimate manner'. She then offered an inaccurate version of Flora's childhood, before pointing the way to other informants, the 'lady friends' in South Park.

Well might Mrs Smith have found her notoriety disturbing. She was now vilified across the press for stirring up Muybridge's passions and driving him 'to the commission of that most terrible of crimes, murder'. One paper called her 'nauseating', another, 'despicable'. If her object was 'to get her fee, let who would be the sufferer', remarked a third, she could be satisfied that her 'peculiar process for collecting a debt' had been 'entirely effective in launching a wretched mortal into eternity'. Nor was that the end of it, when yet another paper added a new crime to the roster: 'The very parties who conveyed his letters when Larkyns failed to remit the heavy black-mail demanded, showed them to the husband. Muybridge was intensely excited by them, and set out at once.' After her immediate efforts to save her reputation, Mrs Smith 'judiciously made up her mind to say nothing further' until she could 'explain in court'. She needed to consider extraordinarily carefully how to restore her name at Muybridge's trial.

Over in Napa that same Monday, the press reported that Muybridge continued to rest 'tranquilly in confinement'. He had been supplied with reading matter and was refusing to give interviews, but he did receive Rulofson that day, who travelled to see him in his cell, no doubt in part to hand back the letters Muybridge had left with him. They discussed Muybridge's 'honor', and talked about Flora too.

Also that day, presumably after this trip rather than beforehand, Rulofson gave his own interview to the *Chronicle*, in a staunch effort at damage limitation. He described how Muybridge had been at Bradley & Rulofson at around half past two on the afternoon of the murder, and how, taking the elevator against his confirmed habit, he had seemed agitated and bewildered, 'pale as marble', with 'eyes glazed like those of a madman', his teeth chattering and his upper lip drawn up 'as rigidly fixed as if he were paralyzed'. In the ladies' dressing room he 'threw himself on a lounge and wept bitterly, moaning', and when at last he could speak, he said: 'Mr. Rulofson, you have been a good friend to me, I want you to promise me that in case of my death you will uphold the good name of my wife, and that you will settle our business affairs with her as you would with me.' Rulofson, deducing that Muybridge contemplated suicide, had asked him why. But Muybridge denied that he was suicidal and, when Rulofson tried to block the door, 'hurled him across the room' with 'almost superhuman strength' and started down the stairs.

Rulofson chased after Muybridge, he said, and at length was able to persuade him to come back upstairs. And between 'paroxysms of grief', his forehead running with 'drops of cold perspiration', Muybridge at last revealed 'that he had been dishonored by Harry Larkyns'. Rulofson protested that it would be hard to be sure, but Muybridge produced proofs. The first line of a letter written by Flora supposedly 'left no room for doubt': this revelatory sentence does not survive. But Muybridge then showed Rulofson what was clearly the letter Harry had sent to Mrs Smith in June. As Rulofson summarised it: Harry 'had heard, he said, that she had been untrue to him, but he did not and could not believe that the mother of his child would forget him or be untrue'.

At the 'astounding revelation' of this correspondence, Rulofson was temporarily 'staggered', he said, and asked Muybridge what he meant to do. Muybridge replied that he intended to track Harry down, 'and that one or other of them must die'. This avowal embroiled Rulofson in a potential murder and, knowing the Vallejo ferry would shortly depart, he claimed to have 'talked against time', even arguing that if Muybridge left at once he might fail in his mission, as he was 'in no fitting condition of mind to undertake a task which required the greatest coolness and judgement'. But with mere minutes to go, Muybridge 'sprang out of the room and ran down the street like a deer'. And this time there was no stopping him.

It is not a given that Muybridge sanctioned this portrait of him as a gibbering madman. What is sure, though, is that Rulofson knew the legal import of the picture he was painting; more particularly, that he knew the value of leavening clear premeditation with implied insanity. In his daily life Rulofson kept well hidden the fact that Edward Rulloff, infamous at the time as a scholar, robber and presumed multiple murderer, was his very own brother. Rulloff had successfully defended himself in several trials; but the most recent of them, in New York in May 1871, had come down to a simple argument over whether, having shot his latest victim in the head, he was guilty of murder in the first or second degree. When Rulloff was sentenced to hang, an argument was propounded in the press that his enormous intellect was grounds for sparing him the death penalty. Mark Twain published a satirical letter on the subject. But this satire came with a measure of ambivalence, and three days before the hanging Twain, still then working on material for *Roughing It*, scribbled a sardonic, anticipatory dedication for the book honouring Rulloff as 'the Late Cain'. Though 'his bloody deed placed him without the pale of sympathy, strictly speaking', Twain wrote, Cain had had the 'misfortune' to be denied 'the beneficent Insanity Plea'. Without doubt Rulofson, too, would have mulled his brother's legal fortunes in painful detail, and therefore understood in his very marrow how sometimes a convincing insanity plea stood to save a murderer from the noose.

During the morning of Tuesday, 20 October, crowds came to Lockheart & Porter to take a last look at Harry and leave flowers, 'until the coffin was covered with wreaths and bouquets'. His funeral was set for 1 p.m. At last 'the coffin lid was screwed down', and his 'intimate friends' carried his body to the hearse. The cortège proceeded to the Church of the Advent on Howard, a single block from where Flora had given birth six months before.

Church of the Advent: photograph by Muybridge

There were ten pall-bearers in pairs: Harry Edwards with Barton Hill, acting manager of the California Theatre; Clay Green, playwright, with Richard Wheeler; Sam Davis with Alfred Bulch, resident clerk at 1010 Montgomery; Walter Fisher with Dan O'Connell; and finally Louis Hamm, an amateur artist, with T. J. Vivian, journalist, statistician and boxing aficionado. The music was overseen by George T. Evans, leader of the orchestra at Maguire's Opera House, a member of the Bohemian Club and the composer, for Jennie Lee, of the 'Kenilworth Galop'. Four superb singers also performed: Mrs Blake and Miss Howell, stalwarts of the city's concert halls, the tenor Alfred Wilkie, recently of the troupe of Madame Anna Bishop, and George Russell, renowned baritone and much Harry's favourite of the California Minstrels.

Four or five hundred people attended, including 'editors and reporters of all the city papers' and others of Harry's friends, all ready to throw 'a broad mantle of charity over his earthly frailties'. Sam Davis later wrote that 'There never was such a mingling of classes as was seen at Larkins' funeral. Millionaires and paupers, society dames and harlots, merchants and thespians, opera singers and dance-hall artists, ministers and newspapermen—every extreme of life produced friends to pay a last tribute to Harry Larkins.'

A solemn Episcopalian service followed. The singers performed a setting of the lines, 'Man that is born of a woman hath but a short time to live, and is full of misery. He cometh up, and is cut down like a flower; he fleeth as it were a shadow, and never continueth in one stay.' The whole congregation sang 'Rock of Ages Cleft for Me'. And at the end, in the most powerful moment of the service, George Russell sang what was said to be Harry's favourite air, 'Flee as a Bird', a piece of music destined to become a jazz standard, at dirge speed, in New Orleans funeral marches. The lyric, drawing on Psalm XI, had been written in 1857 by Mary S. Dana, who then set it to a 'Spanish Melody'. Her words so pointedly fitted Harry's circumstances that it is no wonder the congregation wept:

> Flee as a bird to your mountain,
> Thou who art weary of sin;
> Go to the clear flowing fountain,
> Where you may wash and be clean;
> Fly, for th'avenger is near thee;
> Call and the Saviour will hear thee,
> He on his bosom will bear thee,
> Thou who art weary of sin,
> O thou, who art weary of sin.

As the pall-bearers, in step, began to carry Harry's body from the church, 'a well-known actress of the California Theatre' – Jennie Lee, later reports make it clear – 'leaned from her seat and, sobbing violently, put a handsome bouquet upon the coffin'.

Lloyd's guide to San Francisco included a description of a fashionable San Francisco funeral, packed with smart friends and curious onlookers, professionals singing the requiem, and a profusion of flowers. At the end of such a service, he wrote, a 'grand procession forms, and slowly marches to the cemetery', where 'the remains are deposited in a vault for future disposal'. He also described the city's westerly Lone Mountain burial grounds; its many tombs and monuments, its avenues and paths, disappearing into 'the unimproved wilds'. On the south side was the Masonic cemetery, and it was there that Harry's remains were now taken. A 'long concourse of carriages followed the corpse', and his coffin was displayed outside a vault for the last time. The quartet sang once more, 'Just as I Am, Without One Plea'. Then, after a few 'appropriate remarks' by Alfred Bulch, came a eulogy by Harry Edwards.

Edwards spoke fiercely. Harry had been 'a gentleman in the finest sense of the word', and one who 'in the retrospect of his own sorrows, knew how to find excuses for the follies of his fellow men'. He had been seeking, 'by the energy of his own endeavor', to earn the right to go home to England, honour restored. But those who had known him best knew 'the torments he endured', and 'the wearying conflicts of his one poor heart against a world of selfish, pitiless pride'. He had been a distinguished soldier on the battlefield, but the 'grandest and most heroic struggles of his life were the hand-to-hand conflicts which he waged against those who reviled him here, and who were far beneath him in every point of manliness, and truth, and honor'. Let Harry's detractors know, Edwards continued, that 'no mother's hand ever smoothed his head, no father's gentle voice ever offered him counsel. Those natural protectors and advisers were snatched from him at so early an age that his memory of them was but a faded recollection.' Deprived of their care and counsel, he had had 'to fight the battle of his life alone'. Those now 'gathered in the depth of sorrow around his poor remains' knew how arduous Harry's path had been, and they 'loved and honored him' for it. And so, said Edwards, 'gentle and loving friend and brother, farewell!' By now, wrote Richard Wheeler, 'tears were streaming down the faces of nearly everyone present'. Reportedly, Jennie Lee was the last mourner to abandon the vault.

Benjamin Lloyd could not resist the wry observation that a wanderer among the Lone Mountain headstones must be left with the impression that the Angel of Death admitted to his ranks 'only those whose heavenly virtues rendered them unfit to inhabit a sin-cursed world'. And naturally Harry Edwards was expected to speak highly of the dead. Yet when, a decade later, he published a clutch of his memorial speeches, he was moved to add a singular, impassioned prologue to his words about Harry. Few had known him intimately, he said, but among those who had counted him a 'warm and true friend', his 'unselfish character' remained even now a 'sacred' memory. Harry's knowledge and understanding, in multiple spheres, had been 'refined', 'admirable', 'brilliant'. Unspecified 'influences about him' might have fettered him and prevented him 'from adorning more distinctly the walk of life in which he moved'. Indeed, poverty had so dogged him that 'the generous fountains of his nature' were 'dried up by her touch'. But the cutting-short of his 'great abilities' represented a distressing loss of potential, nevertheless. Edwards finished by observing that 'many who knew and loved' Harry had followed him to the grave, and he said sadly that, if nothing else, then the tremendous 'depth of their sorrow' could be taken as a measure of what had been lost.

15: Misstatements

Word spread fast among San Francisco's Bohemians that Edward Ellis had 'gibbered and gloated' over Harry's corpse. His 'infamy' became a news item, one paper reporting that he had left the undertaker's 'rubbing his hands and grinning like a human jackal'. The young Bancroft assistant Gerald Darcy, though he had never met Ellis, found the stories 'so repulsive' that he 'undertook to thrash him'. Darcy was pale, 'a light weight', with 'whiskers just struggling into prominence, and a self-contained manner'. On the Monday evening he had repaired to the upstairs offices of the *Chronicle* to challenge Ellis: 'You call yourself a representative Englishman?' he said. 'Name your friend. You spat in Harry Larkyns' dead face, and I've resolved to have satisfaction.' Darcy himself named Walter Fisher. Ellis at first 'temporized', then agreed so needlingly to show up for a fight that Darcy twice attempted to bypass formalities and simply give him a kicking that very night. But he was restrained both times by the *Chronicle*'s doughty city editor, Colonel Shaw, soon to become president of the National Rifle Association. As Ellis slipped away, Darcy, held back by Shaw, flung out that Ellis 'wasn't a gentleman, and the Almighty couldn't make him one'.

Ellis was not a character to take insults quietly. The next day he went to the police and laid the double charge against Darcy of using vulgar language, and language calculated to provoke a duel. Though arrests after sunset were proscribed for misdemeanour charges, a compliant officer imprisoned Darcy that night, leaving him no chance to procure bail. The following morning, coupled with its own account of Harry's funeral, the *Chronicle* obligingly printed a letter from Ellis which it headed, 'Baseless Fabrication'. Ellis had expressed no more than 'disbelief' about Harry's death, he wrote. He had been 'accidentally' at the dock when the coffin arrived, had looked at the body 'reverently' and intended to take 'the proper legal steps for my own vindication'. William Paton was outraged into writing a letter that he got the *Post* to print that same evening. Ellis absolutely had 'used many strong expressions', he retorted, had spoken of Harry 'as a swindler, scoundrel, etc.' and had displayed an 'evil animus' utterly unbecoming 'an Englishman, passing himself off as a gentleman'.

There were 'Bohemians of all sorts on hand' over the next two days as the case against Darcy played out in the police court. On day one, the *Alta* carried a singular message in its 'Brevities' column: 'Take a friend's advice, Ellis, and drop that case against Darcy', but naturally Ellis ignored this. The *Post* referred to him as 'The Ghoul' and painted him as affected and portly, with a jet-black beard and a prominent 'sheeny pate'. The *Alta* described Ellis's bizarre servility and 'peculiarity of utterance', and compared him to a comic creation by William Horace Lingard or Charles Vivian. Given that Lingard was a celebrated female impersonator, and given that Charles Vivian had famously been for six weeks the husband of Annie Hindle, foremost male impersonator of the day, this remark seems designed to imply Ellis was, at the least, effete.

Colonel A. P. Dudley, defending Darcy, in order to stay sharp, forsook his usual 'matutinal cocktail'. In a typical performance he might be found to have 'lost the case, his temper, and some gallons of "honest sweat," three waistcoat buttons, and some hair oil'. He now assailed Ellis with combative questions, to which Ellis responded with 'N-e-o-w, Sar' and wriggling half-replies. Ellis denied being a 'bogus correspondent' for the *Chronicle*, but admitted having helped Harry put together one London letter for the *Post*. He denied calling for liquor in the saloon or proposing 'any sentiment' on hearing of Harry's death, only to concede that he had flung his drink over his shoulder, though 'Not exultingly'. Then he flat out admitted that he had often expressed 'detestation' of Harry when alive, 'and would not conceal his lack of regret on his death'. Ellis's lawyer, Oscar Shuck, there to prosecute Darcy, found himself forced to defend Ellis. Consigning Harry's soul to hell might be thought the less offensive, Shuck ventured, given that Ellis did not believe in hell. Here Dudley objected to theological distractions, and the objection was upheld.

Once all the testimony was in, Shuck declined to make a closing argument unless Colonel Dudley planned to do so. Dudley longed to 'scarify the complainant', but 'gracefully subsided'. No wonder

Shuck was chary. His client stood revealed, not only by every witness called but by his own testimony too, as a liar and a disgrace. Yet
even now Ellis may have clung to his chances. The police magistrate
was the same Judge Louderback who had presided in the case
brought against Harry by Arthur Neil. He of all people would know
that Harry really had been a scoundrel.

Unhesitatingly, Louderback threw the case out of court.

Darcy left the building 'the hero of the hour'. Ellis 'walked off
alone', an 'object of execration'. Even the Los Angeles press wrote
him up as a cowardly 'scrub', and 'never the equal in anything
gentlemanly of the unfortunate over whose death he rejoiced'. The
Chronicle, though, uncharacteristically mute, told its readers simply
that Ellis's complaint 'came up for hearing yesterday in the Police
Court and was dismissed, after a somewhat lengthy examination'.

News of the murder itself spread much further, and after a few
days the *New York Times* gave its own account of Harry's life,
under the heading 'A Man of the World'. In India, it said, he had
'hob-nobbed with Begums and Rajahs', coming home to squander
his riches, before showing 'bravery, dash and military skill' among
the sharpshooters in the Franco–Prussian War. The *Chicago Daily
Tribune* took its sources further. Little knowing that one of Harry's
exploits had already featured in a G. A. Henty novel, it called him
a 'real life' hero of Charles Lever, the author of numerous adventure
stories. Mentions of Garibaldi inspired the added assertion that
Harry had 'belonged to Mazzini's secret league'; and that the 'spies
of Europe knew him' because he had 'amused himself with plotting
dire destruction for the crowned heads of Europe'. The *Tribune* also
dished up an imaginary embroilment with an Indian potentate:
Harry 'succeeded to the palace, the harem, and the Treasury of the
man he had expelled', but, after 'six years of solitary splendour', grew
weary of 'barbaric magnificence' and decamped one night to London
with 'a trunkful of diamonds'. There he lost out in an investment,
before winning the Legion d'honneur in the Franco–Prussian war,
and so on, in lurid style, until eventually, 'an oath, a flash and the
dull thud of a bullet, and the man of the world went out of the
world', the 'ghastly end of an odd life'. The account concluded

that 'Among the queerest of the queer crowd that will rise from California soil when the last trump sounds will be the late Larkyns.'

As was his wont, Sam Davis would also muddle the picture with celebratory fictions about his friend. In one small, typical instance he took Muybridge's apology to the ladies after the shooting and gave it to Harry instead, making him break off from his reeling last run to ask their pardon, 'with the hesitation of death in his tones, but with a soft smile playing about his lips': copperplate Victorian bunk.

Flora naturally attracted comment too, much of it hostile. A report wound its way through the press that, with her 'petite figure, and with "tender blue eyes"', she was 'of course the object of much curiosity'. And true enough, as far away as New Zealand a paper explained that 'Larkyns was unfortunately one of those men who could not nicely measure out the quality of his love' after he became 'the object of a most engrossing passion on the part of a Mrs. Muybridge'. A columnist on the *New York Times* wrote: 'I doubt if, in the case of Harry Larkyns, it may not be considered that a very elegant and useful man was wasted on a very silly, shallow fool of a woman', while nearer to home the *Sonoma Democrat* commented slyly that only Flora knew whether or not the 'fault' was 'wholly with' Harry, so that he deserved to be 'shot down like a dog'. Harry would have seethed at being defended like this at Flora's expense. Yet when they were accorded equality, that was not necessarily favourable either. The editor of the *Oakland Transcript*, for example, argued bluntly: 'the woman is as guilty as the man, and should meet with the same punishment'. He explained further that 'It is generally the woman who makes the first advance—certainly no man ever approached a woman unless some sign was hung out. If one deserves death, both are alike unfit to live.' This elicited a withering response from Laura de Force Gordon, a 'championess' of women's voting rights then editing her own newspaper, the *Stockton Leader*. She derided 'the *Transcript* man' for his 'usual stupidity', before laying out impatiently how 'passable-looking' young women across the land, not through hanging out 'signs' but merely by being civil, found themselves harassed in all manner of public places by the 'egotistical male animal of asinine nature'. Several papers raised the spectre of Victoria Woodhull by designating the story 'A Free

Love Tragedy', and the *Oakland Tribune* suggested gloatingly that, as a wronged husband, Theodore Tilton 'could learn a trick or two from our San Francisco chaps'. In 'one act', it said, Muybridge had 'put an end to such skylarkin's with his better (or worser) half', a glib remark that made Flora, as a putative adulteress, 'worser' than her husband, who had committed murder.

It seems to have been Sam Davis, again, who on 9 November launched a terrifically successful falsity in the *Examiner*, ascribing to Harry a poem 'written a short time before he was shot dead' called 'Who Shall Judge?' The lines were actually by a Miss A. L. Muzzey, author also of a poem about the 'pain of childbirth in Want's deepest hells'. But a ghastly fittingness caused the false attribution to stick, so that 'Judge Not', as it came to be called, would be reprinted and anthologised under Harry's name for decades to come: 'How do we know what hearts have vilest sin? / How do we know? / Many, like sepulchers, are foul within, / Whose outward garb is spotless as the snow, / And many may be pure we think not so;' etc. As well as pleading mercy for Harry, these lines raised the critical question of just how 'foul within' Muybridge was likely to be judged to be.

Muybridge had taken only a day or two to retain counsel, the Hon. William Wirt Pendegast of Napa and Cameron H. King of San Francisco. They made no attempt to secure bail. His true intent on the night of the killing had been much debated in the press; but now, 'The defendant, it is stated, denies that he intended only to maim the deceased, but avers that his intention was to kill him.' Muybridge's pursuit of Harry, too, seemingly wishing for a second shot, appeared 'to corroborate the homicidal intent'. At the same time, his 1860 stagecoach accident and subsequent coma was noted as 'material for an insanity defence'.

When a Grand Jury was convened on 8 December, it found that 'Edward J Muybridge' did 'feloniously wilfully unlawfully and of his malice aforethought kill and murder one Harry Larkyns'. He was indicted, to be tried the following February. He remained 'secluded from all but a few intimate friends', and despite the intermittent importuning of journalists, for two months 'refrained from talking about the tragedy, upon the advice of his counsel'. However, in this he was about to be provoked into changing his mind.

Flora had some time since quietly returned from Oregon to San Francisco. And, none too sure that widowhood lay ahead, in mid December she took her first steps towards procuring a divorce. Filing a petition meant putting testimony on record about Muybridge that was likely to be reported. And this left her in a strange position. If she painted him as deranged in the role of her husband, she stood to bolster his insanity defence as a murderer. Still, she was driven forward by the simple fact that she was struggling to survive, and initiating divorce proceedings would allow her to plead for interim support.

Her case was taken by a lawyer called Jesse B. Hart, who was sufficiently confident of her cause to agree to defer payment until after the verdict. The initial filing took place in the Nineteenth District Court on 14 December, presided over by Judge Wheeler, whom the *Post* considered 'painstaking, courteous and honest'. Her petition asserted that in the winter of 1873, Muybridge had 'falsely charged the plaintiff with the crime of adultery, accusing her of being with child by other than himself, and threatened to kill her'. In addition, she had more than once woken in the night to find him watching her while she slept, before stealing away 'to hide this act'. His skulking voyeurism had affected her 'in such a manner that she has ever since been miserable'. Thus she laid the default charge against Muybridge of 'extreme cruelty' towards her, and believed herself 'to be entitled to a divorce'. In supplementary information she disclosed that her child, born within wedlock, was 'in her possession, cared for and supported by her', and that she was 'without the means of support of any kind for herself and child'. She estimated Muybridge's accumulated wealth, along with monies owed to him by Bradley & Rulofson, at $5,000 to $10,000, and prayed 'to be allowed alimony for the support of herself and child'. Judge Wheeler made an immediate order to stop Muybridge collecting the sums held by Bradley & Rulofson, and set a further hearing for January.

Napa's young District Attorney, Dennis Spencer, faced with the job of prosecuting Muybridge, went to San Francisco to consult Flora. When Muybridge received a letter that tipped him off about this meeting he became 'very angry', and raged that 'the conduct of the District Attorney was disgraceful'. Perhaps he felt that Flora betrayed him anew merely by speaking to Spencer. Perhaps he also feared what she might say, false or true.

The very week of Flora's divorce filing, George W. Smith of the *Chronicle* visited Napa and found that Muybridge was all of a sudden now willing to be interviewed. He was keen, he explained, to correct a 'misstatement' or two in the press reporting of his case, especially aggrieved by articles describing him as 'in the employ' of Bradley & Rulofson. Though 'attached to their establishment', he said, he worked for himself. About Flora he remarked: 'I have heard that she is in the city, but we are now, of course, completely estranged, and I do not desire to see her again. Having deceived me so cruelly, I can never have any confidence in her. I am prepared to expect anything from her, even to her taking part in the prosecution at my trial', but 'I defy them to bring anything against me.' He boasted of receiving letters of support, 'piles of them', and of the 'influential and wealthy men' who had offered to raise bail for him, up to $100,000 if he wished it, he said. However, his lawyers had advised against this because a bail application required the disclosure of evidence.

Remarkably, having made this point, Muybridge set out for George Smith various arguments by which he hoped to sway public perception of his deeds, arguments that required him to lie. But then he had had six quiet weeks to think it all through; and having taken the life of his victim, he was not in a mood to throw away his own.

Overarchingly, Muybridge set about making his case according to what was known as the 'unwritten law', by the lights of which a husband who committed murder to avenge his 'honour' was guilty of no crime. There was no actual law to this effect. But local juries were inclined to respect the principle; so much so, indeed, that the *New York Times* had already predicted scornfully that, in the guise of 'injured husband', Muybridge was likely to appeal 'to the fine sense of justice and chivalry which the California public has never been found to lack on such occasions'.

In speaking to George Smith, one of Muybridge's strategies was to shake the established details of the shooting itself. Killing Harry out of the darkness, he had taken every precaution to stack the odds in his own favour. But this had led to adverse press comment that 'The manner in which the deed was done was most cowardly': Muybridge had executed Harry 'without a chance of escape or a word of warning'. Mark Twain incidentally confirms that, among those who roughed it, it was considered 'a most cowardly act' to shoot a man when you were concealed, 'giving him "no show"'. And there was even speculation that 'Had they met on equal terms the ending might have been different, for Larkyns was a man of cool courage, not to be intimidated by the muzzle of a pistol.' Muybridge therefore now explained:

> As soon as he came to the door I said to him, 'My name is Muybridge; I have received a message about my wife—.' Before I could say more he started to retreat into the house, although I had made no demonstration against him. I saw that he would be gone in a moment and that I must act on the instant or he would escape me; so I fired on him. I did not intend to shoot him so quickly but thought to parlay with him and hear what he had to say in excuse or extenuation, but he turned to run like a guilty craven when I pronounced my name and said I had heard about my wife, and I had to shoot him so or let him go unpunished. The only thing I am sorry for in connection with the affair is that he died so quickly. I would have wished that he could have lived long enough at least to acknowledge the wrong he had done me, that his punishment was deserved, and that my act was a justifiable defence of my marital rights.

This account contradicted all witness statements given under oath immediately afterwards and corroborated by the post-mortem: Muybridge shot Harry front on, then Harry turned and ran. And Muybridge then capped his lie by sharing an extraordinary, delusional fantasy in which Harry, with his dying breath, accepted the justice of his own murder – the lack of this crowning flourish being the 'only thing' for which Muybridge declared himself sorry.

To appeal to the logic of the 'unwritten law' it was not enough just to paint Harry as a 'craven', however, whose running away was as good as a confession. Muybridge also needed to counter the idea that he himself bore some responsibility for the failure of his marriage. It was in this interview, therefore, that Muybridge denied ever inviting Harry to his home, and said that he had merely given him occasional advice on art matters, resisting all friendship with him because 'I did not fancy the Major's style of man.' Muybridge also now stated flatly: 'I did not know or suspect that he was visiting my wife or ever went anywhere with her.' But this lie, too, proved impossible to maintain. After all, numerous newspapers had dished up versions of the story that he had come to blows with Harry in the spring; and it was also widely reported that he had sent Flora to Oregon 'in the hope of finally interrupting the scandalous intrigue'. Muybridge therefore immediately contradicted himself, describing the night that Flora had come in late after seeing Adelaide Neilson. 'I asked her where she had been, and she said, "To the theater with Major Larkyns." I then said earnestly, "Now look here, Flo. I don't want you to be going out with any man at night without my knowledge or consent. It is not proper, and will bring you into scandal if you persist in it. Now, do you never go out with him in that way again." She promised me solemnly and faithfully that she would not.' The next morning, said Muybridge,

I went to see Larkyns about it. I met him on Montgomery Street, just coming down from his rooms, and he said, quite gayly, 'Good morning, Mr. Muybridge.' I said, 'I hear that you were at the theater with my wife last night.' 'Yes,' said he, 'but I didn't think there was any harm in that.' I said, 'You know very well that, as a married woman, it is not proper for her to be running about at night with you or any man but me, and I want you to let her alone. Do you never take her out in that way again. I do not request it of you, but I command you to keep away from her and never take her out in this way again. You know my right to speak about it in this manner; you know my rights in the premises as a married man. So do I; and I shall defend them. If you transgress them after this morning I shall hold you to the consequences, and I suppose you know what that means in California.' 'Oh, yes,' said he, 'and if there is any objection on your part to her going out with me I will take her out no more.'

Muybridge, having previously protested total ignorance that anything was amiss, now amended his story to one in which he had had
no suspicions before this incident, and was destined to return to a
state of perfect confidence after it. Awkwardly, this left him issuing
a veiled death threat to Harry, one fine morning, in response to a
single trip to the theatre, conceived of as a property violation: 'you
know my rights in the premises as a married man'. By contrast with
this implausible narrative, Muybridge was able to dismiss Flora's
Oregon visit easily enough. Had he sent her away to separate her
from Harry? 'Nothing of the kind', he said. He had been concerned
about leaving her 'alone with her baby', and had therefore thoughtfully proposed that she should visit her relatives.

After threatening Harry in March, Muybridge said,

> I supposed that they had kept their promise to me. I had no idea
> that my wife had ever went [*sic*] with him again or that there was
> anything wrong between them until I got those letters from the
> nurse on the morning of the day on which the shooting was done.
> I never had entertained any suspicion that my wife was guilty of
> infidelity to me with him or any other man until that time. But the
> letters from her to him and from him to her left me no room for
> doubt. I was thrown completely off my balance. The revelation was
> like a stroke of lightning to me.

George Smith did not point out that Muybridge had just shifted
his last meeting with Mrs Smith from the Friday night, when it
actually happened, to the following morning. But he did press him
to explain why, if he suspected nothing, he had wanted the letters
in the first place. Muybridge was floored by this, and responded
uneasily: 'I will tell you the history of those letters (a pause). Upon
reflection, I think perhaps I had better not state that now.'

As the query implied, Muybridge's story was hard to credit,
especially his claim that the revelation of Flora's purported infidelity
had come upon him like a bolt from the blue. At the same time,
something in the letters did tip him over into committing murder.
Perhaps the true lightning strike to the man who thought of 'the
premises', and the child, as his own was doubt about the baby's

paternity; not only as a fact in itself, but also as placing the start of Harry and Flora's liaison much earlier than Muybridge had thought to fear. Evidently it had been Harry's anguished letter to Mrs Smith that most ate into Muybridge's soul as he travelled the hundred-odd miles to the Yellow Jacket Mine. In it, Harry had written of being utterly desperate to hear from Flora, and this note of despair seems to have been what provoked Muybridge's crowing death sentence: 'This is a message from my wife.'

George Smith must have acted as a sympathetic listener for most of the interview. And he would write up Muybridge as resembling the figure of a 'quiet, good-natured old farmer'. But he did eventually challenge Muybridge on his own ground, returning to the question of his supposed dishonouring by Harry. Especially, Smith wondered how Muybridge could ever have trusted to marital sanctity, or believed that Flora had virtue worth a killing to defend. After all, he said, 'It is intimated that you were the means of her estrangement from her first husband', that 'you instigated and assisted her to get a divorce for the purposes of marrying her; that you knew her character before you married her, and that her alienation from you by Larkyns was of a piece with your conduct when she was Mr. Stone's wife.' Muybridge responded smoothly: 'All of which is untrue.' But he did not say more, merely reiterating the bland statement: 'I was away from home a great deal and, being unsuspicious when at home, it was an easy matter for them to deceive me.'

As for his own relations with Flora, 'we never had any trouble to speak of', said Muybridge, explaining, in a way that once more fails to ring true, that the worst of it had been negligible, with no 'terrible scene' of the kind Mrs Smith had reported. 'I was always a man of very simple tastes and few wants, and I did not spend much money. What I had left after paying my little expenses I gave to her, and yet she was always wanting more. I could never see that she bought anything with it to speak of or imagine what she did with it. We sometimes had little spats about the money, but nothing serious—nothing more than married people have every day and forget the next.'

A California jury inclined to absolve a killer like Muybridge was expected to settle for a fig-leaf verdict of temporary insanity.

Four days after Harry's shooting, the *Russian River Flag*, a local paper, wrote with weary cynicism that the 'murderer will, of course, plead "insanity" on his trial, and, of course, be turned loose, instead of being sent to the insane asylum'. But although Muybridge had just followed the tack his lawyers wished to pursue, and spoken of being thrown completely off balance by a revelation like a 'stroke of lightning', he baulked at being labelled mad, even as the cost of saving himself. As he pointed out compulsively, there was an illogic to getting away with a 'justified' murder by calling the act deranged:

> I objected to the plea of insanity when it was made after the shooting, because I thought a man to be crazy must not know what he was doing, and I knew what I was doing. I was beside myself with rage and indignation, and resolved to avenge my dishonor. I said to Rulofson that morning—and my words have been mistaken in that respect by him—'One of us will be shot.' I did not say as he states, 'One of us must die,' but he said 'For God's sake, don't kill him,' and I answered, 'One of us will be shot.'

Though using the words 'beside myself with rage and indignation' was apparently a sop to Muybridge's pride that conveniently allowed others, still, to characterise him as having been temporarily insane, it remained unhelpful to his cause to broadcast a declaration of his own sanity. He tried to ameliorate the effect of his qualms both by suggesting that he had not declared a positive intent to kill Harry, and by pointing out his own bravery, inasmuch as he had risked taking a bullet himself. Muybridge ended his interview with an outburst worthy of the stage at the California Theatre: 'I loved the woman with all my heart and soul, and the revelation of her infidelity was a cruel, prostrating blow to me, shattering my idol and blighting the bright affection of my life.' In his determinedly self-vaunting way, he added: 'I have no fear of the result of my trial. I feel that I was justified in what I did, and that all right-minded people will justify my action. I am ready and anxious to be tried to-morrow, if possible. There will be no appeal for delay in my case, I assure you.'

*

The print response to Muybridge's interview was swift and mocking. The *Alta* 'Brevities' column stated: 'A gentleman in the Napa jail, who is awaiting trial for deliberate murder, is reported as saying that "all right-thinking men" indorse his conduct. This is a severe rebuke to those who do not believe in murdering those who offend him.' Richard Wheeler, another of the hundred-odd subscribers to Muybridge's 1872 Yosemite expedition, was more personal in the *Stock Report*. Under the title 'Larkyns' Assassin', he wrote angrily that the *Chronicle* interview was 'nothing more than a chance for Muybridge to get in his first plea to the public'. Wheeler was especially offended by the assertion that Harry had run before being shot: 'Gammon.' He had 'taken pains' to investigate, he said. Harry 'went from a brilliantly lighted room out into the darkness, and unable to see his assailant, he asked him to come into the light where he could see him. The reply came in the shape of a bullet which sent him reeling back into the room with his death wound.' Nor was it likely, he added, that someone as brave as Harry on the battlefield would ever run 'like a craven coward'. Wheeler heaped scorn on Muybridge, who, 'after taking deliberate aim and shooting his victim through the heart, regrets that he died so soon'. In future, he said, if Muybridge wished to converse with his victims, he should shoot them in the leg. He even took issue with George Smith's description of Muybridge as looking like a friendly old farmer. Far from it: 'His face wears a sour, morose expression and at times a look of brutal ferocity.' Wheeler finished by clarifying that he was 'writing no defence' of Harry's intimacy with Flora, 'but Muybridge committed a cowardly, cold blooded murder, and for which he should suffer the extreme penalty of the law'.

There were other writers in the press at large who contested the idea that Muybridge was blameless and that Harry had deserved his fate. *The Hawaiian Gazette* held that 'Muybridge killed the wrong man. His own selfish conduct was the real cause of his wife's estrangement, and to have been consistent with himself he ought to have gone for his own scalp.' And Colonel George Thistleton, in the *Illustrated Jolly Giant*, wrote frankly: 'we say it is sad that poor Major Larkyns should have forfeited his life for an offence which thousands of our most influential citizens commit daily'. There was only one crime in this department, thought Thistleton, where a man deserved this punishment: 'where he outrages the virtue of a woman against her will'. *Common Sense*, meanwhile, dedicated to spiritualism and women's rights, scorned the moral interpretation of the case that Muybridge so strongly encouraged. 'The papers speak of Muybridge as having been "dishonored" by Larkyns. How can an innocent man be dishonored? Dishonor attaches only to those who are guilty. He dishonored himself when he committed murder.' The *Chicago Tribune*, by contrast, summarised the nub of the interview as being the doubtful matter of Muybridge's 'wife's reputation for good behavior before he married her'.

Muybridge responded by writing confidentially to George Smith to ask for a correction to be printed, a fractional stroke of retouching designed to enhance his image as a kind, unworldly old soul. Smith complied: 'In speaking of his present relations with his wife Mr. Muybridge was made to say: "I am prepared to expect anything from her, even to her taking part with the prosecution at my trial." His words were: "I am told to be prepared," etc. He added further: "For my wife's present position I have the most sincere pity."'

The fact that Muybridge raised just one important quibble in his letter can only mean that he was content with virtually the whole of the interview as printed. In confidence, he explained to Smith that he had sought the vital correction from a fear that he might 'unnecessarily <u>exasperate</u>, where I have every wish to <u>conciliate</u>': apparently, he believed that it was in Flora's power to attempt to harm him. After insisting on his pity for her, he added that he had only ever thought her 'the unwilling victim of her seducers perfidy', removing all agency from Flora, not to mention from himself. He continued: 'With regard to my interview with Larkyns, I ordered him not only never to go out with my wife, but "<u>never to speak to her or recognise his acquaintance with her under any circumstances or where-ever he saw her</u>"', and noted: 'These were my words, my wife gave me the same promise. <u>He</u> pledged his word not to do so on his "honor as a <u>gentleman</u>".' As for Muybridge's current position, '<u>What regret I may feel, my heart alone knows</u>.' He finished with an unwittingly ironic private message for the *Chronicle*'s proprietor:

'Be kind enough to tender my grateful thanks to Mr. De Young, for the interest he has manifested in my case, and the impartiality and justice with which he views it.'

The *New York Times* piece written after Harry's death, 'A Man of the World', was reproduced wholesale by the London *Times* in mid November. A week or two later, Ray Pelly wrote to San Francisco seeking information. He eventually received an answer from William Lane Booker, the British Consul, who would have known Harry through cricket. As it happens, he had also been a subscriber to Muybridge's 1872 Yosemite expedition. But he omitted to divulge his acquaintance with either victim or murderer, or even to use Muybridge's name. On 7 December he had replied to Miss Larkins, he said,

> and an English gentleman — Mr. Edwards — wrote the same day giving a full report of the circumstances attending the killing of Major Larkyns & his funeral — The deceased spelt his name with a 'y' which prevented my tracing the relatives or I should have advised them promptly of the melancholy affair. I dare say before this reaches you you will have heard all the particulars. I enclose an extract from the Morning Chronicle of today on the subject.

Miss Larkins, Conny, would have written on Henrietta's behalf as well as her own, as they were still living together in Cleveland Square. Conny remained there until 1876, when, aged thirty-four, she went to Georgetown, Demerara, as the third wife of Sir William Snagg, Chief Justice of British Guiana. He was more than twice her age, and he died two years later. Conny returned to Cleveland Square and remained there as the widowed Lady Snagg. She was the beneficiary of two £1,000 life assurance policies, money rooted in the Snagg family's past ownership of slave plantations, and on this relatively scrimping income maintained a spinsterish existence ever after.

The 'extract' tucked inside Lane Booker's letter to Ray was Muybridge's *Chronicle* interview, cut out of that morning's paper. In the same envelope, either Ray or Alice added a clipped-out copy of the *New York Times* account of the 'little tragedy' of 'one Harry

Larkyns'. Both articles must have made extremely painful reading. The second, after a distorted summary of Harry's good and bad sides, remarked: 'He began his career with the intention of seeing life; he saw it. When he had seen it, he died as the fool dieth—in blood and wantonness.'

One British paper that took up the story wrote: 'We learn that the murderer takes things coolly, and confidently awaits his trial for a crime which he feels certain his moral countrymen will view with lenient eyes.' Harry's fate, it continued, ought to be a warning to 'high-spirited British youths'. In particular, 'It is clear that California is not the right place for careless Don Juans. They must confine their operations to Europe for some time to come, inasmuch as husbands in new settlements are apt to be intolerant.' But not all of them were intolerant to the point of murder. Fanny Osbourne's husband, for example, felt no need to slaughter Robert Louis Stevenson; and if he had, there would have been no Long John Silver; no Dr Jekyll and Mr Hyde. Moreover, even if Muybridge did fervently hope that his 'moral countrymen' were going to save him in the 'back of man's beyond', it is hardly likely that his own upbringing in Kingston upon Thames had supplied him with an unthinking belief in the justice of revenge killings.

A decade later, one of Muybridge's actual countrymen, Thomas Arundel Harcourt, faced a similar disaster in his Californian marriage to Fannie Rulofson. After Ambrose Bierce returned to San Francisco in 1875, Harcourt and he became close friends. Bierce's forte was satire, including such witty touches as renaming Leland Stanford, '£eland $tanford', while Harcourt was locally celebrated for translating Emile Zola's terrific novel of degradation, *Thérèse Raquin*. Together, in 1877, in an anonymous prank, they penned a highly risqué little book called *The Dance of Death*, in which they excoriated the waltz. With 'gas-scorched eyeballs', and training 'a beacon over the dark vortex', they felt it imperative, they wrote, to present the reader with a true picture of 'tumultuously' swelling breasts, 'limbs interwoven', women's bodies thrilling with 'amorous contact', and men's expressions 'gleaming with a fierce intolerable lust'. Waltzing at a party, a wife or daughter, temporarily 'enervated, limp, listless, worn out', must 'yield her body' to be 'pastured upon' afresh, and, in short, this 'hideous social ulcer' provided 'a certain physical ecstacy' of a kind that really ought only to be indulged in private, 'and, as some would go so far as to say, under matrimonial restrictions'. Despite its sly jokes about desire and adultery, the book was treated by the innocent as a sermon and 'sold like wildfire'. And, remarkably, the whole project was funded by Fannie's father, and published under his first names, 'William Herman', throwing a curious light on Rulofson as Muybridge's principal defender.

The similar disaster for Harcourt, in 1884, was that Fannie ran away with another man, whereupon, still only in his early thirties, impoverished and miserable, Harcourt unstoppably killed himself. Bierce excelled at waspish epitaphs, one of the most famous credited to him being, 'Here lies Frank Pixley, as usual'. For Harcourt, though, Bierce composed two anguished poems, their mood encapsulated in the couplet:

> From his white lips he smiled and mutely bled,
> And, having meanly lived, is grandly dead.

Another account of Harcourt's end stated more specifically that he 'anticipated the slow decay of alcoholism by jumping out a window'. What Harcourt did not do was to assuage the agony of losing the woman he loved by coldly killing someone else.

On Christmas Eve, 1874, a 'spiritualistic medium' from Chicago, Mrs C. M. Sawyer, undertook, during a nighttime séance at 1145 Mission, to bring forth the 'materialized spirit of Harry Larkyns'. Prominent figures attended, including Joe Goodman, the erstwhile editor of the Virginia *Enterprise* and the first employer of 'Mark Twain'; and Senator John P. Jones, yet another of the subscribers to Muybridge's 1872 Yosemite expedition, and the possessor of a gigantic Comstock fortune: within a year, Jones would demand the return of $50,000 he had invested in the *Post*, precipitating the abrupt end of Henry George's editorship of the paper. Captain Lees also attended, the police detective who had long before tried to help Harry leave the city. They and a few others, including two ladies, formed a committee, tying threads with bells attached across every door in the room and all its moveable furniture. Captain Lees then stuck postage stamps over the loose top of the cabinet from which Harry's spirit was to manifest. Finally, they tied Mrs Sawyer to her chair, after which the room was plunged into darkness, and nothing happened. When the committee agreed to loosen Sawyer, there followed 'a series of raps, voices, "materialized" hands, etc.' But the performance was 'so shallow as to excite ridicule', and at midnight, the visitors 'departed in disgust'.

A few days later, in the new year, Flora's application for financial support, pending divorce proceedings, at last came up for review. Judge Wheeler ordered that Muybridge must show why he should not pay $50 a month interim alimony to support his wife and baby. But 'after argument', Muybridge's lawyer was able to persuade Wheeler that Flora's appeal was insufficient. Wheeler 'denied the prayer for alimony', but he did so 'without prejudice', giving Flora the right to return and plead more strongly a second time. One paper wrote kindly, 'We hope that she may prove her case', but conceded that 'the present outlook' for her was 'very dark'.

After Harry's funeral service, his body had been placed temporarily in a vault in the Masonic cemetery on Lone Mountain, pending instructions from the Larkins family in England. The *Post* explained this in exactly the language Muybridge had used when asserting his rights over Flora: 'The remains will lie in the tomb until the desires of Major Larkyns' relatives are made known in the premises'. There is no evidence that the family did repatriate Harry's corpse; nor does it seem in the least likely that they would have wished to do so. Even Alice was persuaded to destroy a little memoir by Harry that he had left in her safekeeping. Given that Harry Edwards was a leading Freemason, the overwhelming likelihood instead is that, after the winding back and forth of letters across the Atlantic, Harry was in the end buried properly in the graveyard where he already lay. But even if he was quietly interred on Lone Mountain, all the graves there would eventually be dug out, the bones consigned to chaotic reburial beyond the city bounds, the land sold, and the tombstones used as ballast and rubble.

16: Trial

Muybridge's trial was set to be a sensation, with the verdict keenly awaited across the land. The presiding judge, William T. Wallace, a man of 'tremendous size', was a Justice of the California Supreme Court, though his recent politicking had caused the *Post* to declare that he might best serve the state by 'resigning the position he has so conspicuously disgraced'. Dennis Spencer, prosecuting Muybridge, had been elected District Attorney in Napa only two years previously, and was relatively junior. Now aged thirty, and no 'beauty', but a 'little thin built man with a small bullet-shaped head, covered in a thin crop of light hair', he had only a 'local reputation'. And though Sam Davis, retained by the *Post* to report on the trial, was sure that Spencer would prosecute the case 'with all the vim and enthusiasm of his nature', Spencer himself felt the odds were heavily stacked against him. The Board of Supervisors had refused him associate counsel, and he 'bitterly' complained of 'the lukewarmness of Larkyns' friends', who gave him no help in assembling his case. Moreover, while Harry's defenders might deeply regret 'the fate which condemned one so brilliant to such an untimely taking off', those Bohemians who used their press columns to deplore Muybridge's conduct and question his veracity, were not so ready to provide hostile testimony in person. Meanwhile powerful figures from the opposing camp, such as the De Young brothers of the *San Francisco Chronicle*, simply ignored Spencer's subpoenas.

Before 1870, Spencer had trained in law at the firm of Pendegast & Stoney, on Main Street, Napa. And, dauntingly, it was the same William Wirt Pendegast who now led Muybridge's defence team. Pendegast was also in his early thirties, and he cut a remarkable figure. He was tall, with an 'intellectual face and luxuriant hair'. More importantly, though, he had been a State Senator in the California Legislature from the age of twenty-five, and was by common acclaim

'Napa's favorite orator'. Pendegast's second was another ambitious young figure, 'suggestive of the band-box attorney', Cameron H. King of San Francisco, who came from a prominent 'race of lawyers' and had previously been Executive Secretary to his uncle Henry Huntley Haight, until 1871 the Governor of California. Pendegast was assisted by the Napa Court Commissioner F. E. Johnston, and King, by his law partner, Edward Gottschalk, specifically retained to rally witnesses for the defence.

The day before the trial began, a pale Muybridge was taken from his cell in the 'miserable' condemned building adjoining the courthouse and brought in to make his plea. In 'a clear firm voice he enunciated "Not Guilty"'. Then, as he was removed back to his cell, he 'turned to the Sheriff, and said with a quiet laugh, "To kill a man and yet plead not guilty"', leaving at least one reporter affronted: 'He carries himself with the air of a man who had done a noble action, and his deportment is almost comical, so much is it the reverse of what one would expect.'

Only now, at the very last minute, with proceedings already launched, did the Board of Supervisors relent and allow Dennis Spencer a second, to face the defence team of four. He turned to Thomas P. Stoney, his other teacher in Napa, and Pendegast's previous law partner, who seemingly 'assumed the management of the case'. Stoney, rising forty, had been born in South Carolina and had returned to fight with the Confederates in the Civil War. But the eventual repeal of the Test Oath Act allowed him to resume his practice in Napa. He had the reputation of being 'all head', and 'as quiet as a summer afternoon', his forte not oratory but legal logic. Where the defence had 'spent weeks in preparing their case', and intimated that they were confident of an acquittal, Stoney found himself with mere hours to confirm the prosecution strategy. At least he knew Pendegast inside out.

The next day, Wednesday, 3 February, the trial proper began. The court was soon humming with potential jurors, visiting lawyers, general spectators and 'the extensive acquaintance of the principals'. And the morning train brought in a second influx that left people standing in the aisles. Muybridge, in a rough suit and with a countenance like 'bleached muslin', betrayed 'considerable nervousness, although manifestly striving to appear cool'. Though his true age was forty-four, he was described as 'a tall, reserved looking man, about 50 years of age', but appearing 'even older'. He was said to be 'generally esteemed', and, despite not being 'of strong, or even of average social leanings', to have 'numerous acquaintances', as well as 'contact professionally with many influential citizens'.

Muybridge, mid forties, studio portrait by Bradley & Rulofson

In planning the killing, Muybridge must have reckoned that the outside risk of facing instant retribution from roughs in the Pine Flat mining camp, where he expected Harry to be, was more than offset by the advantages of committing murder in a region where a jury was none too likely to be particular. And in the event their selection was swift, with only seventeen men challenged. As for the twelve selected, each in turn professed to have no existing, fixed opinion as to the verdict, and no scruples about the death penalty. Ten were 'bronzed and sturdy farmers of middle age', two were carpenters, and eleven of them were married. Sam Davis, in the *Post*, described them as almost all 'old men, gray headed, and hard fisted, with families'. Witnesses were to be excluded from the courtroom except when testifying. Muybridge stood up as the clerk read out the indictment for murder.

Thomas Stoney gave the opening address for the prosecution. In blunt terms, he laid out the law. He 'wished it to be understood that there were but two parties to the case, the people of the State and Muybridge'. Categorically, the conduct of Muybridge's victim was not at issue. That was for a 'higher tribunal'. In law, 'Nothing but self-defence authorizes a man to take the life of another.' But this shooting had been neither an act of self-defence, nor an accident: 'there could be no pretence of that in this case'. Muybridge had killed in cold blood a victim who was 'quietly pursuing his peaceful avocation, and unarmed'. The prosecution would prove the only relevant part of the whole story, said Stoney, that Muybridge 'was guilty of wilful, premeditated murder, with malice aforethought, and should be convicted of murder in the first degree': that he was, in short, 'just as guilty as possible'.

Muybridge sat behind his counsel, head in hand, nervously straying his fingers through his beard. 'A thousand times his eyes went slowly up and down the lines of jury men at his right.'

The first prosecution witnesses testified to events during the evening and the night of the murder, giving essentially the same accounts that they had provided at the inquest, and had corroborated the following week, talking to reporters. Pendegast feebly proposed in Muybridge's defence that his lack of a coat on the night of the killing, and consequent need to borrow a buggy robe, indicated that his actions had been unplanned. But by the end of that long first day of the trial there was no serious challenge to the prosecution narrative. Even so, press reporters found that 'There are a few who denounce Muybridge, but public sympathy is generally with him.' He himself appeared to be 'in excellent health and good spirits'.

*

The next day, the prosecution resumed straightforwardly. But it would soon find itself in choppy waters. Spencer began 'with a nervous vigor and determined quickness which elicited the gratified attention of all except the prisoner', and matters went well until he started to question Mr McArthur, the man who had disarmed Muybridge and then stood guard over him driving to Calistoga. When Spencer asked what Muybridge had said in the hours after the killing, defence counsel objected clamorously that the defendant's conversation subsequent to the shooting should not be allowed. Stoney appealed to Judge Wallace: 'It is necessary for us, in order to convict of murder in the first degree, to show premeditation.' Wallace ruled that Muybridge's words constituted a voluntary confession, and allowed the prosecution to continue.

According to McArthur, Muybridge 'said he intended to kill Larkyns'. He thought 'miners were a pretty rough lot, and he did not know what the consequences would be, but he had resolved to shoot the Major and take the consequence', making sure, 'if he never returned', that 'his business would all be settled'. When William Sarles asked why he had come in the night 'to alarm everybody', Muybridge replied 'that he did not wish to give Larkyns a chance to shoot him'. He also explained about firing off his gun en route: his pistol 'had been laying a long time unused' but loaded, and his intent had been, if he found the barrel 'foul, or anything wrong with the weapon, to turn back'.

Pendegast now began McArthur's cross-examination. He opened with a leading question, flagrantly appealing to the 'unwritten law', and intended to defend Muybridge by convicting Harry: 'Did he say, as one of his excuses, "This man has seduced my wife?"' Over futile objections from Stoney, McArthur replied that this was what he had understood Muybridge to mean when he spoke of his happiness having been destroyed. Pendegast then elicited from McArthur that Muybridge had also spoken of his suspicions being raised and then allayed, of giving a warning to Harry, and, finally, of intercepting a letter that confirmed adulterous 'intimacy'. He had even garrulously mentioned happier days, apparently, with 'trips photographing, accompanied by his wife'. Pendegast asked McArthur to agree that Muybridge had made no attempt to escape when the wagon was upset, going to Calistoga. Here Stoney, thoroughly exasperated, pointed out that as Muybridge's feet had been tied and the others were armed, escape would have been impossible.

Dennis Spencer now resumed questioning McArthur for the prosecution. Provoked by Pendegast's emphasis on Harry as a figure of dishonour, he took the dubious path of implying that Flora had not been worth fighting over. 'Did he say to you who his wife was before he married her?' he asked, over objections from Pendegast. McArthur replied that Muybridge had told him 'his wife was a divorced woman when he married her'. Spencer asked, 'Did he say where she was living at the time of the shooting?' Once more, Pendegast objected to an 'immaterial' line of enquiry.

Judge Wallace suddenly found he had had enough. 'I think the whole conversation is immaterial', he said. He abruptly reversed his earlier ruling and disallowed all McArthur's testimony: neither prosecution nor defence could draw on Muybridge's behaviour or statements after the murder. Pendegast had made hay with McArthur while he had the chance. Spencer, attempting to undo this, found himself cut off almost before he had begun.

After a few further questions to witnesses confirming uncontested details, Spencer rested the prosecution case. The total effort must have felt worryingly thin, and certainly he and Stoney were hoping to bolster their arguments in cross-questioning the defence witnesses. As the press explained: 'The major part of the proof on that side will come in the rebuttal.' In particular, it was going to be imperative to shake the only conceivable legitimate defence argument: that, for Muybridge, 17 October 1874 had been a singular day of revelation so appalling that it had provoked him to fleeting madness, thereby exonerating him from moral responsibility for Harry's murder.

Judge Wallace was supposedly 'a thorough believer in the deterrent effect of capital punishment', having 'no patience with maudlin ideas regarding criminals'. But whatever authority he possessed had already been weakened in this trial by his dithering over McArthur's testimony. And it was about to be undermined further by Muybridge's lawyers, who had planned a campaign of remorseless disrespect for the law.

Cameron H. King opened for the defence. He was 'frequently interrupted by the Court', and repeatedly told to stick 'strictly to the facts and to what he expected to prove'. But he kept on peppering his remarks with inflammatory irrelevancies and outright lies. He began by saying that they were there to decide 'whether Edward J Muybridge should dangle in mid air from the gallows', or walk free, to 'live as he had ever lived', though presumably not committing occasional murders. King conjured up Flora as an 'unfortunate woman who has fallen by the wiles and machinations of a practiced libertine, whose greatest boast was his power to make women false'. He evaporated her marriage to Lucius Stone: her name had been 'Miss Flora Downs' when Muybridge met her, King said, and she had been 'pure and virtuous', but 'compelled by poverty to earn her bread by honest labor'. Muybridge's 'sympathies were touched. His generous heart could not permit a woman to suffer', and he offered her a position in his gallery 'to color photographs'. Though this was, in fact, the job she already had, King's habit of elision lends weight to the idea that in time Flora worked for Muybridge. He had been 'fascinated' by her, King went on, intimacy ripened into love and, remembering, he repeated, that 'no breath of scandal had ever touched her name', they had married. Flora 'was his soul's idol, and they lived happily together, wrapped up in each other's love'.

Having delivered this mawkish and inaccurate summary, King defied further objections and returned to Harry: he would 'prove that Larkyns was a man of bad character', he said. Long before any 'criminal intimacy', Harry had rented rooms on Montgomery Street, representing himself as married and saying that his absent wife would soon arrive. 'We are prepared to prove that Larkyns succeeded in his devilish plot', said King, that he 'frequently induced' Flora to come to his rooms, and there 'slowly undermined her heart and attacked her citadel of virtue', of which fact 'he boasted to his friends'. Again and again, Stoney and Spencer objected that King was being 'allowed to state matters which would not be allowable as evidence'. He was, that is, maligning Harry as he pleased, knowing that these supposed 'matters', true or false, would never be put to proof.

Judge Wallace upheld the objections, but King forged on with repeated 'attempts to evade the ruling', as when he gave a list of what Muybridge had not known until the day of the murder. He had not been aware, for example, that on the night Flora gave birth she had come directly from Harry's rooms; nor had he guessed, leaning lovingly over her once the baby was born, that 'LARKYNS' KISSES WERE FRESH AND HOT UPON HER LIPS', as press type-setters rendered this flourish. The baby was 'probably the seducer's offspring', King announced airily. But Muybridge had suspected absolutely nothing: 'His whole soul was wrapped up in love for his wife. His confidence in her truth was unlimited.' Harry had pursued Flora with amorous epistles even in Oregon, urging elopement, said King, and 'I feel assured that his death only prevented this.' Yet again Wallace reprimanded King, 'forbidding his stating such matters'.

King now switched to muddling the question of when Muybridge had made 'the terrible discovery of his wife's infidelity'. He explained that Muybridge had refused to pay Mrs Smith her fee, triggering her case against him, because he believed that she had been paid already, and suspected her of a ruse to get her money twice. At the debt hearing, he had been alerted to awful worries by the letters submitted in evidence and, fearing that he had been dishonoured, Muybridge 'dropped all business, took no food' and 'sleep forsook him', said King, rather as though, imaginatively, the next several days had been a unitary, sleepless phase of horror. During this, as it were, single day, Muybridge had been 'wrought up to insanity until his impulse to kill the seducer became uncontrollable'.

As Muybridge had in his interview with George Smith, King now shunted Muybridge's final meeting with Mrs Smith from the Friday evening, 16 October, to the morning of the murder: clearly one of the main planks of the defence strategy. Thus, on the 'fatal Saturday, October 17th', said King, Muybridge, 'trembling in every limb, his brain on fire, his face haggard, his eye wild and glazed', had 'sought this woman, Mrs. Smith, again, and demanded that she should tell him all she knew. "Tell me, woman, great God! tell me the truth!" Frightened by his wild look, and fearful that he would kill himself or her, she fell down and confessed all she knew. The proof was convincing. The grief and suffering he had undergone paralyzed his reason.' Muybridge's idol was shattered, said King: 'His wife was false to him as hell.'

Remarkably, with this Pendegast and King had found a way to make the interests of a natural prosecution witness coalesce with those of the defendant. If Mrs Smith was prepared to testify that Muybridge had terrorised her into betraying Flora and Harry, this would justify her in having handed over their letters, the act for which she had been excoriated by the press. At the same time, if she was willing to shift the scene to Saturday morning, this might nicely contribute to a picture of Muybridge overcome by a brief, ungovernably vengeful fit of lunacy. Meanwhile, to explain the testimony of those who, on the contrary, had considered Muybridge to be his usual self that day, King now described how, after rushing about like a copybook maniac, abruptly he had found himself instead in the grip of 'the terrible calmness and apparent coolness of insanity'. In this second state, apparently quite normal but equally mad, Muybridge had set off to find Harry, to send a 'righteous bullet crashing through his heart'.

Over vociferous objections but before he could be stopped, King now 'exhibited a portrait of a voluptuous looking female for the admiration of the jury': Flora. As one reporter sardonically wrote, the only legitimate use of this photograph would have been in rebuttal of another one, even more suggestive, perhaps showing her 'in tights in the character of Pocahontas, stretched en abandon on a lounge'. King then produced a photograph of the baby, with the name 'Harry' inscribed on the back, and a note to say that it had been sent from Oregon.

To close, King stated that the defence 'would claim an acquittal on the ground of justifiable homicide and insanity'. This was extraordinarily brazen. While Muybridge's sanity was open to legal debate, there was no argument for 'justifiable homicide' in this case, within the law. But 'Who is the man,' King pressed on, 'even though he be of sound mind—that can say he would have acted differently?' Almost as though the person murdered had been Muybridge, he added: 'He is not a man who would not sacrifice himself to save his wife from dishonor and shame', and only a 'coward and a cur' would leave his wife's seducer free to 'boast his conquest' among 'drunken companions over the flowing bowl', free to 'point out the wretched man who walks the streets—a cuckold'. Take Muybridge, said King, wrapping up at last: the defence 'shall show you the depth of his impassioned love of his wife; that he was wrapped up in her and lived only for her'. And, 'Having shown all this, we shall ask you, as the law does, to look upon his acts with mercy.'

Mrs Smith was the first defence witness called. According to the press, Gottschalk, King's second, with his 'carefully frizzled' hair, had been conspicuously 'playing the gallant' with both her and her daughter. And, ominously, Mrs Smith, 'plainly dressed, with flower-trimmed straw hat', was said 'to have about as clear a view of the situation as the Attorneys themselves'.

King asked Mrs Smith whether she had spoken with Muybridge 'on the morning of the killing'. Stoney immediately objected that any testimony designed to show 'provocation or justification' would not constitute 'competent evidence'. But King replied that Mrs Smith would help to establish 'the defendant's frenzied condition and insanity on the morning of the killing'. Mrs Smith now testified 'with considerable dramatic effect', sometimes 'rising from her seat and gesticulating'. She agreed that she had seen Muybridge 'on the day of the homicide and had a conversation with him'. And when she slipped and referred to the Friday night, King steered her back on course: 'What conversation did you have with Mr. Muybridge on Saturday morning and how did he act[?]' Mrs Smith talked about the baby's photograph. Muybridge, 'turning red and pale', examined it and said, 'As I live, "Harry" is written on it in my wife's handwriting.' He 'stamped on the floor and exhibited the wildest excitement', said Mrs Smith. 'His appearance was that of a madman; he was haggard and pale, his eyes glassy; his lower jaw hung down, showed his teeth; he trembled from head to foot, and gasped for breath', and on and on. He came at her with a raised hand, she said, demanding she tell all. 'I thought he was insane, and would kill me or himself if I did not. I then told him all I knew.' 'State all you told him and his actions on hearing the same', said King encouragingly.

Of all the witnesses in Muybridge's trial, Mrs Smith had the greatest chance of saving his life. Along with helpful descriptions of his derangement, she could slip in testimony calculated to make the behaviour of Flora and Harry seem as offensive as possible.

Furthermore, if she was willing, she could strongly reinforce, or even exceed, whatever justification was to be derived from Harry and Flora's letters. One paper compressed her evidence into a vignette in which Muybridge, tears streaming down his face, caught the handle of her front door and said, 'I come to see you about my wife and Mr. Larkyns', Mrs Smith replying to this right out: 'I can convince you of the guilt of your wife.'

Mrs Smith testified that she had told Muybridge how, when Flora was in the carriage in labour, Harry had 'kissed and caressed' her and 'fondled her like a spoiled child'. Contradicting her initial interviews, in which she said that, after bringing a doctor, Harry stayed with Flora only about three minutes, she also now claimed to have told Muybridge that Harry had 'bent over her, when in bed and in the agonies of child-birth; was there more than two hours at a time'. This painful narrative continued, with Harry as a dime-novel villain. When he came to see the baby for the first time, Flora supposedly said to him, 'Major, who is the baby like?' And Harry, with a smile, supposedly replied, 'You ought to know; we remember the 13th of July, don't we, and have something to show for it?' Then 'both cast their eyes on the bed where the baby was lying', said Mrs Smith. Another time she had been called in, she said, 'and there lay Mrs. Muybridge, her bosom bare, and Larkyns with his hand on her shoulder'. Harry had said to her, 'I want you to take good care of that baby. I hold you responsible, for I have got two babies now.' In with this mishmash, Mrs Smith claimed to have remarked coyly to Flora that she 'did not understand this matter of the baby having two fathers'. There was no stopping her. Flora had once said, 'I love Harry better than any man in the world, and if Muybridge knew what I have done he would kill Harry, and me, too.' And Harry had said, 'Why don't the old man go on the railroad and take pictures?' Mrs Smith told him he ought to be careful, to which he had replied, 'Flora and I have fooled the old man so long that we can keep it up still longer.' Mrs Smith claimed to have told Muybridge that Harry went into Flora's rooms 'and locked the door' perhaps 'as much as three times a week'.

Muybridge had asked Mrs Smith, she now reported, whether she knew how Flora had spent the money intended for her own bill 'and other debts'. She could think only of 'the extra washing that was put in accounts for it', and explained to him: 'Major Larkyns sent his old shirts to your house to be repaired and done up. They were sent to the wash with yours', and afterwards delivered to Harry at 1010 Montgomery Street; this pathetic domestic economy, just after Harry lost his job with the *Post*, was the only detail to support a claim Muybridge had made in his *Chronicle* interview, 'on undoubted authority', that Flora kept Harry in 'high style'. When Harry became a circus agent, Flora 'wished me to take charge of the child while the two travelled together', said Mrs Smith. Harry had told Flora he would take her to England 'and present her as his wife, and the baby as his child'. The two of them 'went to a restaurant together two weeks after the birth'. Flora 'slept out of the house for ten nights' when Muybridge was at Belmont; and on it went.

Some of what Mrs Smith said was presumably true, or half true. But how much of it was highly exaggerated, misleading or flatly untrue, and which elements she had genuinely divulged to Muybridge – this, in the circumstances, is hard to guess. 'I told Muybridge many other things. Don't recollect all now', she said to the court, adding that he had 'seemed like one dumbfounded and fell on the floor in a fit. I was afraid he would die.' When he then recovered again, he apparently exclaimed: 'Flora, Flora, my heart is broken. I would have given my heart's best blood for you. How could you treat me so cruelly? If you did not love me you might at least respect me too much to put that man in my shoes.' After this, he supposedly began gibbering again, and 'I thought, and my opinion is,' said Mrs Smith stoutly, 'that when he left me he was insane.' Solicited for more general evidence of his madness, she was slightly thrown, but recalled an incident where Muybridge, 'looking at mother and baby, seemed happy', but then, turning suddenly to their two caged canaries, said to Mrs Smith, '"Why do you give those birds hemp-seed when I told you not?" I replied, "You gave that to your birds last night yourself." "Ah, dear me," said he, "I feel bad here sometimes," tapping his forehead.'

Mrs Smith's cross-examination by Dennis Spencer was barely reported in the press. Apparently he questioned her 'at great length, but her direct testimony was not shaken'. She insisted: 'Never said that if the money due had been paid there would have been no trouble', and clarified that 'All letters were sent to her (Mrs. Smith)—four in number—and were, two from Larkyns and two from Mrs. Muybridge.' She also agreed that she had several photographs given to her by Flora; and that, a couple of months before, Flora had come 'and asked for the pictures, which I refused to give her'. When Spencer tried to produce proofs that Mrs Smith was 'living in open adultery' the judge stopped him, and Mrs Smith later asked to be allowed to 'repel imputations' on her character.

The only two letters brought out in the trial, and then partially replicated in the press, were the Calistoga letter from Harry to Mrs Smith, and the letter from Oregon sent by Flora to Mrs Smith's daughter: in other words, letters that the Smiths possessed by right. Yet, extraordinarily, the copies submitted in evidence, which survive to this day, were not the originals, but transcripts made by Muybridge. He may have written out both letters word for word, though why he should do so there is no saying. But the fact is, he had every opportunity to alter their contents lightly, not only to aid his cause by making them come across as more concrete and damning, but also, quite possibly, to remove damaging reflections on himself.

Mrs Smith's daughter Sarah was next up, and was dispatched pretty swiftly. She had known Muybridge since 1872, she said, and she worked at Bradley & Rulofson. If this was not a coincidence, then it is possible the Muybridges had helped her to secure her job, given that her mother first assisted Flora with a stillbirth late in 1871. She 'Did not know where Muybridge was in July and August, 1873', she said, the span covering the conception of the baby. As for Muybridge himself, like her mother, Sarah Smith fell in line with the requirements of the defence. She had occasionally noticed him to be 'nervous and excitable and eccentric', but 'He was always kind to his wife and always gave her all the money she wanted.'

Up next was William Rulofson, described doubtfully in the press as 'A Cool Witness'. He repainted the picture he had given the *Chronicle* of Muybridge's crazed state on the day of the killing. Rulofson had been surprised to meet him coming down in the elevator, which Muybridge had previously 'always refused' to use. Muybridge had made a circuit of the vestibule three or four times, grinding his teeth and in a frenzy, leaving Rulofson 'really afraid' that 'the quivering of his whole frame was developing insanity', and so on. Rulofson now explained how Muybridge had given a clear account of his wishes should he end up dead; had 'Begged him that in settling up his business he would give everything that belonged to him to his wife "as I have something to do".' Further, Muybridge had asked Rulofson to keep the letters from Mrs Smith. In the event that he should be killed by Harry, or perhaps lynched as his murderer, he 'extorted' from Rulofson a pledge to 'destroy everything that reflected upon his wife's good name' and therefore, in his view, on his own 'dishonor'. Dead, that is, Muybridge wished to be seen as a martyr, protecting the unblemished innocence of his wife. But alive, he would need those letters for his defence, in which case Flora's good name, and how it might reflect on his prospects, would become trickier to negotiate.

Asked about Muybridge's general mental wellbeing, Rulofson replied that he might 'fill whole volumes' with his 'strange freaks' and peculiar actions. Inadvertently, Rulofson here also suggested the pressure on Mrs Smith's daughter, one of his own workers, to fall in with the defence, when he explained that if Muybridge 'took a dislike to any person in my employ, I would discharge the man', sackings that could be 'utterly causeless'; and 'after all was over, Muybridge would break out again about him as though the thing had not been settled.' Muybridge was 'an invaluable assistant', said Rulofson grandly, and was 'strictly honest'. Yet repeatedly, contracts or 'Bargains made one day would be misunderstood and misstated the next.' He believed that for some time, Muybridge had been 'subject to fits of occasional insanity'.

Once again, if the prosecution now scored any points in cross-examination, the press did not grasp this. When Stoney asked Rulofson if that was the total evidence of Muybridge's insanity, Rulofson recalled that Muybridge had once posed for a photograph on what looked like a crazily dangerous pinnacle in Yosemite, and added that, if the prosecution wished, he could reel off further examples for about two years.

Several long-standing friends of Muybridge now spoke about how changed he had been on his return to San Francisco in 1867, and after his stagecoach accident in 1860. Matthias Gray, the music publisher, soon to become a director of the Bohemian Club; Silas Selleck, the photographer, whose friendship with Muybridge predated even his first arrival in San Francisco; Joseph C. Eastland, an associate from the Mercantile Library; and J. P. H. Wentworth, who had run into Muybridge on the Vallejo ferry on the day of the murder: all agreed. Beforehand, they said, Muybridge had been 'affable' and 'a genial, pleasant and quick business man'. Afterwards, with his 'singular' name change and newly grey hair, he 'was very eccentric, so very unlike his way before going', both 'careless in dress' and 'not as good a business man'. In fact, his 'entire sanity' could seem doubtful: 'his ways and expression of face were odd— especially at times'. He became 'unnecessarily excited', and could be 'very violent and excited in an uncalled for manner', particularly showing 'great impatience in all business transactions'.

After a gruelling day in court, an unidentified pressman filed a late telegraph report for the next morning's papers. 'Muybridge is in moderately good spirits and very hopeful. Last night I spent an hour with him. It was very amusing to listen to his experiences in jail.' The prisoner had recounted intervening, with threats of physical force, to prevent other, 'hardened' inmates menacing one another or using profanities: 'Muybridge feels a little proud of his influence in such a place, and says they one and all treat him with marked respect.'

According to Sam Davis's reporting, Dennis Spencer had been caught off guard by the roster of friends of Muybridge prepared to testify to his unhinged manner. Some of those subpoenaed by the defence, including Virgil Williams, had failed to appear; but enough had come. Spencer therefore needed to scramble to muster rebuttal testimony. The reluctance of Harry's friends to testify for the prosecution had extended even to Harry Edwards, who sent word to say he could not attend. But Spencer responded to this with a subpoena and also now summoned a witness he had held in reserve, Dr G. A. Shurtleff, superintendent of the nearby Stockton Insane Asylum.

Friday, 5 February would end up as the last day on which witnesses testified. Contrary to 'the previously arranged plan of the counsel for the defence', first on the stand that morning was Muybridge himself, though, 'upon his request, which was in accord with the secret policy of the lawyers, he was not asked anything about his wife or the circumstances of the killing of Larkyns'. Instead he had finally decided he must collaborate in an insanity defence. He was 'quiet, cool and reserved' as he gave an account of the stagecoach accident in 1860 and his nine-day coma, of subsequent months of unpleasant symptoms, and of the $2,500 damages that he had won.

During a recess, Dr Shurtleff caught up with the previous day's testimony on Muybridge's mental wellbeing, before taking the stand. Stoney, for the prosecution, then asked him whether he thought Muybridge's sanity at the point of murder could be deduced from his behaviour after the killing. As Judge Wallace had previously ruled out evidence of Muybridge's speech and actions after the murder, this led to 'considerable sparring' between the various lawyers, until Wallace himself posed Stoney's question again. With caveats, Shurtleff replied: 'If it was testified by the common observer that he was calm after the homicide, it would lead to the opinion that he was not insane.' Wallace was now faced with deciding whether to reallow evidence that he had ruled out, changing his mind for a second time. He deferred his decision while the prosecution called Harry Edwards to the stand. According to the narrative of Pendegast and King, Muybridge had been maddened to insanity by Mrs Smith on the Saturday morning, appearing at Bradley & Rulofson at 2.30 p.m. a shivering, weeping wreck. Edwards testified that he had known Muybridge 'tolerably intimately' for four or five years, and that he had been 'calm and not excited' during their conversation in the middle of the day.

Wallace now announced to the court that he was 'satisfied that he had erred' in previously restricting permissible evidence about Muybridge, leading to a fresh interleaving of opposed prosecution and defence narratives.

The prosecution recalled several witnesses from the night of the murder, who agreed that, after killing Harry, Muybridge had been, consistently, 'exceedingly cool and deliberate'. Stoney was also now at liberty to call George W. Smith to testify: Muybridge's *Chronicle* interviewer, currently reporting from the press table. Stoney was interested in the letter Muybridge had written to Smith, asking for a printed correction. But before he could go further, Pendegast leapt up and denounced Smith as ungentlemanly for producing a letter marked 'confidential'. Wallace 'severely reprimanded' Pendegast, pointing out that Smith had had no choice but to produce it. Still, Pendegast had successfully thrown a little dust over what Stoney wished to bring to light, that Muybridge had told Smith he 'objected to the plea of insanity'. Stoney next read out sections of the interview itself. But if he tried to wrest advantage from Muybridge's many implausible, contradictory and manifestly false statements, this made little impact on the day's press reporting, and perhaps not much more on the jury either.

The defence now called two witnesses in order to counter the picture of Muybridge's coolness after the killing. Rulofson described how, in jail two days later, Muybridge had broken down in agitated 'bursts of grief', before becoming 'immovable as stone'. His excitement, said Rulofson, 'was peculiarly unlike any one he had ever seen; these paroxysms were only when his wife or his honor were named'. Then the Napa Deputy Sheriff told of Muybridge's fury on learning that Spencer had interviewed Flora.

The prosecution anxiously recalled Dr Shurtleff. But his view of Muybridge remained unchanged: 'it would seem to me that the act was premeditated, and that he exercised his reasoning faculties to accomplish it. I think that he understood the nature of the act and the consequences; think he felt justified in his own mind.' He believed Muybridge 'was not irresistibly impelled, but was moved by passion'. He 'had a motive, which goes against the idea of madness'. In short, he 'was of the opinion that he was a sane man when he committed the act'. King, for the defence, set about reading Shurtleff lengthy case histories from books on insanity. But though Shurtleff accepted the authority of those being cited, he 'explained very clearly where they had no bearing'.

Closing speeches began with Stoney for the prosecution. He had stern words about juries. Men who freed a murderer who had taken the law into his own hands, by their own defiance of the law, matched the 'enormity' of his crime. Stoney 'knew personally, nearly all the jurors' now before him, he said, and hoped better of them than an acquittal. In the present case, insanity was emphatically 'not proven'. Nor had the defence been able to produce any expert witness to support an argument for insanity. Shifting ground, he explained once more that adultery was 'no justifiable provocation to murder, in the sight of the law', so that it had been 'gratuitous' and wrong to 'vilify and abuse Larkyns'. Moreover, because the vilification constituted no legitimate argument, countering it had fallen outside the prosecution brief. Momentarily addressing this asymmetric battle, Stoney did now suggest wearily that if he and Spencer had set about disproving the asserted adultery, this effort 'would have been defeated by the objection that the other side had not attempted to prove adultery, but merely that Muybridge had been told of it'. As he then acidly put it: 'It has been the part of this defence to show one thing and to try to prove another.' At any rate, he said, 'There are friends of Larkyns here, and at their request, I repudiate the imputation on his memory.'

Returning to the actual accused, Stoney put it to the jury that, in choosing to believe, without proof, that his prospective victim was guilty of what was not anyway a crime, Muybridge had illegally and unjustly 'made himself the law, the judge, and the executioner'. As for dressing this up as insanity: 'Could anything', he asked, 'be so puerile?—to attempt to mislead the judgment of twelve sensible men with such a plea.' It was, he said, 'murder in the first degree or it was nothing. Their verdict must bring him in guilty of this or nothing.' He ended: 'You stick to the law, gentlemen.' A jury 'must decide upon the law and upon the evidence, even if it makes their hearts bleed to do it'.

The press rated Stoney's hour-long speech 'able and impressive'. But defence counsel were the real stars, and when King rose to speak after a recess, 'the Court-room was densely crowded and great excitement prevailed'.

King opened by seeming to abandon all question of the 'unwritten law'. He would 'not ask an acquittal on the ground of justification, as he was satisfied that his Honor would instruct them that the circumstances did not amount to a legal justification of the deed'. He might quickly note, he said, that, 'The books' showed 'many cases wherein the contrary doctrine had been held'. And of course, all the evidence demonstrated that Muybridge had had a 'holy and tender regard' for Flora, and Leviticus ordained that adultery was a capital offence: 'the adulterer and adulteress shall surely be put to death'. Leviticus might not be the law in California, although 'I believe it is a safe moral guide', said King smoothly. Still, no, he would stick to the second argument, 'that the prisoner was insane at the time of the homicide'. Once more he read 'pages, almost volumes' of medical testimony intended to 'sustain his position'. And just imagine, he said to the jury, that you, like Muybridge, 'were tottering on the verge of insanity as all great geniuses are', only to have the 'maddening fire of jealousy' applied. Here King, the 'band-box' San Francisco lawyer, riskily switched to deriding the counsel from Napa. Spencer had been chosen by the people locally as their District Attorney for his 'learning and genius'. Why the need for Stoney's help? This betrayed a lack of confidence in himself and, by extension, in those who had selected him. And when it came to Stoney, 'the hired counsel', he had surely demonstrated bad taste in appearing for the prosecution. A local reporter wrote testily that King's 'neatly rounded sentences suffered in the main from being ended by qualifications'. But King ended his speech with 'a pathetic appeal to the jury to consider all the circumstances surrounding this terrible case in the light of merciful consideration'. He had come to 'love' Muybridge, he said, before prospectively polishing him off: 'He has a noble and honest heart; his life's work is done, and he seeks now only an honorable grave in which to lie down to blissful forgetfulness of all his troubles.'

King was directly followed by Pendegast. With 'his tall form towering above the heads of the large crowd present, a silence almost unearthly pervaded the courtroom'. He began by addressing Stoney's argument, that the crime had been outright murder in the first degree or 'nothing', accepting this same stark choice, but rather in the spirit of a dare honourably made by Muybridge himself. 'By the request of the defendant', said Pendegast, the jury should indeed 'either acquit his client of any crime whatever or send him to the gallows'. Pendegast went on to dismiss the insanity defence just presented by his partner, King, as mere quibbling, although he then made a jesting aside that, of course, 'a man must necessarily be insane to permit himself to be interviewed by a reporter of the

San Francisco Chronicle'. After all, though, he said, 'The killing is admitted, as are all, or nearly all the attendant circumstances testified to.' Thus the real question was, had the killing really been a crime?

Though King had just purported to abandon a defence of 'legal justification', Pendegast now launched into a 'thrilling peroration' to this very effect, and began on Harry. Emphasising what he affected to disavow, he said that he was more than happy not to 'drag the character of the dead from his bloody grave', and was in fact 'perfectly willing that he should sleep there till the resurrection', when presumably he would get what was coming to him. Obviously, he went on, 'Larkyns was but one of a class, and that class, in seducing a man's wife, make a dreadful gamble.' By implication, Harry could hardly complain at the outcome: such men 'stake their lives against moments of sensual gratification. He had played and lost, and had to pay the penalty.'

By contrast with Harry, said Pendegast, Muybridge was a man of 'noble, generous impulses, whose ambition was to elevate his art and cherish his wife's affection'. He had

> recognized the difference in tastes and temperaments between his wife and himself. The difference in their ages accounted for these, and he indulged her in all those innocent amusements which she loved, while he cared not for them. He permitted her to go to the theaters and elsewhere, and to enjoy herself in ways which had no attraction for him. He loved her deeply, madly, with all the love of a strong self-constrained man.

Pendegast conceded that, at some point, Muybridge had commanded Harry from his home, but not through suspicion; simply, 'he felt he had the right to select the company of his wife'. And the 'revelation that his whole life was blasted' had come upon him 'All at once, like a clap of thunder from a clear sky.' Though in his opening remarks King had stated that Muybridge endured three terrible sleepless nights after being shown suggestive letters in his lawyer's office, Pendegast now said that Muybridge had been lulled by his lawyer's analysis that they suggested merely a 'harmless flirtation', hence his shock on the morning of the murder. Also contradicting

King's opening assertion that Mrs Smith had been forced into her revelations by Muybridge, 'fearful that he would kill himself or her', Pendegast now claimed that she had 'deemed it her duty to unfold the loathsome, sickening tale', adding, 'whether wisely or not it is not for us to say'. He 'would not even ask that a man on the jury should imagine himself in Muybridge's place at that time', he said; however, it had been from Mrs Smith that Muybridge had first learnt of Flora's falseness, 'even to the extent of palming off upon him as his own the child of her libertine seducer'. Pendegast read from the copy of Harry's letter to Mrs Smith, and commented that 'Muybridge was not only revenging his wrongs when he shot that man dead, but protecting his wife against him in the future.' It was an awful 'shame', he added, that in law a wife was not more completely her husband's property:

> Under the law, if Larkyns, after being forbidden, had wrenched a shingle from the roof of Muybridge's house, the latter would have been justified in shooting him dead. But when he takes the wife of his bosom, writes prostitute upon her brow, blackens the names of the children, and dishonors and ruins the happiness of the husband, that husband is to ask the law to protect him from a repetition of such conduct. As if it could be repeated! This debauchee, this libertine, holds the woman in his arms on the night of the birth of the child, kisses her lips, calls her his baby, intrudes himself into the sacred precincts of the birthchamber and afterwards exchanges with her ribald jokes at the expense of the old man whom they had wronged.

At the end of his oratorical torrent, Pendegast admitted: 'Gentlemen, there is no statute in such cases permitting a man to slay his injurer.' And yet why not? 'Because no law was needed', he said, any more than there was 'a law to compel a mother to give nourishment to a child'. As with the maternal urge, he explained, 'There is a heaven born impulse in every man's breast to avenge speedily and terribly the dishonour of his wife.' By this extraordinary jump from nurturing to murder, Pendegast made Muybridge's 'heavenly impulse' a law in itself, and one that not merely allowed but required him to kill, so that he must obey 'if hell yawned before him the instant afterward'.

Pendegast now felt bound to argue that the testimony of Mrs Smith and of Rulofson 'was worthy of the highest credence', adding, too, that the views of Muybridge's friends on his mental state, having known him for nearly twenty years, 'must outweigh the opinions of a score of doctors who had never seen him save in the court room'. Muybridge had been 'cruelly stricken through the very excess of his love', he said, and although the law might suggest that he had done wrong,

> you, gentlemen of the jury, you who have wives that you love, daughters whom you reverence, will not say so. I cannot ask you to send this man back to his happy home. The destroyer has been there, and has written all over it, from foundation-stone to root-tree, the words, 'Desolation! desolation!' His wife's name has been smirched, his child bastardized, and his earthly happiness so utterly destroyed, that no hope exists of its reconstruction.

Like King, Pendegast now finished by tracing Muybridge's future to its end point, and painted him wandering quietly in heavenly landscapes, 'securing shadows of their beauty by the magic of his art', thereby gaining 'surcease of sorrow' and passing on 'to his allotted end in comparative composure'.

The courtroom, held spellbound for over an hour and a half, 'shook with applause'. Wallace had one man arrested for his excessive demonstrations, though he was shortly released. In the *Chronicle*, George Smith wrote that spectators who, after Stoney's speech, had said that it would be a 'shame and a disgrace' to let Muybridge go free, had their hearts melted by Pendegast's 'wonderful, moving eloquence'. And Muybridge himself, at such a flattering vindication of his savagery, was 'violently convulsed. His head trembled on his hand and he sobbed with grief.'

It was left to Dennis Spencer to close for the prosecution. King and Pendegast had done their utmost to take the wind out of his sails by professing to reject both the insanity and the justification arguments for acquittal, while forcefully promoting both. In response, Spencer adopted an approach of near-capitulation. He was in an 'embarrassing position', he said, having to speak after 'the eloquent gentlemen who had preceded him', and he knew 'that his position was in a manner an unpopular one'. Even so, 'There is no form of insanity which strikes a man like a flash of lightning, compelling him to commit an awful crime, and then passing away like a dream, leaving no trace behind', he said. And anyway, the only 'essential witnesses' to Muybridge's insanity had been Rulofson and Mrs Smith. Rulofson, as an 'intimate friend' of the prisoner, 'might naturally have stretched his evidence'. And Mrs Smith lacked all merit as a witness, 'a traitor to both parties' and 'a postoffice for the guilty couple', he said, carelessly ceding vital ground by characterising them that way. Mrs Smith 'had been their accomplice all the way through', he continued, 'and her daughter too, and the tone of the letters proved it'. He pointed out that Mrs Smith did not, 'as alleged, inform Muybridge of all these facts on the morning of the 17th', adding that if she had, 'the prisoner, immediately after leaving her house, with the filthy details still ringing in his ears, could not have quietly conversed with Harry Edwards, and inquired if he had any business for him. It was impossible.' And again, Spencer seemed unhappily to concede those 'filthy details', against which the passing testimony of Harry Edwards was no great match.

Pressing on, Spencer declared that shooting out of the darkness was 'murderous and cowardly'. Nor was there valid biblical sanction for choosing to kill an adulterer. Muybridge was not above the law, and everything in his actions 'showed deliberate premeditation', so that 'it was high time these high-handed proceedings were stopped'. In a sideways swipe, he pointed out that Pendegast had been a member of the state legislature for four terms; if he really doubted the law that he had been so glibly dismissing, why had he not fought to change it? Spencer also took a stab at Muybridge for hypocrisy: by the 'justification' argument, Muybridge himself 'would not be entitled to a trial' but would merit execution forthwith. And yet, 'The very prisoner, after his act, comes here and avails himself of all the legal safeguards which he denied his victim.'

Spencer's speech lasted a mere forty-five minutes, and the best verdict on his performance was that he was 'a man of promise'. If correctly reported, the final four words he left ringing in the ears of the jury constituted his ultimate rhetorical lapse: 'He asked at their hands no compromise verdict', and concluded: 'If the prisoner was not guilty of deliberate murder, then let him go free.'

Late that night, Wallace read instructions to the jury, providing written forms of the four potential verdicts. Murder in the first degree carried the death penalty, if Muybridge had conducted the killing 'with an abandoned and malignant heart'. Murder in the second degree, if the killing had been unintentional, carried a life sentence. 'Not guilty' was applicable only if someone other than Muybridge carried out the shooting. And finally there was the option of 'Not guilty by reason of insanity.' This option came with the strongly emphasised caveat that Muybridge's avowed belief that he had been justified in the killing was not, in itself, sufficient reason to class him as insane.

The twelve jurors retired to the jury room, adjacent to the court, and 'loud and earnest discussion' could be heard. Wallace cleared all the spectators from the courtroom, fearing an unseemly celebration if Muybridge should walk free. An initial ballot was said to show five in favour of a verdict of murder in the first degree and seven for acquittal. Though a decision had been expected in short order, the jurymen now refused to shift ground.

Muybridge went to Pendegast's office, also adjoining the courtroom, 'accompanied by about twenty of his friends and most ardent sympathisers', 'chatted gaily', and joined in 'joke, raillery and laugh'. But when midnight came Wallace called it a night, and had Muybridge sent back to jail. Outside the courthouse a rump of spectators lingered until 3.00 a.m., while the jurors dropped asleep.

After breakfast the next morning, and a new ballot, the count of five against seven remained the same. Apparently the five who found Muybridge guilty did not consider him culpable; but they could not convince themselves that he was mad either, especially on the word of Mrs Smith, 'none believing in the nurse's testimony'. Involved discussion recommenced, and a third ballot was held at noon. To the surprise of those present, the verdict was now unanimous.

Without the knowledge of the waiting crowds, Muybridge was hastily recalled from his cell, and the courtroom doors were locked to keep the public out. Pendegast and Johnston sat either side of

Muybridge in case he should break down, Johnston urging him in a whisper to stay calm. To this Muybridge replied, 'I feel fully prepared to meet anything except that which we most desire.'

After painfully slow formalities, and 'amid a silence like the silence of death', the verdict was announced: 'We, the jury, find the defendant not guilty.'

Muybridge gasped and 'sank forward from his chair', rendered 'as helpless as a newborn babe'. Pendegast 'caught him in his arms and thus prevented his falling to the floor, but his body was limp as a wet cloth'. That was not the end of it either. Muybridge now 'fell all to pieces and suffered most terrible paroxysms of emotion'. His 'eyes were glassy, his jaws set and his face livid. The veins of his hands and forehead swelled out like whipcord. He moaned and wept convulsively, but uttered no word of pain or rejoicing.' Before his small audience, Muybridge 'rocked to and fro in his chair. His face was absolutely horrifying in its contortions as convulsion followed convulsion. The Judge discharged the jury and hastily left the courtroom, unable to bear the sight.' Johnston, Spencer and some of the jurors also left, while the court clerk hid his face. Pendegast urged Muybridge to control himself and to thank the remaining jurors, but Muybridge was incapable of complying.

Muybridge was now carried to Pendegast's court office, where he was attended by a local doctor, who administered a sedative. Finally, Johnston, in a stern voice, said, 'Muybridge. I sympathize with you, but this exhibition of emotion is extremely painful to me, and for my sake alone I wish you to desist.' Muybridge 'suddenly straightened his form and said: "I will, sir; I will be calm. I am calm now."' Court resumed, the legalities were completed and Muybridge walked free.

The news spread fast. As he descended the court steps, the assembled crowd 'cheered vociferously and long'. Jury members revealed that although their verdict was 'directly contrary to the charge of the Judge', and 'not in accord with the law of the books', they believed it did accord 'with the law of human nature', and that, 'in short, under similar circumstances', at least, as those circumstances had been described to them, 'they would have done as Muybridge did, and they could not conscientiously punish him for doing what they would have done themselves'.

17: Aftermath

The *Alta* 'Brevities' column, remembering Muybridge's stated belief that he would walk free, now interpreted this as having been bravado or calculation. Based on his fit in court, it noted, he 'evidently didn't expect to be acquitted'. Still, travelling back to San Francisco an innocent man, he did speak of plans already made. As soon as possible, he aimed to tie up his suspended arrangements with the Pacific Mail Company and to 'go upon the professional trip through Mexico and South America, which he had in contemplation when the troubles from which he had just emerged came upon him'. He was pressed about Flora too. 'For his wife he uniformly, after his arrest, spoke in pity rather than passion', observed one paper; and 'Since his acquittal he has spoken in the same spirit, saying that he should always regard her with compassion for her fallen estate, and that so long as he lives and has a dollar or the means of getting one she shall not come to want.' Muybridge must have felt invincible as he dished out this lie to reporters. He still had lawyers fighting in the court of the Nineteenth District of San Francisco, making every conceivable argument to help him avoid giving Flora even a cent.

The crowd outside the Napa courthouse, by a visible majority, had approved the jury's peculiar verdict. And other voices agreed. The *Memphis Daily Appeal* said just one word: 'Correct.' The *Territorial Enterprize* also backed an acquittal. 'It looks like a terrible thing to see a man killed as was Larkyns,' it remarked, 'but there are some things worse than that.' Specifically, reporting of the Beecher–Tilton case was proving 'more shameful and infinitely more contaminating' to the young people of America than the example set by Muybridge, so that 'It would have been much better for the world had Tilton, a year ago, blown out Beecher's brains, and then his own.'

There were other favourable points. The Montana *New Northwest* felt that the jury's remarkable decision to ditch the fig leaf of an insanity finding was 'a healthier view of such cases'. The *New York Tribune*, too, respected this bypassing of a 'fraudulent' verdict: 'whether the prisoner was guilty or not, we are free to say that we like the moral courage of calling a spade a spade'. And yet, it continued, this was merely the jury committing 'perjury' once, rather than twice. Setting Muybridge loose 'painfully shocked' the paper's sense of justice, when not even 'beastly and almost total depravity' could justify his recourse to 'Lynch Law'. Henry George, in the *Post*, also wrote with cool contempt that as the judge had in effect accepted a verdict of 'justifiable murder', so 'the next Legislature should recognize such an act'. And the journal *The Pacific Odd Fellows* amplified this thought: 'A man takes a woman for his wife "for better for worse" when he marries', it said, and if Wallace sanctioned this jury's verdict, then 'Away with all arrests, all trials, all judges, all juries in such cases hereafter.' *Common Sense*, on the side of promoting women's rights, wrote with no less disdain: 'another California jury has decided that a man may murder with impunity the seducer of his wife, or even one who is seduced *by* his wife', before adding, correctly: 'The idea seems to be that when a woman becomes a wife she ceases to be an individual, and becomes the property of her husband.' Nor were all the scandalised voices metropolitan. The *Russian River Flag*, local to the murder, wrote that the jury had 'outraged the law and the facts and violated their oaths to set the assassin free'. Moreover, it pointed out, even by the improper lights of the 'unwritten law', the defence had signally failed to show 'whether Larkyns seduced the woman or she him, or whether she was a wife whose loss was worth grieving about'. If a wife was 'untrue', it went on, 'the husband is at fault, or the woman is a wanton. In either case the husband is a lunatic or a murderer to kill a woman's paramour.' The *Lake County Bee*, too, wrote that 'Outside of Napa—where people appear to rejoice at the result—the verdict creates no little surprise', given that the trial had 'clearly proved' a case of 'wilful, premeditated murder'. The *Bee* was wrong about the *Napa Reporter*, at least, which also described the jury's decision as a 'pernicious' example of placing 'the law of nature above the written law of man'.

The debate provoked by Muybridge's trial did not end a pattern in local California courtrooms of absolving killers in similar cases, and in 1880, the *Sacramento Daily Union* railed against the continued defence, as it put it, of 'sentimental murder'. The enduring popularity of these illicit verdicts marked California as uncivilised, said the paper. 'The idea that anyone can prove his worth by taking upon himself the ineffaceable infamy of murder' was 'utterly preposterous', and 'No man's reputation was ever vindicated by washing it in blood.'

For a few weeks after the trial Muybridge 'lived in retirement', squaring plans for his next great trip. The *Chronicle* reported that, because of 'the family difficulty which led to such serious results', he was keener than ever to escape what it called 'the scene of his misfortunes'. And when he discovered that 'unrelenting' Flora had 'resolved on another summary proceedings to get alimony', it continued, Muybridge consulted his friends in 'dismay', conspiring to outwit her. Supposedly, he came to believe that she meant to seize his photographic apparatus, and therefore packed his equipment in Bradley & Rulofson boxes and secretly transferred them to the Panama steamer, set to leave the next day. In a scene that could have been conjured by Dickens, when the steamer set out towards the Golden Gate, a fast rowing boat, bearing a single passenger 'muffled to the chin', pushed off from the isolated Meiggs's Wharf. The little craft chased the steamer down, and when the two vessels met opposite Black Point the steamer 'slackened speed, according to previous arrangement', and 'the muffled man was taken on board'. Even as Flora, 'the relentless wife', sought desperately to 'lay an embargo' through the courts, Muybridge 'vanished in the mists hovering over the bar'.

More certain than this crowing *Chronicle* tale is that on 9 March, with Muybridge long gone, Flora launched a new motion against him for alimony and counsel fees. Five days were awarded for the two sides to file affidavits and counter-affidavits, and on 26 March, just after Flora's twenty-fourth birthday, Judge Wheeler ruled for a second time. Much though her husband was a known murderer, by law he was an innocent man, and so the subject went unmentioned. Thus, Muybridge's lawyer argued against interim alimony on the grounds that the bill suing for divorce did not 'disclose a good cause of action'. This was an objection Wheeler had never faced before; but, acknowledging that 'the authorities were full of opinions on the subject', he succumbed to its lure. He noted that for all Flora's supposed distress early in 1874, she and Muybridge had continued to live together until she went to Oregon in June. And he thought 'a husband had a perfect right to look upon his wife when she is asleep'; this 'could not be construed to be cruelty', let alone 'extreme cruelty'. He explained carefully that, to meet legal requirements, Flora needed to show that Muybridge had induced in her 'such persistent mental suffering' that it would, 'under ordinary circumstances, create mental debility'.

Once more, Wheeler denied Flora interim alimony; but once more, he invited her, if she wished, to 'amend the complaint' and submit a strengthened petition. The *Chronicle* reported this in a misleadingly cartoonish way. Wheeler had found her existing petition 'very shadowy', it said, including her 'main' argument, that 'the horrid husband looked in through a window while she slumbered', but as the judge saw no cruelty in 'a Benedick feasting his eyes on his snoring partner', alimony had been ruled 'out of the question'.

Muybridge was the victor yet again. However, Flora did immediately set about composing a stronger divorce application, which she submitted three days later. Though the process remained a legal chess game, at least she could now argue without the constraint of her husband's murder trial lying ahead; could argue for her freedom, her right to custody of her child and for desperately needed funds. And a palpable bitterness did mark her amplified deposition, as she attempted more thoroughly to blacken Muybridge's name.

It was in this amended complaint, reported by the *Post* under the headline 'Mrs. Muybridge Again', that Flora described how Muybridge had helped her to procure her divorce from Lucius Stone, giving her $30 to spend as he dictated, before he 'abused her' and demanded it back again; here, too, that she explained how he had next 'threatened that if she did not marry him he would be revenged upon her', compelling her to consent because she 'depended upon him for a living', an assertion incidentally strengthened by Rulofson's testimony that Muybridge would agitate for underlings to be fired when they crossed him. She still maintained that in the winter of 1873, Muybridge had 'falsely charged her with the crime of adultery, and that the child she was soon to bear was not his, and threatened to kill her'. And she explained that Muybridge had gone so far as to break 'a pane of glass in order to be able to observe her while asleep', peculiar behaviour that had filled her with alarm. She disputed the charge against her of infidelity, and stated that on 15 April 1874, she 'bore to her husband a child, named George Down [*sic*] Muybridge'. She had then lived with Muybridge 'in fear of her life' until June when, 'So anxious was she to go to Oregon that she went to the boat on foot, carrying her infant, when she was scarcely able to walk', her fears 'increased by her knowledge that Muybridge's character was fitful, violent and jealous'. For good measure, she alleged 'the commission of adultery on Muybridge's part in the summer of 1874'. She then laid out that he had '$10,000 worth of personal property, all of which is common property', and appealed to the court 'for a decree of divorce and the care of the child, and for alimony for the support of the child pending the suit, and for a division of the common property and for permanent alimony for the support of the child'. The *Post* ended its report with one last, incendiary detail: 'She says that while in Oregon she received a telegram signed "Mrs. Smith" dated October 15th: and that since her return from Oregon she has discovered that the body of the telegram and the original was in Muybridge's handwriting, and since then she has become convinced that it was his fixed intention to kill her if he could do so and escape punishment, and that it is still his purpose to do so.' The fifteenth of October 1874 was the day that Muybridge, in the office of his lawyer, read correspondence by Flora and Harry, and two days before he murdered Harry. Not only had he submitted letters transcribed by himself as evidence in order to sway his trial, but it seems he had also falsified a telegram to try to trick Flora into returning to San Francisco.

This is the earliest surviving record of any kind to give a proper name to Flora's baby. She had cleaved to 'George', with such painful meaning for Harry, and had followed this with 'Downs', her maiden name, asserting her own rights, while in using 'Muybridge' she necessarily defended the child's legitimacy too. And there was perhaps poetic justice in this combination, by which her little boy, now aged almost one, gestured to all three people woefully implicated in his entry into the world.

Flora's new petition might appear exaggerated, a desperate attempt to meet the legal definition of 'extreme cruelty', even if Muybridge's old friends had also willingly stood witness to his morose eccentricity, his perverse financial dealings, and behaviour that could be 'very violent and excited in an uncalled for manner'. Outweighing any questions of voyeurism or unreason, however, was her shocking new assertion that Muybridge had faked a telegram, from a fixed desire to kill her too. And yet there seems to have been evidence for at least part of this claim. One of Dennis Spencer's failed subpoenas at Muybridge's trial had attempted to summon an official of the Western Union Telegraph Company, requiring that he should produce the original of a dispatch as from Mrs. Smith to Flora, sent two days before Harry's murder.

Judge Wheeler responded by issuing an order 'directing Muybridge to show cause on Friday, April 2d, at 10 a. m., why he should not pay alimony, fees, etc., during the pendency of the action', which would, Wheeler added, be complying with 'the usual preliminaries of such suits'. And however much Muybridge's lawyer subsequently wriggled, Wheeler did finally rule, on the 30th, that Muybridge should, *pro tem*, provide Flora with funds. He agreed that 'the affidavits went to show that Mrs. Muybridge was without means, and had a child to support', while her husband was 'engaged upon a contract in Mexico', and seemed to be 'both a leading and prosperous man in his profession', earning 'from $200 to $400 a month'. As for the divorce petition, the 'Court did not wish then to take cognizance of the circumstances of the estrangement of the parties, but simply to deal with the question of alimony'. For now, that is, Flora's allegations could wait. Wheeler ordered that Muybridge was to pay her $50 a month as from 1 January 1875, meaning that she was immediately owed $200. And given that the next day was 1 May, within hours he would owe her $50 more.

This victory was entirely empty, and in the absence of Eduardo Santiago Muybridge, as he had become in Panama, Flora continued without means. Her own lawyer, Jesse Hart, patiently and kindly advanced her 'certain moneys' and tried to help during what soon became her 'illness and poverty'. Six weeks later the press reported that 'Mrs. Flora Muybridge, whose faithlessness was the cause of a well remembered tragedy, is living ill and destitute in one of the San Francisco city hospitals.' An Arizona paper later stiffened this to read: 'Mrs. Flora Muybridge, whose illicit love sent Harry Larkyns to the grave with a bullet in his heart and wrecked her husband's life, is now lying at the point of death, alone and destitute, in one of the city hospitals of San Francisco.' There she was visited by Captain Bromley, from whose house she had married, for the first time, eight years earlier. Apparently she said, 'I am sorry.'

A few days later, the *Alta* carried a front-page headline saying simply: 'She Is Dead.'

Flora met her end during the afternoon of 18 July 1875, under the charge of the Sisters of Mercy at the Catholic hospital of St Mary, nine months and a day after Harry's murder. The *Chronicle* reported that she had 'sickened' after Muybridge's trial, her illness

St Mary's Hospital: photograph by Muybridge

developing 'into complication of spinal complaint and inflammatory rheumatism, which baffled the skill of physicians'. Friends had placed her in hospital at the start of May, it said, and there 'she languished in great pain until death put an end to her sufferings'. It added, 'The poor woman was out of her mind a great portion of the time, and was unconscious at the time of her death', though there had been lucid moments, in one of which she had professed to the Sisters that she was at 'peace with God'.

The *Alta* struck a different note. 'Poor Flora is a cold', it wrote, pointedly invoking *King Lear*, and the lines of Edgar, who, brought down by the false accusations of his wicked, illegitimate brother, becomes an outcast and pretends to be mad. She had, it said, entered hospital and 'lingered there and alone for a couple of weeks, suffering from paralysis', when 'death released her of a life that must at least have been a regret'.

Some of the press responses to Muybridge's trial had suggested that Flora deserved to die. One paper, after approving the verdict, wrote that now, 'MRS. MUYBRIDGE should be tried, as an accessory before the fact in the killing of LARKYN.' Another weighed in, saying: 'Larkyns took the chances and lost. No matter how guilty the woman, his crime was none the less. Whose turn next?' Whether or not there was a conscious wish to taunt her into killing herself, it is not hard to imagine that Flora, penniless, severely ill, in mourning and divided from her child, might have sunk the faster for being tormented with public condemnation.

The *Alta*'s 'Brevities' column added a further, withering note: 'When Mr. Muybridge hears of the death of his late wife, he will doubtless feel satisfied that his work is complete, and will be able to begin life anew with an easy conscience and enlarged wisdom.' But there is no evidence that either his wisdom or his conscience were ever troubled in the least degree. The women's literary journal *Golden Dawn* was even blunter when it declared that 'on some one's head rests the blood of at least two persons'.

The *Chronicle* had its own last words on Flora, reporting that, with 'no relatives here except her infant', her 'babe' had been placed 'with a French family at the Mission' who 'kindly cared for it during the illness of its mother, and will, it is believed, adopt it'. And finally,

'Her friends and acquaintances in this city are making efforts to procure the means of giving her remains a burial befitting the station she formerly occupied in life.' Her funeral took place privately on Clementina Street, none too respectable, and from there Flora was taken to be buried in the Cosmopolitan Section of the Odd Fellows Cemetery on San Francisco's Lone Mountain. She came to rest, that is, a short stroll from the vault that had held Harry's murdered body, among the tidy avenues of monuments, but close to the unimproved wilds.

Postscript

If Harry really was the father of Flora's baby, then with her death, George Downs Muybridge became the orphan child of two orphan children. His only definite relatives, the Stumps, who had conspicuously failed to rescue Flora, chose not to rescue the infant who had lived with them either. And though Muybridge returned to San Francisco late in 1875, for some time he too let the little boy be.

In March 1876, Muybridge's lawyer, William Wirt Pendegast, aged barely thirty-five, suffered an apoplectic fit and died. Stoney, opposing counsel at Muybridge's trial, but also Pendegast's good friend, delivered the eulogy at his funeral, and Muybridge wrote to Pendegast's widow declaring his gratitude for the 'noble and disinterested generosity' shown to him by her husband when, as he put it, he was 'bowed down by grief and crushed with broken pride'.

Muybridge had by now taken his business away from another of his defenders, William Rulofson, and was selling instead through the gallery of Samuel Morse. As it happens, Rulofson too would die within a couple of years. Ambrose Bierce wrote sardonically that Rulofson executed his own 'dance of death' when he accidentally fell off the roof of the Bradley & Rulofson building. He left a wife and eleven children.

In September 1876, something caused Muybridge to intervene and place Flora's child, now aged two and a half, in San Francisco's Haight Street Protestant Orphan Asylum. In his trial it had been a strong plank of the defence that Muybridge was driven temporarily mad by discovering the baby to have been fathered by his wife's libertine seducer. Yet Muybridge allowed the child to be registered as a 'half orphan', indicating that he had one parent alive, who could only be Muybridge himself. He also supplied him with a new name, presumably one that he thought the boy would 'not be ashamed to own when a man', and so George Downs Muybridge became Florado Helios Muybridge.

San Francisco Protestant Orphan Asylum: photograph by Muybridge

Given the many shifts through which Muybridge had already forced his own name, this move was no doubt heavily thought through. 'Florado' was not unique; but in the circumstances it gave the particularly elegant sense of combining 'Flora' with 'Eduardo', the Spanish form of Edward that Muybridge had used in Panama. 'Helios', meanwhile, not only invoked his business success, and stamped the child as his own copy or 'print', but also, in barely concealed code, allowed for the whole name to be interpreted as Florado, sun, or 'son', of Muybridge.

In November that year, the *Post* looked askance at what it called 'A Peculiar Motion in the Muybridge Divorce Case'. At the time of Flora's death, Muybridge had still owed her alimony of $350, but the case was dismissed by the court shortly after she died. Yet she had been heavily indebted to her lawyer, Jesse Hart, who had gambled on the justice of her cause, and he was therefore 'asking to be substituted as plaintiff in the suit for divorce, and asking leave to file a supplemental complaint'. As the *Post* explained it:

His object in doing it is to recover certain moneys advanced to Mrs. Muybridge during her illness and poverty, and also to recover payment for services rendered her. Some jocose remarks were indulged in by counsel as to the peculiar position Mr. Hart would occupy if the motion were granted, and the Court gave him until Monday to hunt up and file authorities sustaining his position.

A few days later, Judge Wheeler gave his ruling. Though Hart had 'advanced money and depended on the alimony, which would undoubtedly have been allowed, for his reimbursement', he had done so 'at his own risk'. Wheeler agreed that 'there were in Europe statutory provisions for such a proceeding', but locally, he said, the law was 'silent on this point'. Hart's motion was denied.

The 1880 census listed 'Muybridge, F. H.' among the more than 200 orphans at the San Francisco Protestant Orphan Asylum. He was carelessly registered as a girl, 'F', aged six, with parents French, and unable to read or write. Almost all the children there were under the age of twelve, and Florado left aged nine and a half to become a farm worker. By the time of the 1900 census, when he was twenty-six, he was boarding on a farm in Sacramento, one of a gang of young labourers, hostlers and horse trainers. He now knew to say that his father was English, but still believed his mother to have been French, a misconception that lasted all his life. When Muybridge himself died, back in Kingston upon Thames, in 1904, he bequeathed money to a cousin, but left Florado nothing.

In September 1918, now aged forty-five, Florado acquired a draft registration card, on which he was described as a labourer, of medium height and build, with blue eyes and brown hair. His signature was childlike, and he supplied the wrong birthday: 13 May. For 'nearest relative' he gave 'Miss Garoutte', address 'Sate Librian Sact. Cal', a pathetic detail suggesting that Eudora Garoutte, the State Librarian, and a resolute researcher into the biographies of notable early Californians, had contacted Florado at some point and had remained, in his mind, his best link to anything that might represent his family.

Pendegast's daughter grew up to become an avid keeper of her father's flame and, by extension, a defender of Muybridge as well. She too sent out an emissary to track Florado down. News came back to her that he was a labourer, that he drank, and that possibly he could recall Muybridge bringing him toys in the orphanage; but not much more. Coldly averse to this picture, she put on record that Florado had grown up 'utterly worthless'. The 1920 census captured him as a deliveryman for a grocery shop, living alone. Ten years later, still alone, he was working as a nursery gardener. He died in February 1944, in Sacramento, run over by a car.

The year after Muybridge placed Florado in the Haight Street Orphanage, he and Stanford returned to their experiments in photographing horses at speed. The results catapulted Muybridge to international fame, and from this point on, through various vicissitudes, he specialised in images of locomotion, taking analytical photographs of hundreds of moving bodies, animal and human. Chillingly, these included several versions of shots in series showing naked men bolting away from the camera, as though running

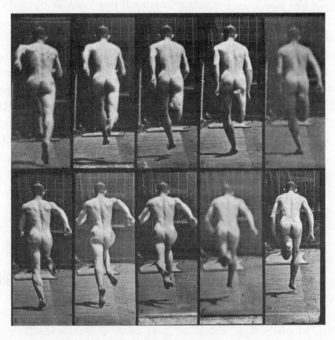

'Running full speed. (Movements. Male).'

for their lives. Another series bore the title 'Turning around in surprise and running away' in which, eyes covered, the figure is unable to see the source of the motivating shock.

In 1880, the *Stock Report*, long since sold by Harry's friend and patron Richard Wheeler, included a humorous note on Muybridge's latest brilliant advances: 'As Mr. Muybridge has succeeded in taking a perfect photograph of a deer at full run, it is proposed to have him try his patent camera on the price of stocks. If he can succeed in photographing them at their present down grade gait, his machine is lightning, indeed.' This joke caught the eye of Sam Davis, now editor of the *Carson Morning Appeal*. He copied and pasted the witticism, but capped it with a growling, unappeased terminal sentence: 'A more surprising feat would be the photographing of the bullet flying from the Muybridge pistol, which killed Harry Larkyns in the dark.'

Acknowledgements

For starting the hare that led me to the subject of this book, my thanks go first to Keith Stern. His willingness to promulgate an underground conjecture about the true identity of Harry Larkyns took my life on an unexpected swerve. I am grateful to him for his generosity in sharing his thoughts with me, and above all for pointing me towards what has ended up as a long spell of pleasure in my work.

The conjecture was that the mysterious Major Harry Larkyns murdered by Muybridge was one and the same as the son, Henry, mentioned in Emma Larkins's famous last Cawnpore letter. As to that letter, I could remember my grandmother showing it to me as a child, she, and therefore I, being descended from Harry's sister Alice. Approaching 'Harry Larkyns' from this angle, it was possible within days to prove definitively who he was. But after this came the challenge to fill in the gaps. I cannot express strongly enough my gratitude to the cousins galore who went to extraordinary lengths to help me in these researches, rifling through attics, cupboards, trunks and cardboard boxes to help me track down surviving Larkins archive materials. From first through to fifth cousins once removed, not forgetting an aunt who is a distant cousin too, these included David Pelly, Philippa Pelly, Mary Miers, Richenda Miers, Nat Low, Ann Scott, Dominick Jones and Stephen Bagnold. Between them they were able to dig out shawls, rings, letters, diaries, photographs, forgotten portraits and more. One branch of the family went so far as to send me eleven crates of jumbled material; but all were unfailingly generous collaborators in a project whose results I very much hope they will enjoy.

I am also grateful to the many librarians, archivists and curators who have helped me in my endeavours: Margaret Makepeace and John O'Brien at the British Library; Mark Willmoth at The Sandhurst Collection Archive; Charlotte Samuels and Seoyoung

Kim at the Kingston Museum, as well as the staff of the Kingston History Centre; Megan Jones, Presley Hubschmitt and Nikelle Riggs at the Napa County Historical Society; Janice Braun at the Olin Library, Mills College; Elena Smith at the California State Library; Kate Holohan at the Cantor Arts Center, Stanford; and, definitely not least, the interlibrary loan staff at the Bodleian in Oxford, and at the Bancroft Library, UC Berkeley – gratifyingly, named after the same Hubert Howe Bancroft who briefly employed Harry to work on his great collection of books.

Andrew Ward was exceptionally generous with his help, time and friendship, ruminating with me on Cawnpore questions, and sending me unpublished schematics about causes of death that he put together for his book, *Our Bones are Scattered*. Equally unstinting was Travis E. Ross, who in 2017, by happy chance, from my point of view, completed a PhD on Bancroft's great history project. Not only did he send me a copy of his intriguing thesis, but he also then went out of his way to give me further leads and clues whenever I assailed him with questions. I was greatly helped, too, by the scholarship of Lawrence I. Berkove, and I am sorry not to have been able to tell him so. Further thanks go to Richard Morgan for allowing me to quote from the diary of John Hatfield Brooks; to Robert Folstein for information on the first run of Offenbach's *La Diva*; and to Bill Woodcock for helping me to orient myself in 1870s San Francisco.

I would also like to register my general gratitude for the invaluable resources offered by today's digitally searchable book and newspaper archives. Those I turned to for my researches included the British Newspaper Archive, with its peerless Victorian holdings, available in hour slots at my local library; and Gallica, which provided a huge range of digitised French materials, including nineteenth-century newspapers. I spent hours hunting through newsprint in the California Digital Newspaper Collection, and in Chronicling America; and I chased obscure books and pamphlets via HathiTrust, archive.org and Google Books. Many of my best finds came about through running searches across these various sites, not forgetting to try 'Muybrldge', 'Larkyne' and other corruptions. This allowed me to turn up material I could never have uncovered in any other way.

There is a group of people whose assistance is not directly evident in this book, because I sent them questions out of the blue that led to dead ends, or on which they drew a blank. I am not any the less grateful to them for the time they took to answer what were often abstruse, long-shot enquiries. This kindly band included Catherine Smith of the Charterhouse Archives; Sarah Hume, Julian Farrance and Ian Maine of the National Army Museum; Brett Payne and John Bradley, experts in British *cartes-de-visite*; Doreen Buxton, historian of Matlock Bath; Peter Judge of the Lloyd's Bank archive, home of the surviving ledgers of Twining's Bank; David Walmsley of the Henty Society; Kurt Gänzl, authority on Emily Soldene; Stephen Herbert and Brian Clegg on a couple of Muybridge obscurities; Alan Griffiths, regarding Bradley & Rulofson arcana; and finally, on the symptoms of poisoning, Andrew Lees.

My great thanks go to my agent, Anna Webber, for her heart-warming encouragement and help from start to finish; and also to Alan Samson, Simon Wright and Jo Whitford, and all at Weidenfeld & Nicolson who contributed hard work and good cheer to this complicated venture.

Finally, I would like to thank the Barrau wing of my family, and especially Julie, for help with the French aspects of this project, and for giving me quarter in Paris. And also, beyond anything, I thank all my family and friends for their boundless support and impressive patience as I grew ever more embroiled in the possibilities of this story. In particular, I would like to thank Helen Small, who responded patiently and expertly to my first draft; and, dearest of all, I must thank Tanglewest and Raymond, to whom, I know, Harry Larkins at times seemed like a wretchedly persistent phantom at the table.

June 2020: After initial publication of this book, I was contacted by the film maker Marc Shaffer, currently working on a feature documentary about Muybridge, who very kindly took time to secure for me the details of various failed prosecution subpoenas from the Muybridge murder trial (*see* Napa County Historical Society holdings 1985.29.1). These oblique puzzle pieces yielded striking new information, and I have altered my text accordingly, pp. 272 and 302. *RMG.*

Notes

INTRODUCTION

1—'a rogue whose tales of his life' ff.: Rebecca Solnit, *River of Shadows* (2004), p. 128.

2—'grandiose': Edward Ball, *The Inventor and the Tycoon* (2013), p. 130.

2—'despicable': Brian Catling, *The Vorrh* (2016), p. 34.

2—'putting his pictures again in motion': (EJM), *San Francisco Examiner*, 6 Feb. 1881, p. 3. (For EJM's authorship of this article, *see* A. V. Mozley, R. B. Haas and F. Forster-Hahn, *Eadweard Muybridge: The Stanford Years, 1872–1882* (1972), p. 119.)

4—'priceless': Solnit, p. 142.

I. CHILDHOOD

9—'to fight the battle of his life': *see* Henry Edwards, *A Mingled Yarn: Sketches on Various Subjects* (1883), pp. 151–4.

9—Conny, also born in India: Constance Marion Larkins, b. 20 May 1842.

9—born Ewart Carnochan: 'Ewart' was taken to be a corruption of 'ye Heart', with an ancestor supposed to have been one of those who attempted to take the heart of the Bruce to the Holy Land; *see* John Alexander Ewart, *The Story of a Soldier's Life* (1881), vol. 1, p. 42.

9—having recently buried a young wife: Eliza Belvedere Battley, of Dublin.

10—George survived being sent into Afghanistan: *see* Francis William Stubbs, *History of the Organization, Equipment, and War Services of the Regiment of Bengal Artillery*, vol. 3 (1877), p. 74.

10—'to strive at all times to please': BL: Mss Eur F732. (For an account of Emma's letters, *see* Sources.)

10—'Uncle Larkins', John Pascal Larkins: *see* Walter Kelly Firminger, *The Early History of Freemasonry in Bengal and the Punjab* (1906), p. 168, etc., and Lynn Zastoupil and Martin Moir (eds), *The Great Indian Education Debate: Documents Relating to the Orientalist–Anglicist Controversy, 1781–1843* (1999), pp. 119–23.

11—Aunt Larkins, born Mary Ann Robertson: her husband's second wife, of many years.

11—slips right out of Conny's correspondence: just once, in 1852, Emma asked Conny in passing, 'do you write to dear little Henry?'

11—Presumably he had been parcelled off: many accounts from San Francisco in 1874 and 1875 indicate that HL called himself an 'Inverness man'. It is possible he received some schooling in Scotland, if this identity was not a ruse.

11— George's sister Henrietta: Emma called her 'my dearest friend, your dearest and best Aunt, & Papa's dearest sister'.

11— she must always keep a carriage: it seems she did, given that in her will Henrietta left £100 to her faithful coachman.

11— the banker John Dimsdale: Dimsdale was a great-nephew of Baron Dimsdale of Russia, a title earned by inoculating Catherine the Great against smallpox.

11— Devonshire cousin, Julia Luke: Julia's mother Georgiana, née Larkins, was Conny's aunt and Henrietta's younger sister.

16— the 'Brazilian in Bloomsbury': *Household Words*, vol. 8, 15 Oct. 1853, p. 162.

16— one of Henrietta's many first cousins: Eliza Susannah Larkins, daughter of William Larkins, d. 1851.

18— some people 'never seem to realise': (HL), *San Francisco Daily Evening Post*, 23 Aug. 1873, p. 1.

18— 'brilliant waif': (Dan O'Connell), 'Town Crier', *San Francisco News Letter*, 4 June 1892, p. 17. (For O'Connell's authorship of this article, *see Our Society Blue Book, The Fashionable Private Address Directory, Season 1892–92*, p. xlvi.)

2. REBELLION

20— 'this cartridge question': London *Times*, 14 Apr. 1857, p. 7.

23— 'There was an immense number': Lydia Hillersdon, 31 May 1857, 'letter 13' in London *Times*, 10 Sept. 1857, p. 7. (In a letter dated 24 May 1857, Emma Halliday included an amateur sketch of crowded figures sleeping in the barracks, Emma Larkins listed among them: *see* Raleigh Trevelyan, *The Golden Oriole: Childhood, Family and Friends in India* (1988), p. 306.)

23— 'kept standing by them all night' ff.: Anon., May 1857, 'letter 22' and 'letter 31' in London *Times*, 5 Sept. 1857, p. 10.

23— 'if the troops do mutiny': Colonel Ewart, 31 May 1857, in London *Times*, 22 Oct. 1857, p. 7.

24— 'not more than 150 fighting men': General Wheeler, 31 May 1857, in London *Times*, 2 Sept. 1857, p. 5.

24— the Cawnpore postal system collapsed: *see* Ewart, 'To-morrow will be the latest safe day', 31 May 1857, in London *Times*, 22 Oct. 1857, p. 7; *see also* London *Times*, 5 Sept. 1857, p. 10, for a Cawnpore letter sent 31 May, received 14 July.

24— 'scattered to atoms': 'H. J. Shepherd' to his brother, 18 July 1857, in London *Times*, 19 Sept. 1857, p. 8.

25— 'standing in the verandah' ff.: Mowbray Thomson, *Story of Cawnpore* (1859), pp. 107–8, 136, 63–4, 77.

25— 'saw their husbands' bodies mutilated': Mowbray Thomson to his mother, Aug. 1857, in *Morning Advertiser*, 25 Dec. 1857, p. 4 (and printed in the *Morning Post* the next day).

26— 'to remain there was to die': London *Times*, 2 Sept. 1857, p. 5.

26— 'incessant bombardment' ff.: Mowbray Thomson, *Story of Cawnpore* (1859), pp. 109, 34, 159, 163.

26— 'after mocking': W. J. Shepherd, *Personal Narrative* (1879), p. 74.

27— immovably lodged in the mud: however, the great fear before this was that any rain might dissolve the entrenchments.

27— 'The infernal treachery': Thomson, pp. 167–8.

27— 'dark complexion' ff.: Shepherd, p. 87.

27— as Lady Wheeler was Eurasian: Saul David, in *The Indian Mutiny* (2003), p. 182, writes that because of this she kept herself apart, and was 'never a welcome guest in cantonment society'. Emma Larkins's correspondence would seem to contradict 'never'.

28— 'burning of the barracks': London *Times*, 24 June, p. 5.

28— out-of-date details: *The Times* first applied the title 'Sepoy Rebellion' on 28 Sept. 1857, p. 6.

28— 'the vortex': *London Evening Standard*, 3 Sept. 1857, p. 4.

28— 'Give full stretch to your imagination': London *Times*, 3 Aug. 1857, p. 5.

29— 'Do not grieve, dear ones': (Emily and Henrietta Streatfeild), *Memoir of the Rev W. Streatfeild, M.A., Vicar of East Ham, Essex; and late fellow of Trinity College, Oxford. By His Daughters* (1869), p. 198.

29— 'Poor young Streathfield': London *Times*, 19 Sept. 1857, p. 8. (After a near-fatal bout of dysentery, Robert eventually made it home.)

29— 'Dear Mamma and her sisters': (Streatfeild), p. 197.

29— Day after day: The time lags were distressing both ways. On 20 July, in Mhow, John Hatfield Brooks noted in his diary: 'Accounts of a fearful tragedy at Cawnpoor', while at the same time observing: 'Mail in. England is still in happy ignorance of all that is going on here!' See Richard Morgan (ed.), *The Diary of an Indian Cavalry Officer, 1843–63: Before, During, and After the Mutiny* (2003), p. 153.

29— 'Sir Hugh Wheeler has been killed': London *Times*, 27 Aug. 1857, p. 7.

29— 'the appalling news': (Streatfeild), p. 201.

29— 'yet direr fate': London *Times*, 29 Aug. 1857, p. 8. (The British goaded themselves with an unsupported belief that the women of the Bibighar suffered rape, yet rejected all idea of the likely rape of Miss Wheeler.)

30— 'We still believe': London *Times*, 2 Sept. 1857, p. 5.

30— 'We think the last gleam': (Streatfeild), p. 202.

30— 'soul-harrowing spectacle': London *Times*, 16 Sept. 1857, 2nd edn, p. 6.

30— 'prodigies and horrors': London *Times*, 17 Sept. 1877, p. 6.

30— 'if they should in future': London *Times*, 19 Sept. 1857, 2nd edn, p. 5.

30— 'high-caste Brahmins': London *Times*, 21 Sept. 1857, p. 5.

31— 'inhumanly butchered': 'H. J. Shepherd' to his brother, 18 July 1857, in London *Times*, 19 Sept. 1857, p. 8.

31— a translated list of names: 'Memorandum', in London *Times*, 21 Sept. 1857, p. 5.

31— 'Major George Larkins and his wife': *see e.g. Evening Mail*, 30 Sept. 1857, p. 8.

32— 'with considerable care': *Homeward Mail*, 16 Sept. 1857, p. 10, and 1 Oct. 1857, p. 20.

3. SCHOOL

33— 'cheaply educated at Brussels': Charles Dickens, *Our Mutual Friend* (1865), vol. 1, p. 11.

33— 'No Vacations': *see e.g. Family Herald*, 5 July 1851, p. 11.

33— 'brought up by his aunt': *see* Kingston: EM5014. (For Kingston *see* Sources.)

33— 'reedy swamps': Charlotte Brontë, *The Professor* (1857; 1991), p. 50.

33— 'a cheap and decent residence': CB to Elizabeth Branwell, 29 Sept. 1841, in Margaret Smith (ed.), *The Letters of Charlotte Brontë*, vol. 1: 1829–1847 (1995), p. 268.

33— 'until she found that they felt more pain': Elizabeth Gaskell, *The Life of Charlotte Brontë* (1857), vol. 1, p. 200.

33— 'his province as a lad': Thomas Westwood, *A Literary Friendship: Letters to Lady Alwyne Compton 1869–1881 from Thomas Westwood* (1914), p. 3.

34— 'He that is low need fear no fall': Brontë meant to invoke the song of the Shepherd's Boy in John Bunyan's *The Pilgrim's Progress*: 'He that is down, needs fear no Fall'.

34— 'extremely cheap there': Brontë, p. 55.

34— 'submit another effort': Sidney Lee and George Smith, *George Smith: A Memoir: With Some Pages of Autobiography* (1902), p. 19. (Smith described how Brontë had an awful ability to 'chill' a party, suggesting that the Jenkins family anecdote was broadly true: ibid., p. 97.)

34— four of his seven boys: Philip Collins, *Dickens and Education* (1963), pp. 27–39. (Dickens would remark on the return of his boys 'after a year's' absence: CD to Angela Burdett Coutts, 10 July 1857, in Storey *et al.* (eds), *The Letters of Charles Dickens*, vol. 8 (1995), p. 372.)

34— 'very pale veal': Henry Dickens, *The Recollections of Sir Henry Dickens, K.C.* (1934), p. 11.

34— 'Second Classman': *Report of Her Majesty's Commissioners Appointed to Inquire into the Revenues and Management of Certain Colleges and Schools*, vol. 2 (1864), Appendix, p. 330.

34— 'Born and established on the Continent': Charles Edward Jenkins, *Colonial Church Chronicle*, Jan. 1871, p. 34.

34— further pickings: for example, he imparted weekly religious instruction at a nearby school for young ladies: London *Times*, 2 June 1868, p. 3.

35— 'deadness'; 'morose nurselings': Brontë, pp. 73, 148.

35— a great advocate: and a 'good amateur' player, apparently: J. R. Scott, *Family Guide to Brussels* (1871), p. 102.

35— 'pure love': (HL), *SF Post*, 6 May 1874, p. 1.

35— 'Though not indigenous': *Bell's Life in London*, 26 June 1859, p. 8.

35— 'Major Larkins, Mrs. Larkins and children': Henry Delafosse, 'Deposition', in London *Times*, 16 Oct. 1857, p. 7.

36— 'if any confirmation had been needed'; 'Do not grieve, dear ones': (Emily and Henrietta Streatfeild), *Memoir of the Rev. W. Streatfeild, M.A., Vicar of East Ham, Essex; And Late Fellow of Trinity College, Oxford. By His Daughters* (1869), p. 203.

37— 'who hopes to escape': here 'hopes' could be read as 'wishes'. (For a Larkins diamond ring supposedly smuggled out earlier, *see* George Trevelyan, *Cawnpore* (1865; 1894), pp. 127–8.)

37— 'there was no ink or pens': W. J. Shepherd, *Personal Narrative* (1879), p. 59.

37— 'so sadly riddled': 'Mr. Sheppard', London *Times*, 7 Nov. 1857, pp. 6–7.

37— 'hopped in the midst': Shepherd, *Personal Narrative*, p. 26.

38— 'defenders': Charles Ball, *History of the Indian Mutiny*, vol. 1 (1858), p. 331.

38— 'I find the officers' servants': James Neill, 1 Aug. 1857, in *Globe*, 26 Sept. 1857, p. 2.

38— 'entrusted to a native servant': (Streatfeild), p. 202.

38— 'the ayah gave the letter': Constance Snagg, née Larkins (BL: Mss Eur F732).

38— 'Bursting into tears': Alice Pelly, née Larkins (BL: Mss Eur F732).

39— 'The four orphan children': *East India: Home Accounts of the East India Company, Ordered, by The House of Commons, to be Printed, 18 June 1858*, pp. 10–11. (In the same year, the Company paid £6,723, nine shillings and two pence for 'Maintenance of lunatics from India'.)

39— a mansion built by Robert Bell: *see* Richard Milward, *Eagle House: A Short History* (2001). (The building was named Nelson House School after a visit by Nelson and Lady Hamilton in 1805, and became Eagle House in 1860.)

39— Arthur Schopenhauer had been sent there: Don Cupitt, *Sea of Faith* (1984), p. 167; *see also* Patrick Bridgwater: *Arthur Schopenhauer's English Schooling* (1988).

39— Rev. John Brackenbury: G. W. de Lisle (ed.), *Marlborough College Register, from 1843 to 1869 inclusive* (1870), p. vii.

40— at full capacity: Brackenbury's moved premises soon after HL left.

40— 'more superficial than sound' ff.: *School Inquiry Commission*, Her Majesty's Stationery Office, vol. 2 (1868), pp. 885–97.

40— 'The "natural enmity" theory': Arthur Granville Bradley, *A History of Marlborough College During Fifty Years: From its Foundation to the Present Time* (1893), pp. 71–2.

40— 'educating expensively': CD to W. W. F. De Certjat, 16 Mar. 1862, in Storey *et al.* (eds), *The Letters of Charles Dickens*, vol. 10 (1998), p. 53.

40— 'I don't think I ever saw': CD to ABC, 21 Jan. 1855, in Storey *et al.* (eds), *The Letters of Charles Dickens*, vol. 7 (1993), p. 508.

41— 'huffed and cuffed': Charles Dickens, *Dombey and Son* (1848), p. 199.

41— 'Now young Dickens': Henry Dickens, p. 12.

41— 'as soon as he is old enough': CD to ABC, 21 Jan. 1855, in *Letters*, ibid., p. 508.

41— 'Fortune, safety, comfort' ff.: Henry Byerley Thomson, *The Choice of a Profession* (1857), pp. 175, 202–6.

41— Addiscombe: H. M. Vibart, *Addiscombe: Its Heroes and Men of Note* (1894), pp. 668, 57.

42— Dr Burney's in Greenwich: *see* George Larkins's cadet papers (BL: IOR: L/MIL/9/150/399–404). (For social relations between the Burney and Larkins families *see* Lorna J. Clark (ed.), *The Letters of Sarah Harriet Burney* (1997).)

42— 'direct cadetship': *see* T. A. Heathcote, *The Military in British India: The Development of British Land Forces in South Asia, 1600–1947* (1995).

42— the philanthropist Angela Burdett Coutts: CD to ABC, 19 Feb. 1856, in Storey *et al.* (eds), *The Letters of Charles Dickens*, vol. 8 (1995), p. 60.

43— 'on the recommendation of his Aunt': *see* HL's cadet papers (BL: IOR: L/MIL/9/250/998–1004).

44— 'a more fearful calamity': *Morning Advertiser*, 10 Dec. 1859, p. 3.

44— 'will fall into that strange life': CD to Walter Savage Landor, 5 July 1856, in *Letters*, ibid., p. 152.

44— 'with unsettled': CD to ABC, 3 Oct. 1856, in *Letters*, ibid., p. 198.

44— 'as little cast down'; 'whether the best definition': CD to John Dean, and CD to William Jerdan, both 21 July 1857, in *Letters*, ibid., p. 382.

45— 'the finest country in the world': Thomas Nicholls Walker, *Through the Mutiny: Reminiscences of Thirty Years' Active Service and Sport in India, 1854–83* (1907), p. 203. (Walker was HL's second cousin once removed.)

45— taken to have inspired the fiction of Trilby and Svengali: ironically, Anna Bishop's husband, Henry Bishop, was the composer of 'Home Sweet Home'.

45— 'electrical effect': (HL), *SF Post*, 26 July 1873, p. 1.

4. BENGAL

46— 'The past is all a dream': John McCosh, *Advice to Officers in India* (1856), p. 41.

46— for another two years: a boy received this pension until he turned eighteen; a girl, until she married or reached twenty-one: Henry Byerley Thomson, *The Choice of a Profession* (1857), pp. 186, 206.

46— His great-grandfather, William Larkins, ff.: *see* Jean Sutton, *The East India Company's Maritime Service, 1746–1834: Masters of the Eastern Seas* (2010).

47— a French frigate *La Piémontaise*: Tom received a gratuitous stab wound after his eventual surrender of 'what remained' of his ship: *St. Helen Gazette*, 18 Sept. 1806 (private collection).

48— By all accounts, it was overwhelming: *see e.g.* James Howard Thornton, *Memories of Seven Campaigns* (1895), pp. 3–6; S. Dewé White, *Indian Reminiscences* (1880), pp. 5–6; McCosh, pp. 50–51.

48— 'condition of India question': London *Times*, 20 Dec. 1860, p. 9, *citing Bombay Gazette*, 26 Nov. 1860.

48— 'discharge or bounty': *see* Peter Stanley, *White Mutiny: British Military Culture in India, 1825–1875* (1997).

48— 'blunderingly resisted': (Charles Dickens), 'The Uncommercial Traveller', *All the Year Round*, 21 Apr. 1860, pp. 37–40.

49— 'sea-hearses': (R. B. Cumberland), 'An Indian Officer', *How I Spent My Two Years' Leave* (1875), p. 4.

50— 'The amount of official correspondence': McCosh, p. 132.

50— 'for the express purpose' ff.: London *Times*, 21 Dec. 1860, p. 5.

50— 'highly delighted with H.M.'s 73rd' ff.: *Homeward*, 20 Dec. 1860, pp. 3–5.

51— 'inferior grain': *Homeward*, 5 June 1861, p. 11, *citing The Englishman* (n.d.).

51— 'insolent threatenings': John Cox Gawler, *Sikhim: With Hints on Mountain and Jungle Warfare* (1873), p. 87.

51— 'The lion has whisked'; 'insults and injuries': *Homeward*, 13 Feb. 1861, p. 13, *citing Friend of India*, 27 Dec. 1860.

51— 'wretchedly poor': *Homeward*, 13 Apr. 1861, p. 6.

52— The superintendent there, Dr Campbell: Campbell was a noted naturalist who had made an earlier risky expedition in the region with the botanist Sir Joseph Hooker.

52— 'the bravery of rashness': *Homeward*, 13 Feb. 1861, p. 13.

52— 'We are rather in a mess' ff.: *Homeward*, 12 Jan. 1861, pp. 14–15.

52— 'efface': *Homeward*, 28 June 1861, p. 2.

52— 'overawe Bhotan': *Homeward*, 17 Mar. 1862, p. 2.

52— rudimentary outstation: Thornton, pp. 161–5.

53— 'snowy peaks, deep dark valleys': Gawler, p. 3.

53— 'waste country': *Homeward*, 21 Feb. 1861, p. 4.

53— 'Wretched cold' ff.: *Homeward*, 13 Apr. 1861, p. 6.

53— 'rotting on the roadside': *Homeward*, 5 June 1861, p. 11.

54— 'The scenery': McCosh, p. 244.

54— 'dull, listless, routine' ff.: McCosh, pp. 109–10 and 70; *see also* pp. 160–65.

54— 'had it not been for the punkahs': *Homeward*, 16 Aug. 1862, p. 4.

55— 'bungalow bestudded steep': William Howard Russell, *My Diary in India, in the Year 1858–9* (1860), p. 144.

55— the San Francisco Minstrels: *Homeward*, 22 Aug. 1862, p. 4. *See also* Bradley G. Shope, *American Popular Music in Britain's Raj* (2016).

55— 'in aid of the unfortunate Lancashire operatives': *Homeward*, 22 Aug. 1862, p. 4.

55— 'foul blot': *see e.g. London Evening Standard*, 1 Jan. 1863, p. 5.

55— Lord Elgin, battled: *Homeward*, 5 Jan. 1863, p. 14; *see also Homeward*, 15 Jan. 1863, pp. 15–16.

57— 'the last of those obtrusive pageants': *Homeward*, 6 May 1863, p. 1.

57— 'full of dusty fugitives' ff.: *Homeward*, 5 June 1863, p. 2.

57— a 'very splendid' fancy-dress ball: (HL), *SF Post*, 11 July 1873, p. 1.

57— 'the order of the day': *Homeward*, 28 Aug. 1863, p. 4.

57— 'The very lax notions': Russell, p. 143. (Russell was famously war reporter for *The Times* during the Crimean War.)

57— 'in the hope of prepossessing': John Lang, *Wanderings in India* (1859), p. 402.

57— 'the place-hunter': Dewé White, p. 17.

58— 'The desperadoes are thirsting' ff.: *Homeward*, 5 Jan. 1863, p. 8, *citing Dacca News*, 23 Nov. 1862.

58— 'equipped for hill and jungle warfare': *Homeward*, 20 May 1863, p. 6, *citing The Englishman* (n.d.).

58— 'Those invincible rebels': *Homeward*, 21 July 1863, p. 1.

58— 'depredations': *Homeward*, 26 Sept. 1863, p. 8.

59— 'I should do my utmost': CD to ABC, 4 Oct. 1857, in Storey *et al.* (eds), *The Letters of Charles Dickens*, vol. 8 (1995), p. 459.

59— 'sun-stroke': CD to Mrs Gore, 7 Sept. 1858, in *Letters*, ibid., p. 654.

59— rewarded with a lieutenancy: CD to W. W. F. De Certjat, 1 Feb. 1859, in Storey *et al.* (eds), *The Letters of Charles Dickens*, vol. 9 (1997), p. 21.

59— 'spends more than he gets': CD to W. W. F. De Certjat, 16 Mar. 1862, in Storey *et al.* (eds), *The Letters of Charles Dickens*, vol. 10 (1998), p. 53.

59— 'with the hectic flush': McCosh, p. 54.

60— who also lived in Cleveland Square: Howard L. Malchow, *Gentlemen Capitalists: The Social and Political World of the Victorian Businessman* (1992), p. 167.

60— The Pelly family had acquired the Upton estate: *see* John Pelly, *The Pelly Family*, 3 vols (1983–91).

60— a mare's nest of intermarriage: the writer Noel Streatfeild was descended from one of these marriages, of a Streatfeild to a Fry.

60— 'so wholly yours': *illeg.* to LP, 29 Dec. 1863 (privately held).

60— 'It is my most painful duty': Arthur A. Adrian, *Georgina Hogarth and the Dickens Circle* (1957), pp. 85–7.

60— 'balance the debit and credit side': McCosh, p. 6.

61— 'poor Walter's wretched affairs': CD to Georgina Hogarth, 12 Oct. 1864, in *Letters*, ibid., p. 438.

61— 'the great amalgamation year': *Homeward*, 8 June 1874, p. 7, *citing Times of India* (n.d.).

61— 'old women and fossils': (Cumberland), p. 5.

61— famed for their élan: *see e.g.* F. W. Pitt, *Incidents in India and Memories of the Mutiny With Some Records of Alexander's Horse and the 1st Bengal Cavalry* (1896).

61— 'Praise to our Indian Brothers': Tennyson, 'The Defence of Lucknow' (1879).

62— 'for having had a sepoy, who shot': *Homeward*, 26 Jan. 1861, p. 3.

62— 'Master Henry Larkins is in debt': RPP to LP, RP, 29 Sept. 1864 (Kingston: EM5014).

62— 'I suppose the Regiment': CD to ABC, 12 Feb. 1864, in *Letters*, ibid., pp. 155–6.

62— 'sacred maxim' ff.: McCosh, pp. 32–3, 109.

63— 'Inventory of Estates': BL: IOR/L/AG/34/27/165.

64— his best bet and only hope: a stray line in Ray Pelly's correspondence of 1865 suggests that Alice was occasionally in touch with HL: 'Alice has got Henrys letter to her great joy.' RPP to LP, RP, 10 May 1865 (Kingston: EM5014).

64— 'Brahmans, Rajputs': A. C. Lovett and G. F. MacMunn, *The Armies of India* (1911), p. 143.

64— 'principally Goorkhas': *Homeward*, 29 Oct. 1857, p. 14.

64— 'semi-mutiny': Lovett and MacMunn, p. 110.

64— 'more enthusiasm than discretion': *Oriental Sporting Magazine*, 16 Mar. 1868, pp. 24–5.

65— 'the late lamented Colonel Bagot': (Cumberland), p. 334.

65— 'Not being able to agree with his colonel': *Echoes*, 12 June 1869, p. 4.

65— Alice's more plausible version: *see* Kingston: EM5014.

65— officers were 'permitted to resign the service': George E. Cochrane, *Regulations Applicable to the European Officer in India* (1867), p. 745; *see also* pp. 366, 1106–7.

5. LONDON

66— 'We Indians': (R. B. Cumberland), 'An Indian Officer', *How I Spent My Two Years' Leave* (1875), pp. 92–3.

66— 'an aunt, colossally rich': *Echoes*, 12 June 1869, p. 4.

66— 'the Cremorne Garden, Argyle Rooms': *San Francisco Chronicle*, 14 Mar. 1873, p. 3.

66— 'Extravagance was evidently his weak point': *see* Kingston: EM5014.

67— 'for 120*l*., being the balance of 196*l*.': *South London Chronicle*, 28 May 1870, p. 3.

67— A successful bookseller: *see* Jennifer Hall-Witt, *Fashionable Acts: Opera and Elite Culture in London, 1780–1880* (2007), pp. 164–8.

67— 'Many an able, industrious': 12 Mar. 1866, in W. E. Gladstone, *Speeches on Parliamentary Reform in 1866* (1866), pp. 53–4.

68— 100 guineas for the season: London *Times*, 16 Mar. 1867, p. 8.

68— 'mere pittance of bread, cheese': CC to Dina Williams Hunt, Dec. 1862, in Sharon Lynn Joffe (ed.), *The Clairmont Family Letters, 1839–1889*, vol. 1 (2016), p. 40; *see also* pp. 23, 631, 671.

68— 'the life of the theatre' ff.: George Moore, *Confessions of a Young Man* (1888, rev. 1926; 1939), pp. 21–2, 163.

69—'westward Hansoms freighted' ff.: William Acton, *Prostitution, Considered in its Moral, Social, and Sanitary Aspects, in London and other Large Cities and Garrison Towns. With Proposals for the Control and Prevention of its Attendant Evils*, 2nd edn (1870), pp. 17, 19, 48.

69—'peculiarly in the way of contact': H. C. G. Matthew, *Gladstone 1809–1898* (1997), pp. 91–3.

70—'inimitable': *Le XIXe siècle*, 13 Nov. 1874, p. 2.

70—'drolleries': *Cheltenham Mercury*, 25 May 1867, p. 4.

70—'Passage des Princes': Jean-Paul Bonami, *La Diva d'Offenbach: Hortense Schneider 1833–1920* (2004), p. 120.

71—'prophet's chamber': Authorized Version, II Kings 4:10.

71—Hagar: *see* Genesis.

71—'so earnestly seeking, <u>now</u> there is no pretence': RPP to LP, RP, 11 Dec. 1867 (Kingston: EM5014). RPP altered the original emphasis of this observation by removing a comma he had placed after '<u>now</u>'.

73—the 'villa' mentality, ff.: Moore, pp. 115, 160.

73—'not only wears as many rings': *Wiltshire Times and Trowbridge Advertiser*, 4 July 1868, p. 2. (Offenbach's 'Infernal Gallop' from his 1858 operetta *Orphée aux enfers* remains the tune most closely associated with the cancan.)

74—'traveled extensively in Europe': *Los Angeles Herald*, 22 Oct. 1874, p. 4.

74—'He had a handsome face and figure': *New York Times*, 28 Oct. 1874, p. 4.

74—'when in Italy, he posed as a great personage': *see* Kingston: EM5014.

74—a 'brilliant fancy ball' in Florence: (HL), 'Ishmaelite', *SF Post*, 24 July 1874, p. 1.

6. PARIS

75—'monster establishments': Charles Dickens (Jr), *Dickens's Dictionary of Paris: An Unconventional Handbook* (1882), p. 118.

75—British press would call 'unpleasant dodges': *Echoes*, 12 June 1869, p. 4.

75—'magnificently furnished saloons': Karl Baedeker, *Paris and Northern France: Handbook for Travellers* (1867), p. 4.

76—'distinguished fashionables': *Baily's Magazine of Sports and Pastimes*, vol. 16, May 1869, pp. 308–9.

76—Queen Victoria wrote to her daughter: 18 July 1863, in Roger Fulford (ed.), *Dearest Mama: Letters Between Queen Victoria and the Crown Princess of Prussia, 1861–1864* (1968), p. 249.

76—die as a chloral addict on the Riviera: *see The Thames Advertiser* (NZ), 12 July 1886, p. 2.

76—'de la plus haute aristocratie d'Angleterre': Louis Arnold, *Le Gaulois*, 30 May 1869, p. 3.

76—'MM. Hamilton et d'autres gentilshommes': Réne de Pont-Jest, *Le Figaro*, 29 May 1869, p. 3.

76—'at a maddening rate of speed': *Melbourne Leader*, 23 Jan. 1869, pp. 26–7.

76— 'fairy city': (HL), 'Special Correspondent', *SF Post*, 14 Aug. 1873, p. 1.

76— 'the highest class of questionable company': W. Blanchard Jerrold, *Paris for the English* (1867), p. 64.

76— 'semi-hemisphere': *Baily's*, May 1869, p. 307.

76— first revealed to a disgusted public: *see* Theodore Reff, *Manet: Olympia* (1976).

77— Victorine Meurent: Meurent was known as 'La Glue', *see* George Moore, *Memoirs of My Dead Life* (1906), pp. 30–32. The model for the maid has been identified as 'Laure'.

77— 'hands full of hair being scattered': (HL), 'Ishmaelite', *SF Post*, 24 July 1873, p. 1.

77— A first ghostly image of Harry in Paris: the following account of HL's shady actions synthesises reporting in *Le Figaro*, 29, 30 May; *Le Gaulois*, 30 May; *Journal des débats*, 31 May; *Le Temps*, 30 May; *Le Voleur illustré*, 28 May (all 1869).

77— 'beauté ravissante': *Journal des débats*, 31 May 1869, p. 3.

77— La Barrucci was a waning figure, ff.: *see* Joanna Richardson, *The Courtesans* (2000).

77— the younger, crazier, Polish 'Marcowitch': *Le Pavé*, 30 Dec. 1868, p. 2.

78— the passing soubriquet *la femme au nègre*: *Le Gaulois*, 30 May 1869, p. 1.

78— *la fée aux giffles*: *Le Gaulois*, 25 Nov. 1869, p. 1.

78— 'well known and very fair Parisian blonde': (HL), *SF Post*, 11 July 1873, p. 1.

78— 'diffused an atmosphere of sumptuous immorality': Ralph Henry Nevill, *The Man of Pleasure* (1912), p. 239.

78— 'Beaux in her string': *Baily's*, Jan. 1869, p. 89.

79— 'a little, insignificant-looking woman': (HL), 'Ishmaelite', *SF Post*, 16 July 1873, p. 1.

80— the jeweller Kramer: *see* Henri Vever, *La Bijouterie française au XIXe siècle (1800–1900), II: Le Second Empire* (1908).

80— he had fallen into near-ruin: *See La Presse*, 23 Nov. 1866, p. 3.

81— 'célèbre boutique': Marie Bashkirtseff, *Journal: Édition integrale Sept. 26 1877–Dec. 21 1879* (1999), vol. 1, p. 143.

82— 'devoted friend': *see Journal des débats*, 31 May 1869, p. 3.

83— 'nobody but Schneider': *Baily's*, May 1869, p. 309.

83— Adolphe Dugléré, described by Rossini: *see* Joanna Richardson, *La Vie Parisienne, 1852–1870* (1971), p. 127.

84— 'partners in pleasure': *see* Louis Arnold, *Le Gaulois*, 30 May 1869, p. 3.

84— 'seething anthill': *see* Georges Cain, *Promenades dans Paris* (1906), p. 165.

84— forced to fight off the sexual advances: Graham Robb, *Rimbaud: A Biography* (2001), p. 47.

84— Mazas: *see* Maxime Du Camp, 'Les Prisons de Paris: Mazas, Saint-Lazare, La Roquette', *Revue des deux mondes*, 2e période, vol. 83, 1 Oct. 1869, pp. 598–634; *see also* Charles Berriat-Saint-Prix, *Mazas: étude sur l'emprisonnement individuel* (1860).

84— 'philanthropie doctrinaire'; 'odeur infecte': Victor Hugo, *Histoire d'un crime* (1877), ch. 15.

84— 'gloomy and repulsive-looking': (Thomas Cook and Son), *Cook's Guide to Paris* (1880), p. 82.

85— 'fumigation sulfureuse': Du Camp, ibid.

86— Blessed are they who remain desperate, ff.: *see* Jules Vallès, *Mazas* (1867).

87— What the press called 'le high-life'; 'proved the nobility of her blood': *see Le Voleur illustré*, 28 May 1869, p. 11.

88— 'un fort joli garçon': *Le Temps*, 30 May 1869, p. 3.

88— 'real distinction and great discretion': *see* Réne de Pont-Jest, *Le Figaro*, 29 May 1869, p. 3.

91— 'éloquent et passionnée': Charles Lachaud, *Plaidoyers de Ch. Lachaud, recueillis par Félix Sangnier* (1885), vol. 1, p. v. (One English observer described a Lachaud performance as 'like a *première*': *see* (Julian Osgood Field), *Things I Shouldn't Tell* (1924), p. 194.)

93— 'tout britannique': Réne de Pont-Jest, *Le Figaro*, 29 May 1869, p. 3.

93— 'extreme limits of delicacy': *see* Louis Arnold, *Le Gaulois*, 30 May 1869, p. 3.

94— 'amiable vampire': *see Le Tintmarre*, 6 June 1869, p. 3.

94— 'tous les lions du *high life*': 'Don Quichotte', *Le Figaro*, 11 July 1869, p. 1.

94— Angelina Fioretti, etc.: *Le Figaro*, 30 May 1869, p. 1.

94— added colour trawled from Pont-Jest's columns: *see* Émile Zola, *Œuvres. Manuscrits et dossiers préparatoires. Les Rougon-Macquart. La Curée. Dossier préparatoire et épreuves corrigées*, 1869–1870. *MS digitzed*, gallica.bnf.fr. (Pont-Jest was later himself defended by M. Lachaud on a charge of sporting unearned honours: *Le Censeur*, Dec. 1881, p. 4.)

94— reputed to have slung plates: *see* (Field), p. 125.

94— a duel: *see* 'Don Quichotte', *Le Figaro*, 11 July 1869, p. 1.

95— *la Déesse de la guerre*: *Le Gaulois*, 31 July 1869, p. 1.

95— 'Tourne-Crême, Fifine du Casino': see Anne Middleton Wagner, *Jean-Baptiste Carpeaux: Sculptor of the Second Empire* (1986), pp. 215 ff., 305, n. 74, *citing* A. Hans, 'Le Groupe de Carpeaux', *Le Nain jaune*, 19 Aug. 1869.

96— a clerkship in a dockside silk house: in *Great Expectations*, Dickens sends a hopelessly compromised Pip to work in a counting house in Egypt.

7. ALAS! MR. LARKIN

97— syndicated a reasonably balanced account: the story appeared in more than twenty papers, including four in Ireland.

97— 'Alas! Mr. Larkin': *Morning Advertiser*, 31 May 1869, p. 3.

97— Emily Soldene: Emily Soldene, *My Theatrical and Musical Recollections* (1897), pp. 62 ff., 82, 137.

98— 'gorgeous kaleidoscope' ff.: *Evening Standard*, 18 Apr. 1870, p. 4; *Daily News*, 19 Apr. 1870, p. 2; *The Era*, 24 Apr. 1870, p. 10.

98— 'landmarks of the representation' ff.: Soldene, pp. 78–86.

99—'gorgeous, merry, sparkling': *Punch*, 31 Jan. 1874, p. 43.

99—'that Goddess of Material Love': *Sporting Times*, 2 Jan. 1875, p. 7.

99—'This lady's legs are as freely displayed': *Sporting Times*, 23 Aug. 1873, p. 5.

100—'gay ladies' ff.: *Daily Telegraph and Courier*, 11 May 1871, p. 2, and *Evening Standard*, 29 Apr. 1870, p. 3.

101—'idle, the vicious, and the intemperate': *Graphic*, 16 July 1887, pp. 18–21.

101—'easy-going, slangish': Angus B. Reach, *Illustrated London News*, 9 Oct. 1847, p. 12.

101—'It sounds so low!': *see* Sos Eltis, *Acts of Desire: Women and Sex on Stage 1800–1930* (2013), p. 78. (Eltis gives an intriguing analysis of *Formosa*.)

101—the case of 'Regina v. Park and others': this summary synthesises *Pall Mall Gazette*, 6 May 1870, p. 5; *Evening Standard*, 7 May 1870, p. 3; *Daily Telegraph*, 21 May 1870, p. 6. *See also* Neil McKenna, *Fanny and Stella: The Young Men Who Shocked Victorian England* (2013).

102—intensely hot morning, ff.: *Evening Standard*, 21 May 1870, p. 6.

102—'The Twins': Montagu Williams, *Leaves of a Life, Being the Reminiscences of Montagu Williams, Q.C.*, vol. 1 (1890), pp. 143–4.

102—'rail compartments mapping out the centre': Reach, *Illustrated London News*, 9 Oct. 1847, p. 12.

103—'*Mr. Harry Larkins*, formerly holding': *Lloyd's Weekly Newspaper*, 22 May 1870, p. 12. For the following account *see also London Daily News*, 23 May 1870, p. 3, and *South London Chronicle*, 28 May 1870, p. 3.

103—'most commandingly situate': London *Times*, 15 July 1872, p. 18.

104—one of the best private banks: John Diprose, *Some Account of the Parish of Saint Clement Danes (Westminster) Past and Present* (1868), p. 249.

104—the two linked by a communicating door: Stephen H. Twining, *Twinings: Two Hundred and Fifty Years of Tea and Coffee, 1706–1956* (1956), pp. 60–62.

105—'impecunious upper and middle class men': Montagu Williams, p. 77.

105—a starry case also presided over by Knox: *Daily News*, 21 Feb. 1870, p. 2.

106—'Azamat-Batuk': *Pall Mall Gazette*, 9 Feb. 1870, p. 6.

106—leaving George Smith privately 'much exhilarated': Sidney Lee and George Smith, *George Smith: A Memoir: With Some Pages of Autobiography* (1902), p. 57.

106—'proud & sensitive': MWS to CC, 2 June 1842, in Betty T. Bennett (ed.), *The Letters of Mary Wollstonecraft Shelley*, vol. 3 (1988), pp. 28–9.

106—'wd destroy me forever': ibid., MWS to AAK, 16–24 Sept. 1843, p. 206.

107—'looked very shocking': ibid., MWS to CC, 15–16 Oct. 1845, pp. 236–7.

107—'is all thrown into the waste gulph': ibid., MWS to CC, 12 Dec. 1845, p. 268.

107—'catch the proper tone of common place': ibid., MWS to CC, 20 Dec. 1845, p. 269.

107—'at times, with the heavy strain': Montagu Williams, p. 225. (Jenny Marx wrote acidly to her father, Karl Marx, about Knox's repressive opposition to an expanded franchise: *see* Olga Maier (ed.), *The Daughters of Karl Marx: Family Correspondence, 1866–1898* (1984), pp. 24–6.)

108—'parties thinking their remedy more convenient': *Morning Advertiser*, 6 Nov. 1871, p. 7. (For a clear-cut example of a plaintiff–blackmailer, *see Evening Standard*, 18 Oct. 1870, p. 7, and the case of Sir Charles Nugent.)

108—'let the thieves pick each other's pockets': William Ballantine, *Some Experiences of a Barrister's Life* (1882), p. 36.

108—he and his partner, Lock, were declared bankrupt: *The Gazette*, 3 Sept. 1872, p. 3917, and *Morning Post*, 4 Jan. 1873, p. 3.

109—'hoped the facts would go forth': *Morning Advertiser*, 6 Nov. 1871, p. 7.

109—Markowich had 'at last' been ordered out: *Reynolds's Newspaper*, 26 June 1870, p. 1.

109—a young American called Ely: *Journal des débats*, 28 Feb. 1870, p. 3.

110—an embarrassing register of all her clients: *Le Gaulois*, 23 Feb. 1870, p. 1.

110—'a second de Sade *without the intellect*': Steven Marcus, *The Other Victorians* (1966), p. 37.

110—Gladstone, to take a single example: H. C. G. Matthew, *Gladstone 1809–1898* (1897), pp. 91–3.

8. WAR

111—France declared war on Prussia: *see* Michael Howard, *The Franco-Prussian War* (2001).

111—'As I suspected Master Harry's latest': RPP to Raymond and Louisa Pelly, 23 July 1870 (Kingston: EM5014). (Ray had at last secured a better living, as vicar of Holy Trinity, Matlock Bath. Despite his stated misgivings, there is circumstantial evidence to suggest that HL visited Matlock to say farewell.)

111—'beggary': *Carolina Watchman*, 24 Dec. 1874, p. 1, *citing* a 'California paper' (n.d.).

111—'esprit aventureux' ff.: *Le XIXe siècle*, 13 Nov. 1874, p. 2.

112—'curiosités indiscrètes': Henri Genevois, *La Défense Nationale en 1870–1871* (1906), vol. 2, pp. 172–3.

112—*Le Figaro* ran an advertisement: *Le Figaro*, 15 Aug. 1870, p. 3.

112—Interior Minister fully authorised *Les Quarante*: *see* (Libraire Militaire R. Capelot), *La Guerre de 1870–71: L'Investissement de Paris* (1908), p. 449.

112—A further announcement: *Le Figaro*, 20 Aug. 1870, p. 2; *see also Le Figaro*, 30 Aug. 1870, p. 2.

113—Those who came forward, *bigarrés*, or a motley lot: *see* 'Grenest', *L'Armée de l'Est: relation anecdotique de la campagne de 1870–1871* (1895), pp. 141–4 (in which HL becomes 'Laskins').

113—James Fowler, a decidedly eccentric American: 'Mr. Fowler crossed from Boulogne to Sandgate, standing in an india-rubber twin canoe (the *Podoscaphe*), in 12 hours, 19 August 1878': *Chambers's Encyclopedia* (1891), vol. 2, p. 718. G. L. called him 'notre brave Peau-Rouge'.

114—'capital material for guerrillas': (G. A. Henty), *Evening Standard*, 25 Aug. 1870, p. 5.

114— printed a memoir two years later: *see* 'G. L.', *Souvenirs d'un volontaire. Campagne 1870–1871* (1872).

114— the proclamation in Paris of the Third Republic: Empress Eugénie fled the country; bathetically, she and her husband later settled in Chislehurst, in Kent.

115— from the local defence force, Mabaret and Michaud: *see* P. Michaud, 'Nécrologie. M. Mabaret,' *Revue des eaux et forêts*, vol. 42 (1903), pp. 730–32.

115— the Eastern Railway Company had agreed: Amédée le Faure, *Histoire de la guerre franco–allemande 1870–71* (1886), pp. 270–71.

115— 'les difficultés sans nombre': Emile Delmas, *De Froeschwiller à Paris. Notes prises sur les champs de bataille* (1871), p. 132.

116— 'a new element of horror' ff.: (G. A. Henty), *Evening Standard*, 3 Sept. 1870, pp. 4, 1, and 7 Sept. 1870, p. 3.

119— their discretion would in the end be praised as merciful: 'Un Ancien Officier de chasseurs à pied', *Les Vosges en 1870 et dans la prochaine campagne* (1887), pp. 162–5.

119— 'infâme commerce': 'Grenest', p. 143.

119— spoke German 'comme Schiller': 'G. L.', p. 108.

120— 'beaucoup d'audace et d'habileté': 'Grenest', p. 143.

120— a new scheme to blow up the Saverne tunnel: Charles Virmaitre, *Paris oublié* (1886), p. 78.

120— 'plus connue': Genevois, p. 40.

120— 'rock tunnel': *see* G. A. Henty, *The Young Franc-Tireurs* (1872).

122— 'Chère Amie' ff.: 'G. L.', 27 Sept. 1870, pp. 104–10.

123— 'volontaires admirablement équipés': 'Un Ancien Élève du Lycée de Strasbourg', *Le Combat d'Épinal (12 octobre 1870)* (1871), p. 7.

123— 'cavaliers d'ordonnance': 'Grenest', p. 144.

124— 'MM. Pistor et Larkyns' ff.: *Le Figaro*, 20 Oct. 1880, p. 5, and 3 Nov. 1880, p. 5.

124— memorably crazy valour: *see* Ladislas Wolowski, *Campagne de 1870–71. Corps franc des Vosges (armée de l'Est)* (1871), p. 17.

124— proved barely willing to cooperate: Ernest Alfred Vizetelli, *My Days of Adventure: The Fall of France, 1870–71* (1914), p. 218.

125— to Garibaldi, 'Illustre citoyen': Le Général Bordone (Joseph Philippe Toussaint Bordone), *Garibaldi et l'armée des Vosges: récit opfficiel de la campagne* (1873), p. 544.

125— the majority of the remaining members of *Les Gris*: Joseph Constant Crouzat, *La Guerre de la défense nationale: le 20e Corps à l'armée de la Loire* (1872), p. 11.

125— 'M. HARRY LARKYNS': (Ministère de la guerre), *République française, décrets, arrêtés et décisions* (1882), p. 397.

126— General Charles Bourbaki, considered dashing by some: for a crushing verdict, *see* Maupassant's widely reproduced short story 'Le Lit 29' (1884).

126—'exposé aux rigueurs': Jean Diez, *Les Journées de la Lisaine: 15, 16 et 17 janvier 1871* (1905), pp. 33–4.

126—what happened on 16 January: René de Belleval, *Campagne de France, 1870–1871: journal d'un capitaine de francs-tireurs* (1872), pp. 178–85. (Belleval had earlier contemplated his own unauthorised assault on 'le fameux tunnel de Saverne': ibid., p. 26.)

126—some simply froze to death in their sleep: Vizetelli, p. 317.

127—'dépression physique et morale': Diez, ibid.

127—'LARKYNS (Harry). Chef d'escadron': A. Martinien, *État nominatif, par affaires et par corps, des officiers tués ou blessés dans la deuxième partie de la campagne (du 15 septembre 1870 au 12 février 1871): guerre de 1870–1871* (1906), p. 170.

128—'l'abomination de la désolation': Belleval, p. 205.

128—'rôle glorieux': *Le XIXe Siècle*, 13 Nov. 1874, p. 2.

128—Decree no. 939: *Bulletin des lois de la République française*, vol. 4, Jan.–June 1872, p. 255.

128—'Harry-Larkins, chef d'escadron': *Journal officiel de la République française*, 7 May 1871, p. 3.

129—'had fought heroically': *see* Kingston: EM5014.

129—'the most beautiful ruin': (HL), 'Ishmaelite', *SF Post*, 31 July 1873, p. 1.

130—'The Storming of Strasbourg' ff.: *see* multiple advertisements, *Evening Standard*, 26 Apr.–1 May 1871.

130—'Poor fellow, he went to the Franco–German War': Emily Soldene, *My Theatrical and Musical Recollections* (1897), p. 86. (N.B. HL was not caught by the British census of 1871, taken at the start of April.)

130—'rendered a good return for the care': *see* Kingston: EM5014.

130—they insisted upon his taking charge of their son: Sam Davis (*see* Sources) had a version of this world-tour story, in which it is Arthur Neil (*see below*) offering money for companionship: *see* (Sam Davis), in Lawrence I. Berkove (ed.), *Insider Stories of the Comstock Lode and Nevada's Mining Frontier 1859–1909, Primary Sources in American Social History* (2007), vol. 2, p. 699.

9. AMERICA

133—'a respectable and wealthy family': *San Francisco Bulletin*, 19 Oct. 1874, p. 3.

133—'sparred his way': *New York Times*, 28 Oct. 1874, p. 4.

133—'dirty and insecure': RLS to W. E. Henley, 23 Aug. 1879, in Ernest Mehew (ed.), *Selected Letters of Robert Louis Stevenson* (1997), pp. 149–50.

133—'matchless marksman' ff.: Mark Twain, *Roughing It* (1872; 1972), pp. 94, 303, 28, 274, 185, 201.

134—Joe Goodman: Goodman later contributed to breaking the code of the Mayan Calendar; *see* Lawrence I. Berkove (ed.), *Insider Stories of the Comstock Lode and Nevada's Mining Frontier 1859–1909, Primary Sources in American Social History* (2007), vol. 1, p. xxxix.

134—'let fancy get the upper hand'; 'I have scarcely exaggerated': Twain, pp. 268, 222.

134—'Adventurers, with keen wits': Ella Sterling Cummins, *The Story of the Files* (1893), p. 116, *citing* Arthur McEwen.

134—unsigned literary snapshot: *see* Berkove (ed.), vol. 2, pp. 577–8. (Berkove notes that he silently corrected 'Larkins' to 'Larkyns', p. 579, n. 5. Here it is silently corrected back again.)

135—these statements are far from wholly false: Phillip Prodger, in *Time Stands Still: Muybridge and the Instantaneous Photography Movement* (2003), p. 258, takes a common line when he writes: 'it is doubtful if any of Larkyns's stories were true', and explains, 'people like Larkyns' found 'willing dupes for their fabulous tales' in the 'partial anarchy of the "Wild West"'.

136—'intricate maze of tunnels and drifts': Twain, pp. 339–40.

136—stands out for being presented as a direct memory: though Berkove credits this piece to Sam Davis (see Sources), Davis was not in Nevada until 1875. Joe Goodman, who also contributed 'By-the-By' columns, and who could have overlapped with HL in Virginia City, was certainly interested in him in 1874 (*see below*).

136—pianoforte lessons at Brackenbury's: Henry Dickens, *The Recollections of Sir Henry Dickens, K.C.* (1934), p. 100.

136—'yarn-spinning': Twain, pp. 191, 275.

137—Neil himself went as a cadet to Sandhurst: *see* Sandhurst Register and records for 1864.

137—'liked each other, and had a good time' ff.: *SF Chronicle*, 14 Mar. 1873, p. 3.

138—'spicy': Edward F. O'Day, *Varied Types* (1915), pp. 67–8, *quoting* M. H. De Young.

141—'the filthy pool of politics': Oscar T. Shuck (ed.), *Representative and Leading Men of the Pacific* (1870), p. 611. (The same Oscar T. Shuck would later represent Edward Ellis in court, *see below*.)

144—to take on more coal: *SF Examiner*, 22 Feb. 1873, p. 3.

144—'for no matter how much he obtained on credit': *SF Chronicle*, ibid.

144—Benjamin Lloyd's 1876 guide: B. E. Lloyd, *Lights and Shades in San Francisco* (1876), pp. 136–9.

145—'a pale-faced young man in fashionable attire': *SF Chronicle*, 15 Mar. 1873, p. 3.

146—supposedly spent a colossal $200: *SF Post*, 15 Mar. 1873, p. 3, said Orr & Atkins 'suffered slightly'.

146—the *Chronicle* slashed its reporting: *SF Chronicle*, 16 Mar. 1873, p. 5.

146—'a great crowd of young city bloods': *Sacramento Daily Union*, 17 Mar. 1873, p. 1.

146—Frank Pixley, ff.: *see* Cummins, pp. 193–4, and *SF Call*, 12 Aug. 1895, p. 1.

146—Judge E. D. Sawyer: *see SF Post*, 15 Mar. 1873, p. 3. (The *Post* wrongly identifies him as 'W. D.')

146— Lizzie Gannon: *see Elevator*, 15 Mar. 1873, p. 2.

147— 'somewhat in the nature of a confession': *Daily Alta California*, 16 Mar. 1873, p. 1. (*SF Post*, 15 Mar. 1873, p. 3, said Neil needed a document to persuade his father that he 'did not squander the money' himself.)

147— 'a reputed widow lady': *Hawaiian Gazette*, 23 Apr. 1873, p. 3, *citing SF Bulletin*, 17 Mar. 1873.

147— 'A Card from the Gallant Major': *SF Chronicle*, 16 Mar. 1873, p. 5.

148— and 'this ended the case': *SF Post*, 19 Oct. 1874, p. 2. (Neil's campaign of 'irretrievable' disgrace was so successful that e.g. Prodger, p. 258, 130 years later, incorrectly labels HL a 'convicted swindler'.)

148— 'soft-headed young Englishman': *New York Times*, 28 Oct. 1874, p. 4.

149— casting himself as a 'retired military officer': Neil's surprising afterlife is deducible from multiple reports in the Isle of Man press.

149— 'A Reporter from Hades': *The California Mail Bag*, Mar.–Apr. 1873, p. 76.

10. BOHEMIA

150— 'a stunning bill at the Occidental': *SF Chronicle*, 15 Mar. 1873, p. 3.

150— offered help to leave town by Isaiah Lees: *SF Chronicle*, 4 Feb. 1875, p. 3.

150— 'desired to assist him in his emergency': *SF Bulletin*, 19 Oct. 1874, p. 3.

150— 'so the Major is to remain with us': *SF Examiner*, 17 Mar. 1873, p. 3.

150— 'the scoundrel that men sometimes spoke of him as': (Richard Wheeler), *SF Weekly Stock Report*, 23 Oct. 1874, p. 3, *citing Daily Stock Report*, 19 Oct. 1874.

150— reduced to 'positive want': *SF Chronicle*, 19 Oct. 1874, p. 3.

150— *How 'Tis Done*: by Bates Harrington; *see* Travis Edward Ross, *History, Inc.—Hubert Howe Bancroft's History Company and the Problem of Selling the Past* (University of Utah, 2017), p. 148.

151— 'the foot of the ladder': *SF Bulletin*, 19 Oct. 1874, p. 3.

151— 'undeserved disgrace' ff.: *SF Post*, 19 Oct. 1874, p. 2.

151— 'discovered by a well known Bohemian': *SF Chronicle*, 4 Feb. 1875, p. 3.

151— 'odd jobs at translating': *New York Times*, 28 Oct. 1874, p. 4.

151— 'Master, happily, of a handsome fortune': Walter M. Fisher, *The Californians* (1876), pp. 183–5.

151— 'queerly decorated': B. E. Lloyd, *Lights and Shades in San Francisco* (1876), pp. 163–5.

152— 'literary workshop': *see* Hubert Howe Bancroft, *Literary Industries* (1890), p. 134. (In 1880, the renamed A. L. Bancroft & Co. would publish an edition of *A Tramp Abroad*, next, after *Roughing It*, of Mark Twain's travel books.)

152— 'records of a vast territory': Henry Lebbeus Oak, *'Literary Industries' in a New Light: A Statement on the Authorship of Bancroft's Native Races and History of the Pacific States* (1893; 1972), p. 4; *see also* pp. 27–8 for the system of paper bags.

152— 'trackless sea of erudition: Lloyd, p. 169.

152— 'no less than six hundred different persons': *see* Bancroft, 'Some of My Assistants', pp. 245–76.

153— 'Harry Larkin': Bancroft, p. 273.

154— 'open to the charge of unfairness': Ella Sterling Cummins, *The Story of the Files* (1893), p. 170.

154— Oak ended his painful accounting: Oak, pp. 34–42.

154— 'was somewhat peculiar': Fisher, pp. 188–91.

154— 'an Irish captain': Bancroft, p. 273.

154— an explosive young man called Gerald Darcy: *Alta*, 23 Oct. 1874, p. 1. (Elsewhere, 'D'Arcy'.)

154— 'of great promise in a literary way': Oak, p. 40.

154— 'principally at translations': (Richard Wheeler), *SF Weekly Stock Report*, 23 Oct. 1874, p. 3, *citing Daily Stock Report*, 19 Oct. 1874.

154— 'gay, dashing and handsome': Sydney *Evening News*, 18 Mar. 1875, p. 3, *citing SF Call*, 4 Feb. 1875.

154— 'From making a translation': *SF Post*, 19 Oct. 1874, p. 2.

155— Being a gentleman scribbler in Grub Street: both lawyers in HL's Marlborough Street hearing earned money as writers on the side. Douglas Straight would go on to edit the *Pall Mall Gazette*.

155— he may have been spurred by contempt: that said, the *Post*, 14 Mar. 1873, p. 2, had itself exploited *Chronicle* material to write up HL's 'cunning devices' in relation to Arthur Neil.

155— 'literary filth': *SF Post*, 21 Aug. 1873, p. 2.

155— 'What the Railroads Will Bring Us': *Overland Monthly*, vol. 1, issue 4, Oct. 1868, p. 302.

155— 'bold, fearless, reform paper': *see* Henry George Jr, *The Life of Henry George* (1900), pp. 180, 255–6, 244–5.

155— 'fearful eruptions of socialism': *SF Examiner*, 30 July 1873, p. 2.

155— 'we should make the rich poorer and the poor richer': *SF Post*, 27 Oct. 1873, p. 2.

155— On board from the start was Dan O'Connell: George Jr, p. 244.

156— Caroline M. Parker: *see Alta*, 21 June 1851, p. 1, and 19 June 1851, p. 2; *Marysville Daily Appeal*, 28 Jan. 1870, p. 3; *LA Herald*, 18 May 1905, p. 3.

156— letter to Charles Darwin: Frederick Burhardt *et al.* (eds), *The Correspondence of Charles Darwin*, vol. 21: 1873 (2014), pp. 254–7.

156— 'kept busy with fights of one kind or another': Cummins, pp. 238–45.

156— in the Mint Saloon on Commercial Street: *SF Examiner*, 10 May 1873, p. 3.

156— 'always palatable': *SF Post*, 26 May 1873, p. 3.

156— 'an absurd mixture of pistols, profanity': (HL), *SF Post*, 23 June 1873, p. 3.

156— 'Surely, if the drama has a mission': (HL), *SF Post*, 20 Dec. 1873, p. 1.

157— 'we will make our mention of her as short': (HL), *SF Post*, 12 Aug. 1873, p. 3.

157— 'up-lifted noses and down-drawn lips': (HL), *SF Post*, 19 July 1873, p. 1.

157— 'musical marvel': (HL), *SF Post*, 18 July 1873, p. 1.

157— California Theatre: *Alta*, 18 July 1868, p. 1, and 19 Aug. 1868, p. 1; *see also* Lloyd, pp. 150–53.

158— 'The dramatic profession': George Moore, *Confessions of a Young Man* (1888, rev. 1926; 1939), p. 183.

158— the family Smorltork, as conjured up by Dickens: Count Smorltork, *The Pickwick Papers* (1837).

158— 'chat about circuses': (HL), *SF Post*, 28 June 1873, p. 1, and 2 July 1873, p. 1. (The awful lion-taming system was not necessarily effective. A couple of years earlier, an assistant of HL's informant had had his leg chewed off, dying the next day.)

159— a lengthy piece on costume: (HL), *SF Post*, 11 July 1873, p. 1.

159— on duelling: (HL), *SF Post*, 14 July 1873, p. 1.

159— on forms of 'street locomotion': (HL), *SF Post*, 22 July 1873, p. 1.

159— On 23 July he turned out an article on spiritualism: (HL), 'Lanyon', *SF Post*, 23 July 1873, p. 1.

160— 'Ouf! How hot it is!': (HL), 'Ishmaelite', *SF Post*, 14 Aug. 1873, p. 1.

160— how to curb the depredations of man-eating tigers: (HL), 'Aladdin', *SF Post*, 8 Aug. 1873, p. 1.

160— 'the Shah, the whole Shah, and nothing but the Shah': (HL) 'Ishmaelite', *SF Post*, 6 Aug. 1873, p. 1.

160— 'a brilliant spectacle': (HL), 'Ishmaelite', *SF Post*, 31 July 1873, p. 1.

161— 'close intimacy': Henry Edwards, *A Mingled Yarn: Sketches on Various Subjects* (1883), p. 151.

161— a leading entomologist: John L. Capinera (ed.), *Encyclopaedia of Entomology*, 2nd edn (2008), pp. 1287–8.

161— 'Few more brilliant waifs': (Dan O'Connell), 'Town Crier', *SF News Letter*, 4 June 1892, p. 17.

161— 'happy-go-lucky' young writer Samuel Post Davis: Cummins, p. 197, *citing* Frank Bailey.

162— on 5 February 1872 ff.: *see* Robert H. Fletcher, *The Annals of the Bohemian Club*, vol. 1: 1872–80 (1898).

163— 'many a pleasant evening': Fisher, p. 192.

163— 'a brilliant writer': Edwards, ibid.

163— 'the froth of the cheap and ever pleasant beer': Fletcher, pp. 107–8.

163— Henry George was an original trustee: Fletcher, p. 28.

163— 'a nicer little spot': *SF Weekly Stock Report*, 27 Nov. 1874, p. 1.

163— 'Start a club, call it Bohemian': (HL), *SF Post*, 7 Feb. 1874, p. 1.

164— 'ocean bath' in the Bay: Lloyd, p. 75.

164— 'Poverty always hung like a gaunt spectre': Edwards, ibid.

164— 'Reckless beyond redemption': (O'Connell), ibid.

164— 'no idea of the value of money': *SF Post*, 19 Oct. 1874, p. 2.

164— 'his generosity led him often far': Edwards, ibid.

164— 'never seemed to own anything that he considered his': (Sam Davis), in

Lawrence I. Berkove (ed.), *Insider Stories of the Comstock Lode and Nevada's Mining Frontier 1859–1909, Primary Sources in American Social History* (2007), vol. 2, pp. 625–6.

164— 'grottoes' and lunch rooms: Lloyd, pp. 62–4.

165— 'more the order of the day than wit': RLS to Sidney Colvin, late Feb. 1880, in Ernest Mehew (ed.), *Selected Letters of Robert Louis Stevenson* (1997), p. 164.

165— 'a heavy-set, black-whiskered': *Alta*, 23 Oct. 1874, p. 1.

165— 'a bad location for Bohemians': *Weekly Oregon Statesman*, 31 Oct. 1874, p. 3.

165— Soon enough, though, Ellis struck lucky: Ellis began his 'Footlight Flashes' column in the *Chronicle* in mid September.

166— 'discreditable notoriety': *Russian River Flag*, 22 Oct. 1874, p. 2. (Even the sceptical *SF Call* would come to accept that Neil's interview had been 'highly-colored and fictitious': 19 Oct. 1874, p. 3.)

166— 'furnished the money of his own free will': *SF Chronicle*, 19 Oct. 1874, p. 3.

166— 'brought all this trouble on him'; 'suffering from an incurable desease [*sic*]': (Richard Wheeler), *SF Weekly Stock Report*, 23 Oct. 1874, p. 3, *citing Daily Stock Report*, 19 Oct. 1874.

166— 'to seek to mate with any woman': (Sam Davis), in Berkove (ed.), p. 699; *see also* (Sam Davis), *Carson Morning Appeal*, 14 Jan. 1880, p. 2.

166— 'stormy introduction': *SF Chronicle*, 19 Oct. 1874, p. 3.

167— 'Warm-hearted, impulsive, sorely tried and hard-working': (Richard Wheeler), *SF Weekly Stock Report*, 23 Oct. 1874, p. 3, *citing Daily Stock Report*, 19 Oct. 1874.

II. FLORA

168— 'a handsome woman' ff.: *SF Chronicle*, 19 Oct. 1874, p. 3, and 4 Feb. 1875, p. 3.

168— 'more than average intelligence': *Pacific Commercial Advertiser*, 31 July 1875, p. 3, *citing SF Call*, 18 July 1875.

168— 'fascinating manner': *SF Call*, 19 Oct. 1874, p. 3.

168— 'good Kentucky family': *SF Chronicle*, 20 Oct. 1874, p. 3.

168— fostered by a Captain Shallcross: Ella Clark, analogue card file, 'Muybridge, Mrs. Edward J', 1927, California State Library, Sacramento. (Clark was a librarian who had known the Shallcross family.)

168— a disaster in 1856, piloting the *Belle*: *Oregon Daily Journal*, 10 Nov. 1913, p. 6.

168— shared the maiden name 'Frazier': Stump m. 'Flora Frazier': *Wide West*, 21 Sept. 1856, p. 2; and Sarah Shallcross willed half her estate to her mother, 'Catherine Frazier': *Sacramento Daily Union*, 11 Aug. 1868, p. 3.

168— 'Flora E. Downs': *Sacramento Daily Union*, 7 Feb. 1863, p. 2. (Separately, there is also a Mrs S. D. Downs listed, possibly Flora's stepmother.)

168— a month off turning thirteen: Gordon Hendricks, *Eadweard Muybridge: The Father of the Motion Picture* (1875), p. 30, calculates her date of birth as 24 Mar. 1851.

168—'the niece of the wife of Captain Shallcross': *Napa Reporter*, 24 Oct. 1874, p. 2.

168—'plying both between Marysville and Sacramento': *Marysville Daily Appeal*, 1 Oct. 1870, p. 3.

169—known for a while as Lily Shallcross: Clark, ibid.

169—'a brilliant scene of gayety and life': B. E. Lloyd, *Lights and Shades in San Francisco* (1876), pp. 83, 86–7, 254, 489.

169—'filled with a set of dissipated': 'Olive Heath', *Marysville Daily Appeal*, 3 Sept. 1868, p. 1.

169—'In this city, July 11th': *Alta*, 12 July 1867, p. 4. (Lucius's middle initial was actually 'D'.)

170—'lived very unhappily and soon separated': *SF Chronicle*, 20 Oct. 1874, p. 3.

170—tricks of the trade: *see e.g.* R. D. Neal, in Edward L. Wilson (ed.), *Philadelphia Photographer*, vol. 9 (1872), p. 100.

170—The Nahls, both classically trained painters: Peter E. Palmquist and Thomas R. Kailbourn, *Pioneer Photographers of the Far West, A Biographic Dictionary, 1840–1865* (2000), p. 415.

171—'painting photographs': *SF Chronicle*, 20 Oct. 1874, p. 3.

171—an upstairs address at 113 Montgomery Street: *Alta*, 31 Dec. 1857, p. 2.

171—a history of the Indian Mutiny: *see* Rebecca Solnit, *River of Shadows* (2004), p. 261.

171—'admirably adapted for placing on the center table': *Alta*, 31 Dec. 1857, p. 2.

171—the suicide of Joseph Washington Finley: *Alta*, 15 July 1857, p. 2.

171—a 'very beautiful photograph': *Alta*, 13 Dec. 1858, p. 2.

172—'dark, uneven, with stairs': Lloyd, p. 294.

172—one of nine directors: *Alta*, 18 Jan. 1859, p. 2.

172—Matthias Gray 'took his store': *Napa Daily Register*, 5 Feb. 1875 (Kingston: 5046/21).

172—Everything, he later said, 'was to my vision two': *see EJM trial testimony below.*

172—'machinery or apparatus for washing clothes': *Repertory of Patent Inventions*, Jan–June 1862, p. 172.

172—a second patent in Paris: *Bulletin des lois de la République française*, July 1862, p. 1198.

172—in an industrial annexe: *International Exhibition 1862: Official Catalogue*, p. 33.

172—'Edward J. Muybridge, Esq. (late of California)': *Money Market Review*, vol. 10 (1865), p. 832.

172—Freeman Harlow Morse: *see* John D. Bennett, *The London Confederates* (2008).

173—a new 'Bank of Turkey': for its collapse, *see Evening Standard*, 25 Apr. 1866, p. 6.

173—'all of the time since 1860': (EJM), *SF Examiner*, 6 Feb. 1881, p. 3.

173— Muybridge arrived back in San Francisco: *Marysville Daily Appeal*, 14 Feb. 1867, p. 3. (He also appears as 'E J Maybridge' 'consignee' per Ivanhoe, in the *Alta*, 1 Oct. 1867, p. 4.)

173— 'an eadvertisement': *see e.g. Derry Journal*, 22 Jan. 1883, p. 6.

173— noticeably grey-haired, newly eccentric: *see EJM trial testimony below*.

173— photographic goods for sale: *Napa Daily Register*, 5 Feb. 1875 (Kingston: 5046/21).

173— 'Mr. Maybridge, of San Francisco': *Alta*, 20 Oct. 1867, p. 1.

174— 'all the eminent artists': *Alta*, 14, 15, 16 Feb. 1868, (all p. 2).

174— 'indefatigable and untiring': Anon., in Edward L. Wilson (ed.), *Philadelphia Photographer*, vol. 6 (1869), pp. 373–5.

174— 'just such cloud effects as we see': *Alta*, 17 Feb. 1868, p. 1.

174— '"Helios" working through the mediumship': *SF Chronicle*, 19 Mar. 1868, p. 3.

174— 'the usual ghastly, lifeless, pallid': Helen Hunt Jackson, *Bits of Travel at Home* (1878), p. 86.

174— 'altogether too gorgeous': Mark Twain, *Alta*, 4 Aug. 1867, p. 1.

175— 'Your worthy ex President': 14 May 1868, in Mary V. Jessup and Robert Bartlett Haas, 'Muybridge's Yosemite Valley Photographs, 1867–1872', *California Historical Society Quarterly*, Mar. 1963, p. 12.

175— 'Helios Rampant': *Alta*, 11 Sept. 1868, p. 1.

175— 'A Gensoul, on Montgomery Street': *Sacramento Daily Union*, 28 Oct. 1868, p. 5.

175— 'a free ticket for him': Lloyd, p. 133.

175— 'issued a decree prohibiting the sale': *Alta*, 8 Mar. 1869, p. 1.

175— 'delinquent' regarding land stocks: *Alta*, 27 Mar. 1869, p. 2.

176— Sarah Shallcross, died: (aged about thirty-eight), *Sacramento Daily Union*, 11 Aug. 1868, p. 3.

176— marrying a Miss Lucy C. Baldwin: *Marysville Daily Appeal*, 19 Jan. 1870, p. 2.

177— 'ulceration of the bowels': *Sacramento Daily Union*, 3 Oct. 1870, p. 3.

177— 'resplendent with gaudy displays': Lloyd, pp. 31, 491.

177— in December 1870 Flora secured a divorce: *SF Chronicle*, 20 Oct. 1874, p. 3. (Hendricks gives the date as 8 December.)

177— 'whereas my wife being Entirely Repugnant': *Sacramento Daily Union*, 14 Apr. 1869, p. 5.

177— 'one divorce granted': Henry George Jr, *The Life of Henry George* (1900), p. 258.

177— 'nothing coarse, nothing depraved about her': Walter M. Fisher, *The Californians* (1876), p. 102.

178— 'She told me that the trouble': (George Smith *quoting* EJM), *SF Chronicle*, 21 Dec. 1874, p. 3.

178— Yet within five years, the 'odor' of trade: *see Alta*, 17 Jan. 1890, p. 1; *SF Chronicle*, 17 Jan. 1890, p. 6; *SF Examiner*, 17 Jan. 1890, p. 3.

178— bought his way into the Bohemian Club: (The Bancroft Company), *The San Francisco Blue Book: Season 1889–90* (1889), p. 235, and *Season 1890–91* (1890), p. 279.

178— Oscar Wilde reputedly quipped: Kevin Starr, *Americans and the California Dream, 1850–1915* (1973), p. 282.

178— Lucius remarried: *Alta*, 6 Apr. 1871, p. 4. (The wedding notice requested 'no cards'. Idelia's name varies from census to census, including 'Ida L.', 'Adela L.' and 'Idella'.)

178— 'I never counselled her to get it': (George Smith *quoting* EJM), *SF Chronicle*, 21 Dec 1874, p. 3.

178— employed, 'by him in his gallery to retouch photographs': *Napa Reporter*, 6 Feb. 1875, p. 2, reporting the defence narrative given by Cameron King, EJM trial. (EJM had previously advertised for his own 'photographic printers-boy': *Alta*, 22 Feb. 1869, p. 2.)

179— 'just the woman to make an impression': *SF Post*, 19 Oct. 1874, p. 1.

179— 'all first class photographic work': EJM to 'EDITORS ALTA', *Alta*, 3 Aug. 1877, p. 2.

179— Flora's own retrospective account: *SF Post*, 31 Mar. 1875, p. 2.

179— the last appeal for emendations: *SF Chronicle*, 19 Mar. 1871, p. 2.

179— a grand 'Peace Celebration': *see Alta*, 22 Mar. 1871, p. 2, and 10 Mar. 1871, p. 1.

180— 'In San Francisco, May 30th, Edward J. Maybridge': *Sacramento Daily Union*, 18 July 1871, p. 2.

180— 'in this city, May 20, by the Rev. Mr. Sawtelle': *SF Call*, 18 July 1871, p. 4.

180— 'liberal terms of communion': *Sacramento Daily Union*, 10 Nov. 1866, p. 4.

180— 'beautiful specimens of the sun painter's art': *Alta*, 29 Jan. 1871, p. 1.

180— '"Helios" hopes to go to the Valley again': Anon., in Edward L. Wilson (ed.), *Philadelphia Photographer*, vol. 6, 1869, p. 375.

181— revealed to the press by the nurse: *SF Chronicle*, 20 Oct. 1874, p. 3. (Susan Smith stated in the autumn of 1874 that she had 'served Mrs. Muybridge in the capacity of nurse' across three years.)

181— 'At the suggestion of several artists and patrons': *see* EJM Scrapbook, p. 15 (Kingston).

182— 'Every photographer was, in great measure': EJM, *Animals in Motion* (1899), p. 1.

182— 'commenced housekeeping': *SF Post*, 19 Oct. 1874, p. 1.

182— Wilson, Hood & Co. commenced suit: *see Alta*, 21 June 1872, p. 1, and *Chronicle*, 21 June 1872, p. 3.

182— 'Industrial Condition of the Slope' ff.: *Alta*, 4 Nov. 1872, p. 2, and 7 Apr. 1873, p. 1.

183— 'not ordinary work': Anon., in Edward L. Wilson (ed.), *Philadelphia Photographer*, vol. 6, 1869, p. 374.

183— Muybridge returned home in late November: *Mariposa Gazette*, 15 Nov. 1872, p. 3, reports 'Mr. E. J. Mybridge' as 'on his way to San Francisco' after a 'six months' professional tour'. *See also Alta*, 9 Dec. 1872, p. 1.

183— 'more particularly due': Lloyd, p. 420.

183— knocked through from 429: Anon., 'Our Prize Picture', in Edward L. Wilson (ed.), *Philadelphia Photographer*, vol. 11, July 1874, p. 208.

184— 'the higher you get, the purer the rays' ff.: *SF Chronicle*, 16 July 1871, p. 3.

184— 'merits of which we cannot even refer to': *Red Bluff Independent*, 12 Sept. 1874, p. 4.

184— employed over thirty artists: *SF Chronicle*, 20 Nov. 1873, p. 2.

184— 'beefy': Emily Soldene, *My Theatrical and Musical Recollections* (1897), p. 181. (*Alta*, 27 May 1877, p. 4, reports her 'First Appearance in San Francisco'.)

184— to make use of the company's superior finishing: *Alta*, 7 Apr. 1873, p. 1.

185— 'shadow behind in this world renowned art gallery': *LA Herald*, 11 July 1875, p. 3.

185— 'gorgeous dresses': *Alta*, 26 Dec. 1872, p. 2.

185— three bold portraits of her to keep: *see* 'Brandenburg Album' in Sources.

185— 'eight hundred of the most perfect': *Alta*, 7 Apr. 1873, p. 1.

185— 'as Mr. Moybridge will be weeks': *Figaro*, 11 Apr. 1873, p. 2.

186— more than $20,000: Jessup and Haas, p. 23.

186— 'a realizing sense of the wonders'; 'in the eternal fitness of things': (EJM), *SF Examiner*, 6 Feb. 1881, p. 3.

186— explained that the *Alta* editors had recommended him: EJM, *Alta*, 3 Aug. 1877, p. 2.

186— 'simultaneously free from contact': EJM, *Animals in Motion* (1899), pp. 1–2.

186— 'Occident is as big a fraud': *SF Weekly Stock Report*, 9 Oct. 1874, p. 1.

186— 'the very poetry of motion': *California Mail Bag*, July 1874, p. 79.

186— 'impossible': *Alta*, 7 Apr. 1873, p. 1.

186— 'swiftly progressive art': (EJM), *SF Examiner*, 6 Feb. 1881, p. 3.

187— 'some special exposing apparatus': EJM, *Animals in Motion* (1899), p. 1.

187— 'A few days ago he announced': *SF Examiner*, 7 Apr. 1873, p. 3.

187— 'Quick Work': *Alta*, 7 Apr. 1873, p. 1.

187— 'probably more important to art': (EJM), *SF Examiner*, 6 Feb. 1881, p. 3.

187— 'singular': *Sacramento Bee*, Sept. 1878, see EJM Scrapbook, p. 32 (Kingston).

188— 'nearly every attitude': *Illustrated London News*, 29 Mar. 1879, see EJM Scrapbook, ibid.

188— 'so many lame cockroaches': Arthur T. Fisher (late 21st Hussars), *Through the Stable and Saddle-Room* (1896), p. 320.

188— 'as such Government photographer': (EJM), *SF Examiner*, 6 Feb. 1881, p. 3.

188— He returned three weeks later: *see Marysville Daily Appeal*, 27 Apr. 1873, p. 3, and 17 May 1873, p. 3.

188—'the grand motor wheel': Orson Squire Fowler, *Sexual Science, Including Manhood, Womanhood, and their Mutual Interrelations* (1870), p. v.

188— to set up as his business manager: *see Chicago Daily Tribune*, 28 Aug. 1881, p. 6.

189—'tolerably intimately' too: *see EJM trial testimony below.*

189— Rulofson, meanwhile, himself a member: Robert H. Fletcher, *The Annals of the Bohemian Club*, vol. 1: 1872–80 (1898), p. 41.

189—'the impression of representing a lady of thirty-five': (HL), *SF Post*, 29 July 1873, p. 3.

189—'fine personal appearance and varied acquirements': *SF Post*, 19 Oct. 1874, p. 1.

189—'constantly making additions': Jessup and Haas, ibid.

190—'never saw a more perfect specimen': (HL), *SF Post*, 7 July 1873, p. 3.

12. AMUSEMENTS

191—'lamentable poverty of principle': *SF Call*, 19 Oct. 1874, p. 3.

192— causing a 'furore': *Alta*, 11 Aug. 1873, p. 1.

192—'I have erred in making <u>horror</u> too predominant': CB to W. S. Williams, 4 Jan. 1848, in Margaret Smith (ed.), *The Letters of Charlotte Brontë*, vol. 2: 1848–1851 (2000), pp. 3–4.

192— fully into the popular realm: *see* Patsy Stoneman, *Jane Eyre on Stage, 1848–1898: An Illustrated Edition of Eight Plays with Contextual Notes* (2007).

192—'who would criticise the setting': (HL), *SF Post*, 9 Sept. 1873, p. 3.

193—'magnificent triumph of scenic art': (HL), *SF Post*, 27 Aug. 1873, p. 3.

193—'in a manner to elicit the highest praise': (HL), *SF Post*, 14 Sept. 1873, p. 3.

193—'It took the versatile Major just two weeks': *SF Chronicle*, 15 Sept. 1873, p. 3; *see also Alta*, 14 Sept. 1873, p. 1, and *California Mail Bag*, Oct. 1873, p. 77.

193—'the justly celebrated': *Marin Journal*, 16 Oct. 1873, p. 3, and 23 Oct. 1873, p. 3.

193—'ventilating her magnificent wardrobe': (HL), *SF Post*, 11 Oct. 1873, p. 3.

194—'vim and force': (HL), *SF Post*, 6 Nov. 1873, p. 1, and 5 Nov. 1873, p. 3.

195—'unlimited, uncircumscribed, everywhere': (CP), 'Our Lady Reporter', *SF Post*, 14 Aug. 1873, p. 1, and 15 Aug. 1873, p. 1.

195—'marriage as an end': (CP), 'Myrtle', *SF Post*, 7 Nov. 1873, p. 1.

195— Flora's pregnancy, now undeniable: EJM's lawyers would claim the baby was 'born prematurely' (*see SF Post*, 6 Feb. 1875, p. 8). If in fact the pregnancy ran full-term, it would now have been four months in.

195— Thomas Maguire: *see* B. E. Lloyd, *Lights and Shades in San Francisco* (1876), pp. 150–54.

195—'leg-itimate' theatre: (HL), *SF Post*, 20 Dec. 1873, p. 1.

196—'All that is Truly Artistic': *SF Chronicle*, 28 Aug. 1873, p. 4.

196—'strange to lament the decadence': (HL), *SF Post*, 29 Nov. 1873, p. 1.

196—'not up to music written for Schneider's contralto voice': (HL), *SF Post*, 25 Nov. 1873, p. 3, and 29 Nov. 1873, p. 1.

197—'Dead broke, Larkins went to work as a stevedore': (Sam Davis), in Lawrence I. Berkove (ed.), *Insider Stories of the Comstock Lode and Nevada's Mining Frontier 1859–1909, Primary Sources in American Social History* (2007), vol. 2, p. 700.

197—'an old soiled print' ff.: Marta Braun, *Eadweard Muybridge* (2010), p. 240, n. 18, puts the opening salvo in the *SF Bulletin*, 26 Nov. 1873. (The *Alta*, 1 Dec. 1873, p. 2, carried the three parts back to back.)

197—'a giant band of giants': *SF Post*, 12 Nov. 1873, p. 3.

198—'regretted not having staid at home': (HL), *SF Post*, 28 Nov. 1873, p. 3.

198—submitted 130 stereoscopic: *Alta*, 20 Feb. 1873, p. 1.

198—Vienna had been an 'unqualified failure': (HL), 'Ishmaelite', *SF Post*, 31 July 1873, p. 1.

198—'Medal for Progress': *LA Daily Herald*, 6 Dec. 1873, p. 1.

198—giant negatives of the Pigeon Point lighthouse: *Santa Cruz Weekly Sentinel*, 13 Dec. 1873, p. 1.

198—'intimacy sprung up': *SF Bulletin*, 19 Oct 1874, p. 3 (said to have been first noted 'about a year since').

199—a 'bright, intelligent lady': *SF Chronicle*, 20 Oct. 1874, p. 3.

199—'Muybridge formed the acquaintance of Larkyns': *Alta*, 19 Oct. 1874, p. 1; *see also SF Post*, 19 Oct. 1874, p. 1.

199—was 'always willing': *SF Chronicle*, 21 Oct. 1874, p. 3.

200—In a much later interview: *see SF Chronicle*, 21 Dec. 1874, p. 3.

201—Harry was had up in the Police Court: *see SF Chronicle*, 28 Dec. 1873, p. 8, and *SF Examiner*, 29 Dec. 1873, p. 3.

201—'caterers': *SF Chronicle*, 21 Sept. 1873, p. 1.

201—'the rest of the San Francisco press': *SF Chronicle*, 28 Sept. 1873, p. 1.

201—Charles Gayler, published a long list: *Alta*, 27 Oct. 1873, p. 1.

201—'weal solid quiticism': *Alta*, 28 Oct. 1873, p. 1.

201—'an obscure city contemporary': *SF Chronicle*, 29 Oct. 1873, p. 1.

201—'spongy brain': *Alta*, 30 Oct. 1873, p. 2.

201—'As rival theatrical critics': *Alta*, 21 Oct. 1874, p. 1.

201—'questionable transactions': *SF Chronicle*, 27 Dec. 1873, p. 3.

201—dismissing Ellis as a 'Flash critic': *SF Examiner*, 28 Oct. 1873, p. 3.

202—Henry George accused the Regents: Henry George Jr, *The Life of Henry George* (1900), p. 280, explains how George was punished for his intervention.

202—'had been "industriously so worded"': *see Appendix to Journals of State and Assembly of the Twentieth Session of the Legislature of the State of California*, vol. 4 (1874), pp. 1–464 (particularly pp. 253, 351).

202—Dion Boucicault, of 'world-wide renown' ff.: (HL), *SF Post*, 15 Jan. 1874, p. 3; 17 Jan. 1874, p. 1; 23 Jan. 1874, p. 1.

203—'I appreciate the compliment': Dion Boucicault, *SF Post*, 26 Jan. 1874, p. 2.

203— 'Kenilworth Galop': *Figaro*, 21 Apr. 1874, p. 2.

204— his mistress, Katharine Rogers: Amnon Kabatchnik, *Blood on the Stage, 1800 to 1900* (2017), pp. 304–5.

204— ruminating on Bohemia: (HL), *SF Post*, 7 Feb. 1874, p. 1.

204— finding wedlock a 'severe' cost: (HL), *SF Post*, 28 July 1873, p. 1.

204— Harcourt married the strikingly beautiful Fannie Rulofson: *Sacramento Daily Union*, 28 Feb. 1874, p. 5. (Rulofson exhibited, by name, photographs of Fannie, and also of his handsome second wife; *see Red Bluff Independent*, 12 Sept. 1874, p. 4.)

204— Shakespeare 'had more divine attributes': (HL), *SF Post*, 14 Apr. 1874, p. 3.

205— 'rank sacrilege': (HL), *SF Post*, 7 Mar. 1874, p. 1.

205— amazed that 'so able and careful': (HL), *SF Post*, 7 Mar. 1874, p. 1.

205— Ellis sneered back: *SF Chronicle*, 15 Mar. 1874, p. 1.

205— 'a fashionable boarding house' ff.: *SF Post*, 19 Oct. 1874, p. 1.

205— a 'frequent visitor': (Richard Wheeler), *SF Weekly Stock Report*, 23 Oct. 1874, p. 3, *citing Daily Stock Report*, 19 Oct. 1874.

206— 'cozy alcoves or stalls': Lloyd, p. 65.

13. UTTERLY MISERABLE WITHOUT YOU

207— 'As related to the writer by Larkyns' ff.: *SF Post*, 19 Oct. 1874, p. 1.

207— 'Neilson was playing her engagement': (George Smith *quoting* EJM), *SF Chronicle*, 21 Dec. 1874, p. 3.

207— 'without a peer' ff.: (HL), *SF Post*, 3, 12, 14, 25 Mar. 1874 (all p. 3).

207— a beautiful '"balcony scene" on either side': (HL), *SF Post*, 23 Mar. 1874, p. 3.

208— 'Muybridge forbid Larkyns coming to his house': (Richard Wheeler), *SF Weekly Stock Report*, 23 Oct. 1874, p. 3, *citing Daily Stock Report*, 19 Oct. 1874.

209— 'What is only folly in man' ff.: (HL), *SF Post*, 11 Apr. 1874, p. 1.

210— 'the Barnum of California' ff.: (HL), *SF Post*, 28 Jan. 1874, and 1, 2, 3, 20 Apr. 1874 (all p. 3).

210— 'old friend of twenty years': (HL), *SF Post*, 14 Apr. 1874, p. 3.

210— 'surmounted by an immense cross' ff.: B. E. Lloyd, *Lights and Shades in San Francisco* (1876), pp. 67–70.

211— 'a furious ringing of the bell' ff.: *SF Chronicle*, 19 Oct. 1874, p. 3.

211— 'held her in his arms, with his coat around her' ff.: *SF Post*, 19 Oct. 1874, p. 2.

212— 'Why Does Not God Kill the Devil?': (HL), *SF Post*, 16 Apr. 1874, p. 2.

212— a 'Dickens Ball': (HL), *SF Post*, 17 Apr. 1874, p. 3; *see also Alta*, 17 Apr. 1874, p. 1.

213— 'The Coming Religion': (HL), *SF Post*, 18 Apr. 1874, p. 2.

213— 'artistic excellence and manly qualities': *SF Post*, 27 Apr. 1874, p. 1.

213— 'bright particular star' ff.: (HL), *SF Post*, 18 Apr. 1874, p. 1; 28 Apr. 1874, p. 3; 30 Apr. 1874, p. 3.

213—'San Francisco, April 15 – Wife of': *Sacramento Daily Union*, 29 Apr. 1874, p. 2.

213—went to Belmont, south of San Francisco: Marta Braun, *Eadweard Muybridge* (2010), p. 91.

214—Harry 'called frequently': *SF Chronicle*, 19 Oct. 1874, p. 3.

214—'very fond of the baby': *SF Post*, 19 Oct. 1874, p. 2.

214—'sent from the room' ff.: *SF Chronicle*, 19 Oct. 1874, p. 3.

214—'inimitable sketches': (HL), *SF Post*, 28 Apr. 1874, p. 3.

214—'John and his magnificent troupe': (HL), *SF Post*, 4 May 1874, p. 1.

214—'pitch-forked on anyhow': (HL), *SF Post*, 18 Apr. 1874, p. 1.

214—choked in 'trash': (HL), *SF Post*, 5 May 1874, p. 1.

215—'just the man his wife would adore': (HL), *SF Post*, 7 May 1874, p. 3.

215—revival of a lapsed California Cricket Club: *see Alta*, 26 Apr. 1874, p. 1.

215—it was 'more than a game': (HL), *SF Post*, 6 May 1874, p. 1.

215—'showed good stuff': *Alta*, 10 May 1874, p. 1.

215—'decidedly Frenchy': *SF Post*, 18 May 1874, p. 1.

215—'ceased his connection': *SF Call*, 19 Oct. 1874, p. 3.

216—'the providential impulses of his friends': William Greer Harrison, 'Biographical Sketch', in Ina D. Coolbrith (ed.), *Songs From Bohemia by Dan O'Connell* (1900), p. 1.

216—'the axiom, "once a spendthrift"': (Dan O'Connell), 'Town Crier', *SF News Letter*, 4 June 1892, p. 17.

216—Charles Pring and Alfred Bulch, became firm friends: *SF Weekly Stock Report*, 23 Oct. 1874, p. 4, citing *Daily Stock Report*, 21 Oct. 1874.

216—'trance and seeing medium' ff.: *Common Sense*, 18 July 1874, p. 116. (At her own death in 1905, CP was noted as being a friend of Florence Nightingale and Elizabeth Cady Stanton: *LA Herald*, 18 May 1905, p. 3.)

217—Woodhull … had hitched up: *see* Mary Gabriel, *Notorious Victoria: The Life of Victoria Woodhull, Uncensored* (1998).

218—'Rather a stout girl' ff.: *Alta*, 2 June 1874, p. 1; *see also Sonoma Democrat*, 6 June 1874, p. 5.

219—'promptly discharged': *Alta*, 6 July 1874, p. 1.

219—'inspired Pythoness': *Common Sense*, 13 June 1874, p. 3.

219—'wine, wit and wisdom': *Alta*, 7 June 1874, p. 1.

219—'In that capacity': *Marysville Daily Appeal*, 22 Oct. 1874, p. 1, *citing Vallejo Chronicle* (n.d.)

219—'A letter received yesterday': *Carson Daily Appeal*, 13 June 1874, p. 3.

219—'We infer that certain young': *Carson Daily Appeal*, 20 June 1874, p. 3.

219—Flora asked her to take care of the baby: *see EJM trial testimony below.*

220—'F. – PINING FOR SUNSHINE': (HL), *SF Chronicle*, 12, 13 June 1874 (both p. 1).

220—'well known upper Columbia river': *Sacramento Daily Union*, 22 Aug. 1876, p. 2.

220— engagement at the Oro Fino Theatre in Portland: *The New Northwest*, 26 June 1874, p. 3.

220— had been negotiating for 'several months': (George Smith *quoting* EJM), *SF Chronicle*, 21 Dec. 1874, p. 3.

221— 'sent his wife on a visit to a relative': *SF Bulletin*, 19 Oct 1874, p. 3.

221— 'F. DO WRITE TO ME. I AM UTTERLY miserable': (HL), *SF Chronicle*, 23 June 1874, p. 1.

221— 'Calistoga Wednesday night': HL to Mrs Smith (n.d.), as transcribed by EJM (Napa County Historical Society: 1985.29.1.6).

223— 'the cry wrung from a doubting tortured heart': (HL), *SF Post*, 5 Mar. 1874, p. 3.

223— 'Look to her, Moor, if thou hast eyes to see': *Othello*, 1.3.293–4.

223— the 'Wood-haul lecture': *SF Examiner*, 9 July 1874, p. 3.

223— 'and present her as his wife': *Napa Daily Register*, 5 Feb. 1875 (Kingston: 5046/21).

223— 'I bring you back the honor': Henry Edwards, *A Mingled Yarn: Sketches on Various Subjects* (1883), p. 153.

224— 'indomitable vim and perseverance': *SF Examiner*, 17 May 1872, p. 3.

224— 'a felon, a confidence operator': (Richard Wheeler), *SF Weekly Stock Report*, 23 Oct. 1874, p. 1.

224— 'an elaborate map of the quicksilver region': *SF Chronicle*, 19 Oct. 1874, p. 3.

224— 'Calistoga and the head of Clear Lake': *Russian River Flag*, 22 Oct. 1874, p. 3.

225— 'topological delineations': *Morning Advertiser*, 10 Dec. 1859, p. 3.

225— 'a substantial start in the world': *SF Bulletin*, 19 Oct 1874, p. 3.

225— 'If the poor girl is in distressed [*sic*] write': *SF Chronicle*, 19 Oct. 1874, p. 3.

225— a letter by Flora: FEM to Sarah Smith, 11 July 1874, as transcribed by EJM (Napa County Historical Society: 1985.29.1.6).

225— a knowing quip ... about the 'unremitting love': *SF Post*, 20 Dec. 1873, p. 1.

226— 'for some of my photos': there is no properly attested photograph of Flora in the literature. Bizarrely, Haas identified her as the subject in photographs of three self-evidently different women, putting all in doubt (*see* Haas, *Muybridge: Man in Motion* (1976), pp. 39–40). Of these, the figure to gain most traction has been the anonymous, wasp-waisted sitter for Bradley & Rulofson's six 'Gold Medal' prize portraits, 1874. (One of these pictures appears beside a shot of Alice Dunning Lingard in the Brandenburg Album: *see* Sources.) Yet the essay 'Our Prize Picture', in Edward L. Wilson (ed.), *Philadelphia Photographer*, vol. 11, July 1874, pp. 205–8, implies that the Gold Medal portraits were specially taken with exceptional care to avoid the need for retouching, in order to impress the judges (who judged by the negatives); and the competition was not announced until Flora was about six months pregnant. A categorically false identification can be found in Edward Ball, *The Inventor and the Tycoon* (2013), p. 156, a picture by EJM that Ball describes as showing Flora and her son. In it, a small child sits up in the grass unaided; yet Flora parted from EJM when the baby was no more than two months old.

227— a scrapbook album she created: *see* 'Brandenburg Album' in Sources.

14. MURDER

230— 'vast mineral resources': *Marin Journal*, 10 Apr. 1873, p. 2.

230— published on 28 Aug.: (HL), 'Ishmaelite', *SF Weekly Stock Report*, 28 Aug. 1874, p. 2.

230— Twain had mischievously accused of tipping sharks: *see* Twain's widely reproduced *jeu d'esprit* 'White Man Mighty Onsartain' (1866). (There was a genuine shark problem at the time: *Alta*, 17 Sept. 1865, p. 1.)

231— For his second letter: (HL), 'Ishmaelite', *SF Weekly Stock Report*, 4 Sept. 1874, p. 4.

233— 'a wild man; his hand *will be* against': Authorized Version, Genesis 16:12.

233— To someone given as 'Dear Old L—': HL to 'L', 28 Aug. 1874, in *SF Post*, 19 Oct. 1874, p. 2. (Also, not quite identically worded, in *SF Chronicle*, 19 Oct. 1874, p. 3.)

233— 'almost became a proverb': (Richard Wheeler), *SF Weekly Stock Report*, 23 Oct. 1874, p. 3, *citing Daily Stock Report*, 19 Oct. 1874.

234— 'He walked among men': Henry Edwards, *A Mingled Yarn: Sketches on Various Subjects* (1883), p. 151.

234— California's 'silver wedding': *Alta*, 10 Sept. 1874, p. 1.

234— Muybridge, back from his lengthy coastal trip: *Alta*, 11 Sept. 1874, p. 1.

234— 'continued to give dinner parties': (Dan O'Connell), 'Town Crier', *SF News Letter*, 4 June 1892, p. 17.

235— 'clasped hands with him and bade him God-speed': Edwards, p. 152.

235— 'luny' ff.: *Sonoma Democrat*, 10 Oct. 1874, p. 1.

235— 'Stewart [*sic*], of Knight's valley': *Sacramento Daily Union*, 16 Oct. 1874, p. 2, *citing Vallejo Chronicle*, 15 Oct. 1874.

236— 'cold sweats, prostrating attacks of cough': RLS to Edmund Gosse, 16 Apr. 1880, in Ernest Mehew (ed.), *Selected Letters of Robert Louis Stevenson* (1997), p. 167.

236— 'right up the mountain' ff.: *see* Robert Louis Stevenson, *Silverado Squatters* (1884). (Stevenson dedicated *Silverado Squatters* to Virgil Williams and his wife, Dora Norton Williams, who, like Flora Muybridge, had worked as a photographic retoucher.)

236— 'more than the $100': *SF Post*, 19 Oct. 1874, p. 1.

236— 'recovered judgement' ff.: *SF Chronicle*, 19 Oct. 1874, p. 4.

236— 'a letter from her to me': *SF Chronicle*, 6 Feb. 1875, p. 3.

237— Ishmaelite's latest long letter: *Weekly Stock Report*, 16 Oct. 1874, p. 8.

238— That same Friday, Muybridge came: newspaper reports synthesised to give the following account are: *Alta*, 19 Oct.; *Napa Reporter*, 24 Oct.; *Russian River Flag*, 22 Oct.; *Sacramento Daily Union*, 20 Oct.; *SF Bulletin*, 19 Oct.; *SF Call*,

19 Oct.; *SF Chronicle*, 19, 20 Oct.; *SF Post*, 19 Oct.; *SF Weekly Stock Report*, 23 Oct. (all 1874). *See also Calistoga Free Press*, 24 Oct. 1874, in A. V. Mozley, R. B. Haas and F. Forster-Hahn, *Eadweard Muybridge: The Stanford Years, 1872–1882* (1972), p. 116, and Post Mortem and Inquest findings, 17 Oct. 1874 (Napa County Historical Society: 1985.29.1.3). *See also below* newspaper reports of trial testimony.

238—'some work in experimental photography': *SF Post*, 6 Feb. 1875, p. 8.

238—'a man of much scientific attainment': *SF Post*, 31 May 1873, p. 3.

238— unknown gall wasp, 'Cynips saltatorius, Hy. Edw': *The Canadian Entomologist*, vol. 23, no. 12, Dec. 1891, pp. 259–67.

238—'nonchalantly said that he had some business': *SF Post*, 19 Oct. 1874, p. 1.

242—'Edward J. Muybridge, a San Francisco photographer': *Pacific Rural Press*, 24 Oct. 1874, p. 1.

242—'It was the old story': (O'Connell), ibid.

243—'trembled before the deceased while he lived' ff.: *Alta*, 23 Oct. 1874, p. 1.

244—'from the almost universal popularity of its victim' ff.: (Richard Wheeler), *SF Weekly Stock Report*, 23 Oct. 1874, p. 1.

244—'large number of gentlemen': *SF Chronicle*, 20 Oct. 1874, p. 3.

244—'big money': (Sam Davis), in Lawrence I. Berkove (ed.), *Insider Stories of the Comstock Lode and Nevada's Mining Frontier 1859–1909, Primary Sources in American Social History* (2007), vol. 2, p. 580.

244—'ideas of correct dealing did not stand him well': *SF Bulletin*, 19 Oct. 1874, p. 3.

245—'Brave, needy, extravagant and reckless': *SF Call*, 21 Oct. 1874, p. 2.

245—'Poor Larkyns': *Oakland Tribune*, 19 Oct. 1874, p. 2.

245—'a cosmopolitan character': *SF Chronicle*, 19 Oct. 1874, p. 3.

245—'idle boasting and fanciful tales': *SF Call*, 19 Oct. 1874, p. 3.

245—'An Aged Nurse Tells What She Knows': *SF Chronicle*, 19 Oct. 1874, p. 3.

246— a corrective interview: *SF Post*, 19 Oct. 1874, p. 1.

247—'The good lady is much disturbed': *SF Chronicle*, 20 Oct. 1874, p. 3.

247—'commission of that most terrible of crimes': *Alta*, 19 Oct. 1874, p. 1.

247—'nauseating': *SF Call*, 20 Oct. 1874, p. 3.

247—'despicable': (Richard Wheeler), *SF Weekly Stock Report*, 23 Oct. 1874, p. 3, citing *Daily Stock Report*, 19 Oct. 1874.

247—'to get her fee, let who would be the sufferer': *Thistleton's Illustrated Jolly Giant*, 24 Oct. 1874, p. 10.

247—'The very parties who conveyed his letters': *Orleans County Monitor*, 9 Nov. 1874, p. 2.

247—'judiciously made up her mind': *SF Chronicle*, 20 Oct. 1874, p. 3.

247—'tranquilly in confinement': *SF Chronicle*, 22 Oct. 1874, p. 3, citing *Napa Register* (n.d.)

247— he did receive Rulofson that day: Rulofson 'went to Napa that Monday': *SF Post*, 6 Feb. 1875, p. 8.

248—Rulofson gave his own interview: *SF Chronicle*, 20 Oct. 1874, p. 3.

249—Edward Rulloff: for Rulloff's identity with Twain's 'Cain', *see* Richard W. Bailey, *Rogue Scholar: The Sinister Life and Celebrated Death of Edward H. Rulloff* (2003), p. 194.

249—'until the coffin was covered with wreaths' ff.: *SF Chronicle*, 21 Oct. 1874, p. 3.

250—Four or five hundred people attended: *SF Bulletin*, 20 Oct. 1874, p. 3.

250—'There never was such a mingling of classes': (Sam Davis), in Berkove (ed.), ibid.

251—destined to become a jazz standard: Louis Armstrong explained its importance in 1950, on the track 'New Orleans Function'.

251—a fashionable San Francisco funeral, ff: B. E. Lloyd, *Lights and Shades in San Francisco* (1876), pp. 110–11, 364–68.

252—'long concourse of carriages followed the corpse': *SF Examiner*, Oct. 20 1874, p. 3.

252—'a gentleman in the finest sense of the word': Edwards, p. 153.

252—'tears were streaming': (Richard Wheeler), *SF Weekly Stock Report*, 23 Oct. 1874, p. 4, *citing Daily Stock Report*, 21 Oct. 1874.

252—'only those whose heavenly virtues': Lloyd, p. 365.

253—'warm and true friend': Edwards, p. 151.

15. MISSTATEMENTS

254—'gibbered and gloated': *SF Bulletin*, 19 Oct. 1874, p. 3.

254—'rubbing his hands and grinning like a human jackal': *SF Examiner*, 20 Oct. 1874, p. 3.

254—'a light weight': *Alta*, 23 Oct. 1874, p. 1.

254—Darcy himself named Walter Fisher: *SF Call*, 21 Oct. 1874, p. 3.

254—president of the National Rifle Association: *see Forest and Stream*, 7 Sept. 1876. (Notoriously, Shaw, in 1896, would describe foiling an abduction attempt by 'warbling' aliens.)

254—arrests after sunset were proscribed: *SF Post*, 21 Oct. 1874, p. 3.

254—'Baseless Fabrication': *SF Chronicle*, 21 Oct. 1874, p. 3.

255—'used many strong expressions' ff.: *SF Post*, 21 Oct. 1874, p. 3.

255—'Take a friend's advice, Ellis': *Alta*, 22 Oct. 1874, p. 1.

255—'lost the case, his temper': *California Mail Bag*, Oct. 1873, p. 6.

255—'the hero of the hour': *New Zealand Herald*, 11 Dec. 1874, p. 3.

256—cowardly 'scrub': *LA Herald*, 25 Oct. 1874, p. 2. Sam Davis took an admission by Ellis in court that he had long ago written as 'Coppinger' (a famous pirate), and elaborated on this to create a tale of HL spitting vengefully down Ellis's throat after Ellis lost him his job (not that he actually did); according to Davis, this earned Ellis the nickname 'Cuspidor Coppinger', a flourish Davis apparently designed as a *post hoc* explanation for Ellis's subsequent wish to 'spit in his dead enemy's face' (*see* Lawrence I. Berkove (ed.), *Insider*

Stories of the Comstock Lode and Nevada's Mining Frontier 1859–1909, Primary Sources in American Social History (2007), vol. 2, pp. 578, 582). Davis plainly muddled the facts, e.g. conflating Ellis's cases against HL and against Darcy, and then sprinkled invention on top. But, following Haas, *Muybridge: Man in Motion* (1976), p. 64, writers on Muybridge have continued to hold this repulsive tale against HL. (Davis, who refers to Ellis as 'vermin', would have seen spitting down the throat as virile; and strangely, at the time, it was a gesture particularly associated with angry journalists, *see e.g. Nashville Daily Union* 19 Aug. 1863, p. 2; *Tennessean*, 7 June 1873, p. 2; Louisiana *Donaldson Chief*, 20 June 1877, p. 1.)

256—'came up for hearing yesterday': *SF Chronicle*, 23 Oct. 1874, p. 3.

256—'A Man of the World': *New York Times*, 28 Oct. 1874, p. 4.

256—a 'real life' hero: *Chicago Daily Tribune* 28 Oct. 1874, p. 4, and 1 Nov. 1874, p. 8.

257—'with the hesitation of death': (Sam Davis), in Berkove (ed.), p. 579.

257—'petite figure, and with "tender blue eyes"': *see e.g. Memphis Ledger*, 9 Nov. 1874, p. 4.

257—'Larkyns was unfortunately': *NZ Herald*, 11 Dec. 1874, p. 3.

257—'I doubt if': *New York Times*, 1 Nov. 1874, p. 2.

257—'shot down like a dog': *Sonoma Democrat*, 24 Oct. 1874, p. 4.

257—'the woman is as guilty' ff.: *Figaro*, 27 Oct. 1874, p. 2, *citing* both (n.d.).

258—'could learn a trick or two': *Oakland Tribune*, 19 Oct. 1874, p. 2.

258—'written a short time before he was shot dead': *Examiner*, 9 Nov. 1874, p. 1; *see also* (Sam Davis), in Berkove (ed.) p. 581.

258—by a Miss A. L. Muzzey: *Phrenological Journal and Science of Health*, Oct. 1873, pp. 8–9. Also (uncredited), *Elevator*, 20 Dec. 1873, p. 1.

258—'The defendant, it is stated, denies': *SF Chronicle*, 21 Oct. 1874, p. 3.

258—'feloniously wilfully unlawfully': Indictment, 8 Dec. 1874 (Napa County Historical Society: 1985.29.1.1).

258—'secluded from all': *SF Chronicle*, 21 Dec. 1874, p. 3.

259—The initial filing took place, ff.: *see SF Chronicle*, 10 Jan. 1875, p. 1, and *Sacramento Daily Union*, 11 Jan. 1875, p. 3, *citing SF Call*, 9 Jan. 1875.

259—'painstaking, courteous and honest': *SF Post*, 13 Oct. 1873, p. 2.

259—went to San Francisco to consult Flora: vaguely reported in early Feb. as 'not a month ago' by *Napa Daily Register*, 6 Feb. 1875 (Kingston: 5047/78).

260—'very angry': *Sacramento Daily Union*, 6 Feb. 1875, p. 8.

260—'misstatement' ff.: *SF Chronicle*, 21 Dec. 1874, p. 3.

260—in the guise of 'injured husband': *New York Times*, 28 Oct. 1874, p. 4.

261—'the deed was done was most cowardly': *Common Sense*, 24 Oct. 1874, p. 1.

261—'without a chance of escape or a word of warning': 'Gossip from San Francisco', 26 Feb. 1875, in *The Queenslander*, 10 Apr. 1875, p. 3.

261—'a most cowardly act': Mark Twain, *Roughing It* (1872; 1972), p. 315.

261—'Had they met on equal terms': *New York Times*, 1 Nov. 1874, p. 2.

265— 'murderer will, of course, plead "insanity"': *Russian River Flag*, 22 Oct. 1874, p. 2.

266— 'A gentleman in the Napa jail': *Alta*, 27 Dec. 1874, p. 1.

266— 'Larkyns' Assassin': (Richard Wheeler), *Weekly Stock Report*, 25 Dec. 1874, p. 1.

266— subscribers to Muybridge's 1872 Yosemite expedition: *see* Yosemite 'Prospectus' with handwritten list of subscribers, in EJM Scrapbook, p. 15 (Kingston).

266— 'Muybridge killed the wrong man': *The Hawaiian Gazette*, 16 Dec. 1874, p. 2.

266— 'we say it is sad that poor Major Larkyns should': *Thistleton's Illustrated Jolly Giant*, 24 Oct. 1874, p. 10.

267— 'The papers speak of Muybridge': *Common Sense*, 24 Oct. 1874, p. 1.

267— 'wife's reputation for good behavior': *Chicago Tribune*, 2 Jan. 1875, p. 5.

267— writing confidentially: EJM to George Smith, 21 Dec. 1874 (Napa County Historical Society: Ephemera Box 36C).

267— Smith complied: *SF Chronicle*, 23 Dec. 1874, p. 3.

268— 'and an English gentleman': WLB to RPP, 21 Dec. 1874 (Kingston: EM5014).

269— 'We learn that the murderer takes things coolly': *The Cambrian*, 27 Nov. 1874, p. 7. (R. B. Cumberland), 'An Indian Officer', *How I Spent My Two Years' Leave* (1875), p. 334, recalled reading in the paper 'of poor wild Larkins having met his death in a violent manner at the hands of some Yankee in the Californian district'. Emily Soldene, *My Theatrical and Musical Recollections* (1897), p. 86, said HL was killed because he 'stupidly took Mrs. Muybridge on a little excursion into the country'.

269— '£eland $tanford': see Bierce's poem 'A Railroad Lackey', in *Black Beetles in Amber* (1892).

269— for translating Emile Zola's terrific novel: *Argonaut*, 23 Aug. 1879, p. 1.

270— 'sold like wildfire': Julia B. Foster, 'Kate Heath', *Sacramento Daily Union*, 25 Aug. 1877, p. 3.

270— 'Here lies Frank Pixley': Carey McWilliams, *Ambrose Bierce: A Biography* (1929), p. 157.

270— two anguished poems: 'T. A. H.' (1884) and 'Reminded' (1903).

270— 'anticipated the slow': McWilliams, p. 128.

270— 'spiritualistic medium' ff.: *SF Chronicle*, 31 Dec. 1874, p. 3. (On 9 Jan., *Common Sense* defended Mrs Sawyer, saying the 'absurd preparations to prevent fraud' had exhausted her 'magnetic power'.)

270— $50,000 he had invested in the *Post*: Henry George Jr, *The Life of Henry George* (1900), p. 248.

271— 'after argument': *SF Chronicle*, 10 Jan. 1875, p. 1.

271— 'without prejudice': *SF Post* 31 Mar. 1875, p. 2.

271— 'We hope that she may prove': Gordon Hendricks, *Eadweard Muybridge:*

The Father of the Motion Picture (1875), p. 74, *citing Calistoga Free Press*, 16 Jan. 1875.

271— 'The remains will lie in the tomb': *SF Post*, 21 Oct. 1874, p. 3.

271— Even Alice was persuaded to destroy a little memoir: presumably written before HL went to war (Kingston: EM5014).

271— Harry Edwards was a leading Freemason: he was 'Scribe' in the SF Chapter of the Masons; *see SF Examiner*, 24 Dec. 1874, p. 3.

271— all the graves there would eventually be dug out: Rebecca Solnit, *River of Shadows* (2004), pp. 242–3, writes movingly about the destruction of the Lone Mountain cemeteries.

16. TRIAL

272— Muybridge's trial was set to be a sensation: press reports synthesised for this account: *Napa Reporter*, 6, 13 Feb.; *Napa Daily Register*, 5, 6, 8 Feb. (Kingston: 5046/21, 5046/20, 5047/78, 5045/35); *Sacramento Daily Union*, 5, 6 Feb.; *SF Bulletin*, 4, 5, 6 Feb.; *SF Chronicle*, 3, 4, 5, 6 Feb.; *SF Post*, 3, 4, 5, 6, 8 Feb. (all 1875). Subpoenas: Napa County Historical Society.

272— William T. Wallace, a man of 'tremendous size': Oscar T. Shuck, *History of the Bench and Bar of California* (1901), p. 188.

272— 'resigning the position': *SF Post*, 15 Dec. 1873, p. 2.

272— elected District Attorney in Napa: (Lewis Publishing), *A Memorial and Biographical History of Northern California* (1891), p. 716.

272— 'little thin built man' ff.: *Napa Reporter*, 13 Feb. 1875, p. 1.

272— a State Senator in the California Legislature': *Marysville Daily Appeal*, 18 Dec. 1867, p. 2.

273— 'Napa's favorite orator': *Mariposa Gazette*, 13 Feb. 1875, p. 2.

273— 'suggestive of the band-box attorney': *Napa Reporter*, 13 Feb. 1875, p. 1.

273— 'race of lawyers': (Western Historical and Publishing Co.), *Master Hands in the Affairs of the Pacific Coast* (1892), p. 45.

273— Stoney, rising forty, had been born in South Carolina: (Slocum, Bowen & Co.), *History of Napa and Lake Counties, California* (1881), pp. 561–4.

273— 'as quiet as a summer afternoon': *Napa Reporter*, 13 Feb. 1875, p. 1.

275— essentially the same accounts that they had provided during the inquest: Dr. Reid, though, expanded on his inquest statement: the bullet entered 'an inch and a quarter to the right and below the left nipple, and about an inch from the sternum', its trajectory, 'inward and upward, penetrating the heart', and 'The ball passed clear through the body.'

277— 'I think the whole conversation is immaterial': though the *SF Chronicle* accidentally attributed this remark to Stoney, the next day Wallace referred back to the decision as his own (as indeed it must have been).

284— not the originals, but transcripts made by Muybridge: noted by Haas, *Muybridge: Man in Motion* (1976), p. 66. (EJM had highly distinctive handwriting.)

286— subpoenaed by the defence, including Virgil Williams: (Kingston: 5050/56).

17. AFTERMATH

297— 'evidently didn't expect to be acquitted' ff.: *Alta*, 8 Feb. 1875, p. 1.

297— 'go upon the professional trip' ff.: *Sacramento Daily Union*, 8 Feb. 1875, p. 1.

297— 'Correct': *Memphis Daily Appeal*: 24 Feb. 1875, p. 2.

297— 'It looks like a terrible thing to see a man killed': *Marysville Daily Appeal*, 12 Feb. 1875, p. 1, *citing Territorial Enterprize* (n.d.)

298— 'a healthier view of such cases': Montana *New North-west*, 19 Feb. 1875, p. 2

298— bypassing of a 'fraudulent' verdict: *New York Tribune*, 10 Mar. 1875, p. 6.

298— 'the next Legislature should recognize such an act': *SF Post*, 6 Feb. 1875, p. 4.

298— 'A man takes a woman for his wife': *The Pacific Odd Fellows*, 13 Feb. 1875, p. 4.

298— 'another California jury has decided': *Common Sense*, 13 Feb. 1875, p. 1.

298— 'outraged the law and the facts': *Russian River Flag*, 11 Feb. 1875, p. 2.

298— 'Outside of Napa': *Alta*, 14 Feb. 1875, p. 1, *citing Lake County Bee* (n.d.).

298— a 'pernicious' and 'dangerous' example: *Napa Reporter*, 13 Feb. 1875, p. 2.

299— 'sentimental murder': *Sacramento Daily Union*, 4 May 1880, p. 2.

299— 'lived in retirement': *SF Chronicle*, 23 Mar. 1875, p. 3. (Gordon Hendricks, *Eadweard Muybridge: The Father of the Motion Picture* (1875), p. 81, argues that EJM departed 27 Feb. 1875.)

300— 'disclose a good cause of action': *Sacramento Daily Union*, 27 Mar. 1875, p. 8, *citing SF Bulletin*, 26 Mar. 1875.

300— misleadingly cartoonish: *SF Chronicle*, 27 Mar. 1875, p. 3.

300— 'Mrs. Muybridge Again': *SF Post*, 31 Mar. 1875, p. 2.

302— 'directing Muybridge to show cause' ff.: *SF Post*, 30 Apr. 1875, p. 2.

302— 'the usual preliminaries': *SF Examiner*, 1 Apr. 1875, p. 3.

302— Eduardo Santiago Muybridge, as he had become: *see* Panama prospectus, 'vistas fotogràphicas', in EJM Scrapbook, p. 15 (Kingston).

303— 'certain moneys': *Sacramento Daily Union*, 11 Nov. 1876, p. 5, *citing SF Post*, 10 Nov. 1876.

303— 'Mrs. Flora Muybridge, whose faithlessness': *Sacramento Daily Union*, 15 July 1875, p. 1.

303— 'Mrs. Flora Muybridge, whose illicit love': *Arizona Weekly Miner*, 13 Aug. 1875, p. 1.

303— There she was visited by Captain Bromley: Ella Clark, analogue card file, 'Muybridge, Mrs. Edward J', 1927, California State Library, Sacramento.

303— 'She Is Dead': *Alta*, 19 July 1875, p. 1.

303— under the charge of the Sisters of Mercy: *see Sacramento Daily Union*, 20 July 1875, p. 2; *see also SF Post*, 19 July 1875, p. 3.

304— 'complication of spinal complaint': *SF Chronicle*, 19 July 1875, p. 3.

304— 'MRS. MUYBRIDGE should be tried': *LA Daily Herald*, 9 Feb. 1875, p. 2.

304— 'Larkyns took the chances and lost': *Marysville Daily Appeal*, 10 Feb. 1875, p. 2.

304— 'When Mr. Muybridge hears': *Alta*, 20 July 1875, p. 1.

304— 'on some one's head rests the blood': *Santa Barbara Daily Press*, 13 Aug. 1875, p. 2, *citing Golden Dawn* (n.d.). (For *Golden Dawn, see The Wasp*, 3 Oct. 1876, p. 7.)

304— 'with a French family at the Mission': *SF Chronicle*, 19 July 1875, p. 3.

305— Her funeral took place on Clementina Street: *see* Rebecca Solnit, *River of Shadows* (2004), p. 147. *See also* Edward Ball, *The Inventor and the Tycoon* (2013), p. 284, for the suggestion that FEM had been living with a 'Mrs. Mary Goss'. (There was on Clementina Street at the time a 'Mrs. Sarah A. Gross, dressmaker'. If this is in fact the same person, then she was perhaps also the previously 'pretended' friend, 'Mrs. Gross', of FEM's letter of 11 July 1874.)

305— Cosmopolitan Section of the Odd Fellows Cemetery: Kingston: 5061/51/2.

POSTSCRIPT

306— Muybridge returned to San Francisco late in 1875: Mary V. Jessup and Robert Bartlett Haas, 'Muybridge's Yosemite Valley Photographs, 1867–1872', *California Historical Society Quarterly*, Mar. 1963, p. 22.

306— William Wirt Pendegast, aged barely thirty-five: *Russian River Flag*, 2 Mar. 1876, p. 2.

306— Pendegast's good friend, delivered the eulogy at his funeral: Kingston: 5063/70.

306— 'noble and disinterested generosity': EJM, 25 May 1876 (Kingston: 5061/84).

306— Ambrose Bierce wrote sardonically that Rulofson executed his own 'dance of death': in S. T. Joshi and David E. Schultz (eds), *A Sole Survivor: Bits of Autobiography* (1998), p. 138.

306— something caused Muybridge to intervene: apparently on 16 Sept. 1876 (Kingston: 5061/51/2; 5061/90).

307— 'A Peculiar Motion in the Muybridge Divorce Case': *Sacramento Daily Union*, 11 Nov. 1876, p. 5, *citing SF Post*, 10 Nov. 1876.

308— Hart had 'advanced money': *SF Examiner*, 18 Nov. 1876, p. 3.

308— Florado left aged nine and a half: Kingston: 5061/90. (Information in a letter about FHM from a 'California State Librarian'. It concludes, 'he was a pitiful specimen of humanity'.)

308— Eudora Garoutte, the State Librarian: Gary F. Kurutz, *California State Library Foundation Bulletin*, no. 111 (2015), p. 28.

309— she put on record that Florado had grown up 'utterly worthless': Leigh also called him 'dissipated and shiftless' (Kingston: 5063/68).

310— 'photographing of the bullet': (Sam Davis), *Carson Morning Appeal*, 8 May 1880, p. 2.

Sources

Sources for the quotations used in this book are given in the end notes, but some of the background information that I drew on is not accounted for in this way. In Part I, thumbnail portraits of minor characters were stitched together from census records, wills where applicable, entries in the *Dictionary of National Biography*, and one or two entries on the website 'Legacies of British Slave-ownership', hosted by University College London. I also derived a huge amount of ancillary information from the digest *Homeward Mail from India, China and the East*, available via the British Newspaper Archive, including such specifics as records of port departures and arrivals. *Homeward Mail*, along with the *London Gazette*, supplied most of the nitty-gritty of Harry's army career; and between them, *Allen's Indian Mail*, the *East India Register and Army List* and the London *Times* supplied the rest, as well as giving the basic details of the careers of other Larkins men, including Harry's father. Jean Sutton's 2010 work *The East India Company's Maritime Service, 1746–1834: Masters of the Eastern Seas* was a further immense boon to me: in it, she builds a whole history on extensive researches into the seafaring members of the Larkins family.

When it came to background reading on events in India in 1857, from the British point of view, I turned to Saul David's formidable *The Indian Mutiny* (2003) and Andrew Ward's, *Our Bones are Scattered: The Cawnpore Massacres and the Indian Mutiny of 1857* (1996), the definitive modern account of the nightmare that swallowed Harry's family. Beyond these, I was excited to discover an unguarded letter sent by Mowbray Thomson to his mother in August 1857, and printed in the *Morning Advertiser* on 25 December 1857, that indicates how far, in his extraordinary book, *The Story of Cawnpore*, written two years later, Thomson actually reined himself in. I was particularly grateful for Peter Stanley's *White Mutiny: British Military Culture in India, 1825–1875* (1997); my attempt to understand military tensions in India immediately after 1858 would have been even more of a headache without it. I did also derive a lot of useful information from George E. Cochrane's deadweight volume *Regulations Applicable to the European Officer in India* (1867); and further insights were delivered rather more agreeably by John McCosh's *Advice to Officers in India* (1856). The British Library's holdings of East India Company materials were extremely useful to me too, in particular Harry's cadet papers and those of his father, which contained all sorts of leads. Now added to this collection is the volume of Emma Larkins's letters that I drew on for this book, transcribed by her daughter Conny, as well as a clutch of surviving original letters, including the last (see BL Mss Eur F732).

My picture of degenerate Paris in 1869 was amplified by reading Joanna Richardson's *The Courtesans* (2000), as well as Émile Zola's *Nana* (1880). Similarly, to understand London's theatres in 1870, I was aided by Jennifer Hall-Witt's *Fashionable Acts: Opera and Elite Culture in London, 1780–1880* (2007), as too by Neil McKenna's *Fanny and Stella: The Young Men Who Shocked Victorian England* (2013). The basic twists and turns of the Franco–Prussian War, dreadfully confused and confusing as they are, I derived from Michael Howard's excellent *The Franco–Prussian War* (2001). And G. A. Henty's *The Young Franc-Tireurs* (1872), though awful jingoistic bunk in many ways, was nevertheless helpful to my project, not only because, amazingly, it retold Harry's exploit in Garrebourg, but also because it provided convincing detail on the hazards of being a sharpshooter in this conflict.

Part II of this book was underpinned all the way through by a great deal of research in the newspapers of the day, including the two that actually employed Harry, the *Post* and the *Stock Report*. To understand San Francisco further in this period I derived information from census reports, and from the excellent annual editions of Langley's *San Francisco Directory*, which listed not only addresses but also the jobs people had. Benjamin Lloyd's anonymous 1876 guidebook *Lights and Shades in San Francisco* proved indispensable too; and the same might be said for Ella Sterling Cummins's *The Story of the Files* (1893), which untangles relations between many of the city's early drudging Bohemians. The PhD thesis of Travis

Edward Ross was tremendously helpful to me: *History, Inc.—Hubert Howe Bancroft's History Company and the Problem of Selling the Past* (University of Utah, 2017). So too was Charles S. Peterson's 'Hubert Howe Bancroft: First Western Regionalist', in Richard W. Etulain (ed.), *Writing Western History: Essays on Major Western Historians* (1991), pp. 43–70.

One vital element in unravelling a convoluted set of misunderstandings about Harry proved to be the two-volume work by Lawrence I. Berkove, *Insider Stories of the Comstock Lode* (2007). This giant compendium happens to rescue four anonymous columns from the *Nevada Mining News* of 1908–9 that contain a set of distorted and exaggerated reminiscences about Harry, columns attributed by Berkove to Samuel Post Davis revising his own earlier journalism. Some of the same stories, seemingly in their original form, were sent years later to the groundbreaking Muybridge scholar Robert Bartlett Haas (see Kingston 5045/70). Haas then imported elements of Davis's concoctions into his book *Muybridge: Man in Motion* (1976), woven together with lurid fantasies about Harry ultimately derived from more or less self-declared romancing by the *Chicago Tribune*, 1 November 1874. Why any of this matters is that these several post-mortem farragos, authoritatively promulgated by Haas, have ossified in the literature since; and even though Haas's dating is manifestly incorrect, they are now endlessly and wrongly presented in writings on Muybridge as the exorbitant lies of a vainglorious Harry himself. Sam Davis was close enough to Harry to be a pall-bearer at his funeral; and he went on to become one of the luminaries of the 'Sagebrush School', whose members, most notably Mark Twain, revelled in hoaxes and absurdities. Thus Davis's literary fancies about his murdered friend should be understood as affectionate yarn-spinning. But by celebrating Harry in the unconstrained way he did, Davis did him an inadvertent disservice, perversely comparable in its ill effects, in the long run, to the deliberate hatchet job of the *San Francisco Chronicle*.

Countless books have been written about Eadweard Muybridge, and despite my caveat above, it is hard to beat Haas's biography *Muybridge: Man in Motion*. Gordon Henricks's *Eadweard Muybridge: The Father of the Motion Picture* (1975), supplies various original insights too, while a more recent judicious contribution to my overladen shelf was Marta Braun's *Eadweard Muybridge* (2010). I also buried myself in the lavish introduction to Muybridge's photographs that is Philip Brookman (ed.), *Edweard Muybridge* (2010), while Peter E. Palmquist's *Pioneer Photographers of the Far West: A Biographical Dictionary, 1840–1865* (2003), was an excellent aid to understanding Muybridge's professional world. Haas's research notes and materials are now in the collection of the Kingston Museum, following a bequest to Kingston by Muybridge himself that includes the extraordinary scrapbook he made of newspaper cuttings about his career. Haas's notes show that he came quite close to working out who Harry was, and it therefore seemed fitting to lodge a slim file with the same collection of copies of all the archive material about Harry used in this book (see Kingston EM5014).

The small set of original documents preserved by the Napa County Historical Society that survive from Muybridge's trial was extremely helpful to my project. As with the various other court cases described in this book, in Paris, London and San Francisco, in order to try to give an accurate account of the Napa trial, I took all the newspaper reports available to me – never covering quite the same testimony; never delivering identical accounts where there was an overlap; often detectably partisan – and strove to devise the most balanced synthesis of this material that I could.

The final source that was brilliantly interesting to me was the 'Brandenburg Album', available to view online via the Cantor Arts Center at Stanford. This anonymous scrapbook was rescued in the 1950s by a collector called Melford F. Brandenburg, who recognised that it contained an exceptional set of original photographs by Muybridge. Before Brandenburg, the album's history remains unknown. But experts attribute it with virtual certainty to Flora, partly because the latest date of any of the Muybridge prints in it fits neatly with the breakdown of their marriage; and partly because the great collection of theatrical portraits that it also contains serves to reinforce the common notion of Flora as a star-struck flibbertigibbet. Casting about for further information, I could find no evidence that anyone had ever weighed up Flora as the likely assembler of the album by analysing the portraits themselves. However, by one means or another, it was quickly possible to identify the figures in roughly half of them. These identities continue to fit tightly to the necessary date span. And beyond this, I found them wonderfully suggestive in seeming to tell something of Flora and Harry's story too.

Index

Page numbers for illustrations are in *italics*.